ALSO BY SCOTT REYNOLDS NELSON

Iron Confederacies

Steel Drivin' Man

A NATION OF DEADBEATS

A NATION OF DEADBEATS

AN UNCOMMON HISTORY OF AMERICA'S FINANCIAL DISASTERS

Scott Reynolds Nelson

Alfred A. Knopf · New York · 2012

THIS IS A BORZOI BOOK
PUBLISHED BY ALFRED A. KNOPF

Library of Congress Cataloging-in-Publication Data

Nelson, Scott Reynolds.
A nation of deadbeats : an uncommon history of America's financial disasters /
by Scott Reynolds Nelson.—1st ed.
p. cm.
ISBN 978-0-307-27269-0
Includes bibliographical references.
1. Financial crises—United States—History. 2. Recessions—United States—
History. 3. Depressions—History. 4. United States—Economic conditions.
I. Title.
HB3743.N45 2012
338.5'42—dc23 2012025264

*Jacket image: Jon Berkeley/Ikon Images/Getty Images; (dollar) Hill Street Studios/
Blend Images/Getty Images
Jacket design by Darren Haggar*

Manufactured in the United States of America
First Edition

Contents

PREFACE

A Republic of Deadbeats

After his first divorce but before he became respectable, my father was a repo man. He did not look the part, which made him all the more effective. He alternately wore a long mustache or a shaggy beard and owned bell-bottoms that were black, blue, and cherry red. His imitation-silk shirts were festooned with city maps, or cartoon characters, or sailing ships. Dad sang in the car, at the top of his lungs, mostly obscure show tunes. His white Dodge Dart had "Mach 1" racing stripes that he had lifted from a souped-up Ford Mustang. The "deadbeats" saw him coming, that's for sure, but they did not understand his profession until he walked into their homes and took away their televisions.

A deadbeat, Dad told me, "was a guy whose mouth wrote a check his ass could not cash." They might be rich or poor, young or old, male or female, black or white, but "deadbeat" was written all over them, and my dad could read it. Florida's Orange, Seminole, and Volusia Counties had plenty of them. And when Dad was working for Woolco, the department store, Woolco got its goods back. Woolco lent appliances to people on the installment plan, and when they failed to pay, ignored the letters and phone calls, refused to answer the door, my father would come by. He often posed as a meter reader or someone with a broken-down car. If he saw a random object lying abandoned in the yard, he would pick it up and bring it to the door as if he were returning it. He was warm and funny, charming, but pushy. He did not carry a gun, but he was fearless under pressure and impervious to verbal abuse. He was earnest about the return of the goods. If the door opened, he was inside; if he was inside, he shortly had his hands on the appliance; the rest was bookkeeping.

As you can imagine, repo men like my father saw people at their worst. He told me that central Florida was full of deadbeats—people who borrowed and borrowed, then lied, hid from their debts, pretended they were solvent, until the guy in bell-bottoms arrived.

My dad was not inclined to be generous about how people got to this place. His own career in repossession began in late 1973, after the first oil shock brought minor financial catastrophe to central Florida. Dad, in fact, had lost a very good job as a regional sales manager at Kimberly-Clark. Repo man was a sudden and severe step down, but there were debts to pay. At the end of 1973, many central Florida families were drowning in consumer debt they had contracted when times were brighter. In this downturn these people certainly had "skin in the game," and it was my dad who did the skinning.

In a certain sense, the story of my dad, Woolco's debtors, and the debts he collected is the story of American history. Americans settled this nation by borrowing goods, land, and more abstract representations of those goods—land warrants, deeds, patents, concessions, and equities. They borrowed with the most optimistic assumptions about their capacity to pay. But when it became clear that Americans were not paying, banks began to doubt wholesalers and called in loans; wholesalers demanded settlement from retailers; retailers sent my dad and thousands like him out into the countryside to recall some portion of their property. Times got hard.

Pundits will tell you that the economic turmoil the nation experienced in 2008–2009 was the first "consumer debt" crash, built on junk consumer debt. These debts were in turn packed into "collateralized debt obligations," or CDOs, paper representations of debt that could be bought and sold as financial instruments. CDOs, we are told, weakened the overall economy by dressing up bad loans as good ones. In 2005 or so, a banker who dealt in junk debt allegedly said: "Give me shit, a blender, and lots of sugar and I will make you a chocolate mousse." In 2008, banks began to figure out just what was in these CDOs. A banking crisis began that brought down multibillion-dollar banking giants like Bear Stearns and Lehman Brothers, as well as causing devastating financial shocks for the thousands of midsized banks and pension funds around the world that held this toxic debt. The federal government, the European Central Bank, and other international government agencies paid for a bailout that has so far cost more than $3 trillion.

The trunk of my father's Dodge Dart suggests that this story of bad debts was not new. In fact, America has seen numerous periods of similar financial decline, and in most cases consumer debt lay at the heart of it. My dad understood consumer debt intimately; tucked back in his trunk was an accordion file filled with photocopies of signed loan agreements for everyday items such as toaster ovens and stereos. These agreements had allowed Woolworth, the parent company of Woolco, to borrow cash repeatedly. Consumer debt had been the source of Woolworth's equity—the basis for Woolworth stocks, for its bonds, for the credit that stereo manufacturers and cosmetics companies provided, and for Woolworth's numerous bank credit lines. All of it rested on documents like the agreements in Dad's trunk, and most of those debts, he said, were good for nothing.

Many economists and historians have written about past American depressions, panics, and crashes. From the 1880s to the 1950s, these scholars have told the history of the nation's economic downturns as the history of banks. This approach was not entirely wrong, but it tended to focus on big personalities or New York institutions. It tended to ignore the farmers, artisans, slaveholders, shopkeepers, and wholesalers whose borrowing had fueled the booms and busts. Then, in the 1960s and 1970s, the so-called New Economic Historians (or "cliometricians") came along with a different story. Using state and federal data, they tried to build simple mathematical models of the nation's financial health. Moving beyond the saga in which banks played the central role, they emphasized what they termed the "real economy," by which they meant measurable indices of growth and profit. Unfortunately, they tended to analyze the data from thirty-five thousand feet, creating a seemingly coherent picture of the entire American economy out of published numbers that were much hazier when viewed up close. These economists sought to estimate such variables as the nation's gross domestic product, its gross income, and its collective return on investment, but none of these figures had been measured directly before the 1930s, and the cliometricians' projections of this data into the past were all based on approximations.

But these models, however scientific they looked, tended to be abstract representations of an economy that was, in fact, more complex and more interconnected than can be predicted or explained with a linear model of inputs and outputs. They tended, for example, to assume that old banks were like modern banks, sharing common accounting principles, or that because banks first issued credit cards in the 1960s, banks had no consumer credit before then. The cliometricians' work was thus often ahistorical. They drilled into historical documents looking for seemingly relevant numbers, then plugged those numbers into a model of a world they understood rather than the economy they sought to describe.[1] And they tended to ignore things that weren't measurable, like hope.

Seldom did these accounts reflect the reality that my dad wrestled with every day: how optimistic assumptions had again and again led Americans to buy millions of shiny new things, and how significant factors outside the banking narrative, such as high commodity prices (oil in Dad's day) and lost jobs (in ours), had turned dreamers into defaulters. In fact, the only panic in which American consumer debt did not figure much was the Great Depression of the 1930s, the only crash that most economists understand.

But as I'll show in the chapters that follow, the nation saw significant economic declines in 1792, 1819, 1837, 1857, 1873, 1893, and 1929. The question in each of these panics boiled down to one my dad well understood. European lenders wondered if Americans would honor their financial promises, or was America simply a nation of deadbeats? That question has been crucial to understanding the history of American financial panics, though most observers have missed it.

For despite the cliometricians' emphasis on the American economy's vital statistics as an indicator of economic health, panics have always crossed oceans. Panics are always and everywhere transnational because credit is transnational. Panic comes from one nation's doubts about another nation's capacity to pay. Were Americans particularly incapable of paying their debts? King George III thought so when he sent Hessian troops to put down the heavily indebted merchants and farmers of Boston and Virginia in the American Revolution. The French revolutionary assembly had its doubts when the Americans refused to reimburse it for the French navies that had rescued them at Yorktown. The first panic in 1792 had everything to do with foreign lenders' doubts about Americans' ability to subdue western Indians who blocked westward expansion. Recovery came when European investors judged New England smugglers to be safer borrowers than French revolutionary assemblies or Saint Domingue slaveholders and put their money back into American banks.

The pattern would continue throughout the nineteenth century. An economic boom after 1815 was conceived in a scheme to sell English woolen coats to Americans on credit. The panic came in 1819 when trade negotiations between America and Britain failed, causing Americans to lose their best trading partners. In the 1830s, British banks with too much cash bet on a speculative bubble in American cotton plantations; British and American banks busted when the Bank of England doubted slave owners' ability to pay. The panic of 1857 resulted from English doubts about whether American railroads had clear title to western lands and whether cash-strapped farmers on railroad land would pay

off their mortgages. And while cheap exports from American farmers contributed to the international panic of 1873, the crash started in
Vienna and sloshed onto American shores when the Bank of England
raised interest rates. The panic of 1893 was largely a by-product of a
sudden drop in sugar-tax revenues from Cuba, and it climaxed when
Europeans doubted if American borrowers would repay their debts in
gold. Finally, in 1928, Americans' doubts about dollar loans to consumers in Germany and Latin America seized up international bond markets and laid the groundwork for the crash of 1929 and the Depression
that followed.

In each case, the documents stored away for safekeeping—whether
a promissory note or a bill of exchange, bank draft, or railway bond—
were viewed as assets by financial intermediaries: merchant banks,
banks of deposit, brokers, moneylenders, and insurance companies.
Other financial intermediaries involved may be unfamiliar—the Federal Land Office, New York wholesalers, midwestern railways, and
Albany insurance companies, among others—but in each case these
financial intermediaries convinced themselves that the financial instrument they had created was sophisticated enough to protect them from
consumer default. And in each case the complex chain of institutions
linking borrowers and lenders made it impossible for lenders to distinguish good loans from bad.

In those crashes in America's past, perhaps a repo man in a Dodge
Dart with a million gallons of gas could have visited every debtor, edged
his way in, and decided who was good for it. But lenders have neither the
time nor the capacity to act with the diligence of a repo man. Instead,
lenders (let's agree to call all of them banks) try to unload the debts,
hide from their own creditors, go into bankruptcy, and call on state and
federal institutions for relief. But banks, as we will see, have routinely
overestimated the collateral—the underlying asset—for the loans they
hold. When those debts go unpaid or appear unpayable, banks quickly
withdraw lending; the teller's window slams shut. As banks suspend
lending, a crisis on Wall Street becomes a crisis on Main Street. Money
is tight. Loans are impossible: crash.

Besides exploring what caused these panics, I'll consider here what
changes these panics caused. Unlike Karl Marx, I do not believe that
all human actions are dictated by economic catastrophes, but it turns
out that panics have changed a lot of things in American history. Marx
predicted that workers and farmers would organize in crises. In fact,
they usually formed unions during economic booms. Unions like the

Brotherhood of Locomotive Engineers, the Knights of Labor, and the American Federation of Labor, for example, all organized during financial upswings.[2]

When busts came, the rules of politics changed as strong political figures emerged who courted farmers, artisans, sailors, and soldiers burned by financial disaster. Many Americans switched parties, since the people in power usually took the blame. Thus in 1793 a political faction appealed to artisans and farmers hurt by that panic; they organized a new party. Labeled "Democrats" by their opponents, they had obtained almost complete hegemony by 1800. In the aftermath of the financial downturn of 1819, the Democratic Party splintered, with the Jacksonian wing ultimately absorbing those with concrete grievances about the economy. After the panic in 1837 wrecked Jackson's party and boosted the newly formed Whigs, the seesawing continued: The 1857 panic caused northern and especially midwestern voters to abandon the Democratic Party for the Republicans, while the crash of 1873 led voters back to the Democrats. After 1893, the wind shifted again as many voters blamed Democrats for hard times. At the same time, both parties saw reform wings within their ranks build a movement called Progressivism. Finally, in 1929, many traditional Republican voters abandoned their party, while a divided Democratic Party found a common theme in reform. The story of American financial panics is the story of politics.

While some parts of this political story may sound familiar, I'd suggest that financial and political history is woven together in ways that are difficult to see at first glance. The First and Second Banks of the United States, the Suffolk Bank of Massachusetts, and the New York Clearing House were all central banks, but they were also political organizations, often covertly intervening in state and federal elections. Criticism of these institutions by Jefferson, Jackson, Roosevelt, Wilson, Hoover, FDR, and others was not just paranoid delusion (though Jackson's paranoia must never be overlooked). Politicians and everyday citizens later exposed how these institutions corrupted American politics. It was not just hyperbole to refer to these banks as political machines. As we shall see, they often were.

I'll also examine here the changes in daily life that panics wrought. For example, controversies over liquor often increased after economic downturns. In the wake of the 1792 panic, for instance, a new tax on alcohol led the whiskey rebels to take up arms against the federal government. After 1819, Philadelphia hospitals received so many out-of-work alcoholics that they learned to plot out the stages of alcohol withdrawal, giving us the medical term "delirium tremens." While the Whigs came to power after 1837 on a campaign of "hard cider," the 1857 panic saw the collapse of an anti-liquor party called the Know-Nothings.[3] The fallout from the panic of 1873 led to the rise of new criminal enterprises built on gambling and liquor in Chicago, while after the 1893 panic the federal government implemented a new tax on liquor to recover lost federal revenue. A constitutional amendment prohibited the sale of alcohol after World War I, but Democrats overturned it, hoping a beer tax would help end the financial crisis of the 1930s. We can also credit financial panics with the creation of the presidential cabinet meeting, the founding of the New York Stock Exchange, the rise of Mormonism, and the invention of the self-service grocery. To talk about American financial panics is to talk about a novel about whales, a guerrilla war over the plains of Kansas, and the invention of the jukebox.[4]

My father died before this book was written, but it is nonetheless my side of a thirty-year-long argument with him. Not surprisingly, he disliked deadbeats, seeing them as the people whose false promises weakened this country. He probably had a point, and no doubt the executives of Woolco would agree. But I find much in them to admire, for defaulters are often dreamers. In viewing America's financial panics through the lens of numerous unfulfilled and forgotten debts that even the oldest banker cannot possibly remember, I hope to provide a perspective my dad would have appreciated: the view from the front porch, the minute he rang the doorbell, when both debtor and creditor prepared their stories.

A Few Technical Terms

A *promissory note* is a promise to pay a debt. The earliest banks accepted them, offering less than the stated value of the debt. When a bank accepted a promissory note, it *discounted* it by subtracting a publicly circulated fee called *the discount.* In American cities until 1913, the *discount rate* was some fraction higher than the discount rate published by the Bank of England. Most of a bank's profit came from the discount rate. In the period discussed here, banks issued their own printed banknotes for the promissory notes they received. When presented with one of its own banknotes, a bank was supposed to provide *specie,* that is, gold and silver coin, for the note. If you were not a stockholder in the bank, there was an additional fee for demanding specie.

A *bill of exchange,* as the term was used most often in the United States in the eighteenth and early nineteenth centuries, was a promissory note from a foreign country, usually Britain. Redeeming it for American dollars at a bank thus involved subtracting the discount rate as well as calculating the exchange rate. For a London bill of exchange brought to a New York bank, you would receive a bit more for the bill if the exchange "favored" London. If the exchange was "against" London, you'd receive less. Merchants and other private *bill brokers* bought up private bills and promissory notes at higher discounts than banks. They then either held them to earn the interest or resold them to banks. Finally, a *banker's acceptance* was (in the American context) a post-1914 term for a bill of exchange in dollars that member banks in the Federal Reserve guaranteed. A member bank would stamp "Accepted" on the note, obliging the bank to guarantee the promise even if the issuer defaulted.

Promissory notes, bills of exchange, and banker's acceptances were, like the signed contracts in my dad's trunk, the promises that banks depended on. Banks recognized that all of their clients and stockholders would not demand specie at the same time, allowing them to issue many more banknotes than the total of bills, notes, and specie they held. This principle is called the ***money multiplier.*** When many borrowers refuse to pay, the money multiplier suggests that the financial impact of this refusal will be many, many times larger than the default. In addition, if it is unclear which institutions' assets are most troubled, ***symbolic doubt*** (my term) will lead lenders, depositors, and stockholders to withdraw even more of their cash. When this happened in the United States in 1792, 1819, 1837, 1857, 1873, 1893, 1929, and 2008, it brought financial depressions. I refer to the political impact of these downturns as ***crash politics.***

A NATION OF DEADBEATS

CHAPTER ONE

Duer's Disgrace

*T*HE NEW NATION'S FIRST financial panic was not long in coming, threatening to reach its climax on the night of April 18, 1792. The shouting started outside William Duer's cell in the "New Gaol," a debtors' prison near the New York City commons at the northeast corner of what is now City Hall Park. A diverse crowd of three to five hundred "disorderly persons" had gathered there to confront him that evening, including cart men, artisans, and slaves. What began with shouts, catcalls, and a few stones tossed at the prison's windows soon escalated into an old-fashioned New York riot.

Colonel William Duer was nearly fifty, a small and delicate man born into a wealthy English family with plantations in the Anglo-Caribbean colonies of Antigua and Dominica. Educated at Eton, Duer had come to New York in 1768 searching for timber for his family's Dominican plantation. Seeing greater opportunities in New York, he had borrowed £1,400 from his sister and established himself the next year on a large plot of land along the Hudson River. With his charming wife, "Lady Kitty," he had defied convention by dressing his servants in livery, creating a family crest of arms, and entertaining aristocrats in a fashionable town house one block north of Wall Street. As the Revolution began, he used his growing social network in New York to become a furnishing merchant, supplying timber, planks, and provisions to the Continental army. By 1780 he was worth more than £400,000, or nearly 2 million. After the Revolution, he had become a member of the powerful Board of Treasury under the Continental Congress, a government bond dealer, and a stock market trader.[1]

But on March 23, 1792, less than a month before the fracas outside, Duer had voluntarily entered the New Gaol to hide from his creditors. By ancient rules of bankruptcy that still applied in New York, debtors' prisons were designed to shake money out of debtors, their friends, and their families.[2] Duer's neighbors in the New Gaol included many who had overleveraged, but no one who had leveraged so much.[3]

At the height of the mayhem outside the prison, some in the crowd reportedly shouted, "We will have Mr. Duer, he has gotten our money." Threatening to remove Duer bodily from his cell, the crowd began to throw paving stones, breaking windows and streetlamps. Well after dusk, "friends of legal restraint and good order" helped the city magistrates to arrest some of the most troublesome members of the crowd, including several artisans, the merchant John Hazard, and Tom, a slave owned by Joseph Towers. For the next few nights, crowds returned to the jail to threaten vengeance. The magistrate assigned Duer his own personal guard, though by the middle of April civil authorities and brick prison walls seemed little protection against a mob bent on repossessing the colonel's assets in this world and sending him to the next one.[4]

At the time he entered prison, it was estimated that Duer, America's first famous deadbeat, had defaulted on promises worth more than $2 million. By some estimates this was more than half the nation's supply of readily available money. For though the American colonies had revolted against the English crown more than ten years earlier, capital, education, and power in America were still concentrated among a small group of insiders. Duer was at the center of this financial network, the man who hired the auctioneers who sold bonds in coffeehouses and shouted current prices from tree stumps on New York's Wall Street. When he placed a bid, every head turned to see which way his money was moving. In today's parlance, Duer was a market maker.

In the beginning of March, Duer and his associates borrowed more than $800,000 to corner the market on U.S. bonds. Few understood that he had bet most of his fortune. When his credit got tight later that month, he had his assistants privately borrow gold and silver at high interest from many of New York's most unlikely lenders. "Besides shopkeepers, Widows, [and] orphans," wrote his associate Seth Johnson, Duer owed "Butchers, Car[t]men, Gardners, market women, & even the noted Bawd Mrs. Macarty—many of them if they are unpaid are ruined."[5]

In addition to the sufferers outside the New Gaol, the nation's tiny financial elite—men who spent their hours and their fortunes in the coffeehouses of Philadelphia, Boston, and New York—faced financial ruin. Scores of Duer's merchant friends along the Eastern Seaboard had signed now-overdue promissory notes on faith under Colonel Duer's name. Most now rued the day they had ever met the man. Some disappeared into the western wilderness or crossed into Canada to escape Duer's fate.[6]

By April all five branches of the newly established Bank of the United States had restricted lending. Lenders demanded immediate settlement in gold and silver. Secretary of the Treasury Alexander Hamilton sought to buoy the nation's tiny stock and securities market by buying back federal Treasuries, but few lenders were accepting anything but gold. In May interest rates on short-term loans approached 96 percent, or 8 percent per month.[7] Soon there were rumors that creditors in Connecticut were demanding that Congress make good on Duer's debts. Many doubted if the new nation could survive its first financial crisis.[8] But that is getting a bit ahead of the story.

HOW TO FUND A REVOLUTION?

AFTER AMERICANS AND BRITISH TROOPS began to exchange gunfire at Lexington and Concord in 1775, merchants with capital had to make a decision: support the Revolution or support the crown? Duer and a small group of New York and New England merchant adventurers with names like Roosevelt, Bleecker, Melvill, and Morris threw their financial backing behind the American partisans. They took enormous risks in challenging the British crown, but many of Duer's associates profited handsomely by providing high-interest loans to this newly formed government.

To be fair, Duer's support for the Revolution put his family in some danger. Indeed he hesitated to take an officer's commission because he feared it would lead the crown to seize the family's plantation in Antigua. Yet as a man with capital, he was in a position to demand a great deal. As companies mustered in New York and Boston, Duer promised provisions but demanded that Revolutionary quartermasters, colonels, treasurers, and comptrollers provide him with negotiable loans and letters of credit, promises of future payment that he could sell to international capitalists in France and Amsterdam.[9] These were the new nation's first debts, and most of them passed through Duer's hands. Of course Duer paid his fellow *colonists* in depreciated colonial currencies when he bought their timber, muskets, and provisions for the Continental armies.[10]

As the man who profited from the nation's debts, Duer had few friends and a host of enemies. Depending on where you stood, men like Duer were either the merchant financiers who had funded the American cause or the speculators who had nearly squeezed the Revolution dry. Those standing outside Duer's jail cell in April 1792 were inclined to see him as the devil in human form. As the Boston *Argus* noted, Duer had long been a swindler who "laughs at the calamity he has brought upon his country; while the bloodsucking brokers in his employ are still hovering round us like *Milton's devils,* pimping, soothing, and promising redress without any intention . . . of ever performing."[11]

Men like Duer were not unfamiliar, even in colonial America. Merchant capitalists like Duer had been secretly doing business with foreign powers for generations. Indeed their covert trading with Dutch, French, and Spanish sea captains had much to do with the crown's imposition of financial regulations that helped cause the Revolution.[12] After the colonies challenged Britain's authority to tax their trade, the hastily created Continental Congress called on militia to assemble. It failed, however, to properly fund the operation. In the past, the colonies had parsimoniously issued small quantities of their own currency, but during the Revolutionary struggle they turned to the printing press, printing unbacked currency to fight the British.

Duer and his friends understood that the colonies in revolt had no currency and banking infrastructure compared with their English opponents. In Britain and much of Europe, printed currencies were strictly regulated by agents of kings and bore the seal of the monarch. For more than one hundred years before the Revolution, colonial currencies changed hands in America, but they were frequently declared illegal by Britain. The value of these colonial currencies rested on either export goods or land. Thus Virginia's first printed banknote was a tobacco receipt issued by the colony's inspection station in Richmond: the state's pledge to pay gold or silver for tobacco deposited in its warehouse. Regular in form and difficult to reproduce, these receipts appealed to Virginians as replacements for scarce gold and silver. To keep up their value, Virginia's treasurer promised to destroy them when Virginians turned them in for taxes (sometimes he didn't). Within a generation Virginia's fledgling private banks held these tobacco receipts in their vaults and issued their own banknotes on their security, a pledge on a pledge. Likewise, New England banks chartered by colonial assemblies took mortgages for land borrowed, bought, or stolen from Indians, giving out currency that could be used to pay taxes. Even before the colonies declared themselves separate nations, they covertly assumed the rights of European sovereigns to make the pledges that became printed money. Colonial currencies were America's first symbolic promises, promises about future tobacco sales, future land values, and the future prospect of property taxes. Imprinting colonial currencies with engravings of painted Indians, tobacco leaves, sailing ships, and sturdy pioneers simply made the metaphor concrete.

Fighting a revolution allowed the colonies to gradually become sovereign in a process both military and monetary. As the battles moved along the Eastern Seaboard, the colonies and their Continental Congress claimed the sovereign power to issue state and national currency to pay for food, guns, and gunpowder. Americans with guns and gunpowder would in turn make their states sovereign by force of arms; sovereign states would then accept their own currency for taxes and unsettled land. As go-betweens in America's first promises, Duer and his friends had their doubts about this circular process of using currency to buy arms to guarantee currency; they speculated in state currencies but refused to take them as payment for the goods they provided. They preferred handwritten promises of future payment: bonds, not currency.

As Duer and his friends predicted, the value of these state currencies fluctuated wildly depending on how the battle with England was progressing, how careful each state was in issuing its notes, and how large its population of currency holders was. In the final analysis, most Americans saw currency for what it was: a measure of the value of land the states claimed but that remained untilled in their westerly reaches, land that states would sell once the shooting stopped. Big colonies had a vast blank check in their thousands of acres of unsurveyed western land. Little colonies had nothing. Rhode Island paper was worthless; Massachusetts notes were respectable; free-spending but well-endowed Virginia was somewhere in between.

When the colonies came together to create the Continental Congress to oversee the fighting of the war, the Congress issued its own currency as well. As a "congress" of independent states rather than a parliament, it had no sovereignty, no direct claim to western land or taxes. The Congress expected that the member states would tax their own lands and then pay the Congress a sum proportional to their population. As it became clear that some states would not pay the debts incurred in the fighting, the value of the Continental dollars plunged after the autumn of 1776. "It is true," wrote the editor of the *Pennsylvania Evening Post,* "that those rags after having gone thro[ugh] a certain mysterious process of *transubstantiation,* under the sanction of Congress are said to be money . . . but since that Popish doctrine with a long name is exploded, and the funds for redeeming these nominal dollars are in the moon, no man but a lunatic will . . . believe that billets of brown paper can really be dollars."[13]

As General Washington's troops suffered for provisions, the Congress tried to prop federal dollars up by authorizing the army to seize the assets of grocers and farmers who refused to take them. The expression "not worth a Continental dollar" became a catchphrase that traveled more widely than the notes did.[14] To make matters worse, the British general Henry Clinton learned to take advantage of the rebels' wartime dependence on paper promises. To simultaneously make money for himself and destabilize the colonial economy, he set up tavern agents to sell knockoffs of American currency for pennies a sheet to unscrupulous buyers.[15]

Duer and many of his friends understood that banknotes issued by states or the Continental Congress were not nearly as reliable as the promises made to foreign states. Indeed, as the fighting continued in 1780, Congress passed the infamous Forty-for-One Act, declaring that it would pay only a dollar in silver for forty continentals.[16] This was hyperinflation of the worst kind. As Revolutionaries like Thomas Paine pointed out, rapid currency inflation was a tax on the poor: the poorest Americans were paid in currency, bought goods with currency, and saved currency that was constantly dropping in value. Rather than hold cash, Duer hoarded assets that appreciated in wartime: gold, silver, timber, or wheat. He especially sought promises that came from across the ocean or promises that could be sold there.

Duer's most spectacular gains came in supplying America's French allies. By agreeing to split his proceeds with requisitioning officers, Duer won lucrative contracts in provisioning French armies and navies. Because he paid with bills of exchange that originated in Paris, he had marketable promises when few others did. He could buy English and Dutch goods with substantial Paris bills, trade those goods for provisions in New York, then charge French forces for the New York provisions, earning what he called "double profits."[17]

In the midst of the fighting between 1776 and 1783, many American promises were made, but few were paid. Courts and legislatures suspended the collection of public and private debts. A few states took strategic advantage of the chaos to favor debtors: North Carolina and New York seized the property of loyalists and forced English creditors to accept the states' depreciated banknotes for it; South Carolina made English creditors accept land in the pine barrens for unpaid promissory notes.[18]

After the Treaty of Paris in 1783, as courts reopened, states began collecting taxes. Creditors—from New York to Liverpool—began to demand repayment. Many private debtors resisted the reckoning.[19] The planter George Mason recalled to Patrick Henry an "absurd question" that one of his constituents had asked: "If we are now to pay the Debts due to British merchants, what have we been fighting for all this while?" Mason was appalled, but there were no repo men or collection agencies in these United States. Between 1783 and 1786 the states were in a tumult over back taxes, unpaid personal debts, and land foreclosures. Armed insurrections against repossessions and property liquidations bubbled up in the western parts of Virginia, Massachusetts, and Pennsylvania. The turmoil made the national government seem all the more ineffective, while anger at creditors like William Duer grew all the more intense.[20]

FROM DEBTS TO DOLLARS TO BONDS

AS UNREST THREATENED, the state governments moved to action. By 1787, in order to "insure domestic tranquility," their representatives convened to draft a new constitution to strengthen the central government. There were other problems to discuss, but considerable heat came from the problem of the nation's unpaid promises. When the dust settled in the drafting of the Constitution, the states would be forced to surrender most of their unsettled land to Congress. This new and more powerful Congress would come together to regulate and tax foreign commerce. The taxes raised would pay creditors and establish a small army, a uniform currency, and a national bank. Not coincidentally, the government's final assumption of state and national debts would turn Duer from a wealthy man into the nation's first millionaire.[21]

Even before the Constitution was written, Duer was already the consummate insider, having served as secretary of the Board of Treasury for the Continental Congress, where his closest associate was another small, slender, and vain merchant: Alexander Hamilton, who became one of the leading figures of the Constitutional Convention. Hamilton, like Duer, was born in the Caribbean. The bastard son of a white Caribbean divorcée, Hamilton had started his career as a teenage bookkeeper for Dutch merchants at the port of St. Croix, where he had watched provisioners, profiteers, and pirates make their fortunes when Europeans went to war. His brilliant, firsthand account of a hurricane in the Caribbean published, in the *Royal Danish American Gazette,* had displayed a keen literary talent and won him the admiration of wealthy New Yorkers, who paid his passage to New York for an education at a grammar school in New Jersey. As a student at King's College (now

Columbia University), he wrote pamphlets in support of the Revolution and became a junior officer in the war and aide-de-camp to General Washington. An assemblyman in the New York legislature, he became one of New York's delegates to the Constitutional Convention. His understanding of finance and trade would make him an important advocate there for a stronger constitution.[22]

Between 1787 and 1788, as the proposed constitution was submitted to the states for ratification, supporters and opponents joined a war of words. Opponents of the new scheme sought to mobilize those with debts to pay. Western farmers who owed on debts and feared future taxes were listening. They might lose their lands if a strong central government sought to repay its war debts too rapidly. Critics of the Constitution assumed names like "Federal Farmer," "Brutus," and "Cato," antique names that suggested a rural opposition to the despotic power of a caesar. They accused the framers of supporting a centralized government in order to benefit profiteering merchants who owned or could easily buy up American debts. This constitution was nothing but a "gilded pill," wrote one author, favored by "holders of public securities, men of great wealth and expectation of public office, B[an]k[er]s and L[aw]y[er]s: these with their train of dependents from the Aristocratic combination."[23] Men, in other words, like William Duer.

Supporters of the Constitution responded under antique names of their own, recalling the founders of the Roman Republic and dwelling on the recurring problems of banking and currency, taxation and bankruptcy, that the Revolution had caused for the colonies. In a series of anonymous articles called "The Federalist," Alexander Hamilton, James Madison, and John Jay defended the proposed constitution.[24] Madison, writing as "Publius," envisioned in Federalist No. 10 that a single large republic could prevent the dominance of the financial cabals that dominated during the revolution, men like Duer, Nicholas Roosevelt, and Robert Morris. In the same year Duer wrote a defense of the Constitution as "Philo-Publius," lover of the public, arguing that the nation ought to court self-interested investors by paying off old debts, for those investors would then strengthen the federal government by continuing to lend to it. He neglected to mention that many of the debts were to him.

All the talk about "virtue" and republican simplicity during these debates was not merely from farmers and merchants who were borrowing ancient Roman language to advance their cause. Opponents like "Federal Farmer" spoke to a concrete problem: wealthy merchants such as Duer had abused their power and traded on inside information. As the head of the Secret Committee of Safety in New York, for example, Duer had sent soldiers to crush the rent rioters on his friends' estates. In negotiating trade agreements across the oceans, Duer and his associates did their own private bargaining beforehand. Using money advanced by Dutch merchants, Duer bought loans that he would later resell to the government.[25] As the secretary of the Board of Treasury, Duer had bought up land certificates just before his committee certified them as legitimate. Indeed, Duer's financial successes and the failure of Continental currencies became joined in the minds of many Americans. While Duer was in prison, many remembered him as the owner of the fast sloop that traveled through the Chesapeake Bay collecting depreciated state notes at knocked-down prices hours before news arrived that the general government would pay them off.[26] (Duer was not the only profiteer of course. Abigail Adams proved an especially astute speculator in the bonds, notes, and currencies that circulated in Boston.)[27] Federalists argued against Anti-Federalists for nearly five years between 1786 and 1791 while delegates convened in the Constitutional Convention and then states debated ratification. When opposition to Duer and Hamilton materialized again a few years later, their critics would draw heavily from the language of the Anti-Federalists.

While Anti-Federalists attacked the virtue of men like Duer on seeming principle, some had their own important interests at stake. Control of the duties in the bustling port of New York City, for example, had allowed Governor George Clinton to create a powerful political machine. Ceding state control of ports, banking, the judiciary, and western lands to the federal government would weaken that power.[28] Farther south, the cabal of Virginia families that ran the House of Burgesses was skeptical of what Patrick Henry called the "ropes and chains of consolidation."[29]

The Anti-Federalists were persuasive, but the currency problems all Americans faced helped Federalists win the day. Federalists dwelled on Revolutionary hyperinflation and the dangers that this new nation faced if it failed to pay its debts. Hamilton in Federalist No. 15 complained about the imbecility of a government whose finances put the country at "almost the last stage of national humiliation." In Federalist No. 23, Hamilton pointed out that the government's inability to "build and equip fleets" came from the state's inability to pay old debts. As James Madison put it in Federalist No. 44, the states had done such a terrible job issuing currency that the power to print money needed to be abandoned, "a voluntary sacrifice on the altar of justice." Under the proposed Constitution the profligate states would be prevented from emitting bills of credit (paper dollars). The proposed national government would be made strong enough to tax, but it would not have the power to issue paper dollars either. Of course, the proposed Constitution raised many issues besides unpaid debts. Arguments about a constitution raised important issues like the future powers of congress, the rights of citizens, and the framework of government. Between 1786, when the war of words commenced, and 1791, when the last state ratified the Constitution, many debts public and private went unpaid.[30]

While supporters and opponents of the Constitution agreed that neither the states nor the federal government could be trusted to issue paper currency, the Constitution left open the question: Who could? State-chartered corporations? Federally chartered corporations? Private owners of funds? Paper money had been around since the seventeenth century in New England; no one doubted that it was needed. In 1791, after the last state ratified the Constitution, Alexander Hamilton and his assistant Colonel William Duer offered their own advice. As secretary of the Treasury, Hamilton was by then one of the most powerful men in America. While the secretaries of state and war played advisory roles, a Treasury secretary was supposed to be independent, akin to a ministerial position in Britain. President Washington treated him as such.[31] The establishment of a bank to repay the nation's debts was the first major project that Hamilton and Duer brought to Congress.

Hamilton proposed that the so-called Bank of the United States (1791–1811) would, to use a modern term, "restructure" America's debt. The new institution would issue printed securities—U.S. bonds—with fixed payment dates. The bank would trade these bonds for the various handwritten federal debts that were circulating in Europe and America; the bank would sell even more bonds to raise cash. The bank would then make loans to the government, to merchants, and to manufacturers. It would also issue a national currency for other banks to use. The nation's first public bank would thus simultaneously act as a Federal Reserve that controlled bank-issued currency; an executive department that could make or break private banks; a private bank to fund trade, both international and coastal; and a fund for encouraging manufacturing. With a capitalization of $10 million to be subscribed mostly by international investors, the Philadelphia institution would dwarf the half-dozen chartered, independent, and state banks then in existence that collectively possessed a capital of less than $2 million.

While Hamilton and Duer's institution was meant to stabilize the domestic economy at home, it was also designed to take advantage of international conflict that had begun to boil around the world. In the summer of 1791, just as King Louis XVI of France was packing his trunks in Versailles in a vain attempt to escape the guillotine, the Bank of the United States opened its books to subscribers. As the forces of the new French Republic sent mass armies across Europe to overthrow ancient monarchies, the bank selected its directors. As the emperor Napoleon's armies closed off English shipping routes and King George's navies shut down French imperial trade, American merchants rushed to fill the gaps. And in the vanguard stood the new Bank of the United States.[32]

"What an age of Wonders and Revolutions," wrote the Richmond postmaster Augustine Davis in the *Virginia Gazette:* "The balance of power in Europe turned topsy-turvy; subjects turned citizens; citizens turned soldiers; peasants turned rulers; palaces turned to prisons; kings turned to dust; titles turned to smoke."[33] In this age of upset and international warfare America, its own revolution concluded, seemed a safe haven for European capital. "The disorders in France," bragged the federal auditor Oliver Wolcott in 1789, "the declining state of the Dutch republic, and the enormous debts which oppress all the great nations of Europe, are circumstances which give the United States a relative importance."[34] With armies storming the capitals of Europe, an American bank would seem as safe as a church. Hamilton was its minister, Duer its deacon.

WHAT IS A BANK?

THE TRULY RADICAL thinking behind Hamilton and Duer's plan can really be understood only by asking, what is a bank, exactly? Banks of the seventeenth, eighteenth, and nineteenth centuries were, to follow the metaphor suggested by Thomas Paine, pawnshops for promises. If, for example, you were having a house built and a carpenter or blacksmith gave you a bill for work he did and you signed the bottom, promising to pay in ninety days, this document would be the kind of two-party note that could provide liquid funds in a world with little coin. A tradesman could bring such a promissory note to a bank, sign it himself, and receive "cash"—the bank's paper money—in exchange for your promise now to pay the note in ninety days. More often the issuer of such a note would be a merchant, and the second person who signed it would be another well-known merchant. While banks held gold and silver in their vaults, "cash" in the form of paper money issued by a bank was light, stackable, and convenient, especially if everyone else in town accepted the bank's note as currency.[35]

Only stockholders deposited their money in banks; banks were primarily lenders. Thus when Duer sought a loan from "the noted Bawd Mrs. Macarty," for example, he would have offered his personal note, payable in ninety days, for the silver she had collected in her bawdy house. If she needed cash sooner than ninety days, she might then bring Duer's note to a bank, sign it underneath, and receive most of that sum in the bank's own paper money. Most banks would hold a Duer promise, confident that a man like Colonel Duer would pay his debts. Dozens of banks did in 1792. In the unlikely event he did not pay, the bank could demand the money from Mrs. Macarty since her signature was below his.

Of course banks had to make a profit. In the jargon of the time these were called banks of discount because they "discounted" the promises they received. In paying Mrs. Macarty, in other words, the teller issued less than the full amount of Duer's promise. Technically, the bank was making a loan to Duer and Macarty by accepting Duer's note. The difference in the face value of the note and what the teller counted out depended on the commonly accepted discount rate, generally just over 5 percent per year in North America. (The rate at the Bank of the United States was usually 6 percent.)[36] Because a ninety-day note is due in a quarter of a year, Mrs. Macarty's payoff would be short by one-quarter of that annual 6 percent. If the bank honored the note and honored Mrs. Macarty, a $100.00 promise from Duer would thus net her roughly $98.50. If she wanted gold or silver and was not a regular customer, banking fees would trim that figure even more. That was called "note-shaving," and banks did it all the time.

This "discount rate" between a Duer note and a bank's paper money is much more important than it may at first appear. Then, as now, it was a barometer of perceptions, a number that told you what borrowers and lenders thought about the financial future.[37] Bankers understood that when "the rate" was high, people had doubts about the future, and credit would be expensive. A high interest rate discouraged merchants like Duer from making promises because paying back a high-interest loan was costly. A high interest rate attracted gold and silver into bank vaults as borrowers came in to pay off their debts to the bank. When the rate was low (and credit was cheap), it did the opposite: it encouraged merchants to write promises to the bank and pulled hard money out of the vaults. Finally, the bank acted as a trusted agent and an enforcer of others' promises. If you had an account with the bank, or represented another bank, you could cash in the bank's own bills for gold or silver. Nowadays a central bank will hold an interest rate down to encourage investment; this was impossible under a gold or silver standard because setting a rate lower than the going rate for private lending would empty the banks' vaults.

For such loans originating abroad, the promissory note was generally in the form of a "bill of exchange" issued and stamped as acceptable from a bank in foreign currency. The price of a bill included the price of international exchange.[38] For merchants who traveled, these bills of exchange were smaller and safer than hard currency. If you came from London to New York with your life's savings in a London bill of exchange, a New York bank might give you a little more New York cash for that bill if the exchange "favored" London. If the exchange was "against" London, you'd get less for the bill of exchange, perhaps a lot less. Finally, merchants and other private brokers would pay in gold for some of a bank's hoard of private bills to earn the interest; they acted as "discounters" for banks and would return the bills for collection a few weeks later. Thus in the early 1790s, when New York merchants were buying lots of goods from London, they favored London banks' promises (the "exchange favored London"), and so the price of London bills was high.

From the 1620s until 1913, London bills of exchange were a vital part of American bank operations. On the one hand, a New York bank that accepted such a bill of exchange was lending to London capitalists by paying American currency for English notes. On the other, when a bank possessed a bill issued by such rock-solid institutions as the Baring Brothers and the House of Rothschild, it held unimpeachable promises whose value grew daily. The stability of a bank's vault of foreign and domestic promises inspired trust among merchants. Trained in commerce, Hamilton and Duer knew that a trusted bank could always issue more bills than all the metallic currency in its vaults. Gold or silver was difficult to move and was often blocked by regulation, and the metal was—in Hamilton's words—"dead stock": it earned nothing as it traveled.[39] Instead of trying to send metal for goods, merchants preferred an account at a bank in the country from which they imported, so they could draw on it for funds. It was safer than moving gold around. Banks, knowing a merchant's preference for a bank balance over gold, safely assumed that merchants with accounts would not all arrive at the banker's till in a single afternoon to demand coin.[40] Thus banks could lend far more than they took in in gold or silver. This was the magic of the multiplying process: $100 of gold or silver in a vault could become $300 or more of bank-issued notes or listed deposits.

The principle made some queasy but not Hamilton. To him, the so-called reserve ratio was the simple science that had made England a commercial empire and would make America one as well. A bank's "emissions," Hamilton declared, "must always be in a compound ratio to the fund and the demand." It was a banker's job to smell the wind and find the right balance: too little and he would not make a profit, too much and he would be embarrassed when asked for his metal.

Of course, given that a bank never had enough gold to satisfy all of its customers at once, the reserve ratio was always a calculated risk. In Hamilton's day, a 3-to-1 ratio was considered conservative enough for any bank, $3 lent out for every dollar coin in the vault. (By the end of the nineteenth century a 10-to-1 ratio was considered adequate. American banks in 2009 averaged 26-to-1 ratios.)[41] Trust was a bank's central asset and, as Duer would learn, its central weakness.

Before the 1850s, banks were notoriously slow moving. They accepted bills of exchange from abroad and promissory notes from men like Duer in the early part of the week. The members of the board met midweek to review them, and at the end of the week they discounted to customers they knew and trusted. If you needed cash instantly, you could cash in a bill of exchange with a bill broker, an individual who did the same thing a bank did, discounting foreign bills for payments in paper money, gold, or silver based on the discount rate and the direction of the exchange, though for a much larger fee. In either case, if you failed to pay your promissory note, the default would be formally "protested" with a notary. Usually, the protest would be posted on the door of the bank and in other public places to alert other lenders.[42]

At a bank with branches in every major port, this discounting function—this willingness to lend to commercial borrowers—eased the path for American merchants to conduct international trade in licit and illicit goods. For Duer, this credit offered him the ability to speculate in land, buy goods to provision armies, or run ships along the East Coast. Merchants were not inclined to hold gold if they could invest a little cash as stockholders, then receive a lot of credit in return. The banknotes rested on two strong pillars: the good credit of the nation and the good credit of its preferred borrowers. Thus Hamilton's Bank of the United States promised to act as a greenhouse for America's growing commercial empire, providing merchants with the credit and currency they needed to send more ships. (Roughly half of its promises in the first six years came from the federal government and the rest from private borrowers.) Trusting in the promises of merchants, the Bank of the United States grew to become the nation's saltwater bank. By discounting notes, it provided credit for a worldwide trade. By the spring of 1792 it had established branches in Boston, New York, Baltimore, and Charleston and provided $6 million to $8 million of yearly credit, mostly to American merchants. Local banks were left to facilitate inland trade that did not pass between these cities, especially for otter, beaver, mink, and flour.[43]

But the Bank of the United States was not just any bank. In designing this bank, Hamilton and Duer did not want to duplicate the European-style institutions of St. Petersburg, Copenhagen, Stockholm, Vienna, Lisbon, and Madrid, each controlled by its national government, each issuing paper whose value was set by government fiat. The issuing of paper by such banks, Hamilton declared, was "seducing and dangerous. . . . In times of tranquility, it might have no ill consequence; it might even perhaps be managed in a way to be productive of good; but in great and trying emergencies, there is almost a moral certainty of its becoming mischievous."[44] The aftermath of the Revolution had brought enough runaway inflation.

The Bank of the United States, as a central bank, would have unique privileges. Hamilton's port collectors would gather gold and silver duties for deposit in the bank, giving the bank liquidity. The bank would issue $5, $10, and $20 notes that would always be accepted as payment for federal taxes, helping ensure their value.[45] Foreign capitalists saw the resources of the new nation and the growing power of its shippers; they either invested by buying stock in the bank or lent by buying bonds from the government. Borrowers included both the federal government and the American sea captains and merchants who provided short-term notes and received ready cash.[46]

Finally, the Bank of the United States would perform some critical functions in the nation's international trade. Bank stock—a voting share in the bank—proved the perfect instrument for that. Hamilton had devised a plan whereby the bank could turn its debts into stock—a bank "share"—that was concrete, divisible, and marketable.[47] Only American holders of Bank of the United States stocks could vote, but like bonds the bank's stock promised a yearly dividend of 6 percent and was easily available on New York's Wall Street.

Further, stock in the Bank of the United States would resolve an American balance-of-payments problem with England, a problem that would bedevil all the other former colonies of Europe. As a developing economy, the American states usually imported more than they exported; they had done so as colonies and would do so again once unified as a nation. In colonial days individual borrowers like Duer, Washington, and Madison relied on British exporters to extend their debts year to year—through either promissory notes or bills of exchange. The rates were 6 percent or more, and even higher when the rate favored England. In most cases these debts could be rolled over from one year to the next with interest accruing. Conflict over those debts to Great Britain helped start the Revolution.[48]

By 1792, stock certificates in the Bank of the United States seemed to be a perfect solution to the international balance-of-payments problem. A merchant whose ships ran the "long haul" from Liverpool to New York would bring English woolens, linens, crockery, and tableware for the Americans. On the ship's return to Liverpool the merchant might load up on American furs, lumber, rum, and potash—a chemical used for binding dyeing agents to wool.[49] Sending other goods from America could be risky. If news from England suggested that food prices were high on the day his ship left New York (roughly forty days earlier), he might gamble and put a little American flour, butter, or fish on board. The merchant then prayed that the English food prices did not fall in the month it took the ship to get to England. But there was little else to transport across the Atlantic.[50]

After 1791, merchants added Bank of the United States stocks to the trade items they sent to England, where an English exporter would accept them for the crockery and woolens he consigned. That exporter was more likely to take Bank of the United States stock if his own bank had American connections. The Baring Brothers in England, for example, could hold an English exporter's Bank of the United States stock certificates, collect the dividends in New York or Philadelphia, and make them payable in pounds to the exporters' Baring account.[51] Everyone would be satisfied with the arrangement, or so Duer and Hamilton thought.

THE "LANDED INTEREST"

ALMOST AS SOON as Hamilton proposed a national bank, suspicions about its potential financial and commercial power emerged in several quarters. Some were old Anti-Federalists, but James Madison, Hamilton's former colleague, soon led them. The core of opposition arose among Virginia tobacco families who feared that a single, central bank would have the outsized political power that the Bank of England had in Great Britain. The Bank of England clearly worked; none of them denied it. Interest rates were low, and the capital market there, in the words of the Virginia planter and physician Walter Jones, could "invigorate circulation, and, probably make a Guinea perform more uses in a week, than it does here in six months." Nonetheless, Jones felt certain that a central bank could be dangerous to "the landed Interest."[52]

In fact, for more than a century Virginia's planter families had performed the function of local banks. Tidewater Virginia plantations, for example, were at the center of regional commerce. The docks of their James River mansions acted as the receiving points for foreign goods and the departure points for Virginia tobacco. Poorer white farmers—remote from the transportation corridors—relied on the big planters to accept and resell their tobacco to foreign purchasers. A hogshead of tobacco stamped with the brand of a prominent Virginia family would command higher prices in London and Liverpool than anything a small farmer could hope to fetch on his own. Control over the tobacco trade became the basis for ascension of the so-called First Families of Virginia.[53]

Besides reselling their neighbors' tobacco, planters provided consumer credit. This was not merchant credit but credit to farmers. Planters operated commissary stores that sold seed and supplies. Farmers borrowed goods, promising to pay with their future crops. The interest rates planters charged would have made a used-car dealer blush. Planters got their own credit and the credit they doled out from commission merchants in England. It was a long line of credit: London banks lent to these English "factors" by extending lines of credit; factors lent to planters by holding the bill of lading for tobacco; planters lent to small farmers by keeping a tally of unpaid purchases in their stores and commissaries. The entire economy of Tidewater Virginia, it seemed, rested on consumer credit.

But the system had begun to change. After 1730, when the Virginia colonial assembly designated certain planters' outbuildings as tobacco inspection warehouses, tobacco towns grew up around these facilities. A farmer could bring in his tobacco and take away receipts for it, which became Virginia's first real currency. Maryland and North Carolina soon followed in designating certain warehouses as official tobacco inspection stations. To the planters' dismay, Scottish merchants soon planted *themselves* in these towns to trade English goods for tobacco receipts. Only the largest planters could by 1750 sell their own sweetened tobacco directly to British creditors to bypass this new "money" economy.[54]

Debt in Virginia's colonial, Revolutionary, and post-Revolutionary economy was always more than money. In Virginia, poorer white farmers' debts to planters were part of a complex web of dependence that stabilized slaveholders' power. To repay debts, the farmer became the jack-of-all-trades of the plantation South—egg vendor, fruit seller, slave patroller, and borrower—while planters formed the political power base.[55] In exchange for this power, planters paid the majority of the taxes in the South, most visibly through a head tax on slaves.[56] Planters' power was hardly total—Jefferson famously claimed that a scion of one of Virginia's First Families would find it hard to win political office—but the roster of America's Virginia-born presidents suggests otherwise: Washington, Jefferson, Madison, and Monroe were all members of Virginia's First Families, their political base further stabilized by the "ghost votes" of three-fifths of every black male slave.[57]

Slavery, staple agriculture, and consumer credit were tightly bound together in Virginia before and after the Revolution. A competing lending institution based in Philadelphia with branches throughout the South threatened the society of planters at its core. Virginia planters also worried that the creation of a central bank would inevitably lead to higher taxes, which they paid disproportionately. If a national bank held the nation's debts, that bank's good credit might encourage further federal borrowing, and federal borrowing necessitated taxes, mostly through a tax on imports. Because planters followed English fashions, filled their households with English goods, and dressed their slaves in English linsey-woolsey shirts, they understood that tariffs on English consumer goods would hit them hardest.[58] According to Jones, higher state and local taxes also encouraged an "emigrating turn in our inhabitants," who would move westward to federal territories where property and luxury taxes could not be levied. This "emigrating turn" had the result of "constantly diverting . . . the sources of populousness and therefore of Arts, Commerce & internal Wealth" away from southeastern states, leaving planters with acres of cheap, untilled land. Antitax sentiment was so strong among emigrants that the federal government provided a tax moratorium for newly admitted states partly to prevent settlers from immediately heading to territories even farther west.[59] Planters may have had a related concern about the growing sentiment in banking circles, for the abolition of slavery. Between the 1770s and the 1790s, most northern states had begun to abolish slavery. Even some southern slaveholders had contributed to what Jones called the "premature & impracticable Steps toward the emancipation of Slaves."[60] Sentiments for abolition appeared strongest among the Anglo-American bankers like Alexander Hamilton and Britain's Henry Thornton (funder of the British antislavery advocate William Wilberforce). A federal bank—which would likely be based in Philadelphia or New York—could threaten the Southeast politically, economically, and socially.

Despite Virginia planters' concerns, most agreed that the federal government needed some sort of semipublic institution to market American debt and issue a paper currency backed by silver and gold. Farmers and merchants along the Mississippi and Ohio Rivers saw the appeal of a bank that could provide credit and transmit money to the West without additional fees: American dollars deposited in a Philadelphia branch could be withdrawn for no cost in Cincinnati, for example. New Englanders saw the bank as an institution that would fund merchant exploration. Some New Yorkers saw the bank as providing stability and legitimacy to their own banks, institutions that mostly lent to their own board members. Ultimately, in a close sectional vote, Hamilton's bank won the support of Congress in 1791, and the Bank of the United States was chartered.

However sound the logic behind his plan for a central bank, Secretary of the Treasury Hamilton had not simply relied on the goodwill of Congress to get his bill passed; half of the congressmen who voted for the measure also got preferred access to bank stock at a time when it remained inaccessible to other buyers. In other words, congressmen got a huge share of the initial public offering.[61] Writing years later, Jefferson condemned the "stockjobbing herd" in Congress that had succumbed to an "engine of influence" stronger than mere individual bribes. "This engine was the Bank of the United States," a "machine for the corruption of the legislature."[62] At the time, the Philadelphia physician Benjamin Rush, James Madison's friend, fumed about how Hamilton used the bank to bribe congressmen. "This influence is not confined to nightly Visits—promises—compromises—Sacrifices—& threats, in New York. It has extended one or two of its polluted Streams to [Philadelphia]." Southeastern planters, led by Madison, remained bitter and suspicious.

By the spring of 1791, Duer and Hamilton had succeeded in pushing their project through, promoting a stable financial institution that had the means to repay the nation's debt (and the prospect of enriching themselves besides). Here was an institution that could convert American promises into bonds, bonds that European merchants would accept without question. But with the establishment of the Bank of the United States, the deepest fears of its critics were soon realized. The Virginia planters' anger at Hamilton's intrigues and their fear of the bank's growing power would quickly turn the bank's opponents from a faction into an opposition political party that would bring Colonel Duer down.

CHAPTER TWO

A Botanizing Excursion

AMILTON AND DUER called them "Democrats."[1] These men set out to destroy Duer, but once they began in earnest, they had little control over the events that followed. Because Duer's power depended on the strength of his promises, two things destroyed him: his role in a military defeat and a run on the New York banks that provided him with credit. In 1792, the panic that resulted became the nation's first crash. A year later the nation was saved by a worldwide war against the revolution in France, but Duer would spend the last years of his life in prison. Duer's opponents used the panic to take control of the nation, build their own banks, and finally kill his beloved Bank of the United States.

On February 28, 1791, three days after President Washington signed the bank bill, Jefferson and Madison reached out to Philip Freneau, the harshest critic of British influence they could find. Freneau was a Franco-American writer whose father and grandfather had been ruined by banks; he also had impeccable Revolutionary credentials, having been locked in a British prison ship during the war. The two Virginians installed him as the editor of a new newspaper in Philadelphia called the *National Gazette;* they promised him public contracts and inside information. The first issue appeared on the last day of October 1791, just weeks after the Bank of the United States had opened its doors.[2] The last page listed without comment the twenty-five board members of the Bank of the United States, six of whom were congressmen who had voted to charter the bank in Congress.[3]

Jefferson and Madison next began a now-famous "botanizing excursion" in late May 1791 along the Hudson River in New York. Their public explanation for their visit to New York was to investigate flora and fauna, particularly the Hessian fly that was invading wheat crops. But their intent was to forge a diplomatic relationship between Virginia and New York that would create the first opposition party in the new nation. Together Jefferson and Madison sought an alliance with New Yorkers who also chafed under the power of Hamilton's bank.[4]

Among the men they visited was New York's "chancellor," Robert R. Livingston, who ran a faction of the powerful Livingston family from the vast family estate Clermont on the eastern side of the Hudson River. The Livingstons were the closest thing to an aristocracy in New York, a family with thousands of tenants along the river, a countinghouse in New York City, and a closely guarded patrimony. Robert Livingston's almond eyes, arched eyebrows, long nose, and undershot chin made him an instantly recognizable figure. Chancellor Livingston had already allied with George Clinton's New York City political machine, which included town artisans and newly rich gentlemen.[5] The upstate Livingstons and the downstate Clinton machine disliked Hamilton for different reasons, but all feared the power and influence of his bank. According to Hamilton's friends, the Virginians also met with the colonel and New York senator Aaron Burr, the man who would be Hamilton's chief rival in New York. As Hamilton's friend put it in a letter at the end of their visit, "There was every evidence of a passionate courtship between the Chancellor, Burr, Jefferson & Madison when the latter two were in town."[6]

Federalists had their own view of this emerging party. According to John Marshall, it was old grievances and a lust for state power that bound the landholders in New York with the planters of Virginia. The two states had, by the standards of the 1790s, a vast amount of western land—New York in what would become Ohio, Virginia in what would become Kentucky. While Virginia and New York had surrendered some land to the federal government in the Constitution of 1787, they kept a great deal. In the words of Marshall, the Madisons, Jeffersons, and Livingstons continued to favor "the undue ascendancy of the states," even after the Constitution. He feared the gentry's "extensive means of influence" in the states "furnished them with weapons for aggression which were not easily to be resisted." Their power, Marshall declared, was "the real danger which threatened the Republic."[7]

To Democrats, however, it was a powerful national government and its bank that represented the greatest threat. Newspapers would be the most important weapons in the war against the bank. The *National Gazette* broadcast every attack on the national bank it could find, calling it "a Hydra [that] wears seven monstrous heads . . . busily engaged in devouring the products of the whole industrious labour of America." This "devouring monster" was "so vastly huge and complicated, that all the Hercules in America would never be able to decapitate him," the paper thundered.[8] Somewhat disingenuously, the new Democratic Party called itself the friend of the people, opponents of "land-jobbers, public plunderers [and] eight per cent loans."[9]

Thomas Jefferson had privately charged that the bank was a "machine for the corruption of the legislature."[10] Investigations by the newspaper editor James Cheetham into Hamilton's past in New York suggested that Jefferson was not far wrong. To hear Democrats tell it, the Bank of New York, chartered in New York in 1784, had already given Hamilton and his friends a near monopoly on credit in New York City. The Bank of the United States just expanded that power. Since 1784, according to Cheetham, the bank had made New York a Federalist "dominion" that funded Federalist candidates. "It was impossible to resist so formidable an engine," Cheetham complained. "No Turkish sultan could be more stern; his speechless messenger of death not more inexorable."[11] Indeed the bank often directly chose political candidates in municipal and state elections, while opponents could find few newspapers to help them. Independent newspapers, always operating on tight margins, found they could not survive without short-term loans, and no one loaned like the Bank of New York.[12]

While the Democrats' war against the Bank of the United States took place in newspapers that the party funded itself, it also took place in the Richmond assembly and the halls of Congress. Shortly after the Bank of the United States was chartered, the Virginia House of Delegates in Richmond passed laws to block such a corrupt institution from operating in the state. Then the assembly instructed Virginia's congressmen to introduce an amendment that would prevent Bank of the United States directors from sitting in Congress.[13]

Next, Secretary of State Jefferson secretly authored a direct attack on Secretary of the Treasury Hamilton that the Virginia congressman William Branch Giles read before Congress. The so-called Giles resolutions laid out Jefferson's case against the bank: Insiders bought bank stock with money borrowed from the bank, which meant that much of the hard currency that supposedly grounded the bank did not exist. Board members, he continued, received generous discounts for borrowing while others paid 8 percent or more. The tone of Giles's remarks was so harsh that it shocked many congressmen. The U.S. auditor's Federalist father called the resolutions "such a piece of baseness as would have disgraced the council of Pandemonium."[14]

In opposing the power of the bank, Jefferson and Madison crafted an argument that came to be labeled "strict construction." Jefferson wrote up a memo to President Washington explaining that because the Constitution had not mentioned a bank, it could not be allowed. His memo became the first statement of a new way of viewing the Constitution. Rather than being a blueprint for government, Jefferson argued, the Constitution precisely specified *all* the future powers of government. The Constitution had not been vague about granting powers and thus forgot the bank, he argued; the document had been deliberately parsimonious. The Constitution gave powers to Congress that were specific and unbendable. Strict construction would be the Democratic Party's gospel.

THE FIRST CRASH

IN LESS THAN A YEAR, the bank faced its first crisis. It began in 1792 after Hamilton's former assistant William Duer resigned from the Treasury to concoct a scheme to corner the market on U.S. 6 percent bonds. The response to Duer's actions among Democrats and some of his financial competitors almost destroyed American banking.

Duer understood that the revolution in France had driven panicked French aristocrats to buy up assets that paid a regular return, Bank of the United States stock in particular. In July 1791 the bank had sold down payments for stock—subscriptions, or "scrips" for short—at just $25. Duer knew that stockholders had to pay the next two installments in January and July 1792. Secretary Hamilton, hoping to boost U.S. bond sales, had specified in the scrip contract that Bank of the United States stockholders would pay a little of the installment in cash, the rest in U.S. 6 percent bonds. Duer figured that bond subscribers in New York and Philadelphia would be forced to buy bonds to make their July payment, and thus that bond prices would *have* to rise. Duer bought contracts in January: he promised to buy bonds in April at January prices. In other words, he bought thousands of bond futures; indeed he hoped to corner the entire market on U.S. bonds available in New York, a market of more than $2 million. If the bond price went up, then he would make the difference between the January and the April price, having put no money down; if the price went *down,* he would owe millions more than he had. In the language of the market he was a "bull."[15]

But by February 1792, Duer was in hot water. The previous fall he had received a lucrative military contract to supply General Arthur St. Clair's expedition against the Indians of the Western Confederacy led by Little Turtle. Duer's agents failed, and failed so spectacularly as to endanger the future of the Republic. They had provided broken packsaddles, insufficient forage, and wet gunpowder; the only provisions that were serviceable, apparently, were the drams of whiskey that Duer's contractors secretly sold directly to the troops.[16]

When St. Clair's army was overwhelmed in November 1791 in what is now western Ohio, Little Turtle's army killed more than six hundred men. Some of them were burned alive, according to retreating soldiers. It was the worst defeat in the history of the U.S. Army and an enormous setback for those who imagined that the United States could confidently blaze a trail over western Indians. By early February, word of Duer's role in the catastrophe had drifted back to North Carolina, New York, and New England. It was also a personal embarrassment to Duer that would undermine the bankers' trust in a man who had borrowed more than $2 million on bull market operations.[17]

On February 2, the North Carolina congressman John Steele asked that a congressional committee be formed to investigate whether "scarcity of provisions and forage" and "the quality of the powder" had been responsible for the defeat. It was a direct attack on Duer, and it set off the first congressional investigation in U.S. history. In addition, President Washington, alarmed by the defeat and the clamor in Congress, summoned his secretaries of state, war, and Treasury to determine how to respond to Duer's mismanagement. This became the first cabinet meeting in U.S. history.[18] By mid-February, his reputation in tatters, Duer could not get credit with his regular lenders for his scheme to buy up the 6 percent bonds. He resorted to borrowing sums as little as $500 from those small lenders, like Mrs. Macarty, who would soon be surrounding his jail.

Duer's reputation was not his only problem. Democrats connected with Chancellor Robert Livingston countered Duer's scheme by trying to withdraw large quantities of gold and silver from the Bank of New York in late January.[19] The move was simultaneously financial and political, the first "bear raid" in American history. When Democrats withdrew gold and silver, the banks lacked specie, and they called in their notes.[20] "I cannot describe to you," wrote one of Duer's associates to another, "the serious effect this great & unexpected depreciation of the moment occasioned."[21] Duer's purchases of U.S. bond futures depended on his pristine public reputation and his preferential access to bank credit. Little Turtle destroyed his reputation; New York Democrats destroyed his credit. His notes were due, his credit had been impeached by the St. Clair disaster, and he had no cash. On March 9 he suspended payment to his creditors.[22]

Duer's mostly Democratic competitors understood that a run on the New York banks could destroy his heavily leveraged fortune. They did not see that a bank panic has a dynamic of its own and would lead thousands of people to hoard hard currency. While a rising tide can be said to lift all boats, few can guess what a tsunami will do. Business was at a standstill. "A Citizen of Philadelphia" wondered in the *National Gazette* in May 1792 what issuing bonds and bank stock had done. It was supposed to "put a stop to speculation" by stabilizing the price of bonds on the market; "on the contrary . . . has it not drawn merchants, lawyers, doctors, parsons, tradesmen, farmers, women, and even apprentice-boys, from their ordinary occupations, to dabble in the stocks, to the disgrace of our country, and to the ruin of many thousands, once valuable and useful citizens?"

In reflecting on those "grossly defrauded and injured" in the downturn, *Dunlap's American Daily Advertiser* suggested that after the downturn the federal government should issue new bonds with

> the following *Devices* inscribed upon [them], according to [their] denomination. 1. The *bloody arm* of a soldier. 2. The *wooden leg* of a soldier. . . . 5. A continental colonel's widow with six children dining on a *salted herring* and *two potatoes*. 6. A continental major *begging his bread* with his family on his way to Kentucky. 7. A continental captain confined *in gaol* for a debt of 50 shillings. 8. A speculator driving his carriage over a soldier on a pair of crutches, in the streets of Philadelphia. . . . 15. A *Ring* to denote the irredeemability of the public debt, or that the evils produced by the certificates will have no end.[23]

As one of Duer's creditors wrote in April, "A general horror has occasioned . . . torpor and indecision among the dealers in stock. . . . The fulfillment of individual engagements is not only suspended but public and private confidence has received such a blow as may eventually stagger the stability of government."[24] In April, Hamilton rushed to buoy up the value of U.S. bonds by having the federal government buy them in New York.[25] Despite his best efforts, by April 1792 the fall of Treasury prices led a decline in bank stock prices traded on Wall Street.

In a desperate bid for liquidity, merchants sought to sell off bank stock and federal bonds to each other to meet the demands of creditors. They might have gathered where they always had, at the auction stalls near Wall Street. But on April 10, in the wake of Duer's failure, the New York legislature passed an "act to prevent the pernicious practice of stock jobbing." The legislature banned the public sale of securities, as well as outlawing futures and options contracts. The chief stock and bond auctioneers on Wall Street—close friends of Duer's—were now discredited. The market for "used stock," what we would call a secondary market, was nearly closed, and so liquidity was nowhere to be found. In March rates on the money market exceeded 1 percent per day with no parties willing to accept stocks or bonds as collateral.[26]

To protect themselves from the public clamor, and the law, bill brokers in New York City gathered at Corre's Hotel to establish a guild that would stop what the New York legislature disapprovingly called "public vendue or outcry" that took place on platforms and corners on Wall Street. The bill brokers formed a committee "to provide a proper room for them to assemble." In selling stocks and bonds indoors, none would charge less than one-fourth of 1 percent commission, and each would give preference for sales to the other brokers in the guild. This brokers' union—conceived as a response to the first American panic—became the New York Stock Exchange.[27]

As the price to borrow money skyrocketed, the Wall Street uncertainty had led to a depression in trade on Main Street by April and May 1792. "Confidence between men and women seems almost ruined," declared a New York correspondent of a Philadelphia paper, "and it would be some consolation if contemptible misers and rich skin-flints had alone suffered in the late failures—Unfortunately the widow, the orphan, and some other characters, who deserve our pity, have been also taken in." By late April widows and orphans were almost certainly among the crowd who rioted outside Duer's jail. In May an anonymous "stockholder in the bank" described in *Claypoole's Daily Advertiser* how "the country is going to ruin by failures." With double-digit interest rates, few would borrow. "Why are you not a commercial man, says one? The answer is, I cannot make more than 5 per cent. net by commerce. Why do you not work at your trade? I cannot make 6 per cent. is the reply. Why do you not build a house? It will not give me more than five per cent. for my money, if rent and repairs are duly considered. Thus all trades and useful occupations are at a stand . . . we are gaping at and abusing each other, while the Europeans and their agents . . . are buying our funds at 50 per cent. under what they are willing to pay for them." The stockholder estimated that Europeans had bought $2 million in public debt at fire-sale prices in the month after Duer's failure.[28]

Credit defaults cascaded through the spring of 1792. Banks or merchants who held "protested" notes from Duer demanded payment from other names on the notes. Thus, while the bawd Mrs. Macarty had lent money to Duer and taken his note for it, after a few weeks she might have turned over his note to a bank for ready cash. Once Duer defaulted, the ancient commercial rules of the two-party note meant that the bank could force her to repay the bank the entire sum, having signed below his note. These second or third signers discovered that they were liable for vast sums, causing further defaults and extending the panic for months. New York City was humbled. "The city is in a languishing condition," declared the *National Gazette* in April, "vessels laying at the wharves without any one to receive their cargoes—the speculators either in jail, ruminating over bushels of loose paper, locked up in garrets, or fled in to remote and desolate parts of Jersey!"[29] The packets of promises that banks and merchants held briefly became bushels of "loose paper." This was the essence of a panic. Let us call it "symbolic doubt": when hope becomes fear, optimism becomes desperation, when the iron gall ink on a note becomes an abstract squiggle, when promises of riches become demands to pay up.

New York was hardest hit, with personal losses totaling close to $3 million. But all the branches of the Bank of the United States contracted their lending by 25 percent and refused to accept notes longer than thirty days. This tightening of lending transmitted New York's financial contraction to Boston, Philadelphia, Baltimore, and Charleston.[30]

Despite the populist outrage outside Duer's cell, widows, orphans, tradesmen, and landlords were not the only ones in trouble. Some of the greatest speculating merchants in America had been taken in by Duer, including Leonard Bleecker, Gulian Verplanck, and George Storer, along with Jacobus and Nicholas Roosevelt (great-grandfather and great-granduncle to Theodore).[31]

The most spectacular loser was Chancellor Livingston's distant cousin the merchant Walter Livingston. Walter was a speculating Federalist in the "manor" branch of the Livingston family.[32] Walter was, he himself admitted later, "nearly allied to Mr. Duer, and persuaded he had been successful in business."[33] Now with his bills protested at the Bank of New York, he was what other brokers referred to as a "lame duck." But Walter, like Duer, had wiles. When his many debts on Duer's speculations came due, Walter hid his assets by secretly conveying them to his son and brother-in-law. In late March he published an advertisement in New York newspapers saying that he had no ready money but he would eventually "give satisfaction to creditors with whom he sincerely sympathizes."[34] Thousands of merchants along the Eastern Seaboard discovered that they were only one or two degrees of separation away from William Duer but that that was enough to bring down their credit. The high price to borrow, or the extreme security demanded, hobbled trade throughout the Eastern Seaboard. These men would be inclined to blame Duer, Hamilton, and the whole body of related Federalists. Jefferson, Madison, and Robert Livingston counted on it.

THE DEFEAT OF St. Clair's men had also roiled the markets for western land. If the Indians of the Western Confederacy under Little Turtle could destroy one-fourth of the U.S. Army in a single battle, could Americans really settle this western land? What value, really, was this western land that Congress claimed to own? In the wake of the panic Congress devoted millions of dollars to funding an expedition under "Mad" Anthony Wayne to destroy the Indians of the Western Confederacy. It was not the first time that Congress hoped that a military expedition might turn the nation's fortunes around.

In 1792, in the nation's temporary capital in Philadelphia, financial destruction sharpened political lines. The panic created the first opportunity for what we might call crash politics in America. New political coalitions would align in opposition to those politicians who could be blamed for the crash. Thus in the president's temporary residence on Philadelphia's High Street, the cabinet members Jefferson and Hamilton sought to block each other's ascendancy to the executive office. Together they persuaded George Washington to run for a second term in the fall of 1792.[35] Each man took the intervening four years to build his party's base. During election season that fall, Philadelphia's Congress Hall rang with charges and countercharges. Virginia politicians blamed New York stockholders for the failure, along with the Federalists Duer and Hamilton. New York Federalists responded that Virginia's First Families used local laws in their state to hoard unused land, thus protecting *themselves* from a sell-off while their poorer constituents were forced to liquidate.[36] Both sides would explain hard times in a narrative that linked speculators to opposing political factions. Political opponents became the heartless villains who had caused the innumerable personal tragedies that followed the crash. Private failure became a public act that the opposing party must have secretly scripted, rehearsed, and then applauded. Crash politics transformed party politics from a contest between professionals into an intense family drama about success and failure, dreams and rude awakenings, life and death.

No issue seemed remote from the issue of hard times. Federalists accused prominent Kentucky Democrats of using the disorder to support separatist movements allied with Spain; they called their opponents the party of anarchy and riot. But the Democrats understood crash politics better: they knew the crash could destroy Hamilton's party. It has been said that success has many fathers while failure is an orphan. In this crash Democrats were prepared to swear out a paternity suit with Alexander Hamilton's name on it. The Federalists, the party of gambling and financial distress, must have caused the panic of 1792.

The Democrats seized upon the failures in New York. "The gambling system," gloated Madison, "which has been pushed to such an excess, is beginning to exhibit its explosions." Duer was "the Prince of the tribe of speculators" and Hamilton's former righthand man. "[Duer] has just become a victim to his enterprizes, and involves an unknown number to an unknown amount in his fate." Hundreds of New Yorkers were "the dupes of his dexterity and the partners of his distress." Madison understood how deep was the rage at Duer: the crowd outside Duer's jail, he wrote, had "every description and gradation of persons, from the Church to the Stews."[37] Could parish priests and the denizens of bathhouses ("the Stews") really join together in a political party? Madison was certain of it. Democrats converted the "Society of St. Tammany" from a small social club into Tammany Hall, the organization that would lure New York mechanics and immigrants away from Hamilton's Federalist Party and into the Democratic fold.[38] The Bank of the United States was still a working political machine, but New York Democrats would build a machine of their own.

Democrats found allies in unlikely places. The bank's demand for hard currency after Duer's downfall in April 1792 pushed revenue agents to enforce existing excise taxes on whiskey and to impose new taxes on locally produced snuff and locally refined sugar. When revenue agents tried to enforce the excise tax on whiskey in August and September, tax revolts followed between 1792 and 1794 in western Pennsylvania and Kentucky. For western farmers whiskey *was* currency. Where roads were bad, where flour was too heavy to ship east, whiskey was a compact store of value that could be traded for necessaries. As they saw it,

Hamilton's attempt to fund his eastern banks by taxing whiskey simply taxed their currency to create his own. The so-called Whiskey Rebellion created thousands of new Democrats.[39]

The luxury tax on sugar also created new opponents in eastern cities. Hamilton and the Federalists felt luxuries like sugar to be obvious sources of revenue, but they failed to take account of city artisans, some of whom worked in these "infant manufactories" and many of whom consumed the "malt, hops, beer, ale, and cyder" that came from refined sugar. These new taxes seemed an enormous burden to them, and many soon deserted the Federalist Party to become Democrats.[40]

By 1794 opposition to Federalists emerged strongest in Jacobin societies formed in Philadelphia and New York. The new societies appealed directly to common workers, or what Hamilton's supporters called the "greasy cap," the "pig tail," and the "democratic TAR."[41] According to a Federalist poet, the financial disorder had led workers to quit their work and interest themselves in efforts to reform the government, work that was decidedly not their affair:

> *Hence, when disorder mars the wheel of state,*
> *Its course impedes, or turns, by force, or weight,*
> *If the ring burst, or if the tiring break,*
> *The spoke is shatter'd or the hub shall crack,*
> *Ballads and pictures, lasts and awls, should fly,*
> *Razors should fall, and puffs neglected lie,*
> *No news should spread, but every arm contend*
> *Who first, and best, the failing wheel should mend.*[42]

According to the Federalist poet, interest by workers in the affairs of state would surely breed anarchy. Federalists, for their part, imagined a vast conspiracy that joined East and West and so blamed the insurrectionary spirit of the so-called whiskey rebels on the Democratic Jacobin clubs in the cities. President Washington agreed. "I consider," he declared, "this [Whiskey] insurrection as the first *formidable* fruit of the Democratic Societies [whose] *artful and designing* members . . . sow the seeds of jealousy and distrust among the people. . . . I see, under a display of popular and fascinating guises, the most diabolical attempts to destroy . . . the government."[43]

Democrats downplayed the exploits of the whiskey rebels while reporting on every move of Duer and his little cabal after the crash. After Duer's promises turned to "loose paper," they wrote, he was still in prison but appeared able to wriggle free from his debts. Democrats claimed that New York's bankruptcy laws had protected Duer's property while hurting those with smaller debts.[44] Democratic newspapers claimed that one Duer associate was commanding a Spanish privateer off the Georgia coast, that another Duer friend had secretly conveyed £70,000 of property to a brother in Canada, while a third was hiding in the wilds of Newark, New Jersey.[45]

Of course, in the case of the Federalist speculator Walter Livingston the Democrats looked less innocent than they had hoped. Walter's cousin Chancellor Robert Livingston had built the Democratic Party to destroy men like Duer, but once Walter Livingston's lands were threatened, the chancellor chose blood and property over party. In 1794, as chancellor of New York, Robert Livingston overturned both the court of chancery and the state supreme court to protect his cousin's property. After Robert stopped the lawsuits, tenants rioted on many of the Livingston family properties upstate. Why did they have to pay their debts if a Livingston was not going to pay his?[46] The legal fallout from the panic of 1792 continued for years.

Creditors found that loose or contradictory bankruptcy laws in the several states made unwinding debts nearly impossible. Too late, many lenders discovered that borrowers could pick an advantageous state, declare bankruptcy there, surrender some assets, and leave all other creditors unfulfilled. Federalists in power, convinced that restoring confidence meant establishing uniform procedures for bankruptcy, sought to bring a uniform bankruptcy law to Congress. In 1792, 1793, 1796, 1798, and 1800, Federalists introduced bills. Democrats continually blocked them until 1800, enjoying making the Federalists twist in the wind. If there was going to be a bankruptcy law, one Democratic newspaper noted, it should "ever prove mild and lenient to the unfortunate, but a scourge to *Evil-DUERS*."[47] A federal bankruptcy act finally passed in 1800. It proposed to settle the debts of insolvents like Duer, yet by 1803, after more than eight hundred suits were tried in federal bankruptcy proceedings, lenders found that they were receiving less than ten cents on the dollar and often much less. Congress overturned the law in 1803.[48]

"FORGED PAPERS AND FRAUDULENT VOYAGES"

THE DUER PANIC was short lived. In part the very downturn itself may have helped prices recover as European buyers snapped up American bonds and Bank of the United States stock at cut-rate prices in the summer of 1792, leading U.S. bond prices to recover somewhat in June. Then, in February 1793, France's declaration of war against Britain and the United Netherlands created much more drastic financial instability in Europe, making America seem a relatively safe haven. In June 1793, Hamilton successfully negotiated a large loan to the Bank of the United States from Dutch capitalists.[49] Luckily for the bank, Dutch investors also got interested. Dutch bankers had previously created funds called *negotiaties:* a pool of mortgages issued on Dutch plantations. But after the failure of the Dutch central bank in December 1790, and then France's declaration of war, Dutch investors sought safer havens. After 1793, Dutch bankers created new *negotiaties* that pooled hundreds of U.S. bonds, state bonds, and Bank of the United States shares. Dutch investors could indirectly invest in American public securities by buying these new *negotiaties,* the world's first mutual funds.[50]

As Duer sat in his cell, the wars of the French Revolution intensified, providing a new opportunity for merchants and a new direction for the bank's investments. Farmers and merchants stood to benefit from foreign wars. "Our object is to feed and theirs to fight," quipped Secretary of State Thomas Jefferson when the declaration of war reached Washington. "We have only to pray that their souldiers may eat a great deal."[51] For more than twenty years, as Napoleon's armies invaded Italy, Prussia, and Russia, Jefferson's prayers were answered as "souldiers" on both sides ate biscuits made of American flour, drank rum manufactured in American distilleries, wore jackets dyed with American potash, and filled their pipes with American tobacco.[52]

But American merchants did not just bring barrels of flour to the victualing yards of Europe; with investment from the Bank of the United States, they now serviced the world. As neutral shippers in a worldwide war, they became lords of the oceans. A few months after France declared war on Britain in February 1793, Britain stopped enforcing the Navigation Acts that had blocked American access to Britain's colonial ports. It gave Yankee ships nearly unfettered access to the British Caribbean. In one year, U.S. trade with the British West Indies increased thirteen-fold. As the war broadened into the Caribbean, Spain, too, opened its ports to enterprising Yankee vessels. Spain's opening of the broad Río de la Plata (Silver River) allowed American ships to trade their flour, rum, and tobacco for Spanish-American silver.[53]

This illicit trade proved vital for the success of the Bank of the United States, which gradually shifted its lending from the government (which could now issue bonds) toward private merchant borrowers.

Back in 1792, 60 percent of the bank's lending had gone to the U.S. government; by 1811, 90 percent of its lending went to the merchant enterprises of its mostly merchant stockholders. Hundreds of thousands of Spanish pesos served as solid backing for American currency and put the new nation on a firmer financial footing than any other former colony before or since. The silver peso became the nation's informal dollar currency, one that could be traded in China, where silver's value was artificially high.[54]

After 1793, trading with the enemies of an international war was certainly dangerous. British naval ships occasionally seized American trading ships that appeared to violate the laws of neutrality. This proved a bone of contention between American merchants and the British navy, in part because Britain and France kept changing the rules. But for every enterprising Yankee caught by British or French ships, dozens more carried flour, lumber, rice, and wig powder to Caribbean plantations. Larger ships risked carting boxes of Caribbean sugar and coffee on the precious "long haul" across the Atlantic, where French, Spanish, or English customers eagerly awaited them. They smuggled French fabrics, Swedish iron, and Portuguese wine back to the Caribbean colonies.[55]

For New England merchants and the Bank of the United States, the wars that followed the French Revolution proved a silver age. As British, French, and Spanish vessels all became targets, neutral American ships quickly became among the most important carriers in the world. "A new power had now arisen on the western shore of the Atlantic," fumed the British Admiralty lawyer James Stephen in his 1805 pamphlet *War in Disguise*. These "enterprising adventurers" carried sugar, coffee, and rum from French colonies to Europe, effectively ignoring England's blockade of France. When imperial powers blocked their cargo, traders set up illicit trading stations on Passamaquoddy Bay in northern Maine and Amelia Island in Spanish Florida.[56]

The reputation of Yankee traders in the freewheeling days after 1793 resembled that of Greeks in later wars: rumrunners, gunrunners, smugglers, and drug dealers. Yankees would trade anything with anyone. By 1807, a vast 1.1 million tons of foreign goods entered U.S. ports. In the same year, the total tonnage of Britain's foreign trade with the world was only 1.5 million tons. In small New England towns like Newburyport, Massachusetts, ships arrived laden with more Caribbean sugar, molasses, gin, and coffee than all of New England could ever have digested. Most of these barrels and boxes were bound for reexport to

Britain, Holland, Denmark, Sweden, and Russia. By passing through New England harbors, the goods proved safer from the depredations of war than they would have been on French or English ships. Merchants paid an import duty to the federal government, then got a large rebate when they shipped the goods out again. The interest the Bank of the United States made on merchant deposits, alongside tariff moneys collected but not yet paid to the federal government, capitalized Hamilton's bank. America's Bank of the United States was built on the profits of profiteering.[57]

As the editor of a New England newspaper put it, "Our fleets visit remotest climes, our national flag commands the respect, and excites the envy, of the most haughty powers of the world." "Respect" might be too strong a word. James Stephen referred to America as a "half-way house" for the "fabrics and commodities of France" to be "re-exported, under the same flag, for the supply of the hostile colonies." American ships would pick up contraband articles at a foreign port, then destroy all the paperwork, picking up "new bills of lading, invoices, clearances, and passports" that suggested the articles came directly from America. After swearing false oaths and forging false certificates, they would carry the goods past English blockades.[58]

Jefferson's party resented these adventures and occasionally tried to block them in the two decades after the panic of 1792. Such merchants used "forged papers and fraudulent voyages," Jefferson declared, and directly interfered with U.S. foreign policy. Undaunted, and backed by the Bank of the United States, these New England merchants turned America's coastal ports into the oriental bazaars of the Atlantic.[59] American ships returning from the Spanish and French colonies brought sugar, silver, and coffee; those from Asia brought tea, pepper, and opium. A newly rich shipper was instantly recognizable in Boston, Philadelphia, and New York. He wore a pipe hat, a long coat, a short coat, and a blousy white shirt. His cotton breeches stopped at the knee, tied discreetly to silk hose and buckled shoes. Jeffersonians abandoned the knee breeches, or "culottes," adopting the long pants of French revolutionary *sans-culottes*. The broadcloth suit was either Prussian blue or Dutch black. Light yellow cotton breeches woven in Nanjing—called nankeen breeches—demonstrated one's refinement. Men in black coats and billowing white shirts counted on trading ships to carry their fortunes. And they counted on the Bank of the United States to guarantee their notes.[60]

The interruptions to America's trade with the world captured the headlines of newspapers and so have entered the history books: the Jay Treaty, the Quasi War, the XYZ Affair, the war against the Barbary pirates, Jefferson's embargo of 1807. But history books often ignore the bigger story: the vast expansion of American shipping that took place in the twenty years of fighting that followed the French Revolution.[61] The great expansion of America's international trade would have been impossible without credit from American banks. The banks relied on credit and capital from Dutch, French, and English investors. During the twenty years of European wars, American shippers' status as neutrals provided high profits and paid the interest on credit. In turn, the consistently high returns made American banks stronger.

American banks and bankers learned from Duer's panic that a tightly connected American merchant elite organized around a single man could not always be relied upon. There was a vast sea of prospective merchants, some newcomers. If carefully watched, these men could provide notes more reliable than Duer's promises. In the years after the panic, as the bank increased its loans to international merchants, a new kind of shipper came to the fore, men who relied on the Bank of the United States for capital, men unconnected to wealthy Caribbean plantations, men sometimes committed to the Democratic Party.[62]

Shippers like John Jacob Astor of New York were cut from a different cloth then Duer and the old Federalist merchants. Astor was short, square headed, and stout, and his foreign accent and uneven spelling made him seem a parvenu among the powdered wigs and snuffboxes of the New York Stock Exchange. Astor had arrived in the profession differently than most merchants, having never worked as a sailor or a quartermaster and having no Caribbean experience. He had left the German town of Walldorf as a teenager and worked briefly for his brother in a London shop that sold flutes. After arriving in the United States, he soon specialized in American furs. He was a peculiar kind of merchant in that after 1797 he became a solid Democrat. Astor was part of a new breed of Democratic merchants who saw opportunities beyond the comfortable confines of the English Empire, English credit, and English banks.[63] When Astor had his portrait painted, he dressed in Democratic trousers and cravat; his hair was not tied back in a queue but swept out front à la Napoleon.

Rather than posing with ships in the background, he posed surrounded by papers and books; his was the new world of bank paper. For Astor, banks facilitated trade and multiplied the capital available to him. He eagerly became a stockholder in the First Bank of the United

States because he understood a central lesson of banks: stockholders are preferred borrowers.[64] As a stockholder, he would help choose whose notes the bank discounted; his own received highest priority. Just as important, any other bank would readily accept Astor's notes drawn on the Bank of the United States. This "public institution," as Astor called it, had a wide reach. Bills drawn from the Bank of the United States allowed him to provide credit to fur trappers and traders deep in the American and Canadian interior. Montreal or Ohio merchants would accept an Astor note drawn on the bank, subtracting very little from the stated value.[65]

By 1795, the promissory notes that had funded Duer's rise had declined in importance, to be replaced by trading documents issued by a crowd of merchants whom the Dutch and English banks might previously have ignored. Bank-issued and bank-accepted bills of exchange funded the vast merchant enterprises that Astor had in mind, enterprises that a single shipowner could never have imagined: otter-killing expeditions to the American Northwest (then under the power of the Russians), china plate manufacture in Hong Kong, pepper harvesting in Sumatra, seal-hunting expeditions in the Antarctic. John Jacob Astor was not the first American shipper to arrive in China—the well-known New England merchants got there quicker—but because the New Yorker had multiple ships and credit with multiple New York banks, he was more successful more often. American bank credit also funded more reliable adventures in selling drugs to eager consumers: South American coffee to Stockholm, Virginia tobacco to Venice, Indian opium to China, Chinese tea to Livorno. Astor would never rival English shippers in the opium trade, but he could usually sell what people craved.[66]

AMERICAN MERCHANTS' PURSUIT of international trade helped buoy the nation out of its first depression as they found new outlets for American staples. With the millions they lent to merchants like Astor, American banks, especially the Bank of the United States, helped participate in that recovery. In the spring of 1799, seven years after the panic, Duer left debtors' prison a free man. He died at home before the summer.

If the bank succeeded financially, it did not succeed politically. By the time of Duer's death Jefferson's generally pro-French, anti–Bank of the United States coalition was on its way to seizing power. In the same year, 1799, the New York Democratic politician Aaron Burr broke the Bank of New York's near monopoly on banking in the city. He pushed a bill through the New York legislature to charter the Manhattan Company, which promised to provide fresh water to a city just recovering from yellow fever. A provision that allowed the "surplus capital" to be "employed in any way not inconsistent with the law" allowed Burr to turn the Manhattan Company into a multimillion-dollar bank, one that also happened to operate a waterworks.[67]

Elected president of the United States in 1801, Jefferson further hobbled the Bank of the United States. He blocked legislation to extend the bank's life, but the bank had enough backing among merchant-Democrats like Astor that Jefferson could not find the votes to end it before its twenty-year charter expired. Jefferson hurt the bank, but he could not kill it.

By 1804, the political conflict between Democrats and Federalists had become deadly and personal. When Burr heard that Hamilton had called him "despicable" and "a dangerous man" who "ought not to be trusted with the reins of government," Burr challenged Hamilton to a duel.[68] When they met on the dueling plains at Weehawken, New Jersey, Burr shot Hamilton dead. As Burr fled, his Federalist opponents accused him of traveling down the Mississippi to create a separate nation for Spain, an echo of the Federalist story about Democratic intrigues in Kentucky.

Democrats quickly distanced themselves from a man who appeared to be banker, duelist, and traitor. Many thought the story of Spanish intrigue absurd, but Jefferson believed it and sought to have Burr tried for treason.[69] Jefferson, Madison, Livingston, and Burr had been botanizing partners just a few years earlier; they had built the Democratic Party together. But by 1804, Jefferson had many reasons to mistrust Burr, who had helped him win the presidency in a way that called Jefferson's integrity into question. Jefferson's experience with Hamilton taught him that a bank could be a political machine that could threaten the life of the Republic. He was inclined to distrust a banker like Burr, a man who knew his closest secrets.

THE LAND RUSH ON $10 BARRELS,
1801 AND AFTER

ONCE THE JEFFERSONIAN Democrats came to power, they created a rival "bank" of their own, the U.S. Land Office. Attempts to sell land after 1798 flagged at first, but at the insistence of Northwest Territorial

Representative William Henry Harrison, Congress converted the land office from a retail land outlet into a bank that lent money to cash-strapped borrowers. Rather than having the Bank of the United States *choose* who might borrow money (and it had a tendency to choose Federalists), Congress passed the Land Act of 1800, which allowed the land office to advance loans to any American citizen.

In May 1801, the land office opened in Chillicothe, Ohio. Crowds gathered in Chillicothe weeks before the first public cry. The register of deeds, lacking the forms and officials on the first day, said he felt "much undetermined as to my duty, [since] not less than two hundred people were in town . . . waiting for the Commencement of the sale." Three weeks after the first plot was cried out, the Chillicothe Land Office had mortgaged off almost 100,000 acres. In paying the first of four installments, buyers entered a claim, then took a note and mortgage. The deed awaited final settlement. The land itself was the security; for those who failed to make payments, the land office would advertise the default, then sell it again in a second sale. This was the Jeffersonian installment plan. If we consider its outstanding loans to borrowers, the U.S. Land Office soon became the largest bank in the world, with millions of dollars in outstanding debts.[70]

The millions owed would soon become tens of millions. Saint Domingue, France's wealthy sugar-producing colony in the Caribbean, was itself revolutionized by the convulsions of Europe. In Saint Domingue, in the words of the historian C. L. R. James, the French Revolution started as a "quarrel between whites and Mulattoes" that "woke the sleeping slaves."[71] The planters were overthrown and many killed in 1793. Even Napoleon's army could not put the genie of revolution back in the bottle. By 1803 the new Republic of Haiti had crushed and embarrassed Napoleon's armies. With his valuable sugar colony lost to him, Napoleon considered his recently acquired Louisiana territories worthless. Why provide timber, pork, and other provisions to a sugar colony you no longer owned? In a fit of pique, and to weaken the English, he sold the Louisiana territory to the United States for just over $11 million. Naturally, the Americans bought it on installments.

Immediately after the Louisiana Purchase, the Democrats' land distribution scheme was extended to all lands south of Tennessee. By 1804 the minimum tract was lowered from 320 acres to 160; the new price was lowered from $2.00 to $1.64 per acre. For a little more than $260, and only $66 down, anyone could own a piece of the West. The potential for profit was real. Between 1797 and 1815, as long as artillery was rumbling and European wheat fields were burning, a barrel of flour could command nearly ten silver dollars in Philadelphia or New York.[72] Depending on the quality of land, rainfall, distance to the mill, the miller's toll, distance to markets, and final prices, a farm family with eighty acres planted might pay off the mortgage in a single good year.

While the wars of the French Revolution initially benefited Federalists and the Bank of the United States, the final victor that would emerge from the convulsions in Europe would be the Democratic Party. Jefferson had built a proxy bank to provide credit to thousands of American farmers. The high price of American flour, cheap western land, and cheap credit would fill the ranks of the new Democratic Party. Federalists who opposed the men they called the "Virginia lordlings"—Jefferson, Madison, and Monroe—would find that cheap land and the promise of riches made the new party unstoppable. Jefferson's "bank" also led to rapid westward movement. As the Federalist Fisher Ames complained, "By adding an unmeasured world beyond that river [the Mississippi], we rush like a comet into infinite space." "In our wild career," he warned, "we may jostle some other world out of its orbit, but we shall, in every event, quench the light of our own."[73] In the aftermath of the first American crash, the bankers and powerful Federalists had lost. The Democratic comet that rushed into infinite space was made of eastern mortgages for western lands. The United States' first real estate boom was just beginning.

Toward the end of Jefferson's second term, the fate of the Bank of the United States became increasingly contentious, its board members increasingly political. In 1807, in order to prevent American shippers from trading with either enemy, Jefferson persuaded Congress to impose a nonimportation policy and finally an embargo on international exports, a strategy the British envoy George Rose called "a sort of Chinese policy [to] shut themselves up from the rest of the world." Furious at Jefferson's ban on their trading, New England merchants and bankers called Jefferson's embargo a tyranny against those "whose farms are on the ocean, and whose harvests are gathered in every sea." Many shippers continued to smuggle, while the bank called in its loans and blamed the Democrats for hurting commerce.[74]

As New England merchants continued smuggling and England began to organize for a war against America, political lines sharpened. Federalists organized hundreds of unemployed sailors in demonstrations against Jefferson's embargo in New York, Philadelphia, and Baltimore. Democrats responded by organizing their own mobs of artisans who rallied in Philadelphia and New York to support the president and

Congress.[75] In 1809 in Norfolk, Virginia, Democrats burned effigies of Francis James Jackson, Britain's minister to the United States who had repeatedly insulted Americans in public.[76] Democratic mobs in Norfolk and Philadelphia emphasized the ruthlessness of the British and the dangers of foreign entanglements. The Democratic press called attention to the partisan nature of the bank, pointing out that nearly all the regional bank directors were Federalists and that the bank had interfered with Jefferson's embargo, had interfered in local elections, and had manufactured memorials to Congress to keep the bank alive.[77]

As the bank itself solicited public petitions for its recharter while war loomed with England, congressional Democrats became increasingly suspicious. Many viewed Federalist and bank connections with Britain as foreign influences that threatened the new nation. In 1810 the Democratic merchant Jesse Atwater published a pamphlet denouncing the bank as "the most monied, most powerful, and perpetual aristocracy in the union." Its loans to politicians and newspaper editors gave it an "everlasting and most baleful influence on our elections." Because it was able to "create artificial scarcity and plenty," he declared, it had the power "of crushing all other banks, of laying under contribution our commercial capitals, of paralyzing our manufactures and of awing our government."[78]

American suspicions about the bank's English sentiments and its outsized influence mixed with suspicions about other British influences in the Americas. Stories circulated in Congress and on the frontier that British officers were providing muskets to Tecumseh's confederacy in the North, the Red Sticks in the South, and the Seminoles in Florida. In Congress, the growing pro-war, anti-bank Democrats quickly earned the name War Hawks. The War Hawk leader, Henry Clay, Speaker of the House, was the chief firebrand. "When a burglar is at our door," he thundered, referring to Britain's alleged arming of Indians, "shall we bravely sally forth and repel his felonious entrance or meanly skulk within the cells of the castle?"[79] Henry Clay voted for sallying forth. The bank remained at the center of all these discussions of war. Eighty citizens of Pittsburgh wrote to Congress that while Britain committed outrages on land and sea, the bank's lending "held in bondage thousands of our citizens, who dared not act according to their consciences, for fear of offending the British stockholders and federal directors." The bank, in asking for recharter in 1810, "opens a modest proposal for the surrendry of our independence."[80]

At the end of 1810, with war looming, the bank lost the crucial support of John Jacob Astor, and that wounded it further. Astor himself was profiteering: funding large-scale smuggling of British goods across the Canada-U.S. border and buying up bills of exchange issued to support the British navy's military buildup in Canada. In December of that year Astor demanded more than $100,000 in silver—apparently to provide cash to discount valuable British notes. Nonplussed, the cashier of the bank asked him to close his account. Outraged, Astor began a public feud with the bank and ironically accused it of supporting the British, a charge the War Hawks quickly repeated.[81] Jefferson's Treasury secretary, Albert Gallatin, a close friend of Astor's, recognized that Astor had actually acted treasonously. In a letter, Astor assured his friend the Treasury secretary, "As to the propriety of my having bought these bills . . . there were circumstances connected with that transaction which are not to be brought before the publick but which I will in a day or two communicate to you." An exasperated Gallatin protected Astor by not revealing his secret deal, but on the back of Astor's letter Gallatin wrote, "I believe that his only explanation will be that he made money by it."[82]

The bank had restructured the debt required to fight one war; it would not survive a second one. Eighteen eleven was the last year of the charter, and War Hawks in Congress doubted the loyalty of a bank with 70 percent ownership in Britain and a tiny portion of its credit in government bonds. War Hawks suggested the bank would use its political power to weaken the government's response to English attacks on shipping and persons.[83] While the British continued to capture American ships and impress American sailors into their navy, the bank, thundered the Virginia senator William Branch Giles, gave "British influence . . . a body and form for action" and was "instrumental in paralyzing every effort of resisting these hostilities."[84]

In a moment of profound irony, John Jacob Astor and his friends promised $2 million to support the U.S. Treasury if the government refused to recharter the bank that had scotched Astor's attempts at profiteering and then closed his account.[85] So just as the storm clouds of Europe threatened to draw the United States into armed conflict, Congress instructed the nation's chartered central bank to shutter its doors. Banks chartered in the states struggled to pick up the slack.

On March 4, 1811, the last day of the bank's charter, Stephen Girard, a one-eyed bastard son of a French nobleman, bought its magnificent marble building. He renamed the Bank of the United States the Bank of Stephen Girard to support his growing merchant enterprise.[86] With no central bank in the country, the state banks, 114 of them in 1811, became more than 140 in 1812. They emerged from the shadow of the Bank of the United States to become the nation's principal commercial institutions.[87] Democrats turned the nation on the path of mixed banking, of a variety of banks with a variety of purposes. When a group of mechanics chartered a new bank in Newark, New Jersey, they declared themselves "aware that the privileges granted to associated companies, under the authority of government, may be the engine of oppression." Banks, in other words, could be political machines. There was only one solution: "In the establishment of new companies, the corrective hand of government will interpose new guards against the evils that a corrupt administration of the authority [has] given to [the] incorporated bodies already established." The only solution to a corrupt party machine such as the Bank of the United States was for the government to charter more party machines to oppose it.[88]

Had Hamilton been alive in 1811, he might have been struck by this extension of logic in Madison's famous Federalist No. 10. Madison argued that in a large republic, many factions would compete and thus prevent control by a single faction that might "concert and execute their plans of oppression."[89] The mechanics of Newark reasoned that if Hamilton and Duer's bank was a corrupt faction (and they believed it was), then the solution was for government to create many corrupt factions, many banks to guard against the evils of all the others. This was the final product of the 1792 depression. Americans, unlike people in most other parts of the world, would have a horde of competing banks to choose from. Each of these banks made its own paper currencies, all redeemable in gold and silver.

Dissolving the Bank of the United States in 1811 was a crucial step toward war. Congress destroyed an efficient financial machine but also—most assuredly—a political one. Some Democrats believed that dissolution of the bank would finally prevent Britain from corrupting the American legislature. Federalists worried that the bank could no longer quiet the rumblings of a war with England. Whatever it meant, the destruction of the bank can be seen as the first shot in what Americans would call the War of 1812.

Yet during the war, even while British and American men-of-war exchanged hot lead and chain shot over Lake Erie, even as American frigates captured English merchantmen in the Atlantic, even as soldiers tussled over Washington City and New Orleans, many Yankee ships and British shippers continued their trading as if nothing had happened. While American soldiers suffered for food, New England merchants were shipping flour to British soldiers and sailors in Portugal and Spain.[90]

By the end of the war New England, whose merchants had traded with the enemy, had a very bad reputation in the rest of the country. Many Democratic newspapers recalled the night in 1813 when merchants in New London, Connecticut, flashed blue lights to the British ships blockading their port, warning them of American warships trying to escape the English blockade. Republicans called the Federalist politicians who favored the Bank of the United States "blue lights."[91] Those blue lights were all that was left of Hamilton's dream, the ghostly reflection of Hamilton's promise of saltwater trade, of triumphant American commerce, and of an American bank that had controlled a nation.

For a while the bank had triumphed. The Napoleonic Wars had provided an opening for the bank and an ambitious plan to turn a new nation into what one historian has called a reexport republic, a republic built on forged papers and fraudulent voyages.[92] This illicit trade, combined with the magical attraction of American bank stocks, built American fortunes and funded American banks. That trade helped the new American republic avoid the fate of so many newly independent nations in the eighteenth, nineteenth, and twentieth centuries. America avoided the receivership, default, and balance-of-payments crises that plagued Latin America, the Caribbean, the princely kingdoms of South Asia, postcolonial South Asia, and much of southern Africa. The fiscal and military state that Hamilton helped create with the Constitution was no accident; his model was to emulate the fiscal and military might of Great Britain. But the bank's capacity went beyond creating a public debt to fight wars and police its borders. This bank would also provide funding for East Coast merchants in a time of international war.[93]

Many Americans viewed this new central bank with suspicion. The Virginians and New Yorkers who in May 1791 joined forces during a botanizing excursion in New York ended Duer's campaign to corner the market in American debt. They contributed to the panic that followed, then built three kinds of institutions to replace it: Tammany Hall, the Federal Land Office, and Democratic state banks like Burr's Manhattan Company.

When Democrats ended the bank's charter in 1811, the United States severed credit relations with many of its English investors. Dozens more banks were created. By the time of the war the New England merchants connected with the bank had grown haughty, financially powerful, and politically ineffectual. Their promises, like William Duer's, were not the guarantees they seemed. Without a uniform national bankruptcy law—like the English and the Dutch had—banks would be more guarded in their lending and less likely to trust the notes of their stockholders. Banks would have to find more trustworthy instruments than the promissory note, and more trustworthy borrowers than William Duer.

After the War of 1812, long-distance trade between the American West and the world, made possible by land grant offices and new kinds of banks, would become the new source of American fortunes. Old Federalists, disgusted with the new banks built during the War of 1812, declared that these banks had become ravenous and destructive. A new "river money" generated by the banks would depend on two new debts: liens against high-value imported goods and loans on high-priced western land. These rock-solid investments would certainly protect America from deadbeats like Colonel Duer, at least until the panic of 1819.

CHAPTER THREE

Monkey Jackets, the Uncorked Mississippi, and the Birth of Caterpillar Banks

IN THE NOVEL *Moby-Dick,* Herman Melville's character Ishmael heads for the dangers of the sea in a monkey jacket. Unlike the long trench coat designed for a life on the land, the monkey jacket is short in the chest. It is perfectly designed for the monkey-like tasks of common sailors: pulling ropes, scurrying across decks, and climbing around in riggings. It was the coat a common sailor wore. After the War of 1812, the monkey jacket began to appeal to workingmen.[1] Its short cut made it especially flattering to a young and single man as it broadened his chest, narrowed his waist, and showed off his legs.

Young Herman Melville knew his jackets not only because he wore one but because his father, his uncles, and his grandfathers had made their fortunes by the sale of finer coats than this, along with buckskin gloves, cambric handkerchiefs, and all manner of decorative Florentines, lutestrings, tastes, and galloons.[2] In the days of the Napoleonic Wars a fine woolen jacket cost as much as $50. This was then a little fortune, a year of a man's wages, the price of a small house. Such goods made Melville's family quite rich.

But the twenty-year war against Napoleon changed everything for the woolen trade and made monkey jackets cheap enough for an artisan or farmer to buy. They were not cheap for everyone. "You will see how shamefully I am treated [by] the commissary," complained Napoleon, who in 1808 was just beginning to recognize that the lack of woolen garments worn by his army as it marched east into Russia would doom his world-grabbing enterprise.

> I have only fourteen hundred coats, seven thousand great coats, instead of fifty thousand; fifteen thousand pairs of shoes, instead of one hundred and twenty-nine thousand. I am in want of every thing. Nothing can be worse than the clothing. My army will begin the campaign naked. It has nothing. . . . My army is naked just as it

is entering on a campaign. I have spent a great deal, which has been money thrown into the sea.[3]

Meanwhile, during the 1808 campaign the forces allied against Napoleon had tens of thousands of English jackets and greatcoats. Government contracts had turned the western side of England into the workshop of Europe. Mechanical innovation in the North of England allowed river factories to turn out what the writer Thomas Carlyle mockingly called the "vestural tissue" for armies and navies around the world.[4] When the war ended in December 1814, the dry-goods market was flooded with partially finished monkey jackets.

The jacket, expensive until 1814 and then "monstrous cheap" in its monkey variety thereafter, would remake the American economic landscape, and remake American banking. Between 1814 and 1818, the jacket's sudden cheapness, its new method of export, and the way in which new competitors sold it all fueled a boom that displaced the Melvilles and dozens of other merchants familiar with the old colonial factorage system. Loans on the shipment of these jackets and other dry goods into the interior would be an important new promise in the arsenal of American banks. The new banks that emerged to fund this trade—called caterpillar banks in their day—created a dollar economy that stretched all the way to Louisiana. It stitched America together east and west of the Appalachian Mountains. But caterpillar banks also provided too much liquidity for stockholders who could not refrain from using it to speculate in land. In the spring of 1818, when Anglo-American conflict over the West Indies trade undermined the market for American wheat just as millions of new acres were opened in the West, American land prices collapsed. The Land Office and the Second Bank of the United States, sensing danger, demanded gold and silver just as land prices were falling. The sudden demand for gold and silver plunged America into the panic of 1819. For many farmers after 1819 their monkey jackets were all they had left.

BEFORE AND DURING the Napoleonic Wars buying and selling a jacket was a gentleman's business. Herman's grandfather Major Thomas Melvill (spelled without the *e* then) sold fine fabrics by the yard on the ground floor of his large and opulent Boston house. In western New York the merchant John Jacob Astor likewise operated a string of "stores" that sold similar goods to farmers and trappers on credit.

In Kentucky and western Tennessee, Congressman Andrew Jackson owned a store or two on his plantations. His stores would have sold on credit as well. The bulk of the capital invested in a store was the fabric.[5] When a farm family wanted English dry goods like woolens or osnaburgs, the storekeeper would measure out the fabric and record the purchase in a country-store ledger book. The goods were payable "at harvest," with considerable interest built into the purchase price.[6]

Rather than buying a finished overcoat, most farm families would agree on a price for cut woolen material, thread, and horn buttons, at more than triple East Coast prices. A mother or daughter would tailor the coat. To settle the account, a rural western family would burn trees to make potash, peel hardwood for barrel hoops, churn milk into butter, or twist hemp into rope. Besides these "country goods," Astor's stores accepted furs, tanned or untanned, of minks, otters, squirrels, and beavers. Astor or Jackson would employ teamsters to transport these high-value, low-weight objects to coastal cities for sale. They would buy their English trade goods ("provisions") in New York or Philadelphia, and sell their country goods ("staples") in Albany or New Orleans.[7]

Thus, even though Americans had won their revolution, American purchases before 1812 rested on a colonial credit system. This system of import and export through colonial stores would have been familiar to British imperial merchants from Mumbai to Montreal. British credit remained so important to American stores that while the U.S. government had proclaimed the dollar the unit of value, many stores still recorded debts in pounds, shillings, and pence.[8]

Before 1812, inland merchants like Andrew Jackson who traded over long distances like these had balance-of-payments problems to worry about. Every year Jackson fretted about whether he had collected enough American staples to match the value of the European provisions he bought and sent west. While he would never admit it in polite company, Jackson was much like the Melvills of Boston, whose trade straddled oceans. Like coastal merchants, he needed banks, but these banks could do him in; in 1795, the twenty-eight-year-old Jackson was nearly bankrupted when the promissory notes he used to acquire Philadelphia provisions proved nonnegotiable because the man who had issued them—a merchant named Allison—had debts great enough to put him in prison. Having "accepted" the notes and then passed them on by signing them, Jackson became liable for them after Allison defaulted. Forced to sell his assets quickly, Jackson just barely evaded debtors' prison himself. In those years he became testier, more concerned about the honor of his signature, and more likely to defend himself with pistols.[9]

The War of 1812 changed that colonial trading system forever. While formally the war resulted from the breakdown of negotiations between the United States and Great Britain, many Americans blamed New England merchants like the Melvills. Merchants like the Melvills had in fact opposed the war, but Americans were sure that their illegal trading with France, Holland, Spain, and their colonies had angered the British ministry and Parliament. Whoever caused it, the easy terms that New England merchants had with their English lenders would be sundered almost completely.

The War of 1812 had many fronts: across the Great Lakes between the United States and Canada, in the Indian lands of the Western Confederacy beyond the Appalachian Mountains, in the Red Sticks territory north and east of New Orleans. Americans fought the British and their Indian allies, sacking the towns and encampments of tribes on the barest suspicion that they had communicated with the British. The war would eventually provide the pretext for a massive expansion of American territory, but challenging the world's naval power was dangerous. After war was declared, American troops sacked Canadian cities on the Great Lakes, and American privateers captured British merchant ships. British vengeance was swift. In 1813, British officers in their surtouts and sailors in their monkey jackets burned the "nest of pirates" that Americans called Baltimore, then looked toward the newly built Capitol in Washington. In August 1814 they invaded the city and set fire to the Executive Mansion.[10]

A war with Britain jeopardized more than the nation's physical infrastructure. Turmoil undermined faith in its currency. As in most wars people hoarded gold and silver, contracts were canceled, banks stopped functioning. In late August 1814, the British burned the city of Washington. As their fires turned night into day, all the banks outside New England suspended specie payments. Secretary of the Treasury Gallatin resigned in frustration.[11] But even in December, after the war concluded, the new Treasury secretary, Alexander Dallas, could not get the state banks outside New England to resume payments. He hesitated to force banks to resume payments, recognizing that a sudden demand for silver would destroy banks good and bad.[12]

The governing wheel was gone. Between 1791 and 1811 the Bank of the United States had enforced interbank settlements, encouraging banks to accept printed currency from one another and occasionally demanding slow-paying state banks to pay silver for land and tariff money they collected. The U.S. Custom House and the Land Office relied on the bank's informal regulation in that the government accepted only printed dollars that the Bank of the United States would accept.[13] But without the Bank of the United States as a bank arbiter and with most states off specie, America's taxing agents—its port collectors and land agents—found it impossible to legally distinguish one bank's notes from another. This awkward interregnum between the First Bank of the United States and the Second saw the birth of a wholly new kind of bank built on an entirely new system of wholesaling and trade. It simultaneously allowed a flourishing of interstate trade and increased the risk of financial panic.

THE OVERSEAS MONKEY JACKET

WHEN THE WAR OF 1812 and the Napoleonic Wars that led to it had ended in 1815, Americans' pent-up desire for British goods surged after twenty years of fighting and embargoes. British sellers were especially eager to unload vast inventories of unfinished woolen jackets that had been fashioned for the soldiers and sailors fighting Napoleon. With Napoleon in exile these unfinished monkey jackets filled warehouses in northern England: the worst had happened for the worsted trade. With European militaries no longer buying, English master clothiers began to dream of knock-kneed American farmers, wives, and children feeding pigs, churning butter, and sharpening their plows—all clad in English wool.

Alexander Brown & Sons can be said to have started the deluge. These merchant bankers of Baltimore got early word of Napoleon's defeat and loaded Brown & Sons ships with crates of English dry goods. Along with the traditional cambrics, sateens, and osnaburgs were crates and crates of unfinished wool jackets. In 1815 half a dozen English ships landed in America with loads of English goods. A year later nearly a hundred ships carried British exports to the United States, exports that had increased tenfold from the average of the previous decade. Alexander Brown & Sons doubled its capital in only two years.[14]

Merchants like the Melvills suffered, pushed to the wall by the flood of cheap imported half-finished goods. They knew the way trade was *supposed* to work, having imported English dry goods before the war. In one year, a blue-stockinged importer would order at least a dozen hair trunks of English dry goods; within the year he would have sold each trunk "by the package" to a wholesaler who would have stored it in a

New York warehouse. Months later the wholesaler would sell the package of folded woolen fabric "by the piece" to a merchant like Andrew Jackson, who would then ship the folded woolen fabric out to stores in the backcountry to be sold at inflated prices on long credit. A group of merchants called this system the best in the world: "Thus the citizen is provided with the foreign products and manufactures which his comfort and convenience require, and disposes of the fruits of his industry in the manner most advantages to himself and the State."[15]

But Brown & Sons and its partners, the English manufacturers, sold the new "cheap" cottons and woolens differently. In the years of the long war from 1797 to 1816, English factories had driven manufactured cotton and woolen prices to less than a third of their previous levels. Highly capitalized English machines helped to spin, reel, and warp thousands of yards of woolens; sweating laborers wove woolens into regular patterns in Yorkshire and the West of England, then napped, dressed, and finished them; Manchester laborers wove the cottons and dyed them; captains of English merchantmen brought these finished, partially stitched goods on regular schedules to the city.[16] Funded at first by fat military contracts, these highly capitalized industries increasingly worked year-round rather than seasonally. That required an expanded market. In 1815 the manufacturers sent local agents—second sons, sons-in-law, and nephews—to New York City where they sold the goods at auction for pennies a pound.

While backwoods merchants could buy these goods at auction, often the intermediate purchaser would be a new kind of man in America's seaport, one who neither owned ships nor saw his final customer. He bought boxes in big lots, "jobbed" the boxes down the street in his carriage, then sold to other merchants. He was a "jobber." Because western merchants couldn't be in town all the time to catch the auction, a jobber with a little bank credit could pick up the jackets at auction, haul them to his warehouse on Pearl Street, and sell in bulk to almost anyone interested in setting up a store in the rapidly expanding West. The old-fashioned New York merchants who, like the Melvills of New England, disliked these new competitors, resented both the English agents and the young and pushy jobbers who bought from them. In a petition to Congress New York merchants complained both about the "ADVENTURERS (chiefly foreigners) [who] import immense quantities of goods" and about the jobbers, "persons unknown to the public, whose names even are not mentioned, and who are responsible for nothing."[17]

Dressed in trousers rather than hose, the jobber represented all the sins of the new city, post-1815. The jobber hired a young assistant called a drummer to troll city hotels and befriend country merchants who visited New York in the fall and the spring. The drummer would then ply the country merchants with sweetened drinks in hotel lobbies and occasionally arrange a discreet rendezvous with a penurious widow. Soon the jobber would lure the merchants into his store. If the country merchant could provide two references, the jobber would sell the goods "on time." In other words, the jobber would accept a note from the country merchant for six months of credit, with the opportunity to extend the credit six months later, and again and again. Jobbers became the key lenders to merchants in the American West. These New York jobbers needed New York banks.[18]

Wartime trade had changed England as well, making the auctioning of goods vital. Sharp merchants like Kleinwort & Sons in Manchester understood the time value of money: no use waiting for merchants like the Melvills to order goods once a year. Instead, they would box up commonly ordered goods in burlap, sell them quick at auction, and invest the cash. Lather, rinse, repeat. Rather than taking a year, the whole operation could conclude in three months if someone could assure speedy, reliable communication across the Atlantic. For this reason Kleinwort & Sons developed a new line of service between New York and Liverpool called a packet service. Before the packet service, wholesalers had relied on slow and uncertain tramp ships. A New York tramp ship bound for Liverpool would advertise a date of departure, then wait and wait and wait for the hold to fill up. Mail, bins of flour, barrels of whiskey, animals, and passengers all queued up until the captain determined that the ship was full enough to cast off. One Kleinwort merchant recalled sending a time-sensitive message every day for thirty days to a correspondent. All thirty arrived at once, months later, when the ship carrying his notes passed through a storm and finally arrived in port.

Kleinwort's inspiration was the English military packet service that sent correspondence and goods on English navy ships at scheduled times. Kleinwort & Sons called its packet service the Black Ball Line and promised that at least one of its four ships would leave Liverpool for New York on the first of every month (a forty-day journey). A different ship would leave New York for Liverpool on the fifth of every month (a twenty-three-day journey). The service began the first day of 1818 in Liverpool with a 380-ton ship. When it started, most thought the ship was too large for the trade; within ten years ships twice the size were far too small.[19]

The Black Ball Line helped change New York from a port city into a metropolis.[20] An English manufacturer with £500 could make, finish, and sell a batch of goods three times in a *single year* even while importers like the Melvills continued the old way, ordering in summer, receiving in fall, selling by winter, collecting in spring. Time was money, and manufacturers who manufactured, delivered, sold, and collected in a single season made a lot of it.

This part of the circuit—the manufacturer, Alexander Brown & Sons importers, and the Black Ball Line—brought the goods more cheaply to New York. But getting a monkey jacket out to a backwoods farmer required other institutions: the auction house, the state bank, and the steamboat. A freezing farmer in Ohio wanting a coat could not have paid cash for it, even if he was prosperous. He had no bank nearby to issue cash in exchange for his promise. The 114 banks in the United States stood mostly on the coast, where they serviced the coastal trade. In western New York, Pennsylvania, or Tennessee cash was scarce. To get it, westerners needed state banks.

AUCTION HOUSE, STATE BANK, STEAMBOAT: THE INLAND MONKEY JACKET

WITHOUT THE BANK of the United States to limit their operations, state banks emerged rapidly to facilitate inland trade and profit by it. Pennsylvania's omnibus bill of 1814 created forty-one banks throughout the interior. The most notorious example was the "litter" of forty banks incorporated in Kentucky in 1817 with a "capital" of $10 million but without a single coin in their vaults. The banks had big plans for the state but no provision for making payments in gold and silver.[21] As citizens of Washington began to rebuild their burned city, independent and state banks expanded, claiming the sovereign power that the Bank of the United States had once claimed. They issued their own currency, which often declined in value. The depreciation of Kentucky dollars hurt anyone obliged to accept them. This included the federal government, as well as artisans and day laborers snookered into doing so. Senators compared the banks to caterpillars, insects that devoured everything in their path. "The banks, pending the war, were the *pillars* of the nation," declared Senator Samuel Smith of Maryland. "Now that we could do without them, they had [become] *caterpillars*."[22] One hundred fourteen banks in 1811 became 208 banks in 1815, and 256 in 1816.[23]

While the caterpillar banks certainly allowed currency inflation, they also allowed the differentiation and specialization of trade that helped to bring monkey jackets to the American interior and drive out the old-fashioned colonial system of importers, wholesalers, and dry-goods merchants. They issued currency—printed bills—that replaced an awkward system of coin and credit.

Before caterpillar banks, money of all kinds was scarce. A farmer or group of farmers would find a store to offer them credit for necessaries like seeds, plows, needles, shirting, and salt. An operator for one of Jackson's stores would then collect the farmer's harvest and pay him what was left with a mix of store credit and silver. In this old-fashioned system of the 1790s, a prominent store owner like Andrew Jackson operated as a wholesaler, retailer, lender, and arbitrageur. Jackson's store advanced credit to farm families, but the families paid high prices for goods, as well as hidden interest rates that approached 50 percent or more.

In the jargon of economics, caterpillar banks "monetized" the debt relationship between the nation's ports and its midwestern cities. Beginning with a small amount of silver, caterpillar banks printed currency and found farmers to lend their printed money to, farmers who would give them promissory notes due in three months or less at 8 percent or more interest, depending on local conditions. Or, as *Niles' Weekly Register* put it, "At first they throw out money profusely, to all that they believe are *ultimately* able to return it; nay, they wind round some like serpents to tempt them to borrow."[24] *Niles' Weekly Register* complained that these "money shops" grew up in every town where there was "a church, a tavern, and a blacksmith's shop."[25] A bank would also establish relationships with the local churches, taverns, and blacksmith shops by promising delivery of silver for their notes at any time while also offering to store in a fireproof safe the silver they received. The bank recognized that all the local houses would not arrive at once to demand their silver, and so it could issue currency beyond the silver it held, often much beyond it. Hezekiah Niles complained that the worst thing about banks was that they created bankers: "A knot of 'little great men' is instantly formed, who withdraw themselves from the 'vulgar,' and ape the manner of 'three tailed bashaws.' "[26]

These caterpillar banks, for all their faults, liberated buying and selling from their colonial dependence on a tiny number of merchant go-betweens. If the Revolution ended America's political dependence on England, the caterpillar banks ended the nation's economic dependence on a few eastern merchants and their English correspondents. Throughout Africa, Asia, and Latin America, former colonies without an independent banking infrastructure continued to rely on a colonial factorage system that gave local monopolies for dry goods, food, or tools. Like America in the age of William Duer, these local commercial cabals were usually tightly tied to rings of political and military men. By expanding credit willy-nilly, caterpillar banks in the American West helped disperse such monopolies, allowing many young merchants the opportunity to open shops by borrowing from the bank. This new credit environment was good for farmers but bad for merchants like Jackson and the Melvills, who had relied on their privileged access to coastal credit.[27]

Three institutions—the auction house, the river banknote, and the steamboat—facilitated this new internal trade in foreign goods. The forty-three licensed auctioneers in New York City were each connected in one way or another to one of the city's caterpillar banks. Auction sales higher than a certain figure—say $100—were immediately accepted as payable in four to six months' time. The auctioneer's bank took the jobber's or merchant's signed bid as an IOU and held it for collection. In this way the banks of New York would accept a bill of credit from a jobber and provide freshly printed New York notes to the English wholesaler or agent, who could spend them in the city.[28] New York banks also helped young jobbers with weak credit by accepting two-party notes signed by a jobber and his backwoods retailer. John Jacob Astor, quicker than most American merchants, saw the writing on the wall. The general-purpose merchant could not survive the onslaught of jobbers, banks, and auction sales where credit was easy and prices cut to the bone. By around 1818 he had sold off his stores in western New York and had auctioneers sell his furs. He invested his proceeds in New York real estate, leasing downtown and midtown spaces to the young, enterprising jobbers—men with ragged hair and trousers like him, men who bypassed the blue-stockinged merchants.

Thus while New York banks advanced consumer credit from English manufacturers that allowed families to move and settle in the West, state banks and steamboats provided the credit for the last mile of settlement. Until 1803, western farms and farm communities tended to spread out from the margins of navigable rivers but they did not move very far inland. After 1803, when American control of New Orleans was more or less established, the Mississippi River became fully "uncorked," in the words of would-be farmers in the Midwest. After that, new shipping and banking facilities provided the last link in the chain of credit.

Without these credit institutions, travel was hazardous. A well-off Kentucky farmer who wanted to bypass a store like Andrew Jackson's could sell his goods downriver in New Orleans by getting a locally built keelboat, poling his way to New Orleans or Natchez, selling his stock, gathering gold and silver, and then poling his way back upriver. Pulling bushes to make his way upriver was called bushwhacking, and it was too laborious and dangerous to travel far. An alternative for returning home to Cincinnati, Louisville, or Nashville meant traveling overland by the Natchez Trace. But a returning farmer traveling over the Trace with a pack of gold and silver was in considerable danger. The Trace was a notorious place for highway robbers like Micajah and Wiley Harpe, named "Big" and "Little" Harpe, who were known for dismembering the bodies of rich travelers. [29]

After 1815, to address the risks of the Natchez Trace, the inland caterpillar banks provided "river money" to farmers. Like all printed money, it was local. It traded along the river and decreased in value the farther it was from the bank.[30] The banks that operated along the river were naturally called river banks.[31] Whichever route a farmer took, if someone stole his river money, he could advertise the denomination, bank, and serial number in a local newspaper, making it difficult for a robber to spend it.[32]

And with his river money he could journey to a river town to buy eastern cottons and woolens from retailers or jobbers who gave reduced rates for cash. He would still sell his harvest in New Orleans or Natchez, but steamboats, waterborne contraptions capitalized after 1815 by the new inland banks, made the upriver trek easier.[33] Midwestern farmers continued to ship their staples downriver, crowding the Mississippi with homemade arks, cotton boxes, keelboats, and skiffs, but after the steamboat arrived, farmers would increasingly sell their homemade rafts to buyers who would keep them as boats or salvage the timber for house construction.[34] A farmer in Vermont or New York who took the Hudson River down to New York City might even travel into Pearl Street to visit the auctions or stop by the retail store operated by David Brooks and his brother Henry, who sold cheap British goods for cash prices. More than a dozen years later Henry's sons would combine to create the trademark "Brooks Brothers" as a symbol of classic tailored suits, ignoring its more tawdry origins. A cheap monkey jacket from Brooks looked better than one the farmer might have made at home, and he could pay for it up front with the Bank of Albany notes in his pocket.

The rise of this paper economy benefited jobbers and retail merchants who became its new middlemen. Of course, the new dollar economy also benefited bankers. "We live in a paper world," the Democratic merchant Jesse Atwater complained before the War of 1812. "The foundations of our houses are laid in bank paper; our splendid carriages roll on paper wheels . . . Thus instead of enjoying a golden, silver, or iron age, we have chosen to make ourselves a paper age." Like paper, the prosperity was fragile, even insubstantial. "If a great fire should be kindled and all the bank paper be thrown into it . . . the charters of all the other banks, together with all the promissory notes, bills and bonds . . . and if the fire should wholly consume them, the *ashes* would add more real wealth to the nation than all of them put together."[35]

After 1815, many western farmers in need of coats and other goods would surely have disagreed. The rapid expansion of river banks certainly led to currency inflation, but reduced prices and the transformation of store credit into a wad of bills allowed families more choices in purchasing. The "dog-cheap goods" one could buy in the river stores were popular, and many came to buy, in the words of local merchants, "pennyworths monstrous cheap."[36] While some worried about the quality of these foreign goods—monkey jackets, "cheap man's cambrics," and "gewgaws rich and rare"[37]—others worried about the underlying value of the banknotes that bought them. For a farmer this new cash economy resembled a game of musical chairs. The river money allowed free and furious exchange, but when the music stopped, the man left holding river money could lose everything.

President James Monroe, responding to the American mania for cheap British monkey jackets, dressed for his 1817 inauguration in a woolen coat, waistcoat, and breeches, all shorn from American sheep, manufactured entirely in America. The tradition of wearing only American-made clothing at the inauguration was one that every president followed thereafter. Monroe became, noted one observer, a "walking argument in favor of the encouragement of native wool."[38]

While farmers may have been happy to be free from store credit, and western merchants were happy to get credit from jobbers, old-fashioned merchants were in trouble. Brown & Sons, Brooks Brothers, and the jobbers made money furiously, but blue-stockinged merchants like the Melvills were nearly done for. Few could adjust to using a bank for credit, buying at auction, accepting that prices could change rapidly, and then selling off inventories as quickly as possible. By April 1817, Herman's uncle Thomas Melvill Jr. was bankrupt. In the same month the State of New York began to change its bankruptcy laws to accommodate the hundreds of New York merchants like Thomas junior who had become insolvent—done in by Black Ball lines, auctioneers, banks, and monkey jackets.[39] Little did anyone know that if the changing structure of the retail economy in 1817 was bad for dry-goods merchants like the Melvills, the Anglo-American trade war that followed would be even worse.

CHAPTER FOUR

The Second Bank, the Monkey Jacket
War, and Tenskwatawa's Revenge

O UNDERSTAND AMERICA'S second panic in 1819, we must follow the career of a dollar bill. We must find a veteran bill, perhaps
from the Bank of Boston. It will be weathered and torn, not as flashy
as a new bill perhaps. Spending it in a rural area—Brooklyn, New York,
for example—would be nearly impossible. But even downtown on Pearl
Street, this dollar would be hard to spend. A young man itching to find
goods might visit the cheap joints—a confectionery, a rag-and-bone
shop, a tippling house—and be unable to spend it because the lady or
fellow at the counter cannot give him change. The Boston dollar must
travel along, wadded in the pocket of his pants, hard up against his
pocket watch, waiting.

At last the young man may discover that great corrupter of youths,
the oyster cellar. He will find it in the rougher part of town, marked by
a light inside a red glass orb. He might first hear a flute playing "Hunters of Kentucky," with a drunken squad of half-grown men howling the
words to accompany it. As he draws closer, he will be assaulted by the
smell of burned tobacco; beneath that the smell of urine, fresh-ground
pepper, and brackish water. Oyster cellars like these were infamous for
separating a boy and his dollar. Not a palace certainly, but a well-lit base-
ment where you could spend your dollar—and thus your evening—with
oysters, chicken, apple whiskey, and beer. The least respectable places
would have dance partners for hire and private rooms in the back. Open
all day and most of the night, a cash business with lots of cash, this was
the perfect place to lay down a Bank of Boston dollar bill and demand
satisfaction, or dinner at least.

Still, this was not a simple transaction. The owner of the establishment would take the dollar bill and look over the engravings on the
edge, perhaps handing it to a fellow who could read the signature. If
it were daytime and the owner did not know the young man, a runner
would take the bill to a bank. If it were nighttime, the proprietor would

demand a "discount," perhaps 20 percent, and would require that the man spend at least half a dollar before asking for metallic change. Spanish doubloons, Mexican pesos, French 5-franc pieces, English guineas, and pennies all changed freely in the city. Credit was also available, if you were known in town. But a Boston dollar bill? Well, foreign money is hard to spend anywhere.[1]

This problem of convertibility did not just irritate any young man wishing to spend money in 1817. It also irritated the U.S. government, which collected tariffs, taxes, and land payments in currencies whose shape, color, and value varied enormously. (Parliament, irritated with "country bank" notes issued during the war, taxed them out of existence in 1815.)[2] It also irritated those who held government debt, especially large bondholders like Stephen Girard and John Jacob Astor. The problem of the unstable value of American dollars led Congress to create a *Second* Bank of the United States, which Congress hoped would crush the excesses of the caterpillar banks and establish a uniform value for American currency. But over-leveraging of land purchases by the Second Bank's own directors coincided with a growing tariff war with Great Britain. When in 1818 a new director of the Second Bank finally tried to discipline both the western branches of the bank and the caterpillar banks just as flour prices were dropping, a financial storm commenced in 1819 that would make the 1792 panic seem short and uneventful.

THE MERCHANT BANKERS Stephen Girard and John Jacob Astor lobbied heavily for the Second Bank of the United States immediately after the War of 1812.[3] During the war they had bought the nation's first Treasury bills in what was called the Sixteen Millions Loan (as the nation's private bankers, they paid less than seventy cents on the dollar for 7 percent bonds, earning them an interest rate close to 30 percent). Girard and Astor wanted an institution that would convert those short-term debts into longer-term debts they could sell. They also wanted a financial instrument like the old Bank of the United States—one with shares that could travel back to Europe to settle trade balances. And they hoped that a new Bank of the United States would impose discipline on the more than two hundred caterpillar banks and push them to return to gold and silver payments for their notes.[4] Congress had its own reasons for supporting a bank: it wanted to prevent farmers from paying for land and tariffs with depreciated notes. The

Treasury could scarcely spend the Kentucky banknotes it received, but rejecting them outright was politically risky.

By 1816, Girard, Astor, and Congress got the bank they wanted, though this new bank, created by a Democratic Congress, differed in important ways from the bank that Hamilton and Duer had built. John C. Calhoun of South Carolina, then a fierce nationalist, wrote the charter. He chartered it not as a saltwater bank but as a bank to bind the nation together. While the old bank had made each of its branches operate separately, allowing each to issue a fixed amount of currency for each dollar of silver in its vaults, the new bank had no such restrictions. This allowed western and southern banks to issue far more currency than the old bank could have.[5] This was only right, according to Congressman Henry Clay and other westerners, who despised the old bank for its conservatism and favoritism of saltwater enterprises. For Clay, the new U.S. bank ought to offer more credit in the West, where it was needed.[6] To prevent Astor or Girard from controlling the bank, Congress also enacted a provision that limited each stockholder to a maximum of thirty votes, whether he had thirty shares or a thousand.[7]

Astor and Girard were not amused. Indeed, the first meeting of the Second Bank of the United States was troubling. Cronyism was rampant, with many shareholders buying additional shares with loans from the banks. One merchant bought 1,172 shares of stock, then registered them under 1,172 different names, assuring that in the directors' election he would defeat Girard, who was limited to thirty votes.[8] The western and southern branches in Ohio and Kentucky issued currency vastly in excess of their reserves.

Congress did not get what it wanted either. The western branches did not force the caterpillar banks to pay in silver in 1817. The Cincinnati branch continued to accept the heavily depreciated currency of the Bank of Kentucky (for example) at par. The Western branches notified the unstable banks that they would hold their weak currency as a "fund," then charge interest for holding their banknotes. As a result, the western branches of the Second Bank kept depreciated state notes on the books without ever settling accounts or demanding silver.

In 1817 the secretary of the Treasury, who called these notes "trash," demanded that the western branches require some sort of security from the caterpillar banks for their depreciated notes. Unfortunately, most of that security was land, valued at prices inflated by the ready availability of river bank money.[9] By this legerdemain the state and local banks *appeared* to have resumed specie payments. In fact, most banks in the West were still almost insolvent, offering land as collateral for notes that might never be repaid.

LEVERAGING LAND: SPECULATIONS BUILT ON SPECULATIONS

THESE DANGEROUS SOUTHERN and western speculations in the Second Bank depended on a second financial intermediary—the U.S. Land Office. Few saw the danger of the link between the Land Office and the Second Bank until it was too late. As the Second Bank began operations, local directors saw an opportunity to leverage the two institutions in a way that Girard and Astor could not have imagined.

Edward King, the son of the prominent Federalist senator Rufus King, did imagine it. As a director at one of the Ohio branches of the Second Bank of the United States, apparently with no money of his own, he took loans from his branch to make down payments on Ohio land he bought on the U.S. Land Office installment plan. Borrowing from a bank for U.S. dollars, he then made down payments on land, using a loan to fund a loan. He was effectively borrowing twice: once from the bank and once from the land office.

His father saw the trouble emerging. He had sat on the board of the First Bank of the United States, which had held first government debt and then mostly ninety-day loans for merchant transactions. Short-term loans like this meant that banks could reduce their loans very quickly in hard times. But the Second Bank, especially in the West, rested much of its lending on long-term loans for land, which meant it had few liquid assets when the government came to collect its funds. When Edward wrote to his father that lending for land helped the people of Ohio (himself foremost) in this way, the elder chastised him: "If they attempt to issue their Paper upon Landed security . . . they will throw themselves into great embarrassment." These were not mortgage banks but banks of discount, and they needed liquidity. By 1819 the Land Office had outstanding loans of almost $22 million. The Second Bank of the United States had loans of more than $10 million, a substantial portion of which were guaranteed with land borrowed from the Land Office, the value of which was far from stable.[10]

Virginia's former governor Wilson Cary Nicholas had tried the same trick. Previously a senator, a port collector, and a congressman, Nicholas had national connections. After serving as the state's governor until

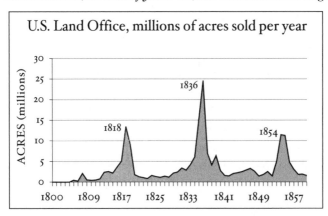

U.S. Land Office, millions of acres sold per year

1816, he took a position as president of the Richmond branch of the Second Bank of the United States in 1817.[11] As a member of the bank's executive, he was entitled to two standing loans of $50,000.[12] In April 1818, Nicholas needed more. He persuaded his friend Thomas Jefferson to guarantee his new loans, declaring that Jefferson would "never suffer the slightest inconvenience from complying with it." Jefferson had qualms, but he owed Nicholas a great deal for helping him out of financial trouble the previous year.[13] Jefferson signed and thus guaranteed Nicholas's down payment for more than a million acres of land in western Virginia.[14] If Nicholas could not continually sell land to make his mortgage payments, he would fail catastrophically.

But as Nicholas should have understood, more and more land was continuing to come on the market. The history of western land in the years after the War of 1812 can be told with a single chart. After the U.S. Army's failure against Little Turtle in 1791, the army had gotten busy. Under "Mad" Anthony Wayne, the army had destroyed the Indians of the Western Confederacy to claim Ohio. In 1805, the Shawnee leader Tecumseh and his brother Tenskwatawa (Open Door) fought back by gathering Miami, Kickapoo, and Potawatomi in a large, pan-Indian village.[15]

In 1811, William Henry Harrison called on the U.S. Army and militia to assemble against the growing threat posed by the Indian presence in Prophetstown in Indiana Territory. The Battle of Tippecanoe followed, a rout for the Indians, making Harrison famous and eliminating concerted Indian opposition to land cessions in the upper Great Lakes. The following year, during the War of 1812, General Jackson destroyed the villages of the Red Sticks in northern Alabama. After 1815, the Land

Office offered up millions of these newly claimed acres in Ohio and northern Alabama. This was a period of unprecedented prosperity in Alabama.[16]

In selling the land, the U.S. Land Office accepted down payments in the circulating notes of both state banks and regional branches of the Bank of the United States. This was dangerous. Though the Land Office recognized that many of these notes had depreciated, it nonetheless took them at face value, because it was in a difficult political situation. For example, if the Land Office took the Bank of Kentucky notes for their face value—a $10 note for $10 in specie—this would encourage speculators to buy the problematic Kentucky notes, make them more valuable, and induce western states to create more caterpillar banks. If, however, the office stopped accepting Kentucky banknotes at face value, knowing they weren't worth the ink used to print them, panicked holders would rush to the Kentucky banks to demand specie. With little silver in their tills, those banks would quickly fold, and the government would get nothing for the Kentucky notes it held. Caterpillar banks like the ones in Kentucky and some branches of the Bank of the United States were on shaky ground.

Congress hoped the main branch of the Second Bank would force both caterpillar banks and the regional branches to resume specie payments and earn the Land Office a hundred cents for every paper dollar it held, but no congressman wanted the notes of his state to receive special disfavor. The land speculators Edward King and Wilson Cary Nicholas stood at the precipice. The independence that Democrats had granted the regional branches gave the directors King and Nicholas little incentive to stop personally borrowing land with borrowed currency or allowing other stockholders to do so. Soon someone would have to point out that wartime wheat prices would have to fall, that low wheat prices could not sustain such high land prices, that land might be overpriced, and that many western banks whose capital depended on loans to land borrowers would be insolvent. And then the Great Spirit would give Tenskwatawa his revenge for Harrison's destruction of Prophetstown.

THE TARIFF WAR

AFTER THE WAR OF 1812 ended, trade between the United States and Great Britain, which had been suspended during the conflict, resumed its brisk pace. The rapid flood of goods across the Atlantic threatened the embryonic American industries that had been seeded during the trade embargo, while U.S. wheat threatened British landowners. Congress and the British Parliament changed the rules of trade by imposing trade barriers; soon the monkey jacket romance ended, and the tariff war began. Together the tariff and the Land Office currency crisis would plunge the nation into a depression.

The British desire to limit transatlantic trade came from large landholders who feared the end of war, and rightly so. During the Napoleonic Wars wheat and flour prices rose quickly, even after wheat from as far away as the Black Sea had been smuggled past French privateers and onto British shores. After the war Russian and American wheat continued to flood Liverpool and London, driving down prices for a 480-pound quarter of wheat from eighty to twenty shillings. English landowners and their tenants soon resented the competition. Parliament—which vastly overrepresented British landowners—responded in 1815 by reinstating the ancient Corn Laws, which blocked imported wheat when prices fell below eighty shillings. More important, when prices were high, it gave preference to wheat and flour from the Canadian colonies.[17]

While Americans along the coast sold a few thousand barrels of flour to Liverpool every year, wheat to Britain was a minor part of American exports before 1868. The crucial American flour market was the British West Indies, especially Jamaica, where hundreds of thousands of barrels of flour went every year, yielding proceeds in the tens of millions of dollars. In 1815, England's Corn Laws were no immediate threat to that crucial trade.[18]

But in 1817 and 1818, a trade war began between Britain and America that would set off the 1819 panic. It started when blue-stockinged merchants hurt by New York auction houses found common cause with American manufacturers of cotton thread, woolens, and fabric. Congress began imposing tariffs on manufactured British goods and placing limits on British trade. In 1817 and 1818 it imposed an American version of the Navigation Acts to slowly and methodically inspect all imported goods on English and other foreign ships. Among the things inspectors searched for were half-finished English jackets that were underpriced or falsely marked.[19] The *Providence Patriot* praised this tough policy with an old poem:

Tender handed press a nettle,
And it stings you for your pains;
Grasp it, like a man of mettle,
And it soft as silk remains.[20]

But Americans *would* be stung for their pains. The promissory notes and bills of exchange that relied on $9 wheat barrels would soon collapse.

In early May 1818, responding to American inspections imposed by the American Navigation Acts, Britain's Parliament closed American merchant shippers' access to the British West Indies. British "orders in Council" were issued at the end of May to enforce the provisions. The British Caribbean colonies were effectively closed to American flour.[21] American merchants rushed to Liverpool to unload American flour that was now unsalable in the English Caribbean, but they were too late. In June 1818, prices on the Liverpool market dropped from a twenty-year average of eighty-eight shillings per barrel to less than forty-four shillings with no buyers.[22] By the end of 1818 hopeful merchants brought nearly thirty thousand barrels of superfine flour to Havana, one of the few markets left, but found no buyers.[23] Between 1794 and the summer of 1818, barrels of wheat had reliably hovered around $9. Those days were over.[24]

CRASH

WHILE THE BRITISH ban on the United States' trade with the Caribbean brought about the panic of 1819, there were other aggravating factors. To make matters worse, the Bank of England was returning to a gold standard between 1815 and 1819 and was paying a premium for gold to do so. That is, it paid more than market rates for gold, drawing the metal from all parts of the world.[25] Any merchant journeying from the United States to England after 1817 would be inclined to take gold back with him instead of either American bonds or English goods.

Then, beginning in January 1818, serious scandals emerged regarding the Second Bank of the United States, particularly the Philadelphia and Baltimore branches. The anonymous letters of "Brutus," published in the Philadelphia *Aurora,* described cashiers accepting promissory notes instead of metallic currency for bank stock, lending without proper collateral, and simply stealing from the till. The detailed descriptions of the inner workings of the bank came from an insider: the son of the Philadelphia branch's cashier who hoped to embark on a literary career with these editorials. The "Brutus" letters had caused a national, and then an international, sensation by the spring of 1818.[26]

Soon the failures mounted even higher. The decline in flour prices and the struggling banks' demands for cash from borrowers reinforced each other, pressing borrowers into a vise. In July 1818 the main branch of the Bank of the United States forced the branches to "curtail" with specie. In other words, banks had to tell borrowers coming to renew their ninety-day loans that their loans could continue but a portion (12.5 percent in this case) had to be paid in cash. Loans could continue, but borrowers needed to bring that much hard metal to the bank as a guarantee. By the end of August 1818, as flour prices fell while word of the bank scandal spread, the main branch ordered the local branches to localize their operations. The eastern branches would no longer give up silver and gold for notes from western branches. Western branches could not fob off eastern notes when asked for cash. Local branches were to become responsible for their own lending, forcing the western branches to drastically withdraw credit. In November 1818, when Congress began to investigate bank operations, the president of the Second Bank resigned.[27]

When Congress's report of the Second Bank's misadventures arrived in England in February 1819, the bloom was already off the rose of the bank's stock—"curious, disgraceful, and instructive," tutted the London *Times*. "The machine indeed appears to be a clumsy and ill-constructed one," wrote the reporter after describing how the branches were separated in August 1818. The congressional report, however, showed that the Brutus allegations were true: the bank's "management was far worse than its construction."[28]

Falling agricultural prices may have mattered more than Congress's investigation of the bank. Shippers, already reeling from the changes in wholesaling and retailing and the failures of New York merchants in 1816, failed rapidly after wheat prices dropped in the summer of 1818. The price of farm products continued to fall for three years, dropping an astonishing 45 percent between 1818 and 1821. "A deep shadow has passed over our land," wrote John Woodward of New York's Tammany Hall in 1819, "a commercial and individual gloom has created a universal stillness. In our remotest villages the hammer is not heard, and in our larger cities the din and bustle of thrifty industry has ceased." Indeed the silencing of hammers directly followed the dropping of wheat prices as commodity prices in food, iron, and timber dropped an average of 31 percent between 1818 and 1821. Twenty percent of the land purchased on mortgage from the Land Office was forfeited between 1820 and 1824 despite repeated price cuts and loan extensions. This was America's second depression and one of the deepest in the nineteenth century.[29]

Langdon Cheves, an opponent of the First Bank, took over the Second Bank in March 1819 after Congress's harsh report. The political economist William Gouge blamed Cheves: "The bank was saved and the people were ruined."[30] A hard-money man, Cheves believed that many of the caterpillar banks were simply money mills. Doing what previous directors had hoped to delay since the bank's founding in 1816, he ordered all branches to demand specie from the caterpillar banks. Caterpillar banks failed, while individuals with loans from the Second Bank's branches were quickly ruined when asked for cash. By August 1819, Rufus King's improvident Ohio son had his notes protested on the door of the very bank in which he was director. He destroyed the vast King family fortune. In the same month Wilson Cary Nicholas proved unable to pay his creditors; all his land and slaves were sold by auction. Jefferson, who had countersigned Nicholas's notes, lost everything as well.[31]

How did it start? Banks are pawnshops for promises, and when external shocks took place like Britain's instant tariff on the Caribbean, Atlantic merchants' ninety-day promises could not be fulfilled. When revelations about mismanagement and extreme leverage inside the Second Bank of the United States were confirmed shortly afterward, symbolic doubt increased: people who held the notes and bills of exchange doubted their value and asked for metal. No bank can possibly turn over metallic currency for all of its outstanding notes all at once because of the reserve ratio—the magic multiplier of the bank. If everyone comes calling, banks must suspend payments.

"A BOUNDLESS EXPANSE OF DESOLATION"

AS MANY CATERPILLAR banks failed in the fall of 1819, the Second Bank began to protest notes of the banks, seize promises held by those banks, then foreclose on property offered as collateral. By 1822 the bank's agency owned most of Cincinnati and more than six thousand acres of good farmland in Ohio and Kentucky.[32] Unwinding the debts took a very long time. Forty years later, in 1862, an organization called the Agency of the Bank of the United States was still selling land in Ohio.[33]

In 1819, state governments in Ohio and Kentucky tried to impose taxes on the Second Bank to prevent it from foreclosing on debtors. The Ohio legislature, in what became known as the "crowbar law," instructed deputies of the Ohio auditor who faced resistance from tellers to break into any room or vault of the Second Bank to collect its yearly tax of $50,000. The Supreme Court then considered the constitutionality of a much smaller tax imposed by Maryland to test the question: Did Congress have the authority to create national institutions exempt from state taxation? In the end, the chief justice of the Supreme Court, John Marshall, a former ally of Alexander Hamilton's, supported the Second Bank, overturning the anti-bank legislation passed by states.[34] He drew an analogy between the national bank and the army, ridiculing the states' rights position of Jefferson and Madison:

> Throughout this vast republic, from the St. Croix to the Gulf of Mexico, from the Atlantic to the Pacific, revenue is to be collected and expended, armies are to be marched and supported. The exigencies of the nation may require that the treasure raised in the north should be transported to the south, that raised in the east conveyed to the west, or that this order should be reversed. Is that construction of the constitution to be preferred which would render these operations difficult, hazardous and expensive?[35]

McCulloch v. Maryland (1819) would be Marshall's most controversial decision. It established the Second Bank's legitimacy in spite of widespread suffering and widespread opposition. This extremely unpopular decision may have been the single most important threat ever to the legitimacy of the Supreme Court. After *McCulloch,* Thomas Jefferson came to brand Marshall's court as "the subtle corps of sappers and miners constantly working underground to undermine the foundations of our confederated fabric."[36]

In May 1819, rumors circulated that two wagons loaded with $120,000 to $140,000 in specie were being spirited from the U.S. branch in Chillicothe to the "mother branch in Philadelphia." Hastily organized state posses failed to stop the shipment. A few months later, officials in Ohio simply ignored the Supreme Court's decision, instructing a deputy to enter the Chillicothe branch in September 1819. According to witnesses, "in a ruffian-like manner," he "jumped over the counter, took and held forcible possession of the vault." The state's deputy then filled his own wagon with bank specie and notes, carrying it the next day to the state bank in Columbus.[37]

In 1820, mobs formed in Cincinnati and Cleveland to stop bank foreclosures. When a parade of citizens headed toward the Cleveland bank bearing a black coffin, the mayor read the state's Riot Act to them, which allowed him to deploy the state militia sent to support the bank. When the militia lined up, the protesters left.[38] Western land prices in parts of Ohio, Tennessee, Alabama, and Kentucky dropped more than 50 percent. "Look at Kentucky," declared one Kentucky correspondent. "What a spectacle does she represent! Nothing is to be seen but a boundless expanse of desolation!"[39]

The suffering continued through 1819 and into the early 1820s. The rapid deflation in agricultural prices idled tens of thousands of East Coast farmers who had depended on high wartime prices. In part because the new lenders—jobbers, store operators, auction houses, and eastern banks—stood between farmers and farm prices, it took almost a year for the crisis to hit the upper Mississippi River.[40] By 1820, jobbers traveled west to find their debtors, shut down their insolvent stores, and sell off their merchandise. "I am sorry I can give you no good tidings of this once flourishing place," wrote a Cincinnati gentleman to his friend in Kentucky. "I will give you a statement of some property sold this day by the marshal, and which I have seen myself ":

> A handsome gig and very valuable horse, sold for four dollars.
> An elegant sideboard for three dollars.
> A fine Brussels carpet, and two Scotch carpets, for three dollars.
> . . .
> A good dining table at twenty five cents.
> I have a little money, and could make a fortune, by attending
> marshals' and sheriffs' sales, could I reconcile it to my feelings.
> This I cannot do.[41]

As the young Bostonian Josiah Warren witnessed in Cincinnati in 1821, "those speculators, to avoid the sheriff, began to scatter like rats from a submerged flour barrel."[42] First the auctioneers saw their notes protested on the doors of New York banks, then jobbers, then western storekeepers, then farmers who had little but their monkey jackets to show for their earlier gains. By 1821 many Ohio towns turned to barter. As Josiah Warren's son put it more than fifty years later,

> A cabinet-maker, for instance, would want two pounds of butter,
> amounting to twenty-five or thirty cents. Without a penny in his
> pocket, he would take his basket, go to the market, find a farmer
> that had some, take two pounds, and give him a table, bedstead, or
> even a bureau, agreeing to take the rest out in truck, as he would call
> it, when he should want it.[43]

In the 1820s, in response to the crisis, Josiah Warren created the first socialist labor bank in Cincinnati, the "labor for labor store."[44] Alabama likewise saw a 50 percent decline in prices and a retreat to barter.[45]

On the East Coast, Philadelphia was probably hardest hit by the panic. Because it specialized in flour exports, the evaporation of the British West Indies market for flour made the scramble for gold and silver even harder. Housing values dropped by 40 percent, according to some accounts. Unemployment in manufacturing may have reached 78 percent, though manufacturing was less than half of the city's overall activity.[46] Thousands headed west to escape creditors. Public hospitals filled up as scores of housewives, merchants, and laborers suffered the effects of trying to drown their sorrows in cheap gin. By 1821, Philadelphia's public hospitals were so full of drying-out alcoholics that doctors discovered that alcohol withdrawal in their patients proceeded in measurable stages. They labeled the new disease delirium tremens.[47]

New England saw its flourishing trade with the world decline considerably. The poet William Cullen Bryant mourned the "paralysis" that fell on what had once been "the flourishing seaports of New England," including "Newburyport, Salem, Plymouth, New London, [and] Newport."[48] When searching for villains, New England merchants looked locally and globally. They blamed the American Navigation Acts that blocked British woolens; they blamed the auction system in New York that allowed goods to be sold below their value; they blamed a banking system that had caused runaway inflation and then collapsed. A few recognized that the boom times of the Napoleonic Wars had created impossible prices for food and that the return to peace, the return to gold in the Bank of England, Britain's ban on America's trade with the Caribbean, and an overly ambitious deflation of currency would lead to crisis. Foremost among them were New Englanders who had never trusted westward settlement anyway. They would soon re-create the banking system on a new foundation.[49]

Although the decline in world trade was punishing, the high-tariff regime that helped create the panic would eventually remake New England. Once behind tariff walls, New England would manufacture most of the woolens and cotton textiles sold in the United States. Manchester, Lowell, Lawrence, and Waterbury would be the new sources of the region's wealth. In 1817, President Monroe's garb of an American-made woolen garment was a gimmick, but by 1830 clothes sewn of all-American fabric would be ordinary.

In New England, the panic of 1819 led to a more stable banking system that came to be known as the Suffolk system. In the early 1820s, the recently chartered Suffolk Bank in Boston became a bank-of-banks. It pledged to accept all paper money printed outside the city of Boston at full face value, but only if that foreign bank kept silver reserves in the Suffolk Bank. In this manner, the Suffolk acted as a central banker, one that would regulate the issue of other banks. For a bank west of Boston the Suffolk Bank provided interest for bank deposits made in silver; further, it would not demand gold or silver in times of financial crisis.[50] By the mid-1820s, then, our traveler arriving in Boston with a pocketful of out-of-town bills would have no trouble spending them. New York City would pass through one more crisis (in 1837) before instituting a similar system.

In western Vermont, which had relied on high wartime prices for wheat, the crisis had hit as soon as England's Corn Laws were enacted in 1815. By 1817, thousands had left the Connecticut River valley—heading west by sleigh to Genesee County, New York, where land was available on Lake Erie in small plots for $2 to $3 an acre.[51] Among the Vermonters were many antinomians expelled from Massachusetts, men and women who believed in signs, had frequent visions, and spoke to long-dead prophets. Some gathered in bands, like the tribe that followed the itinerant prophet Isaac Bullard. The men wore long beards; the women were filthy. Bullock married and divorced them. Others had visions of the lamb of God and listened to the instruction of angels.[52] Among those who came from Vermont was Joseph Smith Jr., a young man who—some claimed—could use a "peep stone" to divine where treasure was buried or where covered-over silver mines lay, mines the "Spaniards" had abandoned centuries earlier.

While many in western New York frowned on the footsore emigrants from Vermont, after the panic some desperate New Yorkers began to find them compelling and believe in their signs and visions. In 1819, a year when land agents, mortgage holders, tax collectors, and sheriffs closed out landholdings for lack of silver, those who promised to deliver silver seemed possessed of magical or divine powers. In a time of bitter disappointment in this world, the Vermont emigrants promised connections to another. Joseph Smith's Mormon Church had begun.

Smith declared that the angel Moroni showed him where ancient golden plates were buried, plates that described an Indian exodus into America. In the 1820s he formed a church based on cooperative principles, one that forsook the individualism and selfishness that had caused the panic. Collective ownership, plural wives, and shared governance would define the group that called themselves the Latter-Day Saints. The Mormon movement was one of the most long-lasting consequences of the panic of 1819.

EXPLANATIONS

ONE WAY TO EXPLAIN the panic of 1819 is as the story of an asset bubble—in this case the asset being land—and the land speculation stories of King and Nicholas certainly suggest that. That is how the Federalist congressman and historian Timothy Pitkin told the story in 1835. Like most Federalists, he thought little of the West and blamed it for inflation. "The advanced price of agricultural productions, during the long wars in Europe, was accompanied by great advance in the price of lands in the United States," he wrote. But "after Europe had settled down in peace, and again returned to her old systems of policy, [flour] was reduced," and so "the price of lands has diminished, since 1815." Peace, and English trade restrictions to the colonies, killed western ambitions and caused the panic.[53]

All that was true, but Pitkin grasped only part of the story. English trade restrictions relocated agricultural benefits rather than destroying them. American wheat was still exported, but it traveled in a different direction. British tariffs after 1817 benefited Montreal millers who brought New York's wheat at cut-rate prices across Lake Erie, then remarketed it as Canadian flour. After 1815 a vast quantity of American wheat exports took place across Lake Erie to Montreal, down the St. Lawrence, and out to the British West Indies, though almost none of this American wheat export is recorded. Britons in Parliament knew all about this smuggling operation, but historians and economists have missed it.[54] This is partly why Philadelphia and New England suffered after 1816, while western New York prospered by comparison.

Another way to tell the story is as a narrative of the bank, with the iron-willed Langdon Cheves driving the other banks to ruin. As Colonel James Taylor put it some fifty years later: "This bank was a large-sized shark, as it ate up all the small banks in the city."[55] But this story of the branches demanding specie from the caterpillar banks neglects the fact that neither Ohio nor Kentucky banks had ever resumed specie payments after the war. They paid interest (usually in silver) on their depreciated paper while hoping to bail themselves out on inflated land prices. Could a western branch of the Second Bank have disciplined the

Ohio and Kentucky banks while creating a stable, slightly inflating currency? Was it possible to help interstate trade flourish on the Ohio and Mississippi Rivers without runaway inflation? Cheves did not think so and watched 7 percent of the banks in the United States fail completely. His successor, Nicholas Biddle, did believe that an increase in western currencies, mild inflation, and close control of banks were possible, as did Henry Clay. They were correct, but a single national institution with the power to investigate lending practices *and* directly control the supply of money had to await the arrival of the Federal Reserve almost one hundred years later.

Another way to tell the story of 1819 is as a cautionary tale of unwarranted inflationary practices: caterpillar banks that needed stomping. This is the Austrian-school argument that most historians have unwittingly repeated, perhaps not realizing the anti-banking principle that underlay it: in the twentieth and twenty-first centuries it has meant a call to destroy the Federal Reserve, stop fractional reserve banking, and bring the nation back to the gold standard. This was also Andrew Jackson's position when he was president. But behind it was an open and personal hostility to marketing arrangements that brought many American farmers their monkey jackets and tried to rescue the American economy from colonial dependence on English credit. The new marketing system, based on readily available paper currencies, hurt the old-fashioned merchants like Andrew Jackson and the blue-stockinged merchants like the Melvills, but it has defined American wholesaling ever since.

PROFITING FROM THE PANIC

New York City saw many of the familiar features of a sell-off, but it rallied more quickly. A young man holding a dollar bill might be sadly disappointed, for most banks' paper money was worthless by 1820. Those with silver and gold could buy almost anything they wanted. Astor escaped the devastation by going to Europe in 1819, where he was unreachable to creditors, even as he continued to acquire land in New York City. As the years progressed, he sold downtown lots for high prices and bought vast holdings farther north on the island. He leased those northern properties out to jobbers and manufacturers, betting correctly that in an era when jobbers needed warehouses and buildings were limited to five stories, midtown values would increase faster than those downtown, because height would impose an upper limit on land prices downtown.

New York City's rapid recovery was assured by a few expediencies adopted as the panic was developing. The cheapness and reliability of the Black Ball Line and other packet ships pulled Atlantic traffic along this narrow corridor.[56] The new auction system allowed anyone with long pants and a little capital to buy dry goods at auction. With ready credit from New York banks, these New York buyers did not need to worry about getting credit from English manufacturers. Most back-and-forth trade with England would become concentrated in the hands of a few large merchant bankers, including Alexander Brown & Sons, Kleinwort & Benson, and the Baring Brothers. The forty-three licensed auctioneers in the city, connected to a few banks, became the destination for English dry goods, the osnaburgs, the cambrics, and the monkey jackets. In 1818, jobbers bought $15 million worth of goods at auction for resale to merchants farther west.[57] In that year alone, the auction tax of just over $300,000 paid for a new shovel-ready experiment—the Erie Canal—that was expected to connect New York City to the Great Lakes.

The State of New York was also protected by the fact that, also before the panic, it had created a new kind of document to resolve the perennial balance-of-payments problems that traders had with Great Britain and Europe. Before the Second Bank had even started, the State of New York had begun to issue state canal bonds, payable out of future canal receipts at 6 percent per year. These became the first state bonds for construction purposes. Within a few years, English merchants with a trade balance in New York would begin to acquire them by the trunk load. They bought them just as their fathers had bought stock in the First Bank of the United States. The Baring Brothers in England guaranteed that London investors would receive pounds for the American bonds denominated in dollars.[58] These New York State bonds—along with auction receipts—paid for the state's portion of the Erie Canal.

By printing a trusted instrument (the state bond) for dealing with balance of payments, regularizing trade between New York and Liverpool, and building an auction system for manufacturers who wanted to sell goods directly and get paid quickly, the State of New York, Quaker shippers, New York bankers, and Manhattan jobbers had usurped the Second Bank of the United States. The proceeds from state bonds paid for a canal system that gave New York access to the Great Lakes market, where food was still cheap and manufactured goods were still expensive. New institutions—caterpillar banks, steamboats, jobbers' shops, dollar bills, and New York auction houses—had allowed Americans to clothe themselves in the "vestural tissues" of the English monkey jacket. The new institutions created a metropolitan system of credit that turned New York into the capital of the nation.

New England merchants and manufacturers displaced by the nation's new monetary and credit system fought back with tariffs and commercial restrictions. The British Parliament was only too happy to respond by severing the United States from trade with the West Indies. The monkey jacket war over wholesaling and retailing, the tariff war, the inflationary measures of caterpillar banks, and the failure of faith in the dollar bill combined to cause a financial panic. Chaos followed. With Anglo-American trade in pieces, some commodity besides flour would have to join the United States to Great Britain. The factory owners of Manchester had something in mind.

CHAPTER FIVE

The Politics of Panic, the Economics of Rags

*T*HE PANIC OF 1819 had dealt a fatal blow to the reign of the New England freebooters who had snuck past empires at war. Captains and merchants in nankeen breeches no longer ruled the country from their quarterdecks. With trade impeded by tariffs, they returned to their towns and endowed private colleges. As ivy covered the walls of academe, American writers like Washington Irving converted the mariners' wistful stories of privateering, international fraud, and treason into homilies on commercial probity.[1]

But while sin slumbered in New England, it would flourish in the cotton fields of the South and the factories of Manchester; all would soon come under the sway of a lucrative international trade in cotton. While Americans tried to understand the panic of 1819 and write recipes for reform, the electorate divided into four hostile camps that—as we shall see—were roughly geographical. After 1825 Andrew Jackson and Martin Van Buren forged these camps into a party that—rightly or wrongly—would blame the nation's financial troubles on New England. In 1830 that party would inaugurate a trade boom large enough to make Americans forget the panic of 1819.

For the next dozen years conflicts between these camps would be about tariffs, canals, and cotton. After the Whiskey Rebellion of 1792–1794 had shown the fierce opposition to internal taxes, the federal government learned to draw most of its revenue from taxes on foreign imports.[2] To the extent that Americans paid taxes, they mostly paid them through tariffs. After 1819, states sought to emulate New York's successful Erie Canal project by stimulating their economies with river improvements, harbor facilities, and canals—an infrastructure economy.[3] Canals and steamboats shrank distances and reorganized trade. The sale of dry goods to the interior allowed New York City to surpass Boston and Philadelphia as the nation's financial center. Infrastructure was key: To the north and west, the Erie Canal gave the city access to the fertile regions around the nation's inland seas, the Great Lakes. South of the Great Lakes, potash, barrel hoops, and wheat traveled east; clothing, metalware, and crockery flowed back. Even more goods were smuggled back and forth between the United States and Canada.

But the most powerful new force in American economic history was the object that benefited from neither tariffs nor canals. It was a crop visible on the decks of every American ship that traveled east: cotton. Some traveled coastwise from New Orleans to New York, then to Liverpool; some flowed directly from New Orleans to Liverpool. America no longer traded everything with everyone. After the monkey jacket war and the tariffs that followed, America traded mostly one thing: American cotton went to Britain and then around the world.[4]

Before the 1819 panic, American food exports were more significant than cotton exports. As we shall see, these proportions changed, so that by the 1820s cotton exports were two to three times as valuable. While wholesale prices for American exports, including cotton, plummeted, the volume of cotton exports would climb.[5] And the cotton that traveled down rivers and along canals would change. Since the 1780s the very valuable black-seed cotton had been grown on the coastal regions of the Old South, but needing high humidity, it could not be grown very far inland. Green-seed cotton, developed thousands of years earlier in the Yucatán,[6] could grow up in the hills but was costly to harvest: its fleecy coating was small compared with the huge seed, and the seed was very tightly attached to the center. When Jackson was a young man, cotton farmers always kept some seed cotton near the hearth for children to separate before bedtime; an hour or more of wrestling might leave behind one ounce of usable lint and three ounces of plump green seeds.[7]

After 1794, green-seed cotton became profitable when Eli Whitney built a sawing cotton engine (cotton gin for short). A roller pushed the cotton down into a box. Rotating hooks pulled the cotton through a wire mesh, leaving the seeds behind. The sawing action of the gin also teaseled the cotton, making it firmer and stronger, better suited for spinning into yarn that was tougher (though never as thin and strong as the yarn that came from black-seed cotton).[8] Similar devices had preceded the gin going back to ancient times, but they had been balky, expensive, and complex. Whitney's combination of cheap metal objects inside a simple wooden box was ingenious.[9] Unfortunately for Whitney, his attempts to control and license the gin failed miserably. South Carolina planters, who resented paying for anything, broke into Whitney's shop and stole his invention; as early as 1810, hundreds of slave and free mechanics throughout the South had pirated the design. Between 1815 and 1819, Americans were exporting a respectable eighty million pounds a year. This, it turned out, was a trifle.

In 1820, in the wake of the crash, cotton prices dropped almost 30 percent, yet ships bound for English ports carried 50 percent more, much of it the cheap green-seed cotton that had been purchased for export before prices dropped. Because it sold for as little as a shilling a pound when it arrived, cotton lay on the docks or in the offices of Liverpool cotton factors, wholesalers, and small dealers. Those thousands of pounds of cut-rate cotton got manufacturers thinking, and a surge of invention followed in Lancashire after 1819.

Two technological revolutions, one on each side of the Atlantic, operated in sync after the 1819 panic. In Britain, the largest manufacturers had mastered the application of waterpower to the mechanical weaving process, mostly for the cheap cottons. While English carding and spinning had been improving for more than a century, the weaving process continued to take place in weaving sheds. Weaving required skilled artisans who selected patterns, watched the weave, and guaranteed the quality of garments. But after about 1819, a series of minor changes allowed the "power loom" to move beyond the cheap calicoes into fancier goods. Steam-powered looms running in their own sheds wove faster, requiring less attention by a skilled weaver. Protest followed.

Hand-loom weavers responded to the emergence of power looms with public meetings and even machine breaking. In 1819, weavers in Manchester, unrepresented in Parliament, planned a series of public protests about wages at St. Peter's Field. The Tory government, fearing anarchy, sent in spies to infiltrate the reformers; they also called in the Fifteenth British Hussars, just returned from war, to police the grounds of St. Peter's Field. As a backup, the Cheshire Yeomanry was brought in, an irregular militia composed of the weavers' enemy: the weaving manufacturers.

As the protest mounted, the Cheshire Yeomanry claimed that the hussars were in danger. They turned on protesters with their sabers, killing eight and wounding more than four hundred in what became known as the Peterloo massacre. "The number of slain and maimed is very countable," wrote the conservative commentator Thomas Carlyle, "but the treasury of rage burning hidden or visible in all hearts ever since . . . is of unknown extent."[10] Peterloo proved an embarrassment for the House of Commons.

The weaving manufacturers were embarrassed by Peterloo, but they

won, and their triumph would assure that green-seed cotton plantations would thrive in the American South. As Carlyle put it, "On every
hand, the living artisan is driven from his workshop, to make room for
a speedier, inanimate one. The shuttle drops from the fingers of the
weaver, and falls into iron fingers that ply it faster." After 1819, iron fingers triumphed. The newest power looms could make almost any sort
of fine cotton goods, including the more fashionable muslins.[11] For
the very best quality goods, hand-loom weavers needed the stronger
black-seed cotton, but by 1819 most manufacturers had adapted their
carding, spinning, and weaving equipment to fit the cheap and abundant green-seed cotton. By 1835, black-seed cotton exports had shrunk
to 2 percent of U.S. exports. American green-seed cotton would act as
warp and weft for a vastly expanded colony of English looms.[12] The
unprotesting power looms hummed along, producing cheap, colorful
goods. Yard upon yard of British textiles filled the square crates that
an expanding British commercial empire delivered to India and to new
markets in Brazil, the Turkish dominions, and Hong Kong.[13]

The price of the underlying cotton was also declining, through
means biological rather than mechanical. After 1820, southern planters
began mixing and cross-pollinating dozens of species of Mexican and
Central American cotton plants, producing plants that could mature
faster, separate more easily, and stand higher. New strains like Petit
Gulf and later Mastodon cotton produced fat, bulbous fruits that were
easier to pluck. These green-seed cottons did not need sea breezes and
could grow far inland. They needed two hundred frost-free days to
thrive, however, limiting planting to south of the 35th parallel. The best
land for cultivation proved to be the black soil in the broad plain along
the Mississippi and Red Rivers, as well as the southern crook of the
Tennessee River in northern Alabama. Some of this was Indian land.

Here a different kind of science — genetic manipulation — cheapened
production. Cotton strains that grew in this rich, alluvial black soil
could grow past elbow height. When a plantation in the "black belt"
of western Alabama or eastern Louisiana was said to be in "high cotton," the cotton grew more thickly and often higher. Slaves did not
have to stoop as low when harvesting. Planters in these high-cotton
regions demanded that slaves harvest twice as much per day.[14] Because
the newer, taller subspecies in the black belt were more compact, slaves
could plant a thousand pounds of seed cotton per acre. Black-belt
planters imposed a more punishing labor regime called the pushing system, in which the daily harvest of a slave was weighed against the fast-

est picker, the previous day's picking, and the previous year's picking. Those who missed their daily quota would be whipped at nightfall.[15]

After being run through a horse-powered "gin," 1,000 pounds of seed cotton became 250 pounds of cotton lint, or more than half a bale. The densely packed and tall cotton of the alluvial plains nearly destroyed the competition farther east, where Virginia and the Carolinas produced impoverished "bumblebee cotton," cotton so low that bumblebees could supposedly sit on the ground and suck the top blossom. And so Virginia, which had produced some cotton in the second decade of the nineteenth century, produced very little by the 1820s. The uplands of South Carolina were the most promising regions in the second decade of the century; but by the 1820s the plantations in the Deep South outperformed them. Manufacturing and biological refinement improved side by side: Mississippi River valley merchants sent cotton samples labeled by subspecies all the way to Liverpool for testing on the constantly improving spindles and looms.[16]

Britain had a tariff on American cotton and Americans had a tariff on British yarn and shirting, but neither seemed to matter. After the panic, cotton exports surged past food exports.[17] It was mostly Americans who ate American food; the rest of the world consumed American cotton.[18] The world's voracious demand for English calicoes gave English manufacturers the capital to tinker with patterns, shapes, and dyes. Manufacturers' demand for southern cotton made southern planters among the richest people in the world.[19]

Before 1817, to put it schematically, American flour had gone to feed slaves in the Caribbean who made valuable sugar and molasses, which New England sea captains used to buy manufactured goods from Europe and slaves from Africa. It was more complex than that, but sugar was nonetheless the crucial intermediate market instrument of the pre-1817 economy. It was as much the coin of the realm as silver.[20] Caribbean slaveholders and New England merchants were the chief beneficiaries of this trade.

After Britain and America imposed tariffs on each other between 1817 and 1819, cotton replaced sugar at the center of the new economy. Southern slaves produced cheap cotton; Manchester textile workers turned it into cheap cotton goods; the low price of these goods gave British shippers access to the trade of the world. Both the old sugar-based and the new cotton-based trade networks depended on slave labor, but the post-1819 cotton network depended on cotton slaves in Alabama or Louisiana rather than sugar slaves in Jamaica or Havana.[21]

After the panic, the entire commodity chain of cotton—from Louisiana fields to quarterdecks to Manchester spindles, looms, and dye rooms—acted as a "global deflator" in the language of today. The combination of cheap land, forced labor, biological innovation, mechanical invention, and clever marketing created an impossibly cheap necessity. In the wake of this chain of force and invention the cheap cotton object—the English calico—became an international best seller. Muslins, osnaburgs, linens, and draperies followed. In India, a five-thousand-year-old carding, spinning, and weaving dynasty began to crumble under the force of it. Yet cotton always needed more markets, and those who made the most from it sought to break down all resistance to the cheap international commodity chain. In England this was the Lancashire "liberals" who sought cheap food, free trade, and a weak English state. In the American Southwest of the early nineteenth century, this was the "Jackson party" that wanted Indian removal, cheap land, and widening of waterways. In the American Southeast this was the "radicals" who wanted a weak federal government and an end to American tariffs. In New York City it was wholesalers who wanted open seas, free ports, and cheap English goods. (When New England textile manufacturers pushed through higher tariffs in 1828, these wholesalers put the flags of American ships at half-mast in mourning.)[22] Cotton was a product, a symbol, and an ideology—an empire that created allegiances that straddled oceans.

"A GENERAL MASS OF DISAFFECTION"

WHILE THE WRENCHING transformation of 1819 helped usher in the beginning of an international cotton economy, the panic also shattered the Democratic Party coalition that Jefferson, Madison, and Robert Livingston had created. In 1820, Secretary of War John C. Calhoun of South Carolina remarked to John Quincy Adams that the nation's politics after the panic of 1819 might never be the same. "There has been within these two years an immense revolution of fortunes in every part of the Union; enormous numbers of persons utterly ruined; multitudes in deep distress; and a general mass of disaffection to the government, not concentrated in any particular direction, but ready to seize upon any event and looking out anywhere for a leader."[23] The leader who would seize on that disaffection and concentrate it would arrive in 1824: a cotton planter, merchant, and presidential candidate named Andrew Jackson.

Indeed the crash politics that followed 1819 created a now-familiar form of American politics that made presidents matter. Before 1819, most American voters considered their governors to be more important than their presidents. States invested millions in infrastructure, while the federal government did relatively little. At the national level the American political system resembled a British one, with a strong parliament at the center of what little national politics existed. Coalitions coalesced and crumbled again: Federalists, Democrats, Quids, Invisibles, War Hawks, and Old Republicans. The nation's early factions ruled through Congress, the American parliament. The executive was a sort of first among equals, a prime minister whom congressmen selected every four years in a caucus. The president was their creature.

The 1819 panic divided the nation into regional coalitions that lacerated one another over issues of taxes and slavery. After a decade of conflict in the 1820s, a new politics emerged, a politics of the masses, federal patronage, and a president who might rule them.[24] As a candidate, Jackson would come to represent the new order: the acknowledged leader of a party, a president who would make foreign trade agreements without Congress, and an interpreter of the Constitution who would routinely veto legislation that Congress proposed. Given the winner-take-all nature of elections, his partisans would make deals with coalitions *before* a presidential election rather than after the organization of Congress. In these ways Jackson made the executive a distinct and separate branch of government. He relied on the splintering of Congress's power after the panic to do so.[25]

Public dissatisfaction with congressional control and party leadership had begun to crumble before 1819. When Congress voted itself a pay raise in 1816, Americans voted out 80 percent of those who voted for the measure.[26] It seemed appropriate to some critics that after England's raid on Washington, Congress met in an abandoned tavern, the walls still stained with lard and grease.[27] After the panic, when, despite widespread dissatisfaction, the Democratic congressional caucus chose the incumbent James Monroe as the 1820 candidate, newspapers openly criticized the caucus machinery. Why should congressmen huddled in a cloakroom bargain over the nation's next president? By 1823, President Monroe could sense the growing revulsion with the machineries of congressional power. He refused to choose a successor, and so in 1823 a halfhearted little minority caucus of Democrats in Congress met to pick the party's official candidate. Most congressmen boycotted.[28]

By that time, crash politics had driven sectional wedges between voters. It began as early as 1819 with memorials—printed addresses—to Congress from manufacturers in New England, New York, and the mid-Atlantic states, all demanding higher tariffs on imported goods. Among these was Herman's uncle Thomas Melvill Jr., who believed that the only solution for a cheap English monkey jacket was a more expensive American one. "Shall we go to Europe and to India for clothing," he railed, "when we have the raw materials, and of the very best quality within ourselves?"[29] (Melvill neglected to mention that the previous year he had begun importing jackets too.) By arguing for tariff protection, he made himself an enemy of southern planters and farmers.

The sorts of tariffs that Melvill advocated had once united the nation. Easier to administer than excise taxes on whiskey, tariffs were also patriotically anti-British. But the panic of 1819 had destroyed that unanimity. The post-1819 memorials described the panic's desolation of northern cities and how a higher tariff could stop it. As a convention assembled in New York put it, "Our commerce is greatly prostrated; our shipping has sunk in value . . . real estate is depreciated . . . [and] numbers of our merchants, manufacturers, and farmers, are reduced to bankruptcy."[30] A higher tariff, the members of the convention assured Congress, would set things right.

In high dudgeon, agricultural societies sprang up in Virginia, South Carolina, and Alabama to counter the charge that a higher tariff would solve the nation's economic difficulties. An increase in the tariff, they complained, made British exported goods more expensive, allowing New England manufacturers to raise prices on Yankee-made boots, shoes, nails, shirting, and carpets. This was nothing but "a tax, in fact, to be levied principally on the great body of agriculturalists, who constitute a large majority of the whole American people."[31] Back and forth flew pamphlets and countercharges about how best to rescue the nation from the depression. A Philadelphia committee referred to the pro-tariff memorials from northern cities as "masterpieces of eloquence." Critics in the Virginia towns of Fredericksburg, Petersburg, and Surry called the same memorials "the undefined projects and extravagant claims of the manufacturing associations."[32]

While the tariff divided Americans along one axis, slavery divided them along a slightly different one. After the 1819 crash, the regional finger-pointing in Congress took place in the shadow of a national squabble about statehood in Missouri. The problem for Congress was numbers. Since as early as 1801, congressmen had apparently agreed on an unwritten rule that newly admitted states would be admitted in pairs, stamped, in the words of the historian James Schouler, "with the alternate birthmarks slavery and freedom."[33] In 1819, when slave-owning Missouri asked for statehood immediately after Congress had accepted Alabama, northern congressmen had balked. Arguments about the future of slavery in the western territory simmered. The fate of the western territories mattered because western land was a blank check for Congress: the only way it could spend its way out of a depression.

Many Northerners argued that the federal government could instruct new territories to abolish slavery. "If Missouri be permitted to introduce and legalize slavery by her constitution," declared a memorial from the Vermont legislature that was read aloud in Congress, "[i]t will bring upon the Constitution and Declaration of Independence a deep stain, which cannot be forgotten or blotted out."[34] Many southern congressmen argued that even a territory was sovereign, so Congress could not legislate on its institutions.

The matter might have ended when congressmen worked out the so-called Missouri Compromise that paired a free Maine with a slave Missouri and established 36°30' as the line above which slavery could not exist. But the printed debates endangered the carefully crafted peace. The debates were printed in political pamphlets that were publicly available in bookstores and lending libraries, even in the coastal city of Charleston. It was there in 1822 that Denmark Vesey, a black man who had won his freedom in a lottery, found an 1819 pamphlet authored by the antislavery senator and banker Rufus King. Impressed by a printed proclamation that described the horrors of slavery, he allegedly showed it to free blacks and slaves in his neighborhood. He may have planned a slave revolt. Whether Vesey actually planned to build a black army, seize the armory, kill planters, and escape to Haiti is irrelevant. In the South, many believed that public discussion of slavery had nearly sparked a bloody revolution. The New York senator Rufus King became an important scapegoat (though the threat to his reputation was nothing compared with the thirty-five slaves and free blacks hanged and thirty-two more sentenced to transportation outside the United States). In the wake of the Vesey insurrection scare, white southerners quaked at the dangers of antislavery memorials laid before Congress and worried about where these inflammatory documents might travel.[35] A stunning shift was beginning in white southerners' views about the value of education, literacy, and frank debate.[36]

So it was perhaps inevitable given the timing of the Missouri question and Vesey's insurrection scare after the 1819 panic that debate
about recovery became sectionalized. These strands twisted together in
complex ways. Thus the Pennsylvania manufacturing advocate Mathew
Carey found that workers responded to his criticisms of Virginia planters who must be "ignorant of this wide-spread desolation" that 1819
had brought to workers, when workingmen "whose sole patrimony is
the labour of their hands [were] reduced to the dreadful alternatives of
starvation, beggary, rapine, or exile." Carey compared the suffering factory worker with the southern slaveholder, who, surrounded "by scores
of slaves, whose labours, employed on fertile soil, cannot fail to afford
you a princely maintenance [cannot imagine] suffering from want of
necessaries."[37]

Even northern farmers who cared little about slavery became suspicious about slaveholders' intentions. As many editorials put it in the
early 1820s, southerners could not stop hungering to fill lands with
half-clad slaves after they expelled half-clad Indians. "These tawny
hunters," complained an anonymous editorial in the *Pennsylvania Gazette*, "are doomed by southern policy to extermination, and the fertile
fields, the rich Savannas, and the majestic forests . . . are destined to
become the miserable abodes of groaning slaves and tyrannic despots."
Other Yankee editorialists complained about southern deafness to the
panic: "They destroy our manufactures, because they say it is better to
send their grain, cotton, and tobacco three thousand miles to feed foreign workmen, while our own are starving for want of employment."[38]

The post-panic national election of 1824 became a bitter, vindictive
campaign. Four men, each claiming to represent the Democratic Party,
declared themselves candidates. While the divisions are complex, it is
possible to locate the candidates as the four ordinal points on a compass.

In the wake of the panic many southeasterners consolidated around
the caucus choice: Secretary of the Treasury William H. Crawford.
Like Washington, Jefferson, Madison, and Monroe, Crawford was born
in Virginia, though raised in South Carolina and Georgia. The six-foot
three-inch Georgia "giant" was a formidable, shambling hulk, his left
wrist having been shattered in a duel with the leader of a Georgia faction that opposed him. After the panic, as Treasury secretary, Crawford
had urged a radical retrenchment of federal expenditure, including
a drastic withdrawal of funds from the U.S. Army, a halt to internal
improvements, and rapid repossession of Land Office properties in

default. Opponents called Crawford's gang of antimilitary, antispend-
ing congressmen the radicals. Most glaringly, the radicals passed the
"Alarm Act" of 1820, which reneged on pensions to veterans, demanding that they demonstrate real poverty before receiving payouts. In the
debt-pinched Southeast he was a hero, but he was not a popular candidate anywhere else.[39]

In January 1823, a newspaper campaign started in the *Washington
Republican* against Crawford. The anonymous author "A.B." accused the
Georgia giant of moving federal deposits to the banks of his political
friends and of hiding evidence after Alabama port authorities caught
his friends smuggling newly enslaved Africans into America.[40] After
a formal inquiry cleared Crawford of charges, one of his friends challenged the originator of some of the charges, South Carolina's George
McDuffie, to a duel. McDuffie was shot and permanently crippled.[41]
Radicals did not forgive or forget; the Georgia giant, having fright-
ened away all critics, suffered a severe stroke at the beginning of the
campaign; they continued to support him. Some gamely said he had
become the perfect candidate because the president should not do
very much anyway.[42] Crawford became the hero of those who believed
that a panic required drastic financial cutbacks.

Henry Clay, also born in Virginia, seemed a more solid choice, but
the panic had hurt his reputation too. A tall and lanky riverboat gambler in his youth, he had a charming demeanor and a quick, broad smile.
Willing to pinch snuff and talk about any public matter, he was one of
the best-known men west of the Appalachian Mountains. Unlike the
stiff Virginia gentry, Clay seemed a deft politician of the new school.
For Clay, like Melvill, the panic could be fixed by what he labeled in
1824 the "American System." An increase in tariffs would protect infant
industries from cheap labor in Europe; the revenue would fund internal
improvements: "We have seen, I think, the causes of the distresses of
the country. We have seen, that an extensive dependence upon the foreign market must lead to still severer distress, to impoverishment, to
ruin. We must then change somewhat the course."[43] Like many north-
westerners of the 1820s, he believed that newer states did not have the
tax base to invest in infrastructure. The federal government, not those
of the states, should invest in canals and public roads that would connect western states to the East.

While Clay saw himself as the western candidate, his call for a
stimulus package of internal improvements made him stronger in the
Northwest than in the Southwest. Many cotton planters in Louisiana,

Mississippi, Alabama, and Arkansas looked south along the mighty Mississippi as their route to cotton markets in New York and Liverpool. Few of these Deep South planters wanted any of Henry Clay's roads. While they wanted local waterways widened, most jealously defended the right of planters to do it themselves and charge tolls.[44] The wealthiest planters had already purchased the land best situated along the Mississippi and Red Rivers. For these men, national roads could be a costly distraction, and national tariffs only increased their costs.[45]

Clay had other deficits as a presidential candidate. As Speaker of the House, he had presided over the Missouri question and brokered the compromise. It weakened his support among extreme partisans of both sides. Just as important, Clay was chief counsel for the Bank of the United States, having defended it before the Supreme Court. Second only to Crawford, moreover, Clay was the West's chief "repo man." In state and circuit courts, Clay's agents had repossessed tens of thousands of acres that had been pledged as collateral. In the 1820s in much of the Northwest any connection to the bank, either as agent or as director hurt one's chances for political office.[46]

At the northeastern quadrant stood John Quincy Adams, who had all the patrician rigidity of his father, the former president John Adams. His opponents called the younger Adams "the professor" for his bookish manner, his obsession with education, and his pompous speech making.[47] Ambitious to be president but unwilling to appear so, he nonetheless had useful qualities. He had vast foreign policy experience, for example, having helped negotiate the Treaty of Ghent. (Clay had gone to Ghent also but had apparently spent his time drinking, playing cards, and propositioning chambermaids.[48]) Adams's blood connection to the Revolutionary tradition and his straightforward commitment to New England endeared him to voters in that region, though he did well in Maryland, Illinois, and even Mississippi.[49]

For Adams the solution to the depression was financial stimulus through infrastructure, but his plan was different from Henry Clay's. Adams imagined that the nation might create a national university, more military academies, a series of astronomical observatories, and a vast number of lighthouses.[50] Which states had a sufficient number of rocky seacoasts and college graduates to accommodate this vast expenditure of federal taxes? New England, of course.[51] While many feared that Crawford might continue a Virginia dynasty, voters outside the Northeast feared that a dynasty run by the son of a former president would be a terrible mistake.

The last candidate, a late addition to the race, was General Andrew Jackson. As a war hero, Jackson was known everywhere, but he polled strongest in the old Southwest, which included a large and consolidated block of Indian country. Jackson and other planters wanted the rich Indian lands of the Five Civilized Tribes—the Cherokees, Chickasaws, Choctaws, Creeks, and Seminoles. Between the Revolution and 1819, southern militias and armies had pushed the Indians northward across Mississippi, Alabama, and Georgia. By 1819, hostile southern planters and farmers surrounded the Indians completely.[52] Much to the dismay of planters, the Cherokees and Creeks began to acquire slaves and grow cotton themselves. A frequent toast among white southerners—who drank frequently—was to "the early removal of the Indians."[53] Though William Crawford was from Georgia, he was weak on the issue of Indian killing. As secretary of war, he had famously suggested that the best way of dealing with the Indians was to intermarry with them.[54] In addition, Crawford's "radical" policy of financial retrenchment threatened to kill southwestern expansion: it prevented treaty payments that facilitated removal and weakened a military that might enforce removal.

Planters and middling farmers from the Southwest who stood behind Jackson were not free-trade radicals. They wanted a state that could sponsor filibustering, or privately organized territory grabs. A filibuster expedition was a military enterprise organized by private investors to invade or seize land from a foreign power, whether in Florida, eastern Texas, Canada, California, or Cuba. For filibusters the American government had to be weak enough to leave them alone but have a strong enough army to back them up in times of peril.[55] For the thousands of planters in the Southwest who saw dollar signs in all the lands circling the Gulf of Mexico that Americans did not own, constitutional scruples and budgetary parsimony would not do.[56] Planters and farmers in the Southwest wanted federal spending in the form of a strong, well-fortified army that would drive out Indian settlements after their volunteer expeditions had made the initial assault. With sufficient private and public force, Cherokee planters, Spanish caudillos, and Mexican farmers could all be expelled from what planters called the Golden Circle around the Gulf of Mexico. The rich tropical and semitropical regions would make way for southern plantations.[57]

Given a four-way race, many expected that the selection for president would be concluded in the House of Representatives, where the Constitution said a close race should be resolved. The candidate Henry Clay, as Speaker of the House, would have tremendous influence over the final tally, but to the surprise of most in Congress, Clay finished fourth in the popular vote, making him ineligible. Even more surprisingly, Jackson won the popular vote, though the general lacked a majority. According to the Constitution, Congress would decide. While the caucus had not selected the candidates, the chief executive would once again be chosen in the alleys, parlors, and hotel lobbies that surrounded the greasy congressional saloon.

As the presidency hung in the balance, Henry Clay had a short and private meeting with John Quincy Adams. Neither Clay nor Adams would admit precisely what was said. Shortly thereafter, Henry Clay oversaw the vote in Congress that named the underdog, John Quincy Adams, as president. Days later Adams named Clay his secretary of state, a position then regarded as a stepping-stone to the presidency. Jackson's followers concluded that the meeting between Adams and Clay was a secret deal that gave the presidency to the Northeast for four years in exchange for the next four going to the Northwest, even though Jackson had won the popular vote! Jackson's supporters from Pennsylvania to New York to Mississippi called it a "corrupt bargain."

As Jackson returned from the Adams inaugural in March 1825, he visited a tavern in Washington, Pennsylvania. A supporter stopped him there to shake his hand, noting: "Well, general, we did all we could for you here but the rascals at Washington cheated you out of it." Jackson replied, "Indeed, my old friend, there was *cheating,* and *corruption,* and *bribery* too."[58] His angry reply was day one of the campaign for the presidential election of 1828.

THE MAN WHO would transform national politics in the wake of the panic, the architect of Jackson's 1828 political campaign, was Martin Van Buren, the short, stout son of a tavern keeper. The Dutch language he had learned at home gave him a strongly accented English, but few spoke the language of American politics better than Van Buren. He had created an Albany political machine called the Bucktails, after the deer tails its faithful wore in their hatbands when they attended party meetings. With their rigidly organized rules and military discipline, these meetings rewarded friends with printing, building, and maintenance contracts. Friends got jobs or postal and printing contracts; in return they were expected to make regular contributions to the party and turn out voters at election time. The Bucktails punished enemies just as harshly. After defeating the Clinton political machine in 1820, they set their sights on creating a national committee that would have the same discipline, state by state, county by county, even school district by school district.[59]

By December 1826, Martin Van Buren, then Senator Van Buren, sat down with John C. Calhoun, who had already moved into Jackson's camp. As a New York free-trade "radical," Van Buren could offer the votes that Jackson would need in the 1828 election. He would show the new party how to build newspaper support, how to reward friends and punish enemies in Congress, how to organize a truly national "campaign," one that resembled a military campaign—with officers, foot soldiers, a flood of campaign literature, and bursts of artillery in the form of carefully leaked and widely disseminated criticisms of the sitting president, John Quincy Adams. Though he claimed the party would represent the old Democratic virtues of Jefferson and Madison, Van Buren had in mind a complex regional coalition whose members would meet regularly in Washington.[60]

As a test of the newly formed coalition in Congress, Van Buren used a couple of Federalist friends to hatch a scheme to propose an outrageous tariff. It was designed to benefit manufacturers of rope, bagging, sail, and iron in the West and the mid-Atlantic and tighten the Jackson coalition. Van Buren knew that New England manufacturers—mostly old-line Federalists—would eagerly vote for it. Jackson supporters in the West would claim credit for voting for it, then call for a "judicious" downward adjustment. At the same time, Jackson supporters in the Southeast and the Southwest could be persuaded to attack the bill as a "Tariff of Abominations" produced by Yankees. It was a complicated gambit designed to identify what political scientists would later call a negative reference group: the elite New England Yankee Adams and his opportunistic western ally Clay. John Randolph of Roanoke, a high-strung, well-educated, and mercurial Virginia senator, coined the name that most critics gave to the victorious Adams and Clay: "the Puritan and the Blackleg." While radicals like John Randolph were a part of Jackson's coalition, they were an unstable part and suspicious of this newly forming Democratic Party. After Democrats passed the tariff, Randolph haughtily declared that the bill "referred to manufactures of no sort or kind except the manufacture of a President of the United States."[61]

American and British tariffs had emerged before, during, and after the panic of 1819, helping reorient Anglo-American trade away from American flour, Caribbean sugar, and British manufactures toward a transatlantic cotton trade and a worldwide market for cheap English calicoes. After the panic, as cotton production became more sophisticated, more regular, and less expensive, it produced fortunes for a small group of radicals, both the planters who settled in the black belt and the free traders of Manchester. By then, the panic had divided the American electorate into four ordinal points of the compass. They differed on taxation (the tariff), and they differed on the financial stimulus it should provide. For planters, would-be planters, and New York merchants, greater trade with Britain promised an international division of labor that might make even greater fortunes. With cotton on their minds, a new and energetic political coalition thus formed among New Yorkers, western farmers, and southern planters under the banner of Andrew Jackson.

In the presidential election of 1828, the tariff that these Democrats had secretly authored and then foisted on New England became the so-called Tariff of Abominations, a symbol of all the secret sins of New England. By then, the man and the hour had collided. Andrew Jackson, who had watched the panic of 1819 destroy thousands of honest men, knew just what to do.

CHAPTER SIX

Leviathan

A NDREW JACKSON fundamentally altered international trade between Great Britain and the United States, making it much cheaper. As this traffic increased, seven merchant houses would create a complex but fragile chain of credit that would further cheapen the price to ship cotton from New Orleans to Liverpool. As a result, the price of American cotton would rise rapidly, causing a price bubble in land and slaves. Rural English banks would invest in the booming cotton trade, and the Second Bank of the United States would grow to profit by it. Once Jackson discovered the political and economic power of the Second Bank, he would try to destroy the institution and then to prick the asset bubble he had helped to create. In doing so, he would nearly destroy his party and usher in the panic of 1837.[1]

Jackson was the candidate who united the interests of the partisans of international cotton. Fittingly, his campaign relied on newspapers, their outrageous stories printed on the ripped and recycled cotton that housewives sold to rag collectors. Jackson's men brilliantly used cheap newspapers to attack his political enemies while remaining vague on issues like the tariff. He directly opposed it in commercial New York while appearing to support it in hemp-growing Kentucky.[2]

The dozens of newspapers created to support the Jackson campaign painted John Quincy Adams as a spendthrift who bought pool tables and fancy drapes for the White House. The papers shocked and titillated readers with allegations that in Russia Adams had surrendered a young American maid to the lechery of the Russian czar. The candidate Henry Clay, meanwhile, was alleged to be a habitué of brothels. Newspapers understood that hard-bitten readers who had lived through the depression of the 1820s would be most riled by stories of spending, luxuriance, and licentiousness that flowed from the "corrupt bargain" that had made Adams president. In time, Adams's newspapers gave as good as they got, but the anti-Jackson stories were often scattergun and outrageous: suggesting that Jackson was a bigamist, that he had a mulatto father, and that his mother was a prostitute. But tales of Jackson's furious outbursts and primal rages appeared only to broaden his appeal. Jackson knew newspapers, and those rags would bring him to power.

Promising to end the corruption in Washington, improve Anglo-American trade, and bring prosperity back to America, Jackson won the 1828 election by a landslide. The steamboat that carried him from Tennessee to Washington for the inauguration had hickory brooms attached to the sides, suggesting that he would sweep the Augean stables of Washington.[3] Before even calling a cabinet meeting, the newly elected Jackson met with the newspaper editors who had made his campaign: particularly Duff Green in Washington and James Watson Webb from New York. He told them his plans, described some financial scandals in the navy, and asked their advice. Though Green was not made postmaster general, Jackson nevertheless gave him full authority to, as Green put it, "reward friends and punish enemies" in the post office. Green compiled a list of federal postmasters and postal employees to be fired, and the list of Jackson loyalists to fill their positions. Jackson's party made the newspapers not just reporters of news but shapers of it.[4]

With backing from the Southeast, the Southwest, New York, and elsewhere, Jackson united what most agreed was a complicated sectional coalition. It included New Yorkers who had profited from the Erie Canal and did not want federally funded internal improvements that might compete with it.[5] It included planters who wanted to see the tariff diminished on goods they imported. It included Ohioans and Kentuckians who blamed the Second Bank of the United States for the panic of 1819, and New Yorkers who saw the bank as a beacon of hope. It included strict constructionists who wanted to diminish the power of a national government. Only New England seemed left out—not surprisingly because Andrew Jackson's policies were formed in direct opposition to those of John Quincy Adams.

"THE ARRANGEMENT"

ANDREW JACKSON'S MANY chroniclers have seldom noticed one of his most important moves in his first year in office, one that proved critical in turning cotton into a long-distance commodity that buoyed American economic growth while lashing the American South even more tightly to the Northwest of Britain.

The key operator was a former Federalist named Louis McLane

who brokered the trade deal of the century, drastically altering U.S. trade and foreign policy with Britain. It was a bold gamble personally for Jackson. His hatred for England was well known. Since his teens he had a dramatic scar on his face that he had received from an English officer's sword; he had fought the British at New Orleans; and as a general in Spanish Florida, he had ordered the hanging of two English officers on suspicion that they had armed the Creeks in the Seminole War. But the new coalition that brought Jackson to power had promised to improve international trade either by knocking down the tariff or by eliminating trade barriers.

Trade between the United States and Great Britain was a perennial problem. In the bad old days, between the Revolution and 1828, Britain and the United States had wrangled over tariffs, but especially over shipping between the United States and Britain's colonies in the West Indies. Britain imposed punishing limitations on American ships entering colonial ports; the United States responded with its own version of the Navigation Acts that harried British ships. The U.S. policy of "reciprocity"—initiated by Secretary of State Jefferson under President Washington and repeated through every administration down to John Quincy Adams—made negotiation nearly impossible. "Reciprocity" as practiced by Americans was really a grown-up version of "punch back," where every British restriction would be met with an American restriction.[6] To the partisans of cotton, all this was destructive; navigation needed to be cheaper; "whatever gives facility and security to navigation," Jackson declared in describing his new policy, "cheapens imports; and all who consume them are alike interested in whatever produces this effect."[7]

McLane would produce the desired effect. Jackson's secretary of state, Martin Van Buren, explained the central principle: Britain and America would prevent port officers from making any distinction between British and American ships. U.S. tariffs on British imports might remain, but all the taxes and special inspections of British ships that had so harried Anglo-American trade between 1816 and 1829 would be rescinded.[8] Britain would likewise lift its restrictions on American ships, and neither could rescind the deal once made. To ensure "the arrangement," as Jacksonians later called it, the ability to make deals would reside with the king on Britain's side and the president on America's side; neither foreign ministers nor legislatures could interfere. McLane brought the deal over when he sailed to Britain in 1829, two months after Jackson's inauguration. McLane was the right choice. He was a well-educated son of a hero of the Revolution, yet a former Federalist with English sympathies. His elaborate manners, attention to form, and sartorial skills were without parallel. His secretary of legation was the well-respected writer Washington Irving, who provided him entry into English society.[9]

McLane was perhaps best at dressing nicely. Before being presented to the foreign secretary, McLane had corresponded with the secretary of state about his attire. Asking how to appear before the British was a grave mistake, given Jackson's personal animosities. President Jackson demanded that he wear a simple black outfit with a white collar and gold stars on the collars. McLane, informed that he might be confused for a doctor or head servant with such a simple outfit, apparently discreetly made his own changes and dressed to British form.[10] When John Randolph of Roanoke, a strong supporter of free trade, later appeared before the king in a simple black outfit with knee pants and white stockings, the king's brother called over Washington Irving. Archly referring to a children's rhyme about the "king of Cannibal Island," the king's brother asked Irving, "Who's your friend, hokey pokey?" Bristling, Irving replied, "That, sir, is John Randolph, United States Minister at Russia, and one of the most distinguished orators of the United States." The king's brother smirked.[11]

The sharply dressed McLane also had what it took to forge the unalterable arrangement. After 1830, English and American ships would be treated as equals in the ports of the other. This introduced more direct competition between British and American shippers, which drastically lowered shipping prices for everything—including cotton—between New Orleans and Liverpool. For Lancashire spinners and southern planters, removing these restrictions was more important than lowering a tariff because it ensured the regularity and thus the cheapness of their shipments.[12]

Asked to authorize the president's "arrangement," congressmen in manufacturing districts were suspicious. On the face of it, the legislation promised American shippers access to the British West Indies. But Representative William Ramsey saw the "free trade" inch that might become a mile, voicing suspicion of a bill reported from the free-trade Committee on Commerce. This committee, he told Congress, might "throw the country at the mercy of foreign nations, and compel us in the interior even to send abroad to have our horses shod."[13] His suspicions were justified. Once signed, "the arrangement" proved unassailable.[14] After the ink was dry, the United States had achieved something like a most favored nation status with Britain without a corresponding need to lower its tariffs. In the 1830s, the price to ship cotton from

New Orleans to Liverpool dropped one-third compared with shipping prices in the previous decade.[15] The combination of high tariffs and cheap trade led to a steep increase in U.S. tariff revenues, so steep that the United States could buy back many of its Treasury bills. By 1831 it was clear that tariff revenues were about to make the U.S. government's debt disappear entirely. A full debt payoff, unprecedented in world history, attracted the attention of bankers all over Europe.[16]

Healing trade relations between the United States and Great Britain ended the squabbles between Britain and its former colony, but it did not end American debates over tariffs and trade. Although the plummeting cost of Atlantic shipping benefited southern planters who exported cotton and imported British-made goods, East Coast planters were not satisfied. For them, the sting of the panic years had not abated. The green-seed cotton boom benefited the planters of the Mississippi delta, not them, but there was nothing they could do about that. What they could affect was the tariff. The English observer Harriet Martineau noted that every time South Carolina planters saw prosperity elsewhere, they blamed the tariff. "Right as the South Carolinians may be as to the principle of free trade, no tariff ever yet occasioned such evils as they groan under." They blamed the 1828 tariff that brought Jackson to power: "Now, when they see the flourishing villages of New England, they cry, 'We pay for all this!' "[17]

And so South Carolina and eastern Virginia became the seedbed of an angry free-trade movement devoted to punishing Jackson for his support of the tariff, his direct-trade "arrangement" notwithstanding. John C. Calhoun, formerly a solid nationalist, responded by creating a theory he called "nullification." In his *South Carolina Exposition,* endorsed and distributed by the South Carolina House of Representatives, he proposed that his state might entirely eliminate any tariff by refusing to enforce it in the port of Charleston. It was a doctrine that extended free trade to its final conclusion: the complete dissolution of trade boundaries. It did so, however, by ignoring federal law. President Jackson labeled it sedition. In 1829, the William & Mary economics professor Thomas R. Dew further extended Calhoun's argument, asserting that tariff measures were an "injustice" that ensure that "the consumers of the South and West would suffer for the gains that are made by the North," as well as "preventing that emigration that would otherwise take place, to those regions of our country."[18]

While the nullification movement had followers throughout the cotton-growing South, few planters in the Southwest saw the advantages of nullification, given the green-seed cotton boom and the growing prosperity that followed Andrew Jackson's 1830 "arrangement." For them, Jackson's stimulus plan had always been about using federal tax money to force the Five Civilized Tribes out of Georgia, Alabama, and Mississippi. It was a promise that Jackson made good on in the Indian Removal Act of 1830, the last and most important step in making available the valuable land along the southern rivers. While such planters appreciated free trade, they also wanted a strong federal government that would pay for Indian removal, as well as back up volunteer incursions into Texas and California and fund the army that would be called on to support them. (Those southern incursions succeeded finally at the end of the Mexican-American War in 1848.) Further stimulus might even realize their dreams of American plantations in the Yucatán and Cuba. This latter stimulus plan never succeeded; southwestern planters still benefited richly from government help.

THE SEVEN HOUSES

AS TRADE RIVALRIES between Britain and its former colony crumbled, and Americans argued among themselves about trade, a few events in England allowed British merchant bankers in the Anglo-American cotton chain to defeat their rivals in the Anglo–*Latin* American trade. Between 1820 and 1824 these wealthy merchant rivals—Sir William Elford, Godfrey Wentworth & Co., and Sir Peter Pole—had rapidly expanded into trading and mining ventures in the newly independent states there. Previously barred from trade in the Spanish Empire, Elford, Wentworth, and Pole extended loans to the new states and helped establish mining companies that expected to use steam engines and modern, British smelting techniques.[19] Eager British investors lent or invested hundreds of millions. Bankers later estimated that English banks and private investors put a stunning £150 million in loans and £200 million in stock subscriptions in these projects between 1823 and 1824. The Bank of England, reeling from the millions of pounds of gold withdrawn for these ventures in the winter of 1824–1825, raised rates and contracted lending. At the same time rumors of revolutionary violence, export bans, and exploded silver mines in Peru surged through the British financial press. An English banking crash followed, destroying more than ninety British banks including, Elford's, Wentworth's and Pole's. The crash after the Latin American bubble briefly hurt cotton prices, leading a few North American merchants to fail as well.[20]

But a few years after the Latin American mining crash, as Anglo-American trade grew, British bankers found a renewed faith in *North*

American borrowers. In the aftermath of 1825 the Anglo-American merchant houses turned themselves into transatlantic merchant bankers who would create new American promises for the trunks of English country banks, this time backed by the future delivery of cotton. English firms like Baring and Brown had been trading in cotton for years. Newcomers followed: Morrison, Cryder & Co.; Lizardi & Co.; Timothy Wiggin & Co.; Thomas Wilson & Co.; and George Wildes & Co. (the last were referred to as the three Ws).[21]

Speculative copper, silver, and gold mines were out; American cotton baled and ready for transit was in. It seemed safe. Especially after Jackson's "arrangement," cotton exports were constantly growing, while the gap between New Orleans and Liverpool prices was large enough that lending to shippers seemed a predictable business. Bank vaults have always held letters of credit and bills of exchange for fixed amounts, due in ninety days. These cotton loans would be the same, only for a longer-distance trip. The seven houses created a bill of exchange "payable on sight." A "sight bill of exchange" was redeemable ninety days after the house "saw" it arrive in Britain. It thus traveled as an interest-bearing note in America for many months, then arrived in Britain, where it could bear interest for another ninety days after arrival.[22] In other words, an established cotton firm calculated the value of a bale or more of cotton on its way to England, handed over a note for somewhat less than its value, then paid the note when the cotton finally arrived. Here was a new promise that banks would hoard.

An American agent of one of the seven houses walking the cotton docks of New Orleans or Mobile was paid to know the volume of cotton traveling across the Atlantic and the current Liverpool price. Seeing a bale for sale on the wharf, he could write up a bill of exchange that multiplied cotton's market price by the bale's weight, subtracting about 20 percent in case prices dropped. The sight bill was a loan for floating cotton guaranteed by the cotton itself. American banks took these promises and held them as their reserve. Indeed an interest-bearing cotton bill of exchange issued by one of the seven houses was better than silver or gold. Once the bill came back to Britain for redemption, British country banks would buy the notes from shippers confident that textile manufacturers would pay the note when they bought title to the cotton bale associated with it. Thus cotton had at least five intermediaries, five individuals or institutions that held the sight bills of exchange: a wharf agent, an American bank, an English country bank, one of the seven houses, and finally the cotton manufacturer.[23]

Rural joint-stock banks in Britain sat on tremendous floating capital reserves and eagerly sought the interest-bearing notes that the seven houses provided. After the Latin American mining panic of 1824–1825, Parliament tried to separate the Bank of England from English country banks with a series of laws. Believing that the Bank of England's sudden retraction of credit was partly to blame for the panic, Parliament allowed joint-stock banks of six or more investors to form, banks that might rival the Bank of England in size and influence. They could then build branches provided they operated more than sixty-five miles from the city limits of London. These joint-stock banks then bought up smaller country banks as branches. Once organized, they sought investments. Given the relative peacefulness of Europe, England's military debts were declining. With English public debt dwindling, the Bank of England could not pay the high interest that rural and country banks wanted. Meanwhile, though American Treasury bonds had served many English banks, the coming extermination of that debt by the Treasury Department put them at a loss for investments.[24]

And so an international investment market on London's Lombard Street came into being. On the "buy side" were English country banks with too much cash seeking relatively high-interest, fixed-return investments. On the "sell side" were the seven houses, with new promises from cotton merchants that would sit in the vaults of British banks until the money arrived from overseas cotton shipments.[25] The seven houses would effectively borrow from the country banks desperate for something more than 3 percent; they would effectively lend to American planters to produce cotton at 8 percent, then bring the cotton to Britain for spinning.[26] This cotton speculation was profitable, but as 1824–1825 had proven, it was also dangerous. The seven houses worked out a scheme for managing risk that will seem very familiar to modern readers.

After 1825 the seven houses off-loaded the risk of trade (or so they thought) by lending their and other banks' money to a special-purpose entity that has often been called a commission house but is better described as an agency house, after its model in the British ports of China and India.[27] It is best understood as a branch bank for a large merchant bank. The agency house of China or India collected porcelain or fine linens, boxed them up, then paid for them with bills of exchange with the name of one of the seven houses on the top. The bills traded as cash in the British sections of these foreign countries. They were not a title to the goods, but the managing house in Britain ensured that the total value of bills issued by an agency house was less than its line of credit. An agent who claimed more cotton than his credit limit could be jailed for fraud. American banks would buy these bills, hold them as they matured, then sell them to local merchants who wanted to use them to buy English goods.[28]

An agency house in New Orleans acted in the same way as a colonial agency house. The New Orleans house received credit—initially £10,000 to £20,000—from one of the seven houses. After Jackson's direct-trade "arrangement" with the crown was completed, no respectable agency house had less than £100,000 of credit. The agency house then located cotton available for sale. Using its credit, the American agency house could issue bills of exchange (up to the house's credit limit) payable sixty or ninety days after they were presented in London.[29] Bills of exchange issued by such reputable agency houses as "J. L. & S. Josephs" were better than cash. "The man who owned an obligation of theirs to $1,000," declared the economics professor Thomas Dew in 1840, "could pay his debts with it, or buy goods, or borrow money on it."[30]

Agency house representatives like Samuel Hermann of Hermann, Briggs & Co. traveled down to wharves along the Mississippi or paid factors (planters' agents) for bales of cotton with the bills that the agency house issued but the seven houses guaranteed.[31] The agency house also paid silver to customers who walked in with a note from one of the seven houses. Of course the agency house took a commission, demanding interest if the note was not due, and charged a fee. American agency houses seemed like banks but were not regulated like them.

An agency house was a lucrative enterprise, and in cash-starved, credit-hungry New Orleans it could make from 5 to more than 25 percent interest on its investment depending on the difference between the Louisiana price it paid and the Liverpool price that the seven houses received. But the agency house was also heavily leveraged; it traded on the name of one of the seven houses, but like a bank it never had enough gold or silver to pay everyone at the same time. As long as merchants, factors, planters, and shopkeepers treated their promises as better than money, the agency houses thrived.

The seven houses also took care of the other side of the business: British goods imported to America. The bills from the seven houses tended to flutter out of American agency houses during the cotton harvest in November to pay factors for cotton on its way to Britain. Factors turned the bills of exchange over to American banks that held them in their vaults as investment-grade securities. Farther north,

New York wholesalers with silver in their tills bought the bills from the banks. Wholesalers bought them because English bills from agency houses could be sent to England to pay for next year's imports. When the bills arrived in England, English bankers accepted them, held them until maturity, then presented them to the seven houses. If the banks quickly needed pound notes or gold, the Bank of England would accept the notes from the seven houses and give up cash. Eventually, the seven houses accepted the bills, sold off the cotton associated with them to cotton manufacturers, and paid off the notes in English pounds or gold.

The bills of exchange from the seven houses proved a workable if ungainly system for funding trade in two directions: southern cotton bales eastward to England and English clothing westward to America.[32] While the U.S. Land Office had provided credit for land before 1819, the agency house offered credit for cotton. Some southern banks acted both as banks and as agency houses. As state-chartered banks, they issued their own banknotes based on the quality of bills in their vaults. The best-known banknotes came from the Citizens' Bank of Louisiana whose $10 notes were labeled both in English ("ten") and French (*dix*). By the latter part of the 1830s, these notes—called Dixies—traveled in the vast region north of New Orleans and south of the Ohio. Steamboat captains began to call the area "Dixie Land."[33]

While the bill of exchange was an ancient financial instrument whose origins dated back to Italian city-states in the eleventh century, there was something new and irregular here. Two chains of banks in two sovereign nations separated by an ocean both funded their banks with bills of exchange. The American bill rested on the credit of the seven houses, which rested on eastbound cotton shipments. This chain of credit rested on the price stability of a single commodity whose value could fluctuate, though it seldom fluctuated wildly. In the words of one contemporary economist "Cotton . . . is the Atlas which upholds our whole commercial system."[34]

The entire system worked rather elegantly if the seven houses diligently evened out their risks across multiple agencies and if they maintained an intelligence network that stretched from Liverpool to Louisiana.[35] But if the Bank of England refused to accept the notes of the seven houses from another bank, or if the Bank of England questioned the country banks' lending practices, or if political controversies caused Americans to doubt the stability of these English instruments, then the chain of promises that built these banks would collapse entirely. All three things would happen in 1836.

For a few years the system worked. The seven houses offered 5 percent loans to agency houses and then let the agency house take the risk of betting on future cotton prices. The agency house borrowed at 5 percent and hoped to make much more off profits from cotton sales; if the southern agency house defaulted, the English house usually held the bill of lading for its cotton and could sell the cotton when it arrived in Liverpool. The system seemed risk-free.[36]

This may look familiar to modern eyes. Banks with lots of capital sought to lend in a highly profitable business but placed an institution (the agency house) and a credit instrument (the bill of exchange) between themselves and the risk. They expected that individual failures would certainly occur: cotton prices might drop when low-quality bales reached Liverpool, for example, so that they were worth less than the handsome figure paid in New Orleans. But the firms believed that by keeping a mix of good and bad loans together, the high profits of one would balance out the losses of the other. In the late twentieth century the institution was a "structured investment vehicle," and the instrument was the "collateralized debt obligation." After 2000 proof of stability was dressed up with a formula borrowed from physics and called a Gaussian copula function.[37] It was equally bogus in the 1830s.

American agency houses, once established, could not resist operating as American banks. After all, they sat on credit from the seven houses, which in turn had credit from English country banks. The agency houses provided credit to anyone who needed ready currency and was willing to pay more than 6 to 8 percent for it. A borrower who came to the agency house for credit did not borrow for a voyage, and so his borrowing ran to the furthest edge that the agency house would allow, usually ninety days. This "accommodation" note was denominated in American dollars and often ran more than $200. At the end of the ninety days, borrowers then paid these bills with a further accommodation note. In other words, they took out a loan to repay an existing loan, usually paying the interest in cash. The slang term, which comes from Ireland, for this kind of accommodation bill was a "kite," and issuing a bill supported by nothing but a future promise to pay was called "flying a kite." And so a system of continual borrowing on the cotton credit chain was established that might continue indefinitely so long as the rates to borrow money in England remained around 3 percent and the rates to borrow in the United States remained at 8 percent or more. If the seven houses could get credit from English banks at low rates, they could lend to their agencies for a few percentage points higher, which could lend to American cotton planters for a few percentage points higher.[38] "If" was the operative word.

THE SECOND BANK IN THE COTTON TRADE

BUSINESS WAS GOOD for the seven houses in the New Orleans trade, but they faced a competitor in Philadelphia, one that also served to limit the expansion of credit. The Second Bank of the United States had proved tremendously capable after the 1819 panic and indeed had helped America escape the difficulties of the 1824–1825 panic in Britain.[39] Like the seven houses, the Philadelphia banker Nicholas Biddle could see the value of bankrolling the import-export trade. "Our great object," Biddle wrote in 1827, "is business men and business paper. . . . [W]e are obliged to keep every dollar we can in a state of activity."[40] While the Barings had stock in Biddle's bank, he was their competitor in this market because he too could borrow on Lombard Street and lend in New Orleans. The Second Bank's charter gave it the responsibility of determining which of the agency bank's notes the U.S. Land Office would receive for land sales. If Biddle refused to accept the notes of a bank, the notes' value declined precipitously. The seven houses watched him carefully.[41]

Nicholas Biddle was a peculiar fellow. His Quaker roots extended back to William Penn's settlement of Pennsylvania. The Biddles had helped found Philadelphia, and Nicholas's uncles had fought in the Revolution. Nicholas entered the University of Pennsylvania at age ten but was not allowed to graduate early. His parents found a lesser institution in Princeton, New Jersey, that allowed Nicholas to graduate at fifteen. He made a grand tour of Europe and was for a short time personal secretary to James Monroe. After 1818, when he finished a brief tour in both houses of the Pennsylvania legislature, Biddle's old-fashioned commitment to Federalist principles apparently made him unelectable.[42] President Monroe, believing him to be a financial genius, made him the government's representative to the newly formed Second Bank of the United States. There he watched President Cheves's hasty retraction of credit to the interior in the 1819 panic. He resolved to do better than Cheves when he headed the bank.

The Bank of the United States had limitations that made Biddle's job difficult. Its charter demanded that Biddle or his cashier sign notes at bank headquarters in Philadelphia. In 1826 he told a friend, "We could at once give to the Southern & Western sections of the country two or three millions of sound & useful circulating medium. But to make two millions of five dollar notes, it would be necessary to sign my name 400,000 times, which . . . is wholly impracticable." In 1827, modeling his behavior on English banking practices, he created something he called a "bank draft" that looked exactly like a banknote but was issued blank—without his signature—to distant branches. When cashiers in New Orleans, Cincinnati, or Pittsburgh needed money, they added their signature in the blank. Because they looked precisely like the banknotes signed by Biddle, Americans accepted them as cash. Like the sterling bills of the seven houses, they would be acceptable as financial instruments at all the bank's branches.

But Biddle's "bank drafts" were more than financial instruments. They did not bear interest like English bills, and they bore the stamp of the U.S. government. Biddle believed that by creating the blank bills himself in limited numbers, he prevented a branch from dangerously overissuing currency. In leaving the bills unissued in the hands of a cashier, he gave the cashiers liquidity when they needed it. Biddle controlled this money supply through his control of his people. The cashiers he appointed to distant branches were born, raised, and trained in Philadelphia; they were loyal, and he trusted them completely. They could expand the money supply to suit the season or the demand for cash. By treating the bank drafts as equivalent to banknotes, Biddle provided a financial instrument that was free from fee, making it desirable as a medium of payment, almost as desirable as a sterling bill of exchange and more desirable than an agency house note.[43]

New financial instruments like the bank draft and the agency house note facilitated the movement of cotton from the American South to the North of Britain. These credit facilities, combined with Andrew Jackson's 1830 "arrangement," helped double the import-export trade with Britain in the decade of Jackson's term. New Orleans's direct trade with Liverpool grew even faster, mostly in English ships. In addition, American trade with the British West Indies increased 2,400 percent in the same decade.[44] Imports and exports surged together as the easy money provided by bills of exchange, agency house notes, and bank drafts allowed American importers to buy vast quantities of British goods on credit.[45]

The credit advanced like a long snake: English country banks lent to the seven houses, which lent to their agencies, which lent to southern planters. Biddle also borrowed from the English country banks and from the seven houses to create his bank drafts. This global chain of cotton credit afforded many white families the capital they needed to enter into the grim business of slave owning.[46]

As capital entered the business, the prices of slaves accelerated, leading some planters to over-leverage; indeed most lived almost entirely on credit. As early as 1829, according to the planter E. O. Blair of Edenton, North Carolina, credit was "ruining all the best families in the County." Blair's friends, "persons who a few years ago were possessed of real wealth are now bankrupt, sold out and subjected to the mortification of seeing their servants, carriages, and furniture purchased by some upstart puppy who has nothing to recommend him but his ill gotten wealth."[47] The internal slave trade increased drastically in the 1830s along with slave prices, each driven up by English demand and the financial liquidity offered by the new bank drafts.

English credit allowed "puppies" with small fortunes, ruthless ambition, and crazy luck to become plantation aristocrats. A hundred years later the novelist William Faulkner documented the rise of these upstart "puppies" when he created the fictional character Thomas Sutpen in his novel *Absalom, Absalom!* Sutpen, born poor in western Virginia, made a quick fortune when he put down a slave uprising in the West Indies. After creating the plantation Sutpen's Hundred, within a generation he could pretend an aristocratic southern lineage. Many such "puppies" with capital and credit built new plantations along the Mississippi and Tombigbee Rivers. Some of them bought estates surrendered to bank and government after the 1819 panic. With enough cash, "puppies" born and raised in New England or Scotland quickly became indistinguishable from the descendants of old families of Virginia and the Carolinas. For white men with cash or good credit, the way was open to buy enslaved workers and start planting. Relatively few poor or middling whites found their way into this credit-based southern aristocracy.[48]

"I WILL TAKE CARE OF THIS"

IN HIS FIRST TERM, as the economy improved, Andrew Jackson had reached a rapprochement with Biddle and the bank. From his personal experience, and as an inheritor of Jefferson's party, Jackson distrusted Britain and the British banking system. While he believed the United States should have a central bank, he thought a branch of the United States Treasury should handle American debt and should discount bills of exchange to facilitate exports. He did not like that Biddle's bank had a private board and issued personal loans; his inner circle was divided about the bank. By 1831, however, Jackson and Biddle's mutual mistrust had exploded into controversy. Biddle noticed in Jackson's second

State of the Union address in December 1830 that Jackson had recommended that Congress replace the Bank of the United States with a national bank—a branch of the Treasury—that might issue land scrip currency but would not allow private loans. Jackson's ally in Congress Thomas Hart Benton then read a florid, daylong speech critiquing the Second Bank as a "moneyed tribunal" that made individual fortunes and "the planetary plague" that caused "sectional jealousy" and "fierce contests for power." While Benton's resolution preventing the bank's recharter was stopped by a close vote in the Senate, Jackson's newspapers widely reprinted the entire speech in February 1831. Biddle, concerned about the future of the enterprise, hired a shadowy lobbyist named Silas Burrows in April 1831 and sent him to New York. Burrows bragged to Biddle that he could make "friends of the Bank" there. "It can easily be affected but must only be talked of," he wrote to Biddle. "I will take care of this."[49]

Burrows soon found his man. He reached out to James Watson Webb, the young editor of the New York *Courier and Enquirer* who was in Jackson's inner circle. Like Biddle, Webb was descended from Revolutionary stock: his father had been an aide to General Washington. Orphaned at five, Webb grew up in Cooperstown, New York, then set out for Washington, D.C., during the panic of 1819. After wheedling a position as a second lieutenant from Secretary of War John C. Calhoun, he briefly served in New York City, then had military adventures in Chicago and Detroit both fighting Indians and challenging his fellow officers to duels. Resigning his commission after he challenged a superior officer, he returned to New York to marry a New York City socialite. His father-in-law helped him buy the editorship of the New York *Courier,* the commercial newspaper that would help put Jackson in the White House. Webb's success in supporting Jackson and the growing circulation of his newspaper made him an insider, with a complete understanding of all the tensions in the newly forming party.[50]

Webb, however, had boundless ambition. As his paper grew larger, he expanded its print run with a steam-powered press, bought a schooner to meet the New York mail packets, and combined a steamship with a pony express to deliver Washington news faster than any New York paper. His circulation soon exceeded the combined circulation of his rivals, but so did his expenses. Webb dealt with that by meeting with Biddle's agent in late March 1831, an event that proved critical to Webb's future success. The Second Bank of the United States would secretly make a loan to Webb's paper, shielded by the agreed-upon fiction that Burrows, Biddle's lobbyist, had a rich father who was funding Webb's expansion; the Second Bank kept the $15,000 loan off the books. As intermediary, Burrows provided both Biddle and Webb with plausible deniability about their relationship. Webb did his part. On April 1, days before the lower house of the New York legislature was to vote on whether to endorse a recharter of the bank, the *Courier and Enquirer* switched positions, supporting recharter.[51] On April 6, Webb's corruption came to light when another editor, John Mumford of the *New-York Standard & Statesmen,* announced that Burrows had offered him a loan in exchange for a change of heart. By the eighth, the other editors in New York felt sure that Webb's position had changed because he had been bought by the bank.

It was at this point Andrew Jackson's ambivalence about the bank hardened into hatred. Jackson wrote to his friend Hugh White of "the corrupting influence of the Bank upon the morals of the people and upon Congress." The bank's influence was everywhere: "Many who you would not have supposed, has secretly enlisted in its ranks." In addition, Jackson had found that someone in the Senate was stalling Benton's efforts to debate the bank's recharter. "Some one of the cabinet may be secretly labouring with Congress to prevent it from being carried into execution," he complained. Fearing that the bank's influence had reached all the way into his cabinet, Jackson asked for the resignations of all of his cabinet members between April and June. He rehired most and then rearranged them.[52] Louis McLane, having helped create "the arrangement" with Great Britain, was promoted to secretary of the Treasury. In the end, the reshuffling proved futile. By the time Jackson's cabinet was approved by Congress in the fall of 1831, it appeared that an even larger part of the cabinet supported the bank.

Convinced the bank had compromised Webb, Jackson cut off all contact with him. Meanwhile, Vice President Calhoun, the now-open author of the doctrine of nullification, had gained the support of Duff Green, and so Jackson also barred Green from the White House. Leaving Webb and Green behind, Jackson created what Nicholas Biddle called sneeringly a "Kitchen Cabinet," a group of advisers who did not meet in the parlor like a formal cabinet would but came up through the back stairs. These advisers—including newspapermen, congressmen, and federal employees—would build the party, promote its official press, and maneuver bills through Congress. Jackson chose its members without congressional review. While most of the cabinet was soft on the bank, most of the Kitchen Cabinet opposed it.[53]

With shocking reports of the bank's influence over Jackson's closest supporters, and concerns that there were supporters of nullification in his own party, Jackson began to see enemies everywhere. He was not far from wrong. The Bank of the United States had indeed hired lobbyists to block state legislatures from sending anti-bank memorials to Congress. Even the folk hero and frontiersman Davy Crockett appeared to be in the bank's power.[54] By April 1832, a congressional committee had found evidence that the bank had tried to buy even more newspaper editors in New York. Jackson was sure that its influence stretched further. As he told Van Buren from his sickbed in July, "The bank is trying to kill me, Mr. Van Buren, *but I will kill it.*"[55]

Days later, near the end of his first term, Jackson vetoed the proposed recharter of Biddle's bank. Biddle quickly printed thousands of copies of Jackson's veto message, convinced it would ruin the general's bid for reelection. Appalled, Biddle discovered that the veto appeared to improve Jackson's popularity.[56] Jackson's growing influence, particularly in Maine and New Hampshire, had much to do with the revelations of Biddle's manipulation of Webb and allegations that Biddle had turned a Pittsburgh paper against Jackson.[57] "The veil has been lifted," railed the *New-Hampshire Patriot & State Gazette,* "the hideous deformity of the institution has been exposed; we feel it our solemn duty to point the finger of detestation at this unparalleled act of enormity."[58] In the fall of 1832, voters in Maine and New Hampshire apparently agreed, adding their electors to a Jackson victory.

But the monster was not yet vanquished. After his reelection, Jackson in May 1833 asked Secretary of the Treasury McLane to remove federal deposits from the bank and place them into banks he named, including the Bank of America, the Bank of Natchez, the Bank of Virginia, the Union Bank of Nashville, and the Planters Bank of Mississippi. McLane refused. Jackson replaced him with William Duane, who also refused to remove the deposits. Jackson removed Duane and replaced him with Roger Taney, who in September 1833 did as the general commanded, placing U.S. deposits into banks that critics would call Jackson's "pet banks."[59] While the credit boom after 1830 had increased the number of banks and their aggregate capital substantially, Jackson's commitment to the "pet banks" led to a flurry of bank charters after September 1833. Three hundred banks in 1830 became 500 in 1834 and 829 by the first day of 1838.[60] If the two Treasury secretaries whom Jackson fired thought that removing the nation's deposits from the bank was unwise and unconstitutional, investors and lenders were apparently troubled as well. From October to December 1833, interest rates on short-term loans in American cities shot up to 10 percent, then climbed from 15 to 34 percent in 1834. Bankers called 1834 a panic year, though it was nothing compared with the hysteria ahead.[61]

Jackson's supporters accused the Bank of the United States of intentionally withdrawing credit to provoke a money panic, a charge Biddle hotly denied.[62] Biddle's supporters countered that the "pet banks" Jackson had supported were curtailing credit in order to unsettle the markets and bring Jackson his victory over the Bank of the United States.[63] The congressional session that had already started in December 1833 was quickly labeled the "panic session," as congressmen debated the wisdom of Jackson's rash attacks, his removal of cabinet members, and what he intended.[64] As Senator William Preston of South Carolina put it, Jackson's men thought

> that the bank had received its deathwound by the veto.... Every body supposed that the monster was drawing near the close of its existence—that he had lain down to die.... At that moment the hunter, keen for sport or impatient for revenge, hurls his dart and rushes upon the dying beast, winding his horn, calling up his huntsmen, and unkennelling his pack; the ebbing energies of the lion are aroused to a new effort of flight, and if in the chase, our corn-fields are trampled upon and our flocks scattered, shall we blame the beast, or his pursuers, who would not permit him to die? It may be sport to the mighty hunter, but it is desolation to the country through which the chase sweeps.[65]

As Preston made clear, Jackson's war with the bank had unsettled national markets.

One might have expected a crash to occur in 1834, but the seven houses appear to have profited from the chaos in the American money markets brought by the contraction. With Biddle's notes declining in volume and capital still cheap in Britain, the seven houses were in the enviable position of borrowing at 4 percent in the United Kingdom and lending at 10 percent or more in America.[66] But many of the agency houses and the houses of American merchants who needed short-term credit predicted that the national markets stood on the precipice of failure. Hundreds of New York merchants from both political parties sent a memorial to Congress warning "of greater impending evils." Borrowing plummeted as lenders demanded an "extravagant premium . . . on the best security." Meanwhile, prices were dropping "in every species of public stocks," while "every branch of business connected with the inland exchanges" as well as those involved in the "purchase and exportation of the produce of the country" were halted.[67] Suddenly many saw the virtues of Biddle's bank drafts: they provided a uniform currency that made inland trade, export, and import possible. "A sound, secure and stable currency," the merchants stated, "cannot be sustained without the agency of the Bank of the United States."[68] As long as the Bank of the United States had its national charter, it determined which of the new state bank issues the U.S. Land Office could accept for land sales; it determined what was sound.

The delivery of New Orleans cotton was the promise at the heart of cotton-based credit, the source of British lending, the source of American borrowing. And so New Orleans stood at the epicenter of the 1834 contraction. "We are," declared Senator William Hendricks of Indiana, "in the hands of the New Orleans market, as the clay is in the hands of the potter. Accounts from that quarter are discouraging at present, and bode worse for the future. Bankruptcies unparalleled in number and extent, are spoken of in New Orleans, and the means of receiving and paying for our produce is believed not to be in existence there."[69] Other produce prices were intimately tied to cotton prices because during boom times cotton planters devoted every acre to cotton, buying most of their food and materials from up north rather than producing them on the plantation. Flour, bacon, and clothing prices depended on stability in the cotton market with its bills of exchange and its bank drafts.

"A VIOLENT AND SUDDEN CHANGE"

MANY WESTERNERS LIKE Hendricks believed that Jackson was trying to force the nation into hard currency as an experiment, an attempt to remove the Second Bank of the United States from the cotton-credit nexus and push the banks toward gold and silver. "However much we may wish the condition of the country to be other than what it is," he told Congress, "we must all admit that gold and silver, to supply the paper system, is not in the country; and that to force, or to attempt to force, a violent and sudden change from the one system to the other, must convulse the country."[70]

But change was what they wanted. When Jacksonian Democrats in Congress blocked the bank's recharter by the congressional recess in June 1834, they sealed the bank's doom.[71] Even if Biddle could get a charter in a state, the bank would no longer have control over the internal credit market. That same summer of 1834, Jackson and his allies sought to change the foundations of American banking with three laws: the Coinage Act, the Distribution Act, and the Specie Circular. Indeed it was the plan's coherence that so troubled his opponents. Jackson had no problem with cotton, with American banking in general, or with Anglo-American commerce. He was not a free state banker nor an anticapitalist nor a financial ignoramus.[72] Yet Jackson doubted whether American banking could rely on a credit chain that stretched all the way to rural Britain. Above all he aimed to destroy an institution that dominated that Anglo-American chain of credit and so clearly interfered in national elections.

To make gold the new basis for American commerce, Congress first passed the Coinage Act of 1834, which went into effect on August 1. It sought to change the relative values of silver and gold coins. Congressional Democrats hoped that newer and smaller gold coins—more convenient than the familiar silver dollars—might replace Biddle's bank drafts. They also hoped that new gold discoveries in Virginia, the Carolinas, and Georgia would make it possible.[73] Under the new rules the mint produced lighter gold coins in eagles, half eagles, and quarter eagles. Friends of Jackson's called the new coins "yellow boys" or "mint drops."[74]

Previously, the official ratio at the mint for silver to gold was 15 to 1, though the actual ratio of values was closer to 15.85 to 1. The Coinage Act changed the ratio to 16 to 1. At the old 15-to-1 ratio, the gold in a $10 gold eagle coin had been worth $10.66, which made the coins quickly disappear from circulation. Revalued at 16 to 1, the newer gold eagle coin was smaller, had less gold in it, and so was less likely to be melted down.[75] The principle involved was called Gresham's law: bad money drives out good. In this case Congress made gold coins worth slightly more than their actual market price as gold. That "bad" and overpriced gold coin would become the common currency. With silver set to a slightly lower price (one-sixteenth of an ounce of gold), the "good" silver in a silver coin would now be too valuable for currency. Silver-standard countries like France and Prussia would buy the undervalued American silver dollars to melt them down for their respective currencies. With gold slightly overvalued, Congress hoped the precious metal would stream in from elsewhere, including gold-standard countries like Britain. In the hopeful words of the Washington *Globe,* "The greatest supply of gold will go to the west. . . . A great stream of gold will flow up the Mississippi from New Orleans and diffuse itself over the great west . . . every substantial citizen will have a long silken purse, of fine open net work, through the interstices of which the yellow gold will shine and glitter." The *Globe*'s critics archly warned ladies away from Democrats' "golden shower"; in Greek mythology Zeus used a "golden shower" to impregnate Danaë.[76]

Democrats hoped that the Coinage Act would make gold more popular than the currency issued by the state banks and the Bank of the United States' own "bank drafts." It worked somewhat. Some American banks shipped out silver and bought gold, importing it from wherever they could. The seven houses, in particular, brought gold to America to cover outstanding debts. Jackson and the Democratic Congress hoped that this gold inflow would reverse the apparent tightening of credit.[77] But hard times would soon drive Americans to hoard both gold and silver, making it disappear as currency for a decade.[78]

The second act designed to stimulate the economy during the expiration of the Second Bank of the United States' national charter was the Distribution Act of June 1836. This act instructed the Treasury secretary to deposit $28 million in tariff and land revenues with the pet banks. While the deposits were listed as low-interest loans to the states, there was no expectation that states would return them.[79] New credit was available with new intermediaries: a collection of untried banks, many newly chartered, which had less experience distinguishing good loans from bad.[80] While some directors would invest in cotton bills of exchange and inland bills, other directors would move into riskier, longer-term investments.

For a short time, the nation had two competing banking systems in place—the Bank of the United States with a Pennsylvania charter and the "pet banks." Both produced currencies, and both chased the same products: land and slaves. Most did so indirectly by taking personal notes and offering credit on cotton bills whose ultimate guarantee was cotton prices. A few foolishly invested directly in mortgages. In the year 1836 alone, 110 new banks were formed to take advantage of Jackson's promise to move American deposits to state banks. Just as in 1819, a speculative real estate bubble had appeared by the end of 1834. In that year the increase in state bank credit fueled impossible increases in sales at land offices in Michigan, Illinois, and Mississippi. While Americans had been buying an average of 1.5 million acres of government land a year between 1828 and 1833, they bought 4.7 million for the year ending July 1835 and 12.6 million for the year ending July 1836, and the number was rapidly accelerating each month thereafter.[81]

Southern banks were the worst offenders. Many of the new state banks in Louisiana and Mississippi allowed stockholders to buy land from the U.S. Land Office for just over $1 an acre, claim the land had a value of $10 or more per acre, and then pledge the land to take out more loans. As stockholders in the banks, this was their right, however much the loans threatened the banks' safety. Many Louisiana and Mississippi banks avoided the short-term loans that banks traditionally invested in; instead, they issued vast mortgages on land and slaves.[82] Other states used the surplus to build railroads to crisscross their states, often without clear surveys or traffic estimates. More railroads were built in 1835 than in any other year in the decade.[83]

Slave prices increased just as rapidly while banks new and old provided the liquid funds for investment. A "prime" male slave in New Orleans had already risen from $500 in 1830 to more than $700 in 1835 on the strength of the Anglo-American cotton trade. In the next two years New Orleans slave prices nearly doubled to $1,250. Virginia and South Carolina had been slave-exporting regions for years, selling slaves "down the river" to Louisiana and Mississippi. As the Deep South sloshed with more and more liquid funds, the differential between low eastern and high western prices increased in 1835 and 1836. Lured by the high differential, hundreds of new men entered the slave-trading business, leading a mass exodus of slaves down to the banks of the Mississippi River.[84] It was a slave boom, one funded by new and old banks' investment in the next season's cotton prices.

Previously, Biddle had held the other banks in check by the chartered power to determine which banks' notes were acceptable at the U.S. Land Office. Now that the power was gone in 1835, Jacksonian Democrats admitted this. "No law of congress," wrote Jackson's representative Thomas Hart Benton, "now that the 14th section of the U. States bank charter is repealed . . . *requires* any description of bank notes to be received in payment of public dues." Dozens of reports came to Congress in 1836, he declared, of

> frauds, speculations and monopolies in the public lands [as] combinations of individuals who, availing themselves of facilities to obtain quantities of what is called land office money, that is to say, *bank notes receivable for public land,* attend the sales, put down competition, monopolize purchases at low rates, and then compel settlers to purchase of them at advanced prices.

With Biddle's control over circulation obliterated by the end of the charter, state banks chased profits by providing banknotes for real estate loans.[85] Some English country banks bought even more American state bonds, given the high apparent returns. Jackson's opponent Henry Clay predicted the coming storm: "From the moment that the Bank of the United States ceased to exist, you gave up the rudder of the national currency, and I greatly fear that we shall see it go on, from worse to worse."[86] Because most banks discounted cotton bills by up to 80 percent of their current market value, they effectively offered loans on future cotton proceeds. If cotton prices dropped 25 percent between the issuing of a bill and the payoff in Liverpool, then bill holders would have to return to cotton planters and demand more cotton. In December 1836 and again in the spring of 1837, cotton prices dropped close to 40 percent.[87]

Jackson's horrified reaction to these "frauds, speculations and monopolies" in land sales resembled Langdon Cheves's reaction to the bubble of 1816–1818. Whereas Cheves had returned banknotes to the state banks demanding silver, in early 1836 Jackson sought legislation that required hard currency for the payment of all land purchases. The Senate rejected it as too extreme. Enraged, Jackson waited until Congress adjourned in July to issue a proclamation, the Specie Circular, which required that all land bought from the federal government be paid for in hard currency.[88] Suddenly all planters with debts needed solid cash for future land payments, a move that would force them to quickly sell cotton or slaves to meet their obligations. Planters needed *gold,* and despite the promises of the Washington *Globe* gold was not streaming up the Mississippi to fly into the webbing of their purses. The sudden rush for liquidity in one market would turn the bills of exchange and Biddle's bank drafts into questionable financial instruments.

1836: SYMBOLIC DOUBT

UNDER THE SECOND Bank of the United States there was a clear separation between seemingly stable notes—those accepted by the Bank of the United States as payable at the land office—and the speculative notes of the wildcat banks. But after the bank was gone, all was confusion. The Specie Circular was a terrible overreaction. Symbolic doubt about the financial instruments at the heart of the cotton commodity chain followed from the radical questions Jackson proposed about the supply of credit. By the spring of 1836, questions also came from the other side of the Atlantic. Some financial insiders noted that some of the seven houses lending money for cotton shipments had relatively few assets. As one contemporary later noted, "By bill-kiting, fifteen or sixteen million pounds had been advanced to Americans by banks whose capital was not one-sixth that amount."[89] Questions soon arrived in Parliament about the banks's lending to the seven houses.[90]

William Clay, a member of Parliament from London's East End, voiced his suspicions on the floor of Parliament in May 1836. "Liverpool and Manchester have witnessed a mushroom growth of schemes" whose "facility of credit" was an "encouragement to speculation." That May, Parliament began an investigation into the joint-stock banks that lent to the seven houses.[91]

Next to raise questions was the Bank of England itself. For most bills on Lombard Street, the Bank of England was the lender of last resort. In times when interest rates rose rapidly, brokers, bankers, and borrowers all relied on the Bank of England to pay gold and silver to trusted brokers, though such brokers had to pay a penalty rate for cash. The basis for that rate, the so-called London bank rate, was published every day in British and American newspapers.

On the same day as Jackson's Specie Circular, July 11, the Bank of England's directors became the third and most important doubter about whether a cotton commodity chain could support a banking system. They stepped in to try to stop what they regarded as an American credit bubble. The London *Times* had already remarked in June 1836 that there was trouble with the credit of the United States and the currency that it relied upon. "The whole of the trading and monetary interest in the union," they declared, "are in an artificial and highly excited state."[92] The Bank of England blamed its shrinking gold supply on American credit problems. It asserted that America's 1834 Coinage Act, in effectively shifting the United States from silver to gold, had encouraged traders to withdraw gold from English vaults to sell to American vaults. For the first time in ten years, the Bank of England raised the London bank rate from 4 to 4.5 percent in July, then to 5 percent in September. This brought gold back to the Bank of England while increasing the price the seven houses had to pay for credit.[93]

In August and September 1836, things went from bad to worse. In August, the Bank of England threw the market for bills of exchange and other Lombard Street bills into a tizzy by rejecting the bills that had been guaranteed and accepted by the rural joint-stock banks. For a month or so afterward, other bill brokers on Lombard Street felt confident that these rapidly growing country banks would succeed and so accepted them at a hefty discount. In other words, the brokers paid gold for Lombard Street notes but at a penalty rate that was substantially higher than the bank's official rate. In August 1836 the Bank of England issued a warning to bankers in the American trade to curtail their credits. It then denied credit facilities to the seven houses in particular.[94]

In September an agitated William Brown of Brown Brothers traveled to London to meet with the bank's treasury committee and convinced the bank directors that the American panic was temporary. He also convinced them to accept the paper of the seven houses.[95] Then somehow the bank's internal audit of the Northern and Central Bank of England in September 1836 was publicly printed. In the audit, the Bank of England declared that the Northern and Central held "a class of paper hitherto unknown to bankers, viz. bills drawn upon America." These, it declared, were very likely worthless. Other banks on Lombard Street then began to question the paper of the seven houses.[96] The joint-stock banks that had been trading on American bonds and cotton bills began to fail. As their banks failed, the textile factors of Liverpool with accounts in country banks, lacking cash or credit, began to suspend their orders.[97]

A rise in London's bank rate was fateful. An observer recalled the prescient statement attributed to the Massachusetts congressman Benjamin Gorham years earlier: "The barometer of the American money market hangs up at the Stock Exchange in London."[98] The chill initiated by the Bank of England's rate, combined with the doubts cast on the American notes, led private bankers to bundle up their coats and hold back cash. This would bring a snowstorm in America. From August to December, the money market in the United States went crazy, with rates as high as 24 percent in August and September and 36 percent in October. The price of cotton dropped 30 to 40 percent.[99] This was death to the agency banks and most of the seven houses. They had provided cash payments to planters for up to 80 percent of the quoted price on cotton. They assumed that in the worst case cotton would never drop more than 25 percent in the month it took to arrive in Liverpool.

What was a cotton bond or a private note worth? No one knew. High rates for cash coupled with anxiety about English bills of exchange, cotton notes, and Biddle's notes. In January 1837 the money market opened up "tight as a drumhead," as one Boston banker put it.[100] With short-term rates at about 36 percent, any merchant who needed to borrow was sunk. Crash was inevitable. In England, the Wildes fell first in

February, the other two Ws fell in March. While cotton prices plummeted, the price of wheat rose quickly, partly because the Hessian fly had returned to damage crops in Pennsylvania, Maryland, and western Virginia.[101]

By March 1837 a parade by radical New York Democrats—the Locofocos—turned into bedlam as rioters burst into a New York flour warehouse and emptied it. Likewise, in the three black-belt counties east of Vicksburg, more than a thousand lawsuits had been brought against Mississippi debtors, totaling nearly $3 million. Citizens there demanded a law suspending debt collection. When the governor refused to call the legislature, mobs in those counties destroyed the courthouses, demanded that the sheriffs resign, and threatened to lynch anyone who took their offices.[102]

Biddle described the symbolic doubt that now plagued the nation in April 1837. "The disasters in New Orleans and in London had nearly destroyed all confidence in private bills," he wrote. Biddle blamed Jackson's "crusade against banks and the discrimination [against paper] at the Land Offices," but he assured European investors that the "cotton bills" that he and the seven banks had created were only "discredited for a moment, [and] would soon become abundant and sound."[103]

As cotton prices plummeted, so too did slave prices. Many English merchant bankers now discovered an ugly truth about the cotton commodity chain: the commodities that planters and factors had pledged to the agency banks for the future sale of cotton were the titles to black men, women, and children. First the agency houses, then the seven houses and the Bank of the United States, and then rural joint-stock banks stood to become the owners of a vast number of slaves.[104]

To prevent that, Mississippi's governor pointed out to the state's legislature that the Mississippi Constitution still prohibited the interstate slave trade. If the legislature simply declared that this prohibition made slaves unsalable, then creditors could not take slaves out of the state to settle debts.[105] He need not have worried: defaulting planters took the slaves off themselves. Scores of slaveholders snuck their slaves out of the state at night to avoid creditors, bound for the contested, but seemingly independent, Republic of Texas. Because the Republic of Texas claimed to be an independent country, and was not yet in the United States, defaulting borrowers who settled there were safe. Their slaves and other movable property were immune from seizure. When sheriffs received writs of collection, they visited the now-abandoned plantations of Mississippi and Louisiana, then returned them with the inscription "G.T.T.": gone to Texas.[106] Residents of the Gulf States coined the term "absquatulate" to describe men who left the state to avoid their debts in order to "squat" in the new republic. The Texas government, desperate for settlers, promised "a labor and a league" of free land (roughly 4,600 acres, of which 177 could be on a river) to any family that rebuilt a plantation there.[107] Independent Texas became a new nation of deadbeats.

Between March and May 1837 the New Orleans failures moved up to New York. New York banks suspended specie payments on May 10, the Boston banks shortly afterward. The panic of 1837 was the first fully national suspension of bank payments in the United States. From 1837 to 1838 it surged across Britain and then continental Europe.[108] In June 1837, the *Leeds Mercury* haughtily complained that "there has been immense *overbanking and overtrading* in America" and that because "the perfectly democratic nature of the American governments is greatly against the adoption of wise and timely measures," their own country banks were doomed to fail. "Our Joint-Stock Banks followed at humble distance," the paper complained, "drawn along in the mighty gulf-stream of American speculation." The paper neglected to mention that the English country banks failed in large measure because they eagerly sought to loan to the seven houses to provide cotton for English textile mills. With cotton so low in price after 1837, a final monetary settlement for the loans would require the sheriff of Leeds to go to the Republic of Texas to repossess slaves and horses, a rather unlikely scenario.

A young Herman Melville saw the crisis firsthand. When his father died in 1832, a twelve-year-old Herman had left school to find work as a teller in the New York State Bank in Albany. He got the position through the influence of his maternal uncle, a powerful man in the Democratic Party. Supported in part by his uncle and his older brother Gansevoort, the scruffy, unkempt Herman spent three years learning the routine of filing, accounting, and discounting notes in Albany. He sought to improve his brief education by joining local debating societies. When Jackson's attack on the Bank of the United States began, he must have marveled at it. But like many soft-money Democrats, he would have worried about Jackson's dangerous obsession.

When the panic hit Albany in May, Herman's mother was forced to make a bond of $50,000 to cover Gansevoort's debts. Herman's paternal uncle, also bankrupted, ran off to Illinois, abandoning the family estate in the Berkshires. Now jobless, Herman returned to the estate while the family scrambled to pay the back taxes on it. Wandering around the old mansion, examining the peeling wallpaper and the family papers, he reflected on the fate of his once proud and wealthy family, humbled once in the panic of 1819 and now in the panic of 1837. After working for a few years as a tutor, he left New York for a life at sea.[109]

Years later, in Pittsfield, Massachusetts, an older Herman Melville reflected on the course of his life with a story that he admitted was partly allegorical. He called it *The Whale*. It was the story of Ishmael, a "simple sailor" from an "old established family" who signs on board a whaling ship led by the "crazy" captain Ahab.

A driven man with a long scar on his face, the captain has a personality that inspires in Ishmael a "wild, mystical, sympathetical feeling." The long scar is the source of Ahab's rage, much like the scar that Jackson received from an English officer in his youth. Among the Democratic crew that works for Ahab, and the New York bankers who support him, few fully understand his reckless plan: "Had any one of his old acquaintances on shore but half dreamed of what was lurking in him then, how soon would their aghast and righteous souls have wrenched the ship from such a fiendish man!" The shipowners, like the Albany Regency under Martin Van Buren, had brought Jackson to power. They "were bent on profitable cruises, the profit to be counted down in dollars from the mint," but Ishmael is learning that crazy Ahab seeks "audacious, immitigable, and supernatural revenge."

Ahab's enemy is a whale, a "murderous monster" that seems to be everywhere and nowhere. The saltwater Bank of the United States provided credit for trade all over the world. The "hated whale has the round watery world to swim in, as the small gold-fish has its glassy globe," Ahab declares, but while "the accountants have computed their great counting-house the globe, by girdling it with guineas . . . my vengeance will fetch a great premium HERE!" he says and pounds his chest.

Ahab's rage is likewise boundless, for he "piled upon the whale's white hump the sum of all the general rage and hate felt by his whole race." In the novel, Ahab nails a gold piece worth sixteen silver dollars to the mast, an echo of the Specie Circular that sought to nail trade to a new form of currency. The man who helps Ahab kill the white whale will receive it.

And so the war between Ahab and this "monster," this "leviathan," comes to matter more than anything. As Melville well knew, the battle begun between captain and monster in 1832 would soon consume them all, driving captain, crew, and whale into oblivion. For while the bank war of 1832–1837 helped consolidate Jackson's power and assure Van Buren's election afterward, the depression that followed Van Buren's inauguration in 1837 tore the country apart. The Democratic Party, like Ahab's ship, would be shattered by the panic.

By 1839, the downturn had brought a new form of crash politics. Jackson's many critics combined to form the Whig Party; his former newspaper ally and sworn enemy, James Watson Webb, had come up with the name. It was a peculiar coalition against Jackson, as the *Richmond Enquirer* noted: "Federalists, Nullifiers, American System men, Bank men, abolitionists, &c." The *Enquirer* was appalled that anyone would vote for them. "Remember that Whigs are Whigs," it declared. Pennsylvania was "bought up by the U.S. Bank—members bribed—whole sections of the country bribed." The Whigs' purpose was to bring back the bank, "that life may be breathed into the entrails of that great Leviathan, to enable it to live another year."[110] But Democrats found that they could no longer make people fear the leviathan. Two years after the 1837 crash Biddle's bank still struggled to exist on a Pennsylvania charter, but his vain attempt to corner the market for cotton to drive its price up again finally destroyed the Bank of the United States of Pennsylvania. It suspended operations in October 1839.[111] But by then the bank was no longer a powerful beast, and no amount of flogging could turn this saltwater bank into a fearsome creature again.

The Whig Party united the wealthiest cotton planters who needed banks to give them credit with nationalistic Missouri merchants like Mark Twain's father, John Marshall Clemens. Westerners who wanted internal improvements sat cheek by jowl in Congress with New Englanders who wanted tariffs to protect eastern industries. After the panic of 1837, the Whigs mastered the stump speeches, barbecues, and coalition politics that had brought Jackson to power. It proved safe to blame an elitist New York Democrat like Van Buren for the bank failure. But the Whig Party needed to find a candidate unconnected with the bank, which had become the party's tar baby. Anyone connected to the bank was unelectable for president. The "great triumvirate" of Calhoun, Clay, and Daniel Webster was all too tightly joined to it. Calhoun had written the charter; Clay had represented it; Webster was now its chief counsel.[112]

Only a war hero without bank connections could allow the Whigs to make the case against the Democratic Party. Luckily, William Henry Harrison could pretend to be a war hero, and he had no ties to the bank. When a Democratic opponent allegedly accused Harrison of having come from a log cabin, Harrison's men embraced a campaign of the Log Cabin and Hard Cider. Democrats had traditionally been the party of drink, but after 1837 Whigs plied voters with drink as well. Harrison won in 1840, only to die suddenly in April 1841.

Unfortunately for John Tyler, the vice president who replaced him, phase two of the crash came weeks after Harrison was in the ground. In the fall of 1841 eight states and one territory failed to pay their debts. Mississippi, Louisiana, Florida, Arkansas, Michigan, Indiana, Illinois, Maryland, and Pennsylvania all suspended payments.[113] They had issued state bonds in rank profusion after 1837, partly to invest funds Jackson had given to the pet banks and partly as stimulus, to spend themselves out of the crisis. By 1841 dozens of railroads to nowhere stretched across their states. Others were surveyed and unbuilt. Indiana had appropriated $10 million for public improvements, an astonishing figure for a state with 100,000 voters.[114] Here was the troubling underside of the infrastructure economy of the 1830s: many states had invested beyond their means in projects of dubious value. Continued tightness in the money market in 1841 prevented many states from paying even the interest on their bonds.[115] The 1841 state debt crisis was an echo of the 1837 crash. (This is very much like the sovereign debt crisis of 2011, which was an echo of the 2008 crash in mortgage lending.) Between 1838 and 1840 states responded to a downturn with an unwarranted expansion in public debt, piling state promises on top of private promises unfulfilled.

In 1841 the governor of Mississippi, Alexander McNutt, coined the term "repudiation" to describe a new policy: completely abandoning a debt. McNutt refused to honor millions of bonds pledged to create the Union Bank of Mississippi. In justification the governor resorted to anti-Semitism, thundering that "the Baron Rothschild" held some of the bonds, a charge that was technically true. "The blood of Judas and Shylock flows in his veins," McNutt declared. "He has mortgages upon the silver mines of Mexico and the quicksilver mines of Spain. He has advanced money to the Sublime Porte, and taken as security a mortgage upon the holy city of Jerusalem and the sepulchre of our Saviour." It seemed preposterous, the governor continued, that a Jew "shall have a mortgage upon our cotton fields and make serfs of our children."[116] Mississippi had received millions from Biddle's bank, which had been rechartered as the Bank of the United States of Philadelphia. By January 1841, with forty-two cents in its treasury, Mississippi stopped payment on its notes. Mississippi's failure finally killed Biddle's bank, which had been struggling since 1839. It failed the following month.[117]

In response to the state repudiations, the world debated the responsibilities of American states. The Reverend Sydney Smith of London, who held discredited Pennsylvania bonds he had bought for his young niece as an inheritance, wrote harshly in 1843:

> Figure to yourself a Pennsylvanian receiving foreigners in his own country, walking over the public works with them, and showing them Larcenous Lake, Swindling Swamp, Crafty Canal, and Rogues' Railway, and other dishonest works. "This swamp we gained (says the patriotic borrower) by the repudiated loan of 1828. Our canal robbery was in 1830; we pocketed your good people's money for the railroad only last year."

Would Americans ever be trusted again? "And now, drab-coloured men of Pennsylvania," Smith concluded, "there is yet a moment left; the eyes of all Europe are anchored upon you,—start up from that trance of dishonesty in which you are plunged; don't think of the flesh which walls about your life, but of that sin which has hurled you from the heaven of character, which hangs over you like a devouring pestilence, and makes good men sad, and ruffians dance and sing."[118]

American lawmakers discussed their fear that foreign powers would send gunboats to invade Mississippi to recover the unpaid debts of American states. In February 1843, Representative John Quincy Adams shocked southern and western representatives by proposing that if Great Britain *should* declare war and send gunboats to Mississippi, the federal government should refrain from interfering and, if war was declared, a repudiating state would "cease thereby to be a State of this Union, and will have no right to aid in her defense from the United States."[119] While some states began to pay interest after a few years, the Mississippi and Florida repudiations remained a sore issue in Europe for more than fifty years. After repudiation, the whale was completely destroyed. Biddle was humbled. Jackson would die two years later. Soft-money Democrats agreed that Jackson's war had destroyed the bank, but had nearly destroyed the party and the nation as well.

Some critics found Melville's novel—when it came out in 1851—to be complex and frankly unbelievable. In one printed version of the book the entire crew dies. But how could Ishmael have narrated the book if the whale dragged the entire crew down? Melville might have noted that in any novel all the characters expire on the last page. Only the reader remains, the witness to the folly and destruction.

CHAPTER SEVEN

Of Swamps and Calculus

YOUNG ELIZUR WRIGHT JR. learned much of what he knew about calculus and religion from his father, a devoutly religious Congregationalist deacon who had taught mathematics at Yale College. Father had instructed son in logarithmic tables and taught him to recite the 107 questions and answers in the Westminster Shorter Catechism. The family was certain that natural logarithms and biblical passages provided all one needed to survive the harsh New England winters. In 1809, Elizur's father, a bearded patriarch with eight children and a young second wife, could see in his own family a logarithmic growth curve that demanded westward settlement. Three hundred measly acres near the Berkshire Mountains would not do, but if the family traded expensive Connecticut land for cheap land in northeastern Ohio, the Wrights could increase their acreage sevenfold. It seemed a biblical prophecy of loaves and fishes. Looking at the children around him, Elizur's father calculated an expansion that stretched scores of years into the future. "O, I remember his manly brow," Elizur junior wrote later:

> *His peaceful look, and words so few and mild*
> *And how he showed me, then a prattling child,*
> *His tables vast of logarithms, and how*
> *He called them Napier's army, rank and file,*
> *To conquer worlds with in the noblest style.*[1]

Ohio was the land, his own family the army. They would cross the Appalachian Mountains and together conquer the wilderness in 1810. Elizur senior arranged to have a cabin built beforehand, easing their arrival. But Elizur remembered that on the day they arrived to see the desolate cabin, his young mother sat down near a tree stump and wept inconsolably. Sometimes even the most gifted thinker could overreach, overcalculate, overspeculate.

Young Elizur learned the cost of his father's miscalculations when he traveled back to Yale College for an education in the fall of 1822. By then the depression that followed the panic of 1819 had reduced the value of the family's homestead considerably. The young scholar carried a bond that pledged one hundred acres of his inheritance as a guarantee that the father would pay for his education at some future date. Dressed in homespun cloth that was dyed with the brown husk of Ohio butternut trees, Elizur looked like an impoverished bumpkin, but his father's teachings would be his staff and shield. He graduated first in his class in calculus, having also convinced his friends to abandon coffee for cold water.

But the challenges at Yale were great. When young Elizur discovered that the Phi Beta Kappa Society was a liquor-soaked bacchanal, he sought to rid the meetings of alcohol. When he disputed a Yale fee supporting athletics, he ran up against Edward Laurens, the conceited son of a wealthy South Carolina planter. Laurens made some remark about Elizur's poverty and homespun clothing. The two exchanged harsh words, then Elizur astonished everyone present by shoving Laurens bodily out of his room. This restless rage at the pretensions of class would define the rest of Elizur Wright's long life. The depression that followed the 1837 panic would almost destroy the young man as he suffered through all the troubles of Job. Only his fierce attachment to logarithms would save him. It would also suggest the solutions to the panic of 1857.

IN 1829, after teaching briefly at Groton Academy, Wright junior returned to Ohio to become professor of mathematics and moral philosophy at Western Reserve College in Hudson, thirty miles south of Cleveland. The family's land farther south stood between two transportation networks. In the south of the state, the river town of Cincinnati greeted steamboats that took wheat and pork barrels south on the Ohio River to southern ports on the Mississippi. This Ohio River town was more properly a southern town, with fiddlers, gamblers, duelers, and whiskey. Slaves worked at the edge of the water, unloading boats, plumbing the depths of the Ohio, calling out the rocks and shoals. Southern Ohio newspapers listed prices current in New Orleans.

Northern Ohio towns, mostly in the Western Reserve that Connecticut had held back from the federal government, snuggled just south of Lake Erie. Cleveland was their most important market town.

Yankee steamboat captains there were less inclined to gamble on cockfights (a grievous sin) and more inclined to gamble by packing and reshipping cheap Ohio wheat for resale in New York (a service to God and commerce).

Middle Ohio was a crossroads between a northern and a southern transportation network. One day, according to those in northern Ohio, cheap Ohio wheat would travel from Lake Erie to Lake Ontario across the Erie Canal and out to Europe, where prices for wheat were high. But the planning for that route had barely begun. The Wright family estate, and the Western Reserve Academy, were too far from Cleveland to profitably sell wheat, and Cleveland was too far from international markets. As young Elizur tried to lure his fiancée to Ohio in 1829, he dismissed the reports of Ohio's roughness: "Never mind the Ohio stories, my love. If Ohio is not yet made, why we will do what we can to make it. . . . Self-denial, economy, prudence, diligence, industry must be our weapons."[2] Over the next twenty years an Ohio bank called the "Ohio Life Insurance & Trust Company" would begin to fund a northern route to Europe, one centered on northern railroads, collateralized debt, and new understandings of risk. Wright was a witness to its difficult beginning.

AN OHIO AWAKENING

MIDDLE OHIO WAS also at the crossroads between slavery and freedom, and the Wright family had been antislavery for as long as Elizur remembered. At Western Reserve College, Elizur's future prospects as a teacher came into conflict with his principles. As a young teacher, he had believed in colonization, the resettlement of free blacks in Africa, as the solution to the ills of slavery. But after 1830, as southwestern Democrats pressed for the removal of the Five Civilized Tribes from the lower South, Wright grew angry. Such removal would kill tens of thousands of Indians, he now saw, and resettlement in the scrublands of Oklahoma and Nebraska Territory would make daily life a constant struggle: all this suffering to free lands for the expansion of plantation slavery?

The removal of free blacks to Africa, he came to see, relied on the same paper-thin arguments—that the races could never settle together, that the darker races were incompatible with civilization.[3] It violated every principle he drew from the Bible, especially the gospels of Paul. But colonization also violated what Elizur Wright called the laws of mathematics. Arguing for the removal of a few hundred black men and women a year, he wrote, was "at war with the combined principles of Arithmetic and human nature." The natural growth curve, as Wright well knew, made siphoning off individuals expensive and ridiculous. Even if the colonization societies could resettle ten thousand free blacks a year, they would scarcely keep up with the natural population increase of slaves already in the South. Putting "these people on their own land and with their own property *in America* would be both more expedient and much less costly."[4]

To the horror of his parents, Elizur's moral awakening about slavery made him skeptical of his own Christian religion. In Connecticut, Massachusetts, and Ohio, Elizur had listened to sermons that opposed sin but endorsed southern slavery. They appalled him. When he taught the Gospels at Western Reserve College, he also lectured to his students about the sins of slavery. Locals in Ohio condemned him for the antislavery principles that he laid out—as "E.W."—in the local newspapers. "If 'E.W.' will set us the example," wrote a correspondent to the newspaper, "by making a negro his intimate companion and friend, and will unequivocally aver his willingness to have a sister or daughter marry one . . . it may be received as a sufficient test of his sincerity."[5] Elizur proved his sincerity by marching through graduation in his faculty robes, arm in arm with a black man. Western Reserve College promptly fired him.

Losing his professorship was not Wright's first setback, nor would it be his last. In 1831, an abolitionist and dry-goods merchant by the name of Arthur Tappan rescued him, hiring him to edit the *Emancipator,* a journal devoted to immediate abolition. In connection with these duties he became corresponding secretary of the American Antislavery Society. Elizur's intelligence was well-known, his pen pointed, and his temper legendary. A magazine described him years later as "endowed with an intolerant pride of opinion, and with a quill like the spur of a 'game chicken,' he is a born wrangler, never so happy as when in a quarrel."[6]

The panic of 1837 was the next setback for Wright: the Tappans who had supported him lost everything. He moved to Boston with his family, then in 1840 helped form the Liberty Party, a political organization devoted to the abolition of slavery. To make ends meet, Wright published an English translation of the fables of La Fontaine, selling copies door to door by subscription. In 1844 he made the bold decision to board a steamer for Great Britain. Carrying his fables and another book written by his neighbor, he hoped to procure enough subscriptions to pay for his trip and to support his family.[7]

A FINANCIAL AWAKENING

WHILE IN BRITAIN in 1844 or 1845, as a favor to a friend in a Massachusetts insurance company, Wright paid a visit to the mathematician Joshua Milne to procure mathematical information. The Massachusetts firm needed proper death tables, and Elizur Wright seemed just the person to discuss the difficult mathematics with the world's foremost expert. His talks with Milne changed everything. Actuarial accounting was complex, accessible only to those with a solid grasp of probability, statistics, and calculus. In Britain, actuaries were a kind of intellectual nobility. "Monthly they enlighten the public," he recalled later, "and particularly the Board of Life-Insurance Directors, with nice discussions, clothed in algebraic symbols, mathematically converting the hair of the subject into fur, and cultivating the reverent estimation in which their important services are held." Wright was most impressed by the fierce disputations over mathematical principle: "They keep up a running dispute, and split into several belligerent sects, on the simple matter of the proper way to ascertain and exhibit the balance between the resources and liabilities of a life-insurance company." Fierce disputes and calculus? Elizur Wright had found his home.[8]

Life insurance would be the basis of Wright's mathematical awakening. Over the next thirty years he would form the mathematical tools that would reshape how Americans understand risk and capital investment. His most important contribution to American finance came when he sought to calculate the value of an insurance policy that had lapsed. If a man contributed $3 a year to a policy, what was he due at the end of twenty years? Wright had to calculate the value of each year's payment, adding the compound interest that accrued between the payment and the lapse. Twenty years of payments of $3 meant $3 plus twenty years of interest, $3 plus nineteen years of interest, and so on. The final number was the "present value." He then subtracted a yearly sum to manage the fund, creating "net present value." According to British mathematicians of this era, while it was possible to calculate the net present value of a stream of payments, the computation would take a lifetime. Wright saw a curve. Using a mechanical calculator of his own invention, and the mathematical labor of his sons and daughters, he began to create present-value tables. Wright also began to build

American mortality tables using census, birth, and death tables in Massachusetts.

Wright's calculation of the present value of a stream of revenue would turn out to have uses far beyond the problem of men who canceled their insurance policies. It could also be used to analyze the performance of vast railroad enterprises that straddled states. That day was not long in coming. To Wright, who believed in free trade, the Britain he visited in 1844 was on the threshold of becoming the center of international trade; high food prices held it back. Many British industrialists agreed with Wright that the British economy was stifled by the high English tariff on wheat. Wright also knew that England's high tariff held Ohio back, for it made it difficult for cheap Ohio wheat to sail to Great Britain.

But an international trading presence built on wheat was possible. Great Britain was wealthy, its population was exploding, and famine stalked its colonial possessions.[9] There was simply not enough land in Europe to feed everyone. In 1845, as Wright was meeting with English authors, book lovers, mathematicians, and actuaries, a potato blight spread rapidly across Ireland. In part because British tariffs on imported wheat hobbled the relief effort, the delay brought hunger and a humanitarian crisis to Ireland.

The Irish famine irrevocably changed the relationship between Britain and the northern United States and helped lead to the birth of large-scale corporations. For more than twenty years working-class Chartists and manufacturers had complained unsuccessfully about Britain's ban on wheat imports, but it was the Irish famine that changed minds. Beginning in 1846, Parliament gradually abolished all tariffs on wheat entering the ports of the United Kingdom. The so-called repeal of the Corn Laws split the English government, nearly destroying Sir Robert Peel's Tory Party, but in 1849 the barriers tumbled down. In that year Greek ships filled with Polish Odessa wheat arrived in Dublin and Cork to end the famine: wheat had traveled across four seas, two narrow straits, and three thousand miles of water to find its market and feed hungry Ireland.

American farmers, wheat merchants, and railroad directors watched this scene with fanatical intensity. They knew that the saltwater journey from New York to the British Isles was only slightly farther than the route from Odessa, with no cumbersome straits to navigate. To sell American wheat direct to Liverpool! It became a dream that fired the imagination of John Murray Forbes and the railroad capitalists of

Boston, New York, Philadelphia, and Baltimore. The Erie Canal could not possibly carry all the wheat needed. Following the repeal of the English Corn Laws, railroad capitalists like John Murray Forbes and Erastus Corning (New York Central), Edgar Thomson (Pennsylvania Railroad), and Johns Hopkins (Baltimore & Ohio) lobbied their state legislatures to allow trunk lines—companies composed of multiple private railroads—to join the roads together to connect the Great Lakes with the Atlantic. With a large enough railroad corridor for shipping wheat, they reasoned, Britons would be buttering English bread that came from the American prairies. Trunk lines were planned to create an international fountain of wheat that would flow from Wright's family farm in Ohio all the way to Liverpool. The process had begun in 1849; it would take more than twenty years and a civil war to complete.[10]

As the railroad barons plotted trunk lines from Chicago to New York, Philadelphia, and Baltimore, Wright continued his bitter arguments with fellow abolitionists. His confidence in his mathematical abilities may even have sharpened his tongue. By 1852 he was ejected from the editorship of the Free-Soil newspaper the *Commonwealth*. To pay for his family's bread while he compiled his actuarial and present-value tables, he worked as the untitled editor of the *American Railway Times* starting in 1853. By then, the trunk lines were forming. What Wright the mathematician saw about the financial side of railway stock and bond marketing troubled him deeply. He learned the "technicalities" of the New York Stock Exchange, as he called them. He learned how some traders ejected from the exchange bought and sold on the street, how railroads procured lines of credit from banks, and how men with small capital could engage in puts and calls on the future value of stock. "It is a species of betting about on a par with 'roulette,'" he grumbled.[11] The role of banks in speculative investment for railroads was the most confusing part of the post-1837 economy. It would also prove the most dangerous.

The Ohio Life Insurance & Trust Company best demonstrates the perils involved in speculative railroad investment. After 1834, when President Jackson removed federal deposits from the Second Bank of the United States, New York capitalists created the institution to fill the void as a lender. While this trust company would help fund the continuing movement of American exports, it would also be the largest bank, and largest mortgage lender, west of the Appalachian Mountains.[12] Ohio Life Insurance & Trust Company was not, in fact, an insurance company at all. State charters prevented or severely restricted mortgage lending by any institution that called itself a bank.

But after the panic of 1837 insurance companies, trust companies, and loan companies quickly took over the functions of banks, particularly in states with restrictive charters such as Missouri and Ohio.[13]

Just like the agency house banks during the cotton boom of the 1830s, these "trust and loan companies" that blossomed after the repeal of the English Corn Laws provided a way to lure foreign capitalists to invest in the American land boom. Here again, Britons could invest in Americans' future earnings. No foreign investor could offer a mortgage himself. As one early booster put it, "*First,* they cannot receive title on a foreclosure; and *secondly,* they could not, at such a distance, conveniently or safely manage the investment." But the trust company could "step in between the borrower and the lender . . . as trustees for both."[14] With a trust company like Ohio Life, foreign capital could earn 6 percent on western mortgages that charged borrowers 9 percent or more. By charter, the trust companies could grant mortgages for up to half of the value of any property. While many European investors doubted the validity of state bonds after the repudiations of 1842 and 1843, the trust and loan companies had held up. The Ohio Life Insurance & Trust Company proved the most visible and successful of these enterprises in Britain, a bank that provided financial services to the newly emerging trunk lines.[15]

COLLATERALIZED DEBT OBLIGATIONS

WHILE THE REPEAL of the English Corn Laws in 1849 made the export of American wheat to Britain possible, the trunk lines and Ohio Life created the financial infrastructure to make it possible, especially in allowing English investors to participate in the midwestern land boom. The U.S. Congress provided the final key. It began offering free land to railroads in 1850. The first railroad chartered was the Illinois Central, a road that would run from the northern to the southern tip of Illinois. Congress provided the land in a checkerboard pattern, with alternate plots available free to the railroad and for sale to the public. For railroads the millions of acres of western land near their tracks provided collateral but not capital. How could they turn these pledged assets into ready money?

The railroad bond proved a way of collateralizing debt obligations. With vast quantities of land deeds, railroads could issue mortgages to would-be landowners in the wheat belt at 7.5 percent. Five hundred thousand acres of land valued by the railroads at roughly $7 an acre and mortgaged to buyers could be pooled together into a bond issue of roughly $3.5 million. Offering 6 percent interest or more, the bonds looked attractive to European lenders.[16] The companies did not bother to mention that the revenue from the bonds came as settlers paid off their five-year mortgages. Europeans lent by buying railroad bonds; Americans borrowed by assuming a five-year mortgage from the railroad. In connecting European lenders with American borrowers, the railroad looked exactly like a twenty-first-century savings and loan bank, one that offers mortgages to local homeowners and then quickly resells them.

The bonds were guaranteed—"collateralized" in modern terms—by the land given to the railroads by the government. Because a steady stream of revenue came from the mortgage payments American farmers paid, the revenue would pay off the bondholders. There were a few problems: The presumed increase in value from the government's standard price of $2.50 an acre to the railroad's valuation of $7.00 an acre depended on the railroad's being completed, and it was difficult to calculate how much the land value would increase once it was. In addition, the mortgages were for five years but could be automatically extended if one paid the yearly interest, much like a credit card.[17] Just like the life insurance tables of Elizur Wright, the calculations were impossible by contemporary mathematics. The land was priced as a guess; the yearly payments also. The Illinois Central, the first land grant railroad created, explained the matter in this way to English investors:

> It is estimated that when the railway shall be completed the lands will be saleable at prices considerably exceeding the seven dollars per acre required to reimburse the whole issue of bonds. Indeed, it is well known that land in the United States, through which railways have been constructed, has increased in value from five to ten times more than it was previously worth.[18]

Not all railroad companies could sell bonds directly to English investors like the Illinois Central could. Trust companies like the Ohio Life Insurance & Trust came in to extend credit as an intermediary; they could sell bonds to English investors and then use their capital to make loans to railroads. Ohio Life & Trust took railroad bonds unmarketable in Europe as collateral for loans. It lent railroads up to half of the market value for bonds given to them. This was known as a call-loan market, modeled after British practice. Once trusts like Ohio Life began offering high-interest loans to railroads, many New York banks followed their lead. New York was the center of the action because New York City banks had the loosest charters in the country. New York's Free Banking Act of 1838 (created to resolve the 1837 panic) had assured that.

After 1850, every railroad that needed ready capital kept a New York City office in order to borrow from Ohio Life or any of the other New York banks that specialized in on-call loans for bonds. A railroad turned over its bonds for cash—usually post notes or checks—which it could spend in New York. If the trust company needed liquid funds, it could "call" on the railroad to pay off the loan. If the trust company got no immediate response from the railroad, it would sell the bonds on the New York bond market.[19] All of this worked when bond prices were high. After 1851, over a dozen New York banks competed in the on-call market. They borrowed on the New York and European markets, then re-lent those funds to the high-flying railroads.[20]

And so began the 1850s model of collateralized debt obligations, railroad bonds whose underlying value rested on mortgaged land. The asset was no longer future cotton, which had caused the 1837 panic, but railroad land in the northern Midwest, which seemed safer. The ultimate value of the land rested on the prospect of selling wheat to the East Coast and England. American and British trust companies sought out the railroads and their bonds because, in the words of one financial journalist, "railroad companies are willing to pay high rates for money, and they are therefore considered very profitable customers."[21] What could go wrong?

The railroad bond based on deeded federal land became a vast money machine. Railroad barons like John Murray Forbes, hungry for land grants and the capital that land grant bonds provided, ruthlessly took over any railroad that had a land grant. In the 1850s, Forbes had to acquire these land grant railroads secretly; it still violated state charters for one railroad to own or be owned by other railroads. His acquisition of a railroad in Missouri would ultimately lead to bloodshed on the plains of Kansas.

THE SOUTHERN HANNIBAL

AFTER THE 1837 CRASH, many northern states had competitive elections with Democrats and Whigs blaming each other for the depression. Control passed back and forth between politicians who called themselves Anti-Masons, Know-Nothings, Whigs, or Democrats. As a result, the northern states had many more freshmen congressmen with short terms, while southern states had more stable political coalitions.

Since 1787 the three-fifths compromise had given extra votes to slaveholding states, often overpowering potential opposition from hill-country farmers. Silk-hat planters who had loathed Jackson's bank war still clung to the Whig Party. But growing antislavery sentiment in the North gradually drove many of them into coalitions with the Democrats. Planters were enjoined to vote Whig in state elections and for a pro-slavery northern Democrat for president. A string of "dough-faced" northern presidents emerged in the late 1840s and the 1850s (the reference was to the dough faces that actors wore). According to their detractors, the doughfaces looked like free northern men but quoted the lines given them by their pro-slavery southern backers. So despite northerners' growing numbers in the House, southerners' unity in both houses of Congress combined with their control of the presidents to solidify the South's power from the 1840s to the 1850s. Southern representatives quashed antislavery petitions, dreamed of a southern empire, and startled at night with nightmares of slave revolts.[22]

In 1850 a committee of southern congressmen created the "Address to the People of the Southern States" to drive out the southern moderates. It asked state governments to instruct their congressmen to "act in conformity" with extreme pro-slavery principles. If congressmen did not obey these resolutions in every vote, they would be forced to resign or face recall. In less than a year, southern moderates disappeared from Congress.[23] The Deep South needed no such reinforcement, as these states sent the same congressmen year after year to Congress, where seniority gave them influence in congressional committees, including the powerful Committee on Public Lands.

Mission control for the southern congressional power was the F Street Mess, a boardinghouse in Washington with four southern senators, led by the young, handsome, and headstrong David Rice Atchison of Missouri. Because of the F Street Mess's control, when land grants to railroads began in 1850, most went either through southern states or toward them. The "Illinois Central," for example, started in Illinois but only connected northern to southern Illinois. The F Street Mess assured that any land grant for a "Yankee" railroad pointing west—toward the newly discovered goldfields in California—would be lost in committee.[24]

But Atchison's land lay in western Missouri; from his plantation in northwest Missouri he could look across the Missouri River onto the vast and fertile Platte River valley in the West. An apparent mountain gap near what is now Denver, Colorado, seemed the most logical point for a railroad to the West. In 1850, Atchison sponsored the land grant that would provide 600,000 acres for a railroad to stretch across northern Missouri, joining the town of Hannibal on the Mississippi River to the land of his neighbors, the hemp-growing slaveholders of northwest Missouri. It would be called the Hannibal & St. Joseph Railroad.[25] A young, short Illinois senator named Stephen Douglas helped Atchison get the railroad approved. The so-called Little Giant crossed from the Senate chamber into the House to persuade northern Democrats to favor the line, and the Hannibal & St. Joseph received its acres in June 1852.[26]

Missourians like Atchison imagined that slaveholding travelers in the Mississippi River city of Hannibal could, like the ancient conqueror, cross the mountains and sweep into the center of the world. It was not Rome that the residents of Hannibal sought but the vast goldfields of California, just discovered in 1849. The path to the West was an old dream in Missouri. The lawyer and dry-goods merchant John Marshall Clemens had first proposed the railroad line years earlier. Samuel Langhorne Clemens was only eleven when his father died in March 1847, but the son followed the fortunes of his father's pet project with considerable interest through the 1850s. The younger Clemens visited Washington in 1852 when the Hannibal & St. Joseph Railroad bill went through Congress. Twenty years later Sam Clemens described how the railroad had gotten its grant:

> A Congressional appropriation costs money. Just reflect, for instance. A majority of the House committee, say $10,000 apiece—$40,000; a majority of the Senate committee, the same each—say $40,000; a little extra to one or two chairmen of one or two such committees, say $10,000 each—$20,000; and there's $100,000 of the money gone, to begin with. Then, seven male lobbyists at $3,000 each—$21,000; one female lobbyist, $10,000; a high moral Congressman or Senator here and there—the high moral ones cost money, because they give tone to a measure—say ten of these at $3,000 each, is $30,000.

All told, Clemens estimated, the bribes necessary to get backing for a new railroad totaled $118,000. The young and idealistic Clemens had by then become the writer Mark Twain. He coined the term "the Gilded Age" to describe the corruption engendered by hunger for western riches. The Gilded Age began—for Twain at least—with the corruption of his father's dream in 1852.

Atchison imagined a convenient slaveholders' route from the South up the Mississippi and across the mountains to the goldfields of California. After he got the bill passed, however, continuing the line west from St. Joseph presented a problem: The town of St. Joseph, on the eastern side of the Missouri River, was near the 40th parallel. While the Missouri Compromise made slavery legal on Atchison's side of the river, the same compromise ended slavery on the other side of the river, ending it hundreds of miles south at the dividing line 36°30'. In an indignant 1849 speech to his Missouri constituents Atchison had thundered, "Congress can no more constitutionally prohibit the slaveholder from Missouri from settling in the Territories of the United States with his slaves, than the Rhode Islander with his machinery, or the Methodist, Presbyterian, Turk, or Mormon with his religion."[27]

Just west and south of St. Joseph stood the Wyandot tribe, which had purchased the land from the Delaware Indians. In 1852, the Wyandots sent their representative Abelard Guthrie to work out an agreement with Congress about selling some part of their land on the Kansas River to American settlers. But before Guthrie even got out of Missouri, he met Atchison on a riverboat, and the senator calmly and pleasantly informed him that he would see the Wyandots' land "sunk into hell before he would vote for it" to be sold to Yankees "as a freesoil Territory."[28] According to Atchison, the Missouri Compromise blocking slavery's expansion west of Missouri stood in the way of any settlement. Atchison, wrote Guthrie, "asks the repeal of that act before anything shall be done for Nebraska."[29]

The man to give Atchison what he wanted, to open a slave owners' corridor to the Pacific, was his colleague Stephen Douglas. Douglas had sponsored the organization of the territory but had been stopped by southern votes. After talking over the matter with Atchison and the Kentucky senator Archibald Dixon, Douglas promised to explicitly repeal the clause in the Missouri Compromise that barred slavery above 36°30', though he predicted it would "raise a hell of storm." The storm began in January 1854. Douglas's bill split the territory in two: Kansas and Nebraska. Kansas's northern border at 40 degrees latitude assured that if Kansas became a slave-owning territory, the Hannibal & St. Joseph Railroad could provide a slaveholders' route to California. Both Kansas and Nebraska territories would obey the principle that Atchison had articulated in a speech to constituents the previous summer: "The people who may settle there, and who have the most interest in this question, shall decide it for themselves."[30] Kansas, as Atchison saw it, would be for slaveholders. Yankees could safely keep Nebraska. From January to May, Congress argued over this principle of popular sovereignty, slavery, and Congress's power over both of them.

HANNIBAL COMPROMISED

ATCHISON, for all of his understanding of whom to bribe when it came to congressional politics, never saw the Boston capitalists coming. The land grants to the Hannibal & St. Joseph were too enticing for them to pass up. In March 1854, as Congress was debating the territorial status of Kansas, John Murray Forbes and Nathaniel Thayer took over the Hannibal & St. Joseph to use its land as collateral. Then, to the horror of Missouri stockholders, they made it a zombie.[31] The Boston group worked through a railroad surveyor, a Mr. Duff, who had surveyed the route but had not been paid in years. In a shocking takeover, Forbes used the surveyor's claim to put a lien on the railroad, used the lien to buy a majority stake in the company at a deep discount, quickly voted to change the directors, then created a "fiscal agency" of the company that would meet in New York to settle Duff's claim. The New York fiscal agency became the *actual* board of directors that then demanded payments from all the Missouri stockholders who had stock but had only paid the 10 percent down payment. If the remaining payments were not made immediately, then the agency threatened to have stockholders arrested for breach of contract. In this way it effectively voided most of the stock held in Missouri.[32] Forbes envisioned an interstate railroad system that would head west from Chicago with two branches: one directly west into Iowa and Nebraska, another that stretched south into northern Missouri, then through Hamilton and St. Joseph and into the territory that was likely to be named Kansas.

While the question of slavery in western territories meant everything for an abolitionist like Elizur Wright, slavery did not appear to be a concern for Forbes and Thayer at first. The Boston financiers had two goals. On behalf of the company, they wanted the Missouri land to convert into bonded debt for sale in New York and London markets; this English lending would get the railroad built. Privately, they wanted a railroad trunk line that would export wheat to the Liverpool Corn Exchange ("corn" being the English word for what Americans called wheat). Indeed, Forbes and Thayer secretly stored wheat under assumed names to hold for when wheat prices rose in Britain, a fact they did not reveal to stockholders or bondholders.[33]

Forbes and Thayer did not fear Atchison; they feared other railroads. The competing trunk lines from New York to Chicago occupied their attention. To entice immigrants to use their Missouri railroad to settle farther west, plant wheat, and ship it back over their Chicago route, Nathaniel's distant cousin Eli Thayer created the Massachusetts Emigrant Aid Society. Chartered April 26, 1854, the aid society appeared to be an organization to help lure European settlers to move into western lands. Its charter promised to protect emigrants from enticement from competing railroad and steamboat companies. The society would be an all-purpose settlement agency, designed to direct emigrants to Missouri, Kansas, and Nebraska land owned by the railroad; it said nothing about slavery. It was formed, wrote the agency's secretary, "to impart information to Emigrants arriving in this country, and to protect them from fraud; also to direct attention at the present time, and to afford facilities to persons emigrating to Kansas and Nebraska." The agency's facilities had everything to do with travel and land acquisition, as it was created "to procure for them cheap fare and good accommodations on the route; to secure for their benefit, by purchase or otherwise, advantageous locations as landing-places, a general rendezvous for outfitting purposes &c.; to erect Receiving Houses for the temporary convenience of settlers' families; to establish Furnishing Stores, at which, on reasonably low terms, the necessaries and comforts of life may be purchased."[34] This joint-stock company would be an adjunct to the trunk railroad, driving people west, sending goods west, selling people provisions for farming, and bringing their wheat back east. A wheat railroad funded by Yankees and filled with immigrants was not the kind of railroad that Atchison envisioned at all.

By May 1854, as confidential agents of the railroad began measuring out Missouri land for the bonds, Missourians who had hopes for a railroad to California suspected something was up, in part because the Hannibal & St. Joseph's new board had issued no communication in Missouri. The *Missouri Courier* asked its readers if anyone had heard from "the Boston Convention of capitalists" who had become interested in their railroad. "We feel satisfied," it continued, "had anything transpired *favorable* to our road, that the public would long since have been enlightened."[35] By June 9, the U.S. Land Office had given the Hannibal & St. Joseph its preliminary list of lands.[36] With this land quickly collateralized into railroad bonds, the line was now prepared to market the bonds in New York, Boston, and Europe.[37]

Atchison, who imagined that the lands west of Missouri would be open to slave-owning Missourians, was floored. Twain's father, John (now dead), would also have been appalled. The Hannibal & St. Joseph, a railroad Atchison had sponsored in Congress, was now in the hands of others. He saw the railroad's adjunct, the Emigrant Aid Society, as a direct threat both economically and politically. By June 19, 1854, he had helped form a "Squatter Association" three miles west of Fort Leavenworth, which claimed that Missourians, including slavehold- ers, had already occupied Kansas as squatters who would later pay for land when the Land Office organized it. The association wrote a con- stitution declaring that slavery already existed in the territory. It was a clever if dangerous countermove to the Boston capitalists. The St. Louis *Republican* justified it, comparing it to the perfidious actions of Thayer's Emigrant Aid Society: "They have as much right to go upon Kansas Territory with their slaves and other property as any fanatical son of New England, and this right they will assert at all hazards."[38] Who would have preference for the land? Missourians or foreigners shipped overland by a Yankee trunk line? Missourians crossed the border into Kansas territory to ensure that these lands would belong to them. The Republican newspaper editor Horace Greeley of the *New-York Tribune* responded tartly: "The disciples of Atchison are to cross right over into that Territory with their slaves, and hold them in bondage there by vir- tue of their Bowie Knives and revolvers. This is as we have expected."[39]

Missourians had the advantage at first; in less than an hour they could cross the Missouri River to vote in territorial elections. They formed the "city" of Atchison south and west of St. Joseph in Septem- ber 1854.[40] By then, even non-slaveholding Missourians resented the interference of the New Englanders, the loss of thousands of acres of Missouri's federal land to Boston capitalists, the loss of the state's investment in the road, and the loss of their railroad to private own- ers. "Only think of it, people of Missouri," railed the *Missouri Courier* in September 1854, *"that eight hundred thousand acres of your richest lands, one million and a-half of your State credit, and about two millions* of pri- vate subscriptions have been locked up" in a railroad that was not even finished. Blame "the trickery of some bluebellied Yankees. . . . [G]ener- ous and magnificent donations of public lands to the road, are tempt- ing baits for Yankee cunning and intrigue."[41] Only one counterattack seemed possible. White Missourians with no direct interest in the Kansas lands could squat, elect territorial representatives, and return home the next evening. They did so in November 1854 and again for the constitutional convention and territorial assembly elections.[42] In

November the *Missouri Courier* told its readers they had been "sold to Boston." Fears were widespread that "we've been *euchered* by eastern capitalists."[43]

For Forbes and the Thayers much more was at stake than slavery in Kansas, which they cared almost nothing about. Forbes and Thayer's investment of over $1 million in the Hannibal & St. Joseph was in danger. To protect it, Eli Thayer converted the aid society into an antislavery scheme, realizing that antislavery New Englanders with no stake in their railroad might invest in the aid society as a way of fighting slavery. Forbes and the Thayers appropriated the term "free soil" for themselves, seeing in the term that Elizur Wright and his friends had coined in the 1840s a clever marketing tool for their western railroad ambitions. What the railroad and the aid society provided on their expensive railroad corridor—with sequestered town lots, Emigrant Aid Society-owned hotels, gristmills, and company-owned grain elevators—was "free soil," albeit free soil that people paid for, in five-year mortgages. By 1855 abolitionists who had formed the Free-Soil Party were willing to accept the financial, political, and even military help of Boston capitalists. Within a year the aid society began sending rifles to Kansas. Antislavery radicals like Elizur Wright and John Brown found some extremely unlikely bedfellows in the New England capitalists whose only interest lay in building a trunk line through Missouri and Kansas.

By 1855 the conflict between Boston capitalists and their former allies in Missouri had become a guerrilla war. Missourians squatted on land and claimed to represent the territory. Southern planters funded small armies and brought partisans from as far away as South Carolina to protect the settlers, as well as to harass foreigners who arrived to settle in Lawrence. New England and European settlers called them bushwhackers. Northern aid companies also funded small armies that would violently raid southern settlements in retaliation for bushwhacker raids. In one such raid John Brown and his sons hacked apart Missouri settlers with their swords. Southerners called these northern guerrilla armies jayhawkers, referring to a mythical hawk that worried its prey by pecking, rending, and gouging it.[44]

For David Atchison, all the vote buying that had been done to get the Hannibal & St. Joseph passed through Congress threatened to become a millstone that would drag him under. In January 1855, when the Missouri legislature met in St. Louis to choose its senator, Atchison made it known that he would be proud to be reelected. Then the Democrat Benjamin Gratz Brown of the *Missouri Democrat* rose up in the Missouri

The author's father, John R. Nelson, dressed in the outfit he wore when doing repossessions for Woolco in Orange County, Florida, 1974.

This painting of Colonel William Duer comes from a locket that was owned by Duer's descendants. It shows him at the height of his power, shortly before his defaults led to the 1792 panic.

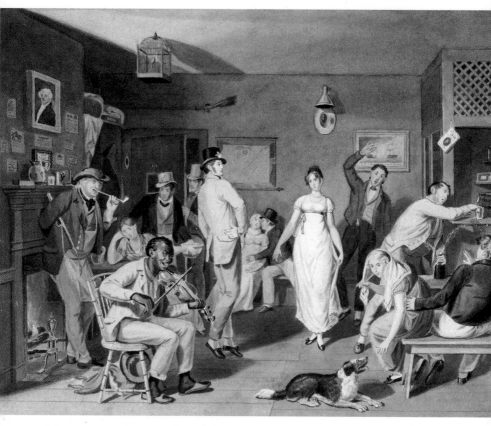

John Lewis Krimmel's painting *Barroom Dancing* (c. 1820) depicts life before the panic. Under George Washington's portrait, a gentleman with riding crop and mechanic's apron represents the passing revolutionary generation. The rifle over the door shows the revolution's conclusion. A black man fiddles enthusiastically for a boisterous generation. A wall map shows settlement into new territories; ships at war depict the just-ended War of 1812. The dancing man in the waistcoat is surrounded by four friends wearing imported blue monkey jackets. They sport silk hats, spit curls, sideburns, cravats, and dancing slippers while the women wear fashionable Regency dresses. The Farmer's Almanac of 1820 tells us that the year is 1819. A barkeep uncorks champagne and reaches for a glass as bubbles splash. By 1820, a nation's long hangover will begin.

US CURS in full YELL, or a WAR-WHOOP to saddle on the PEOPLE, a PAPPOOSE PRESIDENT.

This 1824 pro-Jackson print illustrates the fracturing of the Democratic Party after the 1819 panic. Each dog that bares its fangs wears a collar with the name of a newspaper. The big pack on the left constitutes the supporters of John Quincy Adams, while on the right are the equally treacherous supporters of Henry Clay. In the background, nearly out of the picture, is the crippled William H. Crawford sitting in a papoose outside his office in the Treasury Department, which is providing his pap, or baby food. Jackson represents the fourth faction. He stands on his own two feet. His sword is inscribed "Veni, vidi, vici," or "I came, I saw, I conquered," recalling his victory at the Battle of New Orleans.

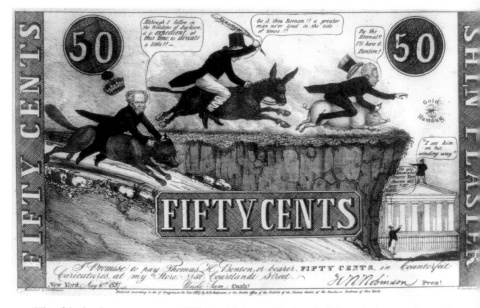

This fake banknote represents Whig criticisms of Jackson's folly in helping to bring about the panic of 1837. Together Jackson, riding a pig, and Thomas Hart Benton, riding a donkey, head over a cliff chasing after the "gold humbug," which represents Jackson's attempt to replace the seemingly stable banknotes of the Second Bank of the United States with gold coins. Nicholas Biddle stands atop the bank watching the coming calamity. Soft-money Democrat Martin Van Buren finds it "expedient, at this time, to deviate a little."

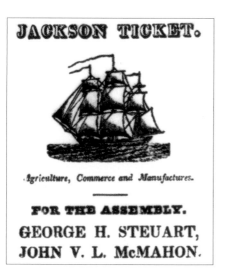

This 1828 ticket brought Jackson to the White House, promising prosperity not just in agriculture and manufacturing but also in commerce. Trade agreements with Britain led to a boom in American cotton exports; American and British banks' attempts to capitalize on this volatile and lucrative trade laid the groundwork for the panic of 1837.

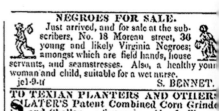

The agency house banks of the 1830s provid[ed] easy loans to southern planters, who bou[ght] slaves in large numbers. Credit came from co[un]try banks in the north of England. This e[asy] credit caused a boom in slave prices betwe[en] 1830 and 1837. While the bank loans mostly res[ted] on future cotton sales, the underlying assets m[ost] planters owned were slaves purchased with c[ot]ton credit. This advertisement appeared in [the] New Orleans *Picayune* on June 7, 1837.

"SOBER SECOND THOUGHTS"

Depicted in this Whig cartoon are unemployed sailors, carpenters, masons, and other laborers who are now having second thoughts about their support of Democrats Andrew Jackson and Martin Van Buren. The Whig Party grew quickly after 1837.

Bankers, bill brokers, women, and children gather around the Seamen's Savings Bank, one of the firms that crashed in the 1857 panic. A garbage collector picks up once-valuable railway bonds that now litter the street.

FRANCISCUS-JOSEPHUS I.

PAX — LABOR — PROGRESSUS.

WILLKOMMEN ALLEN VÖLKERN.

This printed welcome to all people to the Vienna Exposition of 1873 portrays the dreams of the Austro-Hungarian Empire in its bid to become a great European power, the rival of the French, Prussian, and Russian empires. The muses of theater, the graphic arts, and literature surround Franz Joseph in his trademark beard shaved at cheekbones and chin. In the background a modern railway engine and cars pass over a steamboat on the Danube.

THE GREAT FINANCIAL PANIC.—CLOSING THE DOORS OF THE STOCK EXCHANGE ON ITS MEMBERS, SATURDAY, SEPT. 20th.

By midday on September 20, 1873, the New York Stock Exchange had attracted a vast crowd of dealers hoping to sell shares for cash. That afternoon it closed its doors and remained closed for ten days.

Though immigration declined in the years immediately after the panic, a growing number of central Europeans immigrated to the United States under labor contracts. The large family here seeks directions to their final destination in the Midwest. Many rode in closed compartments reserved for immigrants. One route west is advertised on the sign on the left.

IN A STRANGE LAND—ASKING THE WAY.—[DRAWN BY THOMAS WORTH.]

An international crowd hurries to the opening day of Chicago's World's Columbian Exposition on May 1, 1893. As in Vienna in 1873, the world exposition coincided with a financial crisis.

In May 1894, workers protested wage cuts at the Pullman Palace Car Company. George Pullman closed the gates to his factory rather than bargain with employees. The lockout became a strike. The American Railway Union soon joined, calling on railway workers throughout the country to stop work. The long summer of discontent in Chicago shut down interstate railroad traffic across the country.

THE RECENT PANIC—SCENE IN THE NEW YORK STOCK EXCHANGE ON THE MORNING OF FRIDAY, MAY 5th.
[DRAWN BY A ARTIST. REPRODUCTION FROM SKETCHES ON THE SPOT.—[SEE PAGE 436.]

A drastic reduction of the sugar tariff was a gambit by Henry O. Havemeyer of the Sugar Trust to destroy a West Coast competitor. The tariff reduction nearly emptied the U.S. Treasury in the years between 1891 and 1893. When gold in U.S. Treasury vaults dropped below $100 million in April 1893, doubt followed, and American interest rates rose quickly. Just days after the Columbian Exposition opened, a panic on Wall Street commenced on May 5, 1893.

In January and February 1894, Congress debated a progressive income tax to restore federal revenues after the 1893 panic. In this political cartoon Andrew Carnegie, John D. Rockefeller, and Henry O. Havemeyer point to a poor farmer, with his hungry son behind him, and declare, "He should pay the taxes." A tax on incomes of more than $4,000 (accounting for just over one percent of the American public) was soon invalidated by the Supreme Court as "class legislation." Nearly a decade later the Sixteenth Amendment finally authorized a national income tax.

Above: In 1931 a crowd of small depositors protest outside the failed Bank of the United States. In 1928 the bond market seized up as foreign borrowers (Germany especially) began to default; banks then provided high-interest call loans to speculators in the stock market. Stock valuations doubled between 1928 and 1929 and then crashed. With both kinds of toxic assets on their hands, hundreds of banks like the Bank of the United States failed between 1929 and 1933.

e page: Here, J. P. Morgan, flanked by his daughter and son, is called to testify
he Pujo Committee hearings. After a sharp split in Republican ranks in 1912 allowed
ats to seize both houses of Congress and the presidency, Congress created the Pujo
ttee to investigate American banking practices. Following the hearings, Democrats
d the formation of the Federal Reserve, a separate national institution that would
he bankers' acceptance, a document that capitalized on America's international

This photograph (c. 1933) by photographer Mark Barry shows unemployed workers in an unnamed American city. In cities like Chicago, unemployment reached 40 percent in 1931.

Chicago machine politician, political reformer, and mayor Anton J. Cermak Jr. in February 1933. After his successful mayoral campaign in 1931, Cermak brought the urban anti-Prohibition activists, called the "wets," and the municipal reformers, called the "sewer socialists," into a coalition with Democratic candidate Franklin Delano Roosevelt.

legislature to point out that the railroad Atchison had sponsored was now in the hands of Boston Free-Soilers like Nathaniel Thayer. Not only that, declared Brown, but the Hannibal & St. Joseph Railroad had spent $15,000 in "buying a land bill through Congress," and part of that bribe went directly to David Rice Atchison. President Robert Stewart of the Hannibal & St. Joseph then stood up and declared, "It's a lie and a damn lie."

Lie or not, David Atchison's future political chances in Missouri were over. Samuel Langhorne Clemens was not the only one who knew how the Hannibal & St. Joseph legislation had been secured. Despite the aspersions cast upon Atchison for taking bribes from a railroad and then surrendering it to Yankees, his supporters continued to back him for the Senate. The Missouri legislature was by then thoroughly splintered: ultra-southern Democrats like Atchison, anti-slavery Democrats like Benjamin Gratz Brown, and the mostly urban, mostly German-American Whigs who would soon become Republicans. Brown prevented Democrats from uniting under the discredited Atchison, while Atchison's friends prevented the Whigs from uniting with the moderate Democrats.[45] Because of the deadlock, Missouri had an empty seat in the Senate for two years thereafter.

Each escalation in the guerrilla war in Kansas has been told as a story of unselfish New Englanders committed to antislavery and the perfidy of Missouri slaveholders who used their non-slaveholding allies—the "Pukes"—to build an illegitimate slaveholding territory while claiming land they did not own. There is a little truth to it, but it is also a tale that was designed to help New England bankers sleep at night. New England bankers used antislavery activists to build a railroad from Kansas to the East Coast. Committed antislavery men and women like Frederick Douglass, Elizur Wright, and Lydia Maria Child found themselves quickly outspent and outmaneuvered by the Boston bankers. The so-called Boston Associates, previously investors in textile mills who supported slave-produced cotton, now arrived on the scene as liberators promising "practical" antislavery. They quickly took control of the Republican Party. Longtime abolitionists were reduced to supernumeraries; Forbes and friends had become the movement's conductors and principal protagonists.

But in the game for control over access to the West, Forbes's opponents had a final ace up their sleeves. There were problems with the title to the Missouri lands. The southern railroad land grants of 1850–1851 and the northern railroad land grants of 1856 had both been passed after an 1850 act of Congress that was poorly framed and little understood: the Swamp Act. This little act declared that states could acquire any swamplands in the public domain that Congress still owned. Counties needed only to identify the swamplands, drain them, then develop the lands themselves or resell them. Unfortunately for the railroads, the men assigned to identify the swamplands were state employees. The predictable result was that many state agents declared hundreds of thousands of acres to be swamp, land they had never seen. One federal land official pointed out that parts of the Ozark Mountains were "sworn to as a swamp" by Arkansas officials.[46] The title controversy was compounded by the fact that the railroad land grants claimed much of the same federal land as the Swamp Act. Neither the states nor the railroads had done complete surveys. Whose land was it?

Here was the opportunity for southern slaveholders' revenge. By 1857 the Free-Soil settlers had nearly won the bloody struggle over Kansas. By then they constituted the majority in the Kansas Territory and would soon vote out a pro-slavery Lecompton Constitution that Atchison had helped author. But the House Committee on Public Lands was still chaired by Williamson Cobb of Alabama. His committee drafted an addendum to the Swamp Act, the Swamp Act of 1857. He was strongly supported by Jacob Thompson of Mississippi, a former committee member, and the recently arrived secretary of the interior. This second Swamp Act declared that all lands claimed by the states would, by the end of 1857, belong to the states, even if the land claimed was not actually swampland. This would effectively invalidate all railroad claims to lands contested between the railroads and the states. The law was passed on the last day of Congress, March 5, 1857.

For the next eight months Arkansas, Illinois, and Missouri hurriedly declared even more federal land to be swampland, much of it already claimed but not yet marked out and platted by the railroads.[47] By the late spring many bondholders understood what the Swamp Act of 1857 meant. The bonds issued by the railroads rested on prime western land granted to them by the government; they depended on settlers's marking out their land and making their first mortgage payments. But after March 5, apparently, much of this land, claimed but not platted by the railroads, now no longer belonged to the railroads! Railroad stock and bond prices tumbled all spring and summer of 1857.[48] The Ohio Life Insurance & Trust Company suffered first. It had been aggressively lending on the call market to the speculative railroads in Michigan, Ohio, and Illinois.[49] Ohio Life tried to call in its loans in the summer of 1857, but railroads had no cash to pay, and their loans went to protest. By August 1857, the railroad stock and bond prices were now valued at less than the loans outstanding. Fourteen railroads suspended interest payments on $190 million worth of bonds.[50] When bond payments on seemingly solid railroads were suspended, panicked bondholders, unsure of which were threatened, rushed to unload them. When the Ohio Life Insurance & Trust Company failed, the panic of 1857 began. The other banks that had been lending on the call-loan market folded after that.

An organization created in 1853, the New York Clearing House Association, helped some of the less speculative New York banks weather the 1857 panic. Big New York banks had created the institution to emulate the London Clearing House. After October 11, 1853, every business day at ten, "settling clerks" from every member bank in New York entered the crowded room of the Clearing House at the corner of Wall Street and Broadway. With a list of the previous day's transactions with other banks, the clerks would determine by the end of day how much each bank owed the other. To avoid the movement of silver and gold, the Bank of America became the coin depository for the member banks. Member banks deposited their coin in special fireproof safes at the Bank of America. The Bank of America issued "bank certificates" in denominations of $1,000, $5,000, and $10,000 that represented the coin. This was the currency banks used to settle their debts to one another.

In 1857, just four years after the Clearing House started, its members voted that a crisis had arisen. They created a loan committee to operate for the duration of the crisis. As long as panic was declared, banks in trouble could turn in solid but temporarily low-priced loans and bonds. The loan committee valued them and converted them to "loan certificates." These loan certificates resembled the bank certificates that regularly moved between member banks in good years, and all the member banks were obliged to accept them as if they were "bank certificates" until the crisis passed. These loan certificates became a new kind of panic money that allowed New York banks to pay individual creditors in gold in 1857.[51] Those banks most involved in the call-loan market for railroad securities found that the loan committee's assessment of their loans made the difference between prosperity and ruin. A conflict over Missouri land grants put railroad's bonded debt into question and propelled the nation into a financial crisis; ad-hoc loan certificates issued by the New York Clearing House slowed the contagion. The battles over Kansas were just a sideshow to the financial fight between Missourians and Bostonians, but it was a sideshow that would soon bring Civil War.

GENERALLY ACCEPTED

ELIZUR WRIGHT WATCHED the gambling system of the New York banks and trusts with some amusement and a little fear. While he had little interest in the gambles of Ohio Life or the Hannibal & St. Joseph, he was concerned about life insurance companies. They offered policies for men and women who were not directly speculating on stock prices. But policyholders speculated indirectly and innocently through the actions of the boards of their insurance companies. Many of these companies' portfolios consisted of bank and railroad stock, or state and railroad bonds. Yet their financial capacity was a question mark. Insurance companies only occasionally listed where their assets were invested, what their costs were, and what their total policy commitment was. Some time before the panic began, Wright wrote up a bill for the Massachusetts legislature that would regulate these firms. Any insurance company that wanted to do business in Massachusetts should give a full accounting of stocks and bonds held, outstanding claims, number of policies, and maturities. A trained state actuary would then calculate the value of the policies, subtract operating costs, and arrive at the "net present value" of the company's assets. He would compare them with the expected return on investment of the current funds.

These metrics would assure transparency of assets and liabilities for insurance companies. As Wright understood it, there were two fundamental problems—one was the instability of certain companies, the other was the opacity of their books, which made it impossible for investors or policyholders to know which were unstable. When trouble loomed, market participants faced symbolic doubt. Financial institutions—whether insurance companies or banks—often depended on vagueness during booms; they suffered for it during busts.[52] Investors, troubled by the opacity of the instruments (which were safe?), hoarded gold and silver. Only transparency would clear this up.

The insurance companies strongly resisted Wright's proposed regulation, but when the panic of 1857 hit, the Massachusetts legislature was inclined to listen to the man whose editorials in the *American Railway Times* seemed to have predicted the crisis. Wright became the first insurance commissioner of Massachusetts. He calculated the stability of insurance companies using two new metrics: return on investment and net present value. After the 1873 crisis, national banks were required to adopt what we now call "generally accepted accounting principles." After the 1929 panic, all publicly traded companies were required to do so. Wright's metrics are now taught as fundamentals in American business schools. Eventually, in other words, Elizur Wright, the crusading socialist, abolitionist, and actuary, would succeed in merging ethics and mathematics. In the meantime, however, not even his powers of prediction could stave off disaster.

The panic of 1857 hit New York in August, days after creditors posted protests on door lintels and notice boards of New York banks that Ohio Life was not paying interest on its obligations. By September the reputation of American securities in London had been destroyed. A huge sell-off followed in Britain, making the U.S. market for railroad securities drop even more.[53] By October 13, New York banks had suspended payment of specie. Britain's chancellor of the exchequer acted quickly, coming in as a lender of last resort and issuing £2 million in excess of the Bank of England's statutory limits. He thus indirectly bailed out New York banks on the verge of default. The Exchequer justified financial intervention by blaming the crisis on the failure of joint-stock banks in Scotland and Ireland, though he cast the greatest suspicion on the firms connected "with the American trade." His actions quelled the panic in Britain, and when money market rates stabilized there, they stabilized in the United States. By the middle of December, after only four months, the New York Clearing House ordered banks to redeem their loan certificates for bank certificates again. The Boston and New York banks resumed specie payments. By then, however, there had been more than five thousand bankruptcies in the United States.[54]

In the 1858 session, Congress debated two separate sets of bills, what we would now call stimulus packages. The recently formed Republican Party—containing Free-Soilers, Barnburners, Hard Shells, Know-Nothings, and many others—proposed spending all the resources that Congress possessed. Some land would be given to a nationally chartered railroad to the Pacific; western land would go to each of the states to create agricultural and technical colleges; more land would be given free to settlers in a homestead act. Democrats suspended consideration of all of these bills.

The Democrats had a very different stimulus package. They proposed annexing Cuba so that more slaves would be available for the

Deep South states. This would lower the price of slaves and thus allow poorer men the chance to become cotton slaveholders. Democrats in the Senate blocked all bills about western lands until the status of Cuba was resolved. By 1859 many northern Democrats began to fly from a party that was now so clearly under the control of southerners. For the majority of Americans in the North who cared little about slavery, such a stimulus bill seemed offensive, evidence perhaps that abolitionists were right in arguing that a "slave power" controlled the Democratic Party.

In 1857, Elizur Wright imagined he could see the defeat of two institutions that threatened the future of mankind: slavery and opaque financial accounting. Both represented a failure to protect the collective labor of millions of men and women. Slaveholders stole that labor directly. Insurance boards stole that labor indirectly by denying policies to policyholders if they missed a single payment or by siphoning off workers' income in excessive fees.

In the Free-Soil Party, Wright would have to embrace the board members like John Murray Forbes to destroy the slaveholders. After millions lost in blood and treasure, he would see one kind of vampirism destroyed. Another kind of vampirism would become fixed in the American political landscape. Wright would regret his decision to embrace the capitalists of Boston and New York, and he would fight against them for the rest of his days. Perhaps because Elizur knew his death tables, he knew what killed people: strong drink, overeating, lack of exercise, city air. Elizur Wright long outlived John Murray Forbes, the Thayers, and all his antagonists. But still they won. These men—with their trunk lines, opaque financial operations, and inside dealing—had unwittingly helped to start a civil war, and their financial institutions would outlast Elizur Wright. Indeed the war empowered the type of finance capitalism that Forbes's railway bond represented.

In the months leading up to the Republican convention in May 1860, there were many obvious choices for the next presidential candidate: New York's William Henry Seward, Ohio's Salmon Chase, or Pennsylvania's Simon Cameron. But for the railroad men of Boston, Philadelphia, and New York who now had so much influence in the Republican Party, there was only one lawyer in the crowd who stuck out. His specialty was supporting railroads in their claims against the Swamp Acts of 1850 and 1857. He was just their kind of man. His name was Abraham Lincoln.[55]

CHAPTER EIGHT

Ceres Americana

Two economies collided in Kansas in 1857. One relied on the labor of slaves and produced raw materials: cotton above all else, but also sugar, hemp, and rice. Each year some of these slave-made goods went north, but two-thirds or more of the entire cotton crop went to Great Britain.[1] Exports, declared the South Carolina planter and senator James Henry Hammond, depended on the South: "The strength of a nation depends in a great measure upon its wealth, and the wealth of a nation, like that of a man, is to be estimated by its surplus production." And in 1857 the South was the nation's strongman. Of the $279 million worth of exports for 1857, Hammond declared, nearly $158 million came from southern states.

While the cotton boom had plummeted in 1837 after reaching a zenith in 1836, it had been steaming forward since then. Indeed southern exports in 1857 outstripped the entire nation's yearly exports for any year before 1856. To cotton, the 1857 panic was a nothing. Northern criticism of cotton was empty. "No, sir, you dare not make war on cotton. No power on earth dares make war upon it. Cotton is king." Hammond and other southern planters laughed at the panic of 1857.

> When the abuse of credit had destroyed credit and annihilated confidence, when thousands of the strongest commercial houses in the world were coming down, and hundreds of millions of dollars of supposed property evaporating in thin air, when you came to a dead lock, and revolutions were threatened, what brought you up? Fortunately for you it was the commencement of the cotton season, and we have poured in upon you one million six hundred thousand bales of cotton just at the crisis to save you from destruction.[2]

The wheat-export economy that railroad directors, midwestern farmers, and coastal merchants hoped to build was an ambitious and delicate thing. Grains harvested on the grasslands of the Midwest were packed in railroad cars. Shipping these easily spoiled goods over vast distances for a Liverpool price seemed a slender reed on which to build a way of life, an export economy, and a new party. Congressional land grants on "supposed property" made it all possible: wheatland was given to the railroad, settlement was bankrolled by English investors, mortgages were offered to farmers. The entire apparatus depended on the railroads' title to land. It was a harvest easily trampled.

When the dissenting factions of Whigs and Democrats formed the Republican Party in Pittsburgh in February 1856, this new party sought to build an economy out of wheat, even if it meant a war on cotton. With the support of John Murray Forbes and his railroad minions, the Republicans would block the spread of plantations over the grasslands of Missouri and Kansas. The soil would be "free" in that free white families would settle there, but it was a monocultural environment built and sustained by English, Boston, and New York investment. Settlers who bought land on five-year mortgages would do the planting and harvesting. Forbes's associates provided capital, connections, and land. This vast number of mortgage-holding settlers imagined themselves to be independent farmers. And they voted.

After the Forbes family took a Missouri railroad out from under them, enraged Missourians crossed the border to vote in Kansas. The battle quickly became a national one, not over a cotton kingdom versus a heartland of wheat but over the future of the West, as well as the power of foreign corporations, federal states, and families.

Both northerners and southerners in Kansas were filibusters. Since before Andrew Jackson's day, land speculators had funded filibustering expeditions. They recruited in colleges (for officers) and slums (for soldiers) to build an army to battle foreign powers and claim land. In the boom before 1819 they had taken Florida. In the boom before 1837 private southern armies had battled Mexico to create the Republic of Texas. In Canada as well, private armies had been recruited in New York in 1837 to help Louis-Joseph Papineau take Montreal and then to help William Mackenzie take Toronto. Both filibuster raids in Canada failed. When Papineau's conspirators were hanged, their last words were "Je me souviens"—I remember. The phrase is still on license plates in Quebec. Filibusters did not forgive; they did not forget.[3] But it was the arrival of two competing filibuster armies in Kansas, one northern, one southern, that brought a civil war.

From 1855 to 1857 these two filibuster armies fought over the same place.[4] The abolitionist general James Lane's northern filibusters came from Boston, Philadelphia, and Albany. Their financial backers, including evangelical antislavery churches and the Forbeses and Thayers of Boston, shipped rifles to Kansas in boxes marked "Bibles." Men had fought one another for land since the days of Duer, but rarely had they been so well armed. General Atchison's southern filibusters came to fight them in bands as small as two or three; they hoped to win Kansas and a slave-based route to California. Never before had pro-slavery and antislavery filibusters faced each other directly. Southern Democrats briefly challenged the Republican victory over Missouri and Kansas with the second Swamp Act of 1857. And that caused the brief depression that James Henry Hammond was laughing about.

The 1860 election became a referendum on stimulus packages, in the North and in the South. It was by then also a referendum on the violence over the plains of Kansas. Southern Democrats walked out of the Democratic convention in 1860 after the rest of the party refused to endorse slavery as a positive good. Southern Whigs and southern Democrats, unwilling to join together but unwilling to fuse into a coalition with their northern neighbors, divided the southern vote. The southern candidates John C. Breckinridge and John Bell would be the only candidates listed on most ballots in the South. The northern candidates Douglas and Lincoln would be the only candidates listed on most ballots in the North.

As Abraham Lincoln, sometime lawyer for the Illinois Central Railroad, accepted the nomination as standard-bearer of the Republican Party, he refrained from attacking slavery directly, declaring only that he would not permit it to move west. He would allow southern states to protect slavery where it existed, but he and the tens of thousands of settlers in Kansas saw the protection of land from slave owners as a principle. They would brook no compromise about the West being preserved for western railroads, American wheat, and free settlers.

Just like the 1824 election after the 1819 panic, the 1860 election after the 1857 panic saw candidates again split in four directions. But in 1860 the conflict was not just about how to respond to financial catastrophe. Shots had been fired, and the election became an argument about the future of slavery. Lincoln received enough votes to claim the presidency despite not appearing on ballots in the lower South.

James Henry Hammond's prediction of southern secession came true. Southern legislatures, then conventions, then armed bodies of men declared that they would not stand for a Republican president's inauguration. They proposed to separate from the nation to create an empire around the natural center of the cotton market—New Orleans, at the mouth of the Mississippi River. According to Hammond, a new free-trade, riverine civilization would dominate the world. It would resemble the United States, though its central government would be weaker, and it would declare slavery a permanent institution. By 1860 plans to create the Confederacy imagined its capital at Montgomery, Alabama. Finally, Virginians, ambivalent about secession at first, demanded that Richmond become the capital of the new Southern Confederacy.

The secessionists had seen in the mortgage bond panic of 1857 a reason for hope in that the South, without collateralized mortgage debt, might escape from financial ruin. But they failed to fully reckon with the European memories of the deadbeats of 1841: the politicians of the American South. In 1841, Senator Jefferson Davis of Mississippi had declared that his state was right in repudiating its debts to foreign capitalists. When the members of the Confederate Congress chose him as their provisional president, they failed to consider how European capitalists would take the news of a Confederate state headed by a repudiator. Because of Davis's position on the Mississippi defaults, the Confederacy had found it nearly impossible to float the loans it needed to fight a war against the Union.[5] In the end the Confederacy could float only a single loan, one that had to be guaranteed by future cotton delivery. By comparison, a Republican corporate railroad lawyer who had defended the sanctity of the Illinois Central's bonds seemed a safer bet. Hundreds of European investors took federal bonds in the markets of Hamburg, Amsterdam, and Paris and sometimes London.

Two civilizations faced each other, but with rather different standings in the markets of Europe. What next but secession, and bloody civil war?

CERES AMERICANA

IN THE UNITED STATES, the railroads that started the conflict had been built to meet what the railroad director John Denison called "a foreign demand for bread stuffs."[6] While the panic of 1857 slowed down the drive to bring midwestern wheat to Europe, the Civil War provided a fresh opportunity for drastic federal, state, and private investment in the infrastructure that made that delivery possible. A wartime Congress fulfilled the 1859 Republican promise of a stimulus package that would bring American prosperity. By 1873, that American prosperity would destroy the European balance of trade and usher in another depression.

Before the Civil War, despite the best efforts of the trunk line financiers, most midwestern wheat and flour still followed gravity and the Mississippi River to New Orleans, where merchants bought it for resale in the South or the Caribbean. But once the South seceded, the Mississippi River became a war zone. By April 1861, shipping anything south from Chicago had become dangerous. With only smugglers sending goods on the Mississippi, the Great Lakes route to the coast bulged with wheat. New York's exports of wheat increased more than tenfold, advancing from two million bushels in 1860 to twenty-one million in 1861. The wheat passing through the Great Lakes to Buffalo increased by two-thirds in a single year from thirty-two to fifty-two million bushels, thoroughly overtaxing Buffalo grain elevators, the Erie Canal, and wholesale merchants.[7]

Once the Southern states seceded and their representatives left Washington, the Thirty-Seventh Congress became a war Congress dominated by northern Republicans. That Congress determined to build an American export crop to replace cotton. Between 1862 and 1865, Republican lawmakers passed the stimulus provisions that Southern Democrats had blocked in 1858, broke the limits Congress had imposed on federal spending, and turned the United States into a wheat-export powerhouse. Congress began by asking President Lincoln to have his diplomats report on European state investment in food exports. John Bigelow, the United States consul at Paris, highlighted imperial investment in railroad infrastructure as the most important competitive threat to America. Cotton, he assured them in 1861, would no longer be the nation's central export. Experienced cotton brokers in Britain had predicted that "at the close of this war one half of our cotton business [will have] been transferred to India." Meanwhile, much of Europe was investing in its own railroads to export wheat: "Russian roads will lie opened through the whole region of the Terre Norre, from the Black sea to the Baltic, which, from its rich bottomless soils, will yield incalculable quantities of food now inaccessible." Likewise, France was "pushing her railway system down into Spain, and, in concert with that Government, is opening up vast regions hitherto uncultivated, which would grow wheat enough to feed all Europe." America's export trade in wheat, according to Bigelow, could only be "preserved by a railway system proportioned to the magnitude of our

territory and its natural resources, by which everything that the industry of the country can produce can have its market."[8]

With the help of Congress, the American Midwest would feed all
Europe. As the Reverend E. W. Hutter put it in his Thanksgiving ser-
mon in Philadelphia, American farmland could already feed "a family
outnumbering fourfold the present population of the entire globe."[9]
The nation's food harvest would pay the Union's bills. To fund the war,
Congress would issue more than $1 billion in bonds and other pledges.
To pay off those debts, American farmers, supported by Congress,
would feed the globe for the next dozen decades. "Large exports of
Northern produce," exclaimed the *Philadelphia Inquirer* in 1861, had
already begun to give the North "extraordinary strength" to fight a war.
Given the "stringent money market" that "checks all imports, and gives
us the price of our exports in bullion," the Philadelphia paper predicted
that breadstuffs would be America's new bullion.[10] With southern cotton exports suspended, food would keep gold flowing into the nation.

Wheat production and export became the national government's
top priority. Congress funded the survey, charter, and construction of a
Pacific railroad. The Homestead Act provided free prairie land to prospective wheat farmers on both sides of the Missouri River. The Land
Grant Act created land grant universities whose agricultural and technical colleges would increase crop yields in every state. President Lincoln
created the "Department of Agriculture," which would provide seed
samples, measure temperatures, follow international markets, provide
regular crop reports, and predict international prices. A cash-strapped
Congress taxed everything else that came out of the ground, then doubled the tariff on imports. Wheat alone was effectively exempted from
taxation to encourage its growth.[11] The Republican Party was not—as
some historians have suggested—a captive of northern industrialists.
It was devoted to investing in the infrastructure that would allow it to
compete on the wheat markets with Russia, France, British India, and
Austria-Hungary. It succeeded beyond its wildest imagination.

Indeed the Homestead Act provided a perverse incentive to grow
wheat on the plains at any price. To "prove up" or gain one's farmland,
a farmer needed only to plant a crop and build a house. Gaining this
free land meant selling a year's crop, so that even selling at a loss was
profitable if it guaranteed your claim. Common wheat made the perfect frontier crop in the plains. Wheat is, after all, just a weed. It is
easily planted, needs relatively little moisture, thrives in cool weather,
and is easily harvested.[12] The mechanical improvements of the 1850s in

the harvesting and binding of wheat worked best on flat prairie land.[13] Once the war began, the reaper-binder-harvesters made it possible for farm families to grow wheat even with husbands and sons at war. The arid western plains also appeared less hospitable to the red parasitic fungi called wheat rust, which intermittently ravaged the Banat region near Austria-Hungary's Budapest.[14]

Further manufacture of agricultural products became America's most significant specialty during the war. Manufacturers learned to turn carloads of wheat into wagonloads of flour, then turn flour into warehouses of hardtack. Wartime American industry was built on food.[15] Gustavus Swift, Philip Armour, Gail Borden, and Gilbert Van Camp learned the techniques of mass production in boiling, salting, and canning goods for hungry Union soldiers camped on the battlefields of the South. This manufactured and branded food would be the other foundation of America's future exports after war was concluded.[16]

A Republican-controlled Congress also facilitated wheat exports by creating a banking infrastructure that ended the days of free banking with multiple currencies. The Senate Committee on Ways and Means first resolved to create a long-term currency, the federally designed and printed National Bank Note. These National Bank Notes were designed to marry private banks with the federal government. Banks, previously chartered by the states, would receive federal charters, issue notes payable for all debts except tariff duties, and call themselves national banks. Then, borrowing regulations that New York introduced for its state banks in the 1830s, Congress allowed the national banks to hold government bonds—not just gold—as a portion of their reserves. Banks thus became eager purchasers of government bonds.[17]

But as the bill was working through Congress, disaster struck in 1861. A string of Confederate victories prompted fears that the Civil War would last longer than a few months. By December thousands of individuals had begun to hoard gold and silver; on December 31 all the private banks in New York suspended specie payments. Congressman Elbridge Spaulding, chair of the Committee on Ways and Means, took the drastic step of bringing a bill to the House floor without the consent of his committee. With the backing of Secretary of the Treasury Salmon Chase, Spaulding proposed the creation of a temporary note—the "Legal Tender Note"—that would be payable for all debts public and private. This currency would be "backed" not by gold or silver but by the pledge of the central government. Representative Erastus Corning of New York, president of the New York Central Railroad and the Bank of Albany, strongly opposed the measure but was stuck in Albany attending to his bank's failure to make gold payments when the emergency legislation passed.

Thus, on the first day of 1862, American currency was off the gold standard. In other words, the notes were no longer "backed" by gold at the Treasury. Because the notes were printed front and back with green dye, the unbacked currency quickly acquired the humorous name "greenback." This new currency would allow the federal government to pay the $2 million a day required for contractors, employees, and soldiers in the field while the national bank bill worked its way through committee. The United States would be off the gold standard from 1862 to 1879.[18]

Like the river money issued after the War of 1812, greenbacks depreciated in value. Ironically, state banks like Corning's compounded the inflation. They accepted greenbacks at their counters, often demanding a discount of 10 percent or more to accept them, and then put them in a "special reserve." The state banks argued that because Congress had designated the greenbacks payable for all debts, they were as good as gold. The state banks then issued multiples of their own state currencies using greenbacks as a reserve. When asked for specie, they turned over greenbacks.[19] This dodge allowed state banks to furiously issue more currency with none of the restrictions imposed on national banks, a result that led California's attorney general, Frank Pixley, to urge Congress to cancel state bank charters and "sweep the rags of private banks from the moneyed circles."[20]

The greenback notes proved extremely popular, a common dollar currency that spent the same in Chicago and New York. After the National Bank Act created National Bank Notes, both sets of federal dollars, endorsed by the federal government, facilitated the interstate movement of goods.[21] The depreciation of the American greenback further helped exports by cheapening the dollars that grain exporters paid to American shippers while increasing the relative value of the pounds sterling they got for wheat sold in Liverpool.[22]

John Murray Forbes and the railroad minions of the five trunk lines did the rest. They claimed military necessity to consolidate railways, bridge rivers, and lay tracks through cities. They replaced iron rails with expensive but longer-lasting steel rails, replaced wood-burning with coal-burning locomotives, bulked up the size of railway cars, installed grain elevators at major junctions, and purchased lines of steamships to shuttle goods between New York and Liverpool.[23] As the historian

William Cronon has suggested, wheat became something like a liquid during the 1860s: individual bags of labeled wheat became an anachronism. A farmer had his wheat inspected and graded and poured it into a grain elevator. He left with dollars.[24]

The rest of wheat's journey to Britain got cheaper and cheaper, and so American wheat—what Anthony Trollope whimsically called *Ceres Americana*—began to move like a flood toward the East Coast and the ocean beyond. By the end of the Civil War a few interstate railroads struggled for control of the corridor from Chicago to New York; the New York Central, the Erie, and the Pennsylvania battled one another by lowering shipping prices, cheapening delivery, and using mechanical devices to minimize the energy expended in the long-distance distribution of wheat kernels. In the spring and summer the railroads even competed with a cheaper, all-river route through the Great Lakes to the Erie Canal.[25] By 1880, grain made up nearly three-fourths of all the goods sent east on trunk lines.[26] Petroleum was a distant second to wheat as a trunk line export. In the early 1870s the B&O projected a "pipeline" for oil through western Pennsylvania, one that passed under Pennsylvania Railroad track en route to Philadelphia. The war between the railroad corridors occasionally became physical when, for example, employees of the Pennsylvania Railroad pulled up B&O pipes as fast as they were laid.

For wheat, the railroad itself was the pipeline. In Chicago railroads planted gigantic grain elevators on the slips of the southern branch of the Chicago River, elevators that could hold 1.25 million bushels of wheat.[27] A seven-hundred-horsepower engine turned a three-hundred-foot-long, four-foot-wide belt. The belt carried wheat on an endless band of tin buckets, dropping each grade of wheat into one of twenty-six bins. Another contraption poured wheat from elevators directly onto steamboats or railroad cars, depending on the season and the comparative price of shipping. The price to transfer from a railroad car to a warehouse or a steamship was just one-quarter of one cent per bushel. The new method was less than one-tenth the price of using men's shoulders, and because delivery was nearly instantaneous, ships could arrive in port and ship out the next day, saving boat captains tens of thousands of dollars. Thus a cascade of wheat could make a journey from a grain elevator in Kansas or Iowa all the way to Liverpool for just eighteen cents (nine pence) per bushel. And because wheat in Liverpool trended as high as $2 a bushel depending on the season, the four-thousand-mile journey was usually well worth the trip.[28] At first railroads and grain elevator operators made the most from these transactions, but gradually the price between Chicago and Liverpool wheat converged, lowering the per-pound profit of those who moved the grain.

Union troops fed on hardtack, tinned beef, and tinned vegetables finally overwhelmed a Confederate army that starved in 1864 and practically deserted the gates of the Confederate capital at Richmond in 1865. So ended James Henry Hammond's dream of a cotton empire, and so ended the system of slavery that had made it possible. Cotton made from forced labor in India and Egypt competed with the southern empire's fleecy staple. From 1866 to 1890 a glut in international exports caused cotton prices to slowly drop around the world. Cotton was no longer king. As the war concluded in April 1865, a Republican-dominated Congress had drastically reshaped the nation's agriculture, its system of government, and its system of finance. It funded universities to increase crop yields, supported the consolidation of interstate railroads to export wheat, chartered new railroads to the West Coast, and created the greenback to act as a ready currency to buy American wheat at the grain elevator.

Between the war's end in 1865 and 1869, twenty-four million bushels of wheat left American shores for Britain: a bushel for every human being then living in Britain. This was just the beginning—in thirty years that volume would increase twenty-fold—but it was an important beginning. Railroad companies competed with one another by building steam-powered ships that brought railroad grain to Liverpool. Transatlantic freight rates were cut in half between 1860 and 1870 and kept dropping. A rate war between the three major trunk lines—New York Central, Erie, and Penn—began in the winter of 1871–1872. The early 1870s saw the largest drop in the price of food in Europe since the Neolithic era, a development that was distinctly dangerous for those who produced it anywhere else.[29] Like Austria-Hungary.

CHAPTER NINE

A Storm of Wheat

ON MAY 9, 1873, Anton J. Cermak Jr., son of a coal miner, and the future mayor of Chicago, was born in the smokestack town of Kladno, in the hills west of Prague. Tony was born a Bohemian subject of the vast and brutal Austro-Hungarian Empire. The trappings of that empire were everywhere. Every pound of coal Tony's father mined underneath the Vrapice Hills belonged to Franz Joseph, the king of Bohemia, Hungary, and Lodomeria and the emperor of Austria-Hungary. On the day of Tony's birth, the German-speaking emperor was five hours away at the Vienna Exposition, in its ninth day, an international festival devoted to industry and science. Anton's parents had certainly read of the wonders of the exposition in the Czech newspapers. They might have even seen the stalls of downtown Kladno filled with commemorative plates, medals, and prints featuring the tall and handsome emperor in what is now called the Franz Joseph beard: with long sideburns but shaved at the cheekbones, chin, and throat. The beard was everywhere in Bohemia. German-speaking aristocrats, bureaucrats, and junior officers throughout the empire emulated the style to make them stand out from the Bohemian miners, farmers, and butcher boys.[1] One hundred years later the beard reappeared as a style among professional wrestlers, pimps, and members of motorcycle gangs.

While their Viennese king was almost two hundred miles south of Kladno, in the German-speaking city of Vienna, the Cermaks would have followed the news of the exposition, for Vienna was the empire's capital city. Two hundred miles was not so far away, really. The Royal and Imperial Austrian State Railway Company reached from Kladno to Vienna, and Kladno coal was the brightly burning brown lignite that the emperor proudly exhibited there. Kladno coal would also have fueled the steam engine that pulled the little tram that carried visitors to and from Vienna's Prater, or public park.[2]

Franz Joseph had planned the Vienna Exposition to celebrate the twenty-fifth anniversary of his seizure of power. The Cermaks, like many Czechs, still resented the emperor for having abolished the liberal constitution that he had pledged to protect.[3] For many of the miners of Kladno, the Vienna Exposition celebrated six years under a sham constitution, one that provided no rights to citizens; during that time the Czech miners' union had been suppressed, their criticism of the crown censored, and their right to assemble strictly limited.[4]

In vain and glorious Vienna, however, things looked different. Imperial pennants flew on the streets, brass bands marched through town, and tourists stopped in studios to have their silhouettes made before they visited the exposition grounds. The government had spent millions of florins to build Czech, Hungarian, Polish, Slovak, and Tyrolean pavilions in the Prater, each to celebrate the king's enjoyment of the quaint customs of the distant reaches of his empire. On May 9, the opening ceremony was over, but the pageants, brass bands, and outdoor suppers continued.

Vienna was supposed to be the center of a new kind of Europe. Three ungainly empires had emerged, each committed to what European historians call the "liberal revolution," a combination of strong monarchies, weak elected legislatures, and free trade. Franz Joseph emulated Louis Napoleon of France and Kaiser Wilhelm of Prussia in appearing to embrace free speech and public courts — though he heavily censored the press and had the most brutal police in Europe. Vienna would be a capital to rival Paris and Berlin. In a symbolic gesture to demonstrate his commitment to free trade, the emperor had ordered the medieval wall around the city of Vienna removed and replaced by a grand boulevard, the Ringstrasse. A free and open Viennese capital would be a model for a free and open Austria-Hungary. As the last touch, a tall iron fence was discreetly added around the imperial grounds to keep out the riffraff.

New banks, state supported and stockholder owned, were established in Austria-Hungary and Berlin that followed the French Crédit Mobilier model.[5] As the liberal critic and novelist Victor Hugo described the same work under the French emperor, "He needs what he calls 'men.' Diogenes sought them with a lantern, he seeks them with a banknote in his hand."[6] Each emperor personally endorsed new lending institutions. The banks then issued mortgages for municipal and residential construction to build up their capital cities.[7] Vienna's Ringstrasse, like the newly created boulevards of Paris and Berlin, quickly filled up with grand residences, opera houses, and cafés.

While the mines of Kladno provided much of the coal and iron used in the monarchy, the center of Austro-Hungarian prosperity had much to do with the fine flour produced on the fertile wheat fields of Banat south and east of Budapest. Banat wheat was ground in Budapest using the closely guarded secret of "high grinding" that separated wheat into eight grades of flour, supposedly one grade for each of the sharply divided classes of the Austro-Hungarian Empire. Even in times of famine, Austria-Hungary still exported Franz Joseph's patented "Kaiserauszug" super-white flour, a brand prized by bakers and confectioners throughout Europe.[8] But the empire's prosperity proved as delicate as a Viennese torte.

Just west over the Ore Mountains from Kladno in nearby Prussia, the active figure in the liberal revolution was Chancellor Otto von Bismarck, whom Europeans called the "German Dictator."[9] The Prussian banks, like those in Vienna, depended on French models. They also depended on French gold. After Bismarck's army invaded France in the Franco-Prussian War of 1870–1871, France was forced to make vast "reparations" payments to the country that had sacked it. With so much French gold flowing into Berlin, German-speaking Vienna quickly became a target for land speculation. Building and loan associations, which had existed for a dozen years or so in central Europe, built up more capital than they knew what to do with. Thousands of Viennese builders could obtain mortgages.[10]

Through the 1860s and early 1870s land values seemed to climb and climb. At its height a square "fathom" of land along Vienna's Ringstrasse cost more than 700 florins, or nearly $400.[11] Borrowers ravenously assumed more and more credit, using unbuilt or half-built houses as collateral. The most marvelous spots for sightseers in the three cities today are the magisterial buildings erected in the so-called founder period.[12] Newly rich financiers like Paris's George Eugène Haussmann, Berlin's Gerson Bleichröder, and Vienna's Bethel Henry Strousberg built vast train stations and imposing imperial centers.[13] Few understood that the entire edifice of imperial pretension was in danger from competition from abroad. Austro-Hungarian and Russian wheat was expensive, and American wheat would soon be cheaper.

"IT IS NOT THE OAK"

ODESSA GRAIN MERCHANTS saw the change first. Britain, the biggest importer of wheat, shifted to the cheap American stuff quite suddenly around 1871.[14] By 1872 kerosene and manufactured food were rocketing out of America's heartland, undermining prices for rapeseed, flour, and beef, Austria-Hungary's biggest exports.[15] Europeans would later call this the American "Commercial Invasion." A new industrial super-power had arrived, one whose low costs threatened European trade and Europeans' way of life.

Russian banks, many just chartered in the late 1860s, were the first to fail. Somewhat different from the banks of the three empires, these Russian banks lent money directly to thousand-acre estates in Russia's breadbasket. While the black soil of southern Russia (now Ukraine and Moldova) supported enormous wheat estates along the rivers that emptied near Odessa on the Black Sea, the sudden appearance of bank credit led to a banking bubble in 1871 and 1872. "The projectors of these establishments," wrote Richard Clayton Webster, Britain's representa-tive in southern Russia, "would have delighted [the eighteenth-century speculator] John Law." All had access to paper money, including "every person who had a house, or even a hovel." Besides mortgages, Russian bankers discounted short-term loans but based the loans on the most extravagant expectations about wheat prices. Every nobleman signed the bills of his neighbors as a guarantee against default. If noble fami-lies appeared overextended, Webster complained, "they might get their coachmen to sign their bills." When the harvest came in October 1872, Russian banks proved unable to collect the interest on most of their loans to Russian noble families.[16] Foreclosures on mortgages caused nearly six thousand estates to come up for sale. Buyers, however, were few.[17] The London *Times* called the Russian failure the "great stagna-tion."[18] It was a portent of things to come.

The novelist Victor Hugo predicted the failure of the liberal revo-lution in Europe, noting that, like the Russian banking boom, it was built on promises that could not be fulfilled. Ridiculing the exploits of France's Louis Napoleon, who sought to ape the first Napoleon, he wrote, "The toadstool sprouts at the foot of the oak, but it is not the oak."[19] Louis Napoleon's building was based on no real capital, Hugo asserted. The toadstool growth of the founder period could not last. May 9, 1873, the day of Anton Cermak's birth, became noteworthy for the events of the afternoon. In the morning, news arrived that the stocks and bonds of one hundred insolvent investors would be sold on the Vienna Stock Exchange to cover their debts. Prices wobbled in the morning and crashed in the afternoon.[20]

By midday on Anton's birthday traders were crowding the Ring-strasse outside the Vienna Stock Exchange, shouting to sell off thousands of shares in public railways and banks. One bondholder grabbed a well-known financier by the throat, demanding his money. Late in the afternoon, after a few such scuffles, the exchange stopped all trading.[21] Thereafter, Anton's birthday would be known throughout Europe as Black Friday.

The *Krach,* or crash, of 1873 caused a money crunch that would make the Vienna Exposition an object of ridicule. Despite all the Vienna newspapers' predictions, fewer than a third of the predicted visitors arrived. American bartenders who had bribed U.S. officials to set up concessions in the American exhibition in Vienna demanded their money back. The U.S. government promptly suspended the American commissioner for accepting bribes in the first place.[22]

The weak showing of the exposition in Vienna helped feed widespread doubts about the financial future of central Europe.[23] Within hours, the news of the Vienna *Krach* traveled by telegraph and word of mouth north and west toward Kladno. Stories of the suicides of traders on the Vienna Stock Exchange came farther north on the Vltava River, where peddlers, merchants, teamsters, and ship captains brought word to the miners and burghers of nearby Prague.[24] Telegraph wires carried the news farther along the Elbe River to Prussia, then out across the Atlantic on the new transatlantic cable. While much of the intelligence that passed back and forth from Britain to the United States had to do with grain prices, newspaper correspondents also managed to buy enough time on the wires to transmit details about the start of the world's first great depression.

Days after the Cermak family read about the panic, they would have seen the drop in the tonnage rate paid for coal. The drop in coal prices dashed the plans of hundreds of Kladno mining families who had hoped to buy land and move out of the town's cramped and overpriced rental housing.[25] The Cermaks, who lived in a two-room cottage, may have wondered if their son was born under an ill sign.[26] Within a year, Tony and his family would take the route that gossip made: north on the Vltava River to the Elbe; then from Hamburg they would cross the Atlantic, continuing on land to Chicago. On the day he was born, Tony opened his eyes at the start of the panic of 1873. Before the panic, America saw fewer than a third of a million permanent European emigrants a year, mostly from England, Ireland, and Germany. In the forty years between the 1873 panic and World War I, America received more than fifty million permanent migrants, the majority coming from inside the boundaries of the Austro-Hungarian Empire.[27] It would signal the start of one of the greatest mass movements in the history of the world.

In the nineteenth century most financial crises came after an omnipresent commodity suddenly became cheap. Buyers appreciated the plummeting prices, but someone usually suffered. Those who had considerable investments of time or money in an older manufacturing or harvesting process failed, inducing a widespread disillusion in the value of debts and shares. On the Vienna Stock Exchange the cornerstones that crumbled were the agency banks (Maklerbanken) that were heavily invested in Austro-Hungarian exports. Merchants forced to liquidate quickly sold their land for cash, leading land prices to fall. The building and loan associations, with investments in inflated land prices, followed the next day.[28] When capital committed to a particular enterprise could not be sold and reinvested, when nothing seemed recoverable, financial crisis commenced.

No amount of imperial intervention appeared to help. The emperor Franz Joseph hastily helped to create a fund of 20 million florins to back his state banks; he then met Queen Victoria in an elaborate ceremony to discuss international trade. He could do nothing. "The movements of the Money Market are," declared the London *Times* smugly, "as little affected by Imperial and Royal festivities as the tides of the sea."[29]

As the banks of Vienna and Berlin tumbled in May, the Bank of England held emergency meetings. Since the 1830s, the Bank of England's discount rate had set the floor for rates in the European capital market. England, after all, was the biggest importer and exporter in the world. Unsure of which institutions were most involved in the central European bank crisis, the bank's court of directors voted to increase the discount rate, effectively raising it everywhere in Europe and North America. Having just raised the rate from 4 percent to 4.5 percent on May 7, they raised it to 5 percent on May 10, 6 percent on May 17, and 7 percent on June 4. By November 7 it would be 9 percent, the highest rate in the century. When the Bank of England upped its rate, it quickly drove up the cost to borrow money from other banks—what we now call the interbank lending rate.[30] As the Bank of England directors saw it, an increase in the rate guaranteed that borrowers would scale back their operations, for few could borrow at 6 or 7 percent. Gold would return to the Bank of England, protecting it against a run. The price of lending rose, and the circulation of money dropped. It was a recipe for international panic.

"WHAT A SURPRISING LOTTERY IT HAS BECOME"

BY THE FALL OF 1873, the commodity and banking crisis that cheap American wheat wrought in Vienna returned to the United States in the form of increased bank rates. Railroad companies were most at risk. They had recovered from the 1857 panic and had earned the confidence of European investors after the peace of 1865. But while many railroad bonds in the 1850s had relied on mortgages on government-granted land, after 1865 railroads were casting about for new bonds to issue. They crafted complex financial instruments—gilt-edged bonds—that promised a high fixed return but had little or no underlying assets. While European investors were eager to participate in the American boom, few of them understood that many of the postwar American railway bonds had no salable assets in case of default. The Pennsylvania Railroad, for example, issued bonds for most of the subsidiary railroads it controlled. Insiders in Pennsylvania understood that the underlying assets were a tiny fraction of the value printed on the bonds, but the power of the Pennsylvania Railroad's name had made the bonds sell well.[31]

Jay Cooke was the finance banker who had achieved the most success in selling American bonds during the 1860s. With his trademark gray slouch hat, cowhide boots, black cape, and long white beard, he stood out like a patriarch on the exchanges of Philadelphia and New York. During the Civil War he had learned to market U.S. war bonds directly to Americans, especially to midwestern merchants. Advertising heavily in local newspapers, he used a network of subagents he called "minute men" to sell American bonds in Middle America.[32] After the war, Cooke moved into railway finance, where his innovative techniques for selling bonds at home and abroad seemed destined to make him America's most important financier. The pet project he adopted in 1869, the Northern Pacific Railroad, promised to connect the Great Lakes to Puget Sound. As construction slowed and financing proved difficult, he used his brother's position as a board member of the federally sponsored Freedman's Savings and Trust Company to pump up his faltering Northern Pacific bonds. On behalf of thousands of newly freed slaves who had invested their savings in the bank, Cooke's brother invested in his brother's risky Northern Pacific bonds at the top of the market.[33] These unbacked, gilt-edged bonds did well. At first.

But doubts about the railroads came from many directions. A newly formed banking partnership headed by J. P. Morgan and Anthony Drexel sought to unseat Jay Cooke's monopoly on American financing by sowing seeds of doubt about his western railroad. Philadelphia's *Public Ledger,* a newspaper staked by Drexel and Morgan, spread rumors false and true about Cooke's problems selling bonds in Europe. Independent American commentators had begun raising doubts as early as 1872 about many of the proposed transcontinentals. E. L. Godkin, the widely respected editor of the free-trade, Republican magazine *The Nation,* noted that railroad bonds from the American West seemed vastly overpriced. "How far the railroad mania has there gone, and what a surprising lottery it has become, is, in the almost total absence of reliable statistics, not easily estimated," Godkin wrote. "We by no means seek to imply that much money has not been made," he continued, "[b]ut unless we are greatly deceived, within the next few years a great many very handsomely engraved railroad bonds will go to protest, and certificates of stock by the million will find their way into the hands of the trunk makers."[34]

Godkin's skeptical reports suggesting that American railway securities would soon be lining suitcases made an irresistible image. Railway magazines and financial newspapers on both sides of the Atlantic reprinted the argument, if only to dispute it. But Godkin and others planted seeds of doubt in investors' minds.

As investors began to question the values of the many competing American bonds on the market, railway presidents found it harder to sell them. Many presidents like Jay Cooke of the Northern Pacific, Thomas Scott of the Penn, and C. P. Huntington of the Chesapeake & Ohio were forced to take on short-term loans on the money market to continue blasting through mountains and laying track.[35]

Thus, when short-term lending rates doubled in England in 1873, the railroads were in trouble. Unable to pay off or refinance the Northern Pacific Railroad's debt, Cooke's was the first major firm to shutter its doors. The failure of Jay Cooke's bank was announced on the floor of the New York Stock Exchange on September 19, 1873. "This announcement," according to one observer, "was followed by a short silence, and then there arose an uproar which soon spread throughout the country." A selling frenzy proceeded on the exchange and then out on the street. The fall of Jay Cooke, financier of the nation, seemed impossible. When a newsboy in Philadelphia shouted "Extra—All about the failure of Jay Cooke," the Philadelphia police arrested him.[36] Hundreds of American banks failed over the next three years.

The New York Clearing House, created in 1853 and successful at saving some New York banks in 1857, rushed into service. It created a loan committee to determine the values of the bonds banks held, then issued "loan certificates," which other members of the Clearing House were obliged to accept as hard currency for the duration of the panic. The rapid actions of the New York Clearing House protected some downtown New York banks while banks in Philadelphia and Baltimore, lacking loan certificates, faltered. In late September, Philadelphia's and Baltimore's Clearing Houses quickly created loan committees that emulated New York's system. New York banks had resumed specie payments to each other by January 14, 1874, but the downturn continued for more than four years in the United States and for nearly six years in Europe.[37]

WHAT CAUSED THE AMERICAN CRASH?

CRASH POLITICS in the U.S. Congress quickly turned to nasty debates over greenback dollars. These debates pitted farmers, shippers, and merchants of the Midwest who attributed the crash to deflation against railroad directors, bankers, and farmers in the East who blamed the crash on inflation. Many midwesterners believed that the wartime National Banking Act had concentrated capital in New York City, causing midwestern bankers to lodge their investments there. Each year during the harvest, though, New York banks returned massive quantities of currency to western banks to pay farmers for their crops, causing a credit crunch every October. According to midwesterners, it was obvious why the 1873 crash took place in October: the seasonal crunch was exacerbated by Britain's raising of interest rates, causing the panic. Only a more flexible monetary policy would prevent this massive, seasonal drain on assets. Their answer: put more greenbacks in circulation until the crisis abated.

Easterners, particularly those with transatlantic connections to grain and capital markets, blamed the instability of the dollar. They noted the gap between the price of gold and the price of greenbacks, which made selling on international markets a guessing game. As long as the United States was still off the gold standard, railroads that marketed their bonds in England had to denominate their bonds in pounds sterling and pay back lenders in gold. Any inflation of American currency would make paying down their gold debt more costly. In other words, American inflation effectively drove up the interest they paid on their debt to Europe. Bankers who borrowed in Europe and lent in the United States faced the same problem: any inflation would drive up their payoff costs. These bankers also argued that because America depended on English capital markets, doubts about the dollar would make interest rates more volatile. The 9 percent bank rate in Britain in 1873 had caused an 18 percent rate on money in America. Previous monetary inflation (caused during the Civil War) made the European panic hit the United States harder because of doubts about American dollars; further inflation would just make things worse. As long as the value of the dollar was in doubt, it would be prone to European interest rate shocks. Only a return to the gold standard would prevent it.

Name-calling was frequent. Easterners accused westerners of being chronic debtors who wanted to pay their dollar-denominated debts with cheap currency. (This was mostly untrue. Rapid inflation raised interest rates. Because western mortgages were usually for five years, any inflation benefits would evaporate the next time a farmer negotiated his mortgage.) Westerners accused easterners of being moneylenders who wanted their dollar-denominated interest to be worth more than when they lent it. (This described relatively few individuals in the Northeast.) Easterners emasculated their opponents with sexually tinged language. They called themselves hard-money men while their opponents were "softs," who wanted to hold on to the "rag-baby" of paper money. "Hards" dubbed the congressional debates in 1874 the "Inflation Session" because of western proposals to further increase the supply of greenbacks. This "money question" sharply divided Republicans (and would soon divide Democrats). The two sides of the Republican Party reached a careful compromise that slightly inflated the currency. President Ulysses S. Grant—a hard-money man—vetoed it, nearly shattering his own party. With the Republicans in disarray the Democrats took control of the House and gained important seats in the Senate in 1874. The power of the Republicans over the presidency and both houses of Congress, won by war and sustained by victory, was now over. The crash had done them in.[38]

BOHEMIA   HAMBURG   AMERICA

IF TIMES WERE hard in the Bohemian lands around Kladno as well as the United States, then why did the Cermaks come to America? They might have gone anywhere, but the transport companies offering the cheapest passage from Europe were the American steamships that brought the wheat that crushed European prices. American ships brought ruin and took away those who had been ruined. Despite the panic, cheap American commodities continued to flow into Europe throughout the 1870s. Among the beneficiaries were international shipping companies that effectively subsidized the export of central European immigrants. The most spectacular rise came from the Hamburg-American Packet Company (HAPAG), a Hamburg-based steamship company that brought cheap American wheat, beef, pork, and kerosene to Hamburg. The firm found that after 1871 or so it had little to send back from Europe on its massive steamships. But after 1873, it found a way to profit from the crash: its return cargo could be central and northern Europeans, men and women whose livelihoods had been destroyed by plunging food and commodity prices.

HAPAG engineers redesigned the ships' holds to accommodate this two-way traffic. They continued to carry freight from America to Europe, but then with minor mechanical adjustments made in Hamburg, each ship would be ready to carry European men, women, and children back to America. The holds of the ship—called the steerage—could carry people. When the steamship reached New York, the steerage section would be refitted again for freight. Although sending people back to replace goods was a story as old as the Scots-Irish migration to Pennsylvania in the 1740s, the ingenious refitting of ships' holds gave HAPAG an edge over its competitors. By the 1870s HAPAG could charge as little as ten American dollars for a one-way ticket from Hamburg to any point in the United States, a price almost one-eighth of the prevailing price in the 1860s.[39]

After 1870 the cheap delivery of Bohemians, Poles, and Russians to the United States through the ports of Hamburg and Bremen changed the face of American emigration. Along with the Swedes and Norwegians on the north side of the Baltic, ships in the "emigrant trade" brought newcomers from farther away. The few thousand Czech, Russian, and Polish pioneers who had established themselves in the 1850s acted as the drummers, chaplains, rabbis, and storekeepers who made "Amerika" more familiar, an object in which anxiety and interest, fear and love constantly alternated, changing "Amerika" as much as it changed their home countries.[40]

While Danes and Swedes had numerous antecedents, these former subjects of the Austro-Hungarian Empire who came in the backwash of American food exports ordered their groceries, quieted their babies, and sang tavern songs in Czech, Hungarian, Polish, and Slovak. The

Austro-Hungarian constitution of 1867 sped their departure by providing that all citizens could leave freely.[41] Besides the new cheapness of travel arrangements after the American export boom of 1871, political and economic events further conspired to attract central Europeans like the Cermaks to America. While the emperor Franz Joseph's constitution had expanded voting to all adult men, "reforms" instituted after 1870 restricted voting to landholders who paid more than 10 florins a year in taxes.[42] Landless urban workers were infuriated. The financial panic in 1873 only added economic grievances to their political ones.

WHO BROUGHT THE Cermaks? Based on the dates of their arrival, it was probably the Chicago, Wilmington, and Vermillion Coal Company (CW&V), a firm owned by the Chicago, Burlington & Quincy (CB&Q) railroad barons John Murray Forbes and the Thayers of Boston. Their agent managed both their railroad and the coal companies from CB&Q headquarters in downtown Chicago. The synergy between coal company and railroad was obvious: the CB&Q railroad network had tracks across the plains, where wood was so expensive that all the trains ran coal-fired engines.[43] Variations in coal prices strongly affected both railroad and mine because the slightest change in coal prices could drastically change operating costs. In the winter of 1873–1874, when the crash hit Chicago, Forbes's agent complained that hundreds of Chicago families failed to pay their coal bills: "The demand for coal [is] light and collections for what is sold exceedingly slow."[44] He was sure that CW&V had to push down the piece rate paid to miners during the contract talks scheduled for June 1, 1874. But he was also sure that the Irish, English, Scottish, and Welsh miners of Braidwood, Illinois, would stoutly resist.[45]

Their solution was to bring in strikebreakers in advance of a strike. For as little as $10 apiece, they could get central European miners all the way from Kladno with little more effort than sending a telegram.[46] Workers came overland to Hamburg, overseas to New York, and overland again to Chicago, all on a single pouch of tickets issued by confidential railway agents, men who made a 2.5 percent commission.[47] In June 1874, one thousand Kladno miners arrived to be deposited at the CW&V town of Braidwood, about sixty-five miles southwest of Chicago.[48]

The Kladno miners followed the paths traveled by the CB&Q's

rural settlers; the only difference was their final destination. Like the immigrants bound for farms, the miners would have made a minimal down payment for a package that included passage to America, tickets to Chicago, and the half-acre plots of land that the company mortgaged to the miners of Braidwood. Immigration agents in Castle Garden, New York, regularly accepted these through tickets and mortgages as evidence that immigrants already had jobs waiting for them and generally admitted them through to Chicago without further inspection. Over a few years, the cost would be taken out of their pay envelopes.[49] It was not until 1885 that the Foran Act made this mortgage-transportation-contract system illegal, though employers continued to use it to attract workers from over borders and across oceans.[50]

In the spring of 1874, before Tony was a year old, an American railway agent contacted the Cermaks. It was an old pattern: since the 1850s American railway agents of the New England Emigrant Aid Company had been dispatched to the countryside in Britain, Prussia, Norway, Sweden, Denmark, and Austria-Hungary to find distressed (but not impoverished) farmers to grow wheat on the prairies of Kansas and Iowa. Farmers from as far away as Poland, Hungary, or Bohemia made down payments on Iowa or Nebraska land, then paid for the land and their passage over a period of less than five years. The aid associations, as agents of the railroads, shipped immigrants with their household goods all the way to the Missouri River plains, where they could begin planting.[51] Railway agents in Europe could issue tickets for HAPAG, Lloyd, or Cunard steamers, earning 2 to 10 percent of the price of the ticket.[52] A contract labor law passed by Congress in 1864 allowed railway agents to make the same offers to emigrant workers. In Europe, employers could offer a worker a half-acre mortgage on a small plot in a company town; the price of transportation tickets was simply added onto the mortgage price. By this device workers were not technically indentured servants but settlers who worked off their land claim through hourly wages.[53]

When an agent approached Anton's father about traveling to America at a discount rate, the family made a decision. Anton would not grow up in a country where he could not vote but would have to fight if a pointless war broke out with the Prussians, Russians, or Turks. In late April 1874, they left on a train for Hamburg, a steamer for New York, and an emigrant train to Chicago. "I didn't come over on the Mayflower," Cermak later joked, "but I came over as soon as I could."[54]

Anton would have come with his parents in a sealed third-class train from Prague, across the Austrian-Prussian border, to Hamburg.[55] There they would be inspected at the docks before entering a ship in steerage class, a place belowdecks with airholes that let in the salt breezes. For eleven and a half days they would move between the cheap bunks and the standing area, cheek by jowl with thousands of other westbound travelers.[56] On Anton's first birthday, a New York state physician examined him and his parents.[57] After their inspection, railway employees locked them into American immigrant cars—boxcars with benches nailed to the walls, holes in the floor for human waste, and small airholes cut into the sides. After thirty-six hours of nonstop travel they arrived in Chicago.[58]

After the infant Anton and his parents arrived in Chicago, they waited briefly before the CW&V shuttled them onto railway cars bound for the mining town of Braidwood.[59] Tony's father was thoroughly familiar with coal mining; at age twenty-six he would have had more than sixteen years of experience in Bohemian mines, but he and his neighbors may not have suspected that John Murray Forbes and Nathaniel Thayer were bringing them to Braidwood to be strikebreakers. The miners may have guessed it when they saw armed agents of Pinkerton's Detective Agency waiting for them outside the cars. They would have been certain when they realized the Pinkertons were guarding them against the immigrant English, Irish, and Scottish workers gathered at the loading dock outside town. Pinkerton's men were bolstered by Chicago toughs who had been issued guns in Chicago and given the authority to ensure that the CW&V railroad got its coal, that the CB&Q trains ran, and that Chicago wheat got to Liverpool.[60]

As a skilled miner, Tony's father would certainly have realized that their arrival threatened the Braidwood strikers. Despite the language barrier, the strikers tried to convince the new arrivals to return to Chicago by offering to pay their rail fare.[61]

It must have been a peculiar exchange indeed. As the emperor Franz Joseph knew, Kladno miners were among the most militant workers in Austria-Hungary. Some were already members of the workers' educational organizations that had formed in Prague in 1872 to demand a ten-hour workday and a reduction in housing rents. In that year their newspaper and the printed speeches of their chief theoretician, J. B. Pecka, had already been confiscated and banned by the Prague police. While Anton's father was no communist, some who traveled with him certainly were.[62] One can only imagine the scene at the CW&V mining company when the superintendent learned that the men he had brought from Kladno to break the Braidwood strike included some of the best-organized socialists and communists in Europe! In any case, it appears that the Bohemian miners refused to break the strike.

Quite against the expectations of the CW&V, the Braidwood strike and lockout ended in a draw. The company was forced to make concessions, the most important of which was that the management sit down to talk with the leaders of the strike. The rate for coal fell slightly while the company made concessions on the price paid to mule drivers, the boys who drove the carts from the coal face to the trains.[63]

In less than ten years this would be young Anton's job. Meanwhile, his father and his neighbors built a house on their half acre of land. Because Anton's father could not afford to carpet the floor, he painted the floors yellow to give the house the appearance of having carpets. Over the next dozen years the family bounced between Czech neighborhoods in Chicago and the Braidwood mines. While wages were high in Chicago, high prices, cramped housing, and uneven employment sent Anton's father back again and again to the coalfields one hundred feet below Braidwood.[64]

In the mostly Czech neighborhoods of South Braidwood, Chicago's Pilsen, and Chicago's Little California, Anton's father and mother could speak their own tongue, a Slavic language with words in common with Russian and Polish. Tony's father and mother never learned more than a few words of English. As former subjects of Franz Joseph, they would have spoken a little German, but like many Czechs they shied from German as the language of the official bureaucracy and ruling class. Young Anton's education was limited to less than five years.

CRASH POLITICS

UNSANCTIONED PRIVATE ARMIES proliferated in the wake of the 1873 panic. While the Pinkertons had failed to break the strike in Braidwood, they succeeded in breaking the Workingmen's Benevolent Association in Pennsylvania.[65] In the former states of the Confederacy, private militias were bringing an end to the political power of former slaves.

The crash had brought the reemergence of Democrats in the 1874 Congress, and their growing power there led to a rethinking of Reconstruction. In 1875, 1876, and 1877, Democrats in the House withheld military appropriations, leaving soldiers unpaid for months at a time.

While small companies of Union soldiers had been stationed in southern states to protect the voting rights of African-Americans, there were
fewer than a thousand in the southern states after 1873, and even they
were being rapidly demobilized.[66]

In the South, declining commodity prices for cotton met rising state
costs for education and railroads. The economic downturn whipsawed
the rural South. Anger at Republicans in power in the South reached
a high point. While the Klan had disappeared before the panic, after
the panic southern Democrats in South Carolina, Florida, and Louisiana organized into "gun clubs" that openly terrorized black voters and
threatened Republican control of legislatures. These gun clubs began
to destroy the legitimacy of the fragile coalition between white and
black southerners that had created the Republican Party in the South;
they would make for the bloodiest election in the history of the nation.
In South Carolina alone, these armed white gangs put down a strike
wave in coastal areas of the state, initiated the "Ned Tennant Riots,"
and started the Hamburg riots. Scores of black men were disarmed and
killed. After the 1876 election, two governments—one Democratic,
one Republican—operated side by side in South Carolina and Louisiana for months, each claiming legitimacy and calling on military appropriations to put down the other. When the outgoing president, Ulysses
S. Grant, failed to act, Democratic militias claimed all three states in
1877. They called their seizure of power "Redemption."[67]

In business terms, the long-term effects of the panic of 1873 were
perverse. For the largest manufacturing companies in the United
States—those with guaranteed contracts and rebate deals with the
still-surviving railroads—the panic years were golden. The Chicago,
Wilmington, and Vermillion Coal Company grew rapidly. Likewise, the
steelmaker Andrew Carnegie and the oil refiner John D. Rockefeller
had contracts with the Pennsylvania Railroad and thus enough working
capital to finance their own continuing growth.[68] For smaller industrial
firms that relied on seasonal demand and outside capital, the situation
was dire. As capital reserves dried up, so did their industries. Carnegie
and Rockefeller bought out their competitors at fire-sale prices. This
was the beginning of the period of industrial concentration that has
sometimes been called the Gilded Age.

It should not be surprising that the most successful oligopolists
after the panic relied on regional railroad monopolies that had been
built before then. Thomas Scott of the Pennsylvania Railroad is a name
that is little remembered; he lost a fortune in 1873, though he kept his

position as vice president. His old friends succeeded, however. His telegrapher, Andrew Carnegie, had first acted as a "beard" for Scott in the late 1860s, receiving preferential contracts for the rolled steel and bar iron that the Penn required and secretly kicking back fees to Scott. John D. Rockefeller, too, participated in the South Improvement Company, a plan inspired by Scott and the Pennsylvania board to monopolize the transportation of oil from western Pennsylvania to the coast. As Scott's complex steel and petroleum monopoly schemes faltered, the beneficiaries who picked up the pieces were Rockefeller and Carnegie. The panic of 1873 converted them from functionaries into capitalists.[69] Posterity—and a little philanthropy—turned them from capitalists into visionaries.

As the panic deepened, ordinary Americans who worked in the hundreds of thousands of smaller firms suffered terribly. A cigar maker named Samuel Gompers who was young in 1873 later recalled that with the panic "economic organization crumbled with some primeval upheaval." Between 1873 and 1877, as many smaller factories and workshops shuttered their doors, tens of thousands of workers—many former Civil War soldiers—became transients. The words "tramp" and "bum," both indirect references to unemployed former soldiers, became commonplace American terms. Relief rolls exploded in major cities, with 25 percent unemployment (100,000 workers) in New York City alone. Unemployed workers demonstrated in Boston, Chicago, and New York in the winter of 1873–1874 demanding public work. In New York's Tompkins Square in 1874, police entered the crowd with clubs and beat up thousands of men and women. The most violent strikes in American history followed the panic. In 1875 the secret labor group in Pennsylvania's coalfields known as the Molly Maguires exchanged gunfire with the Coal and Iron Police, a private force commissioned by the state.

If violence appeared the most direct result of the 1873 downturn, some entrepreneurs found new ways to profit from the sorrows of the poor and the newly rich providers of cheap wheat. In Chicago, alcohol became a much more regular part of city life after the panic. When the mayor and reformer Joseph Medill hurriedly left the city after a physical breakdown in 1873, a new form of machine politics came after him. At the head of the machine was the political boss, gambling parlor operator, saloon keeper, and all-around crime lord Michael C. McDonald. Newspapers called him a protector of criminals and "King of the Tigers" who ruled the city from a collection of bordellos and gambling dens in downtown Chicago called the Store. McDonald had gotten his start as a child when he peddled candy and newspapers on the Chicago, Burlington & Quincy Railroad. He soon learned that the wealthy farmers who came to Chicago to sell their grain could be easily conned; he called these easy marks the "Granger element," after the independent political movement of Illinois wheat farmers. By the end of 1873, McDonald provided liquor, gambling, and prostitution to Grangers easily relieved of their money; for those who resisted his wiles, he also controlled an underworld crew of bunko artists, confidence men, and corrupt policemen who could shake down the rest. The financial power of the McDonald operation, along with his many employees, business associates, and suppliers, helped him assemble a multiethnic political machine that controlled Chicago's First Ward. Political opponents referred to organized crime's control of the Chicago Democratic Party in the first decade after 1873 as McDonaldism.[70]

To combat such institutions, a female reform organization, calling itself the Woman's Christian Temperance Union (WCTU), formed in 1874. It was a confusing organization; newspapers labeled it a "women's crusade." Some of its members believed that male workers' hard times could be attributed to their own vices, vices that they passed down to their children. Others pointed out that women and children in particular suffered when men turned to alcohol in times of economic distress. Female reformers in the WCTU would stand outside saloons in the winter and try to record the names of men who entered, pray for their recovery, and seek to persuade barkeepers to close down.[71]

In central and eastern Europe, times were even harder. Many political analysts blamed the crisis on a combination of foreign banks and Jews. Rather than blaming the chancellor or the emperor, German politicians began to refer to the system of imperially supported banks as the Strousberg system, lashing the name of a Jewish railroad promoter to the crash. Perversely, conservatives blamed Eduard Lasker, a Jewish member of the Prussian parliament, for calling attention to the corruption in the imperial railway system in January and February 1873, arguing that his criticisms had somehow caused the crash in May.[72] Throughout central Europe and Russia, nationalistic political leaders (or agents of the Russian czar) embraced a new, sophisticated brand of anti-Semitism that proved appealing to thousands who had lost their livelihoods in the panic.[73]

By 1881, an eight-year program of vituperation against Jews reached its zenith. A few months after Czar Alexander II was assassinated by revolutionaries, anti-Semitic leaders throughout the Russian Empire convinced peasants that Jews were behind the killing. The anti-Semites claimed that before he died, the czar had signed a document calling for Orthodox peasants to seize what they labeled "the ill-gotten wealth of the Christ-killers." Murder, rape, and pillage followed in the Jewish pogroms of 1881–1882. In the heartland of Russia as in the American South, rural people had found a scapegoat for the crash: aliens in their own midst.

1877

IN MARCH 1877 the so-called Railway Kings finally agreed to stop their rate war. Cornelius Vanderbilt of the New York Central, Hugh J. Jewett of the Erie, John W. Garrett of the Baltimore & Ohio (B&O), and Thomas Scott of the Pennsylvania abandoned attempts to divide the proceeds of Chicago's coastal traffic by percentage and instead agreed to turn over the forwarding of goods to a central pool, which they called the Trunk Line Association. As Garrett put it to his banker Junius Morgan, "The great principle upon which we all joined to act was to earn more and to spend less."[74] The pooling of resources also apparently involved a joint agreement to lower wages across the systems and the creation of a fund that railroad managers could draw from in the event of a strike.[75] After 1877, many manufacturers would embrace the "pool" as a model for preventing competition and raising prices.[76]

Thomas Scott of the Pennsylvania Railroad decided that he would be the first "to earn more and to spend less" by cutting pay an additional 10 percent for all of his workers. He and the other railroad presidents had already done so in the panic month of October 1873. By 1877, he presumed, with tens of thousands laid off by other, smaller railroad lines, unemployed workers willing to accept these lower rates would be readily available. Scott reached a special deal with the locomotive engineers—the elite among railway workers and the hardest to replace—but he fully expected the freight handlers, firemen, brakemen, and other yard workers to balk. On June 1, 1877, he announced the second 10 percent cut.

When news of the pay cut arrived, workers were prepared to push back. Some of Scott's workers had joined the new Trainmen's Union, a secret organization open to all workers. Earlier in the year the Trainmen's Union had learned of the Trunk Line Association's plan to coordinate pay cuts across the railroads. The union's president, Robert

Ammon, predicted that if engineers and brakemen walked out, the train would simply run "doubleheaders," long trains with two engines. President Ammon later said that union members agreed "that if the railroad companies [put on doubleheaders] that they would kick." In other words, they would strike. In the 1870s, unions were rather different from today: a mix of social club, insurance organization, and burial society. Most states treated them as illegal "combinations." To protect themselves, they instituted secret rituals for joining and made members swear never to reveal brother members. Scott learned of the organization in May, then hired private detectives from Pinkerton, the same agency that had been hired to put down the miners' strike in Braidwood. A few Pinkerton agents posed as railroad workers, infiltrated the Trainmen's Union, and identified its leaders. By the time of the pay cut in July, the organization had spread to other lines, including John W. Garrett's Baltimore & Ohio, which was also thoroughly infiltrated by the Pinkertons.[77]

In July 1877, firemen on the B&O began stepping off their trains at Martinsburg, West Virginia, the central repair shops for B&O trains between Chicago and the East Coast. Some were inspired by the Trainmen's Union, others by the actions of their brother workers. Dozens of cars quickly piled up. Local people—women, children, families of the strikers, and unemployed workers—joined in the protests. While the Trainmen's Union tried to coordinate a national strike, the line between a strike and a mob was difficult to judge. There was general rowdiness in Martinsburg, with buildings broken into and tracks torn up to prevent the trains from moving. It is difficult now to understand how widely despised the so-called Railway Kings were. Their trains passed through many cities day and night at forty miles per hour often without signals or crossings of any kind, regularly killing children and horses.[78] Not surprisingly, the strike became a vast and formless riot.

It spread from there. President Rutherford B. Hayes, a Republican, called on federal troops to restore order, but the unrest continued through July. Democrats in Congress claimed that there had been a deal—called the Compromise of 1877—that had given Hayes the White House in exchange for the removal of federal troops from the South. Hayes, believing there was no such compromise, had refused to do so. Democrats in control of the House blocked army appropriations.[79] So when Hayes called in troops to put down the 1877 strike that had moved from Martinsburg to Baltimore, Pittsburgh, and Philadelphia, most of the soldiers had not been paid for months. The Sixth

Maryland Regiment fought strikers in Baltimore while federal troops fired into the crowds in Philadelphia. Hayes's use of federal troops infuriated workers—many of whom had served in the Union army just over a decade earlier. The crowds grew larger. In late July, mobs burned railroad shops in Baltimore, Albany, Pittsburgh, and Martinsburg. In Pittsburgh, Chicago, and St. Louis sympathy strikes by miners, steelworkers, and other workers followed. Only New England and the Deep South were excluded from the violence. By August, more than one hundred locomotives and two thousand railway cars had been destroyed.[80]

The 1873 crisis thus helped to bring about the first national strike in the United States. The strike led states to reorganize their state militias into national guards to stiffen their resolve against striking workers. State militias in West Virginia, for example, had disbanded and joined the strikers. That would end. The National Guard, composed of professionals and equipped with modern weapons, would be used in industrial disputes more than one hundred times over the next twenty-five years. Armories were built in major cities in the North to ensure that troops would be on hand and well armed for later strikes. So while antagonism toward African-Americans increased in the South and anger at Jews percolated in central and eastern Europe in the 1870s, the lavish funding for National Guard units after 1877 suggests a general unease about immigrant, industrial workers and the mobs that might form around them.[81]

While industrial workers participated in a large number of strikes after 1873, this seldom translated into political organization, unlike the experience of workers in Europe, Australia, or even Canada. For industrial workers after 1873, neither political party was fully available to them. The largely immigrant Catholic Irish and Italian workers continued to vote Democratic. The generally Protestant German, Swedish, and African-American workers tended to vote Republican.[82] The new immigrants of Austria-Hungary would bring a different dynamic to politics in American cities. Cheap American wheat had destroyed the livelihood of their parents; ships bearing American wheat to Europe bore them back in its wake. It would take another financial crisis to bind this substantial group of industrial workers together. When that crisis came to Chicago in 1893, Anton Cermak and millions like him who had left Europe as subjects of German-speaking emperors only to become the subjects of Boston-owned coal companies were finally positioned to demand a different kind of life.

CHAPTER TEN

Crosses of Gold

EW WOULD HAVE expected Anton Cermak to become mayor of Chicago if they had seen him in the year he earned his "M.D.," as he later called it, at age thirteen. That year he began work as a mule driver in a mining shaft for the Chicago, Wilmington, and Vermillion Coal Company.[1] At the tender age of fourteen, Cermak was well known in the coal town of Braidwood as a prankster, a gang leader, and a very mean drunk. At fifteen he was getting into fights and sassing constables.

"When he had a little beer," declared an old friend, "he couldn't be handled by God, by the boss, by anybody." When Cermak and his teenage friends were nearly broke, they would squat behind a Braidwood bar and "shoot the can"—passing cheap, canned Chicago beer from mouth to mouth.

The ethyl alcohol that Cermak swallowed was produced by a complex reaction. Someone first harvests the fungi that form on sugarcane stalks, then mixes them with sugar, water, hops, and malt. The fungi then absorb the sugar, expelling alcohol and carbon dioxide until the concentration of alcohol is so high that it kills the fungi completely; at this stage the mixture is suitable for human consumption. When Cermak raised the can to his lips, the alcohol quickly crossed from stomach to bloodstream, then crossed the blood-brain barrier. If young Tony overdid it, those distilled sugars made him unsettled and violent.[2] Sugar and its by-products have had a long and interesting career in human history.

We should not be surprised to find that sugar, just like wool, cotton, and wheat before it, could be at the center of a financial crisis. Whether raw or in its distilled form as beer, rye, and rum, sugar had helped turn nearby Chicago from the wheat entrepôt it was in 1873 into the caloric export city of the world. By the 1890s Chicago exported concentrated, liquefied, and canned calories. Sugar lay at the heart of American industrialization, forming its most crucial international export: manufactured food. And sugar in both crystal and alcoholic forms neatly divided the nation's politics. The sugar lobby, the strongest in America, had a lock on the most powerful faction of the Republican Party. The beer lobby, the second-strongest lobby in the country, would be Cermak's route to power in the Democratic Party. Partisan conflicts over the sugar that passed into Chicago and other food-exporting cities brought about the most devastating and confusing financial panic America ever experienced.

Tony Cermak was a "hoodlum," a term first coined by the upstanding citizens of San Francisco to describe the epidemic of gangs of children, led by teenagers. In the 1880s, Cermak's gang of Czech, Irish, and Scottish children was known as the "tough babies," and he was its undisputed leader. He schooled his young charges in the sorts of lessons all hoodlums needed to know: how a broomstick could knock the tiles off a roof and which offensive Czech curses when shouted from an alleyway would stop a man in his tracks. Only in Braidwood, it was said, did young Irish boys assimilate by learning Czech. When an Irish-American justice of the peace hauled Tony into court for disturbing the peace, the officer could not pronounce the boy's last name, calling him "Sharmock." The name stuck.

But destroying roofs wasn't Tony's only forte. In 1889, Tony's fellow mule skinners elected him to negotiate a pay increase with the foreman. It did not end well. "So you want a raise, do you?" the foreman shot back. "I'll give you a raise—right up the shaft." Tony quickly found another job, only to lose it again when word got around that young "Sharmock" was a labor agitator. At age sixteen, his days in the mining town of Braidwood were over.

Shortly afterward, Tony snuck onto a boxcar and rode it to Chicago. The young man marveled at the city at first. He was drawn to Pilsen, the Czech section south and west of the city center. He would soon dominate it. In 1890, after a brief career driving a horse for a streetcar company, Tony bought a $3 horse and launched his own scrap-hauling business. He also joined another saloon gang at Hvorka's Tavern in Pilsen; Hvorka's was his entrée into politics. In the Czech slums of Pilsen young Tony Cermak became a minor functionary—a ward heeler—in the Democratic Party's political machine. The combination of careers—freight hauling and politics—proved rewarding. Tony's wagon became the official wagon for the party; from it he doled out firewood and coal before elections. His political connections helped him secure exclusive contracts to collect the refuse wood from the McCormick Reaper Works and the Teckmeyer Box works, both adjoining Pilsen. His hauling business and his political influence grew together.

By 1890, the Czech town of Pilsen was no longer on the outskirts of the city of Chicago. The reaper works, stockyards, and breweries were at the center of the city's working life. Chicago by then was one level up in the food chain from the wheat fields of the Midwest: it was the beef, pork, and manufactured food metropolis of the Western Hemisphere. Less than a mile south of Pilsen stood Chicago's Union Stockyards, a broad and muddy field established by the railroad trunk lines for the delivery of live animals from as far away as Texas. Buyers wandered through the labyrinth of mooing and squealing animals offering prices by hand gestures. A nod and a written ticket closed the deal.[3] When wheat prices were low, the slaughterhouses would collect the lesser grades as feed; after a brief period of fattening, the animals would be herded into factories to be lifted upside down onto a revolving chain, from which position they would be scalded, skinned, and dismembered by men bearing sharp blades. Because the variety of animal sizes prevented automation of these tasks, blood-soaked workers tore at the animals as if driven by demons. This was the new Chicago.[4]

Tony had arrived in the city just a few years before another international exhibition, an event just as daring and confident as the one Franz Joseph had planned for Austria in 1873. Eighteen ninety-three was four hundred years after Columbus's arrival at Hispaniola, and Chicago planned to celebrate all that the great man had discovered before his troops killed all that island's inhabitants. In the swamp south and east of the city, Chicago architects would build an orderly "White City," one that would show off the mechanical inventions of a truly modern age. Like the emperor's exposition of 1873, it would display the variety of languages, foods, and clothing of the world. Organized by the architect Daniel Burnham, this "Paris on the Prairie" would boast magnificent sheds dressed up with plaster of Paris to look like multistory buildings. Visitors would marvel at replicas of old sailing ships, massive landscape paintings, manicured gardens, and the first Ferris wheel in the world. (A jealous Franz Joseph saw it in 1893 and had one built in his old exposition grounds in Vienna a few years later.) Snuggled next to the actual Chicago—now knee-deep in animal blood, taverns, whorehouses, and gambling parlors—the exposition would demonstrate all that the wickedest city in the world could aspire to. Luckily for Cermak, Pilsen was next door to the White City, and there was a great deal of actual cleaning required to build a spotless paradise in the swamps of Lake Michigan. Cermak, with more than a dozen horse-drawn wagons, had secured the cleaning and hauling contract from the city.

It was easy then and it is easy now to dwell on the White City and miss the real and ugly work of American industrialization in the late nineteenth century. We are accustomed to viewing America as the nation of the lightbulb, the Ferris wheel, and the elevator, all of which were on display. But as Cermak would have noted, the fair made its meager fortune on overpriced food, the leavings of which he and his men had to clean up. Indeed, from 1871 until World War I, America's most important and fastest-growing export was manufactured food, mostly canned, bottled, and preserved. This export's value far exceeded finished manufactures until 1900. Only America's export commodities like corn and cotton were larger.[5]

"Food manufacture" took place in the gritty parts of town, not its temples. The slaughterhouses and canneries of Chicago, Cleveland, St. Louis, and western California exported food that could be preserved on shelves and in cupboards for months at a time, and they required wagonloads of sugar. Fructose and sucrose had been key to canning since the Middle Ages, when cooks made "preserves" by boiling down fruits and vegetables into a sealed gelatinous mixture so sludgy that bacteria could not successfully reproduce in it. While some fruits had enough natural sugars to preserve themselves, most canning required extra doses of sugar to set.

Beer too required large quantities of sugar. This was no small matter to Chicago's Democratic machine. The South Side machine, all the way up to Pilsen, was run by "Fatty" Cerveny, a 450-pound agent of the Monarch beer company, one of the largest breweries on Lake Michigan. Saloons were a key organizing place for the Democratic Party in Chicago and elsewhere. Saloon keepers gave free food to drinking customers, provided space for meetings, organized railroad excursions for picnics, made bathrooms available, and even provided small loans to workers down on their luck. Small wonder that the saloon keepers—usually dedicated to a single brewery—often became political figures.[6]

The Democratic Party latched onto one kind of caloric politics—the beer voters—and never let go. But beer was not the only lucrative and politically sensitive part of America's dependence on manufactured food. Because cane sugar required a tropical climate, the United States could produce little of it domestically. Thus manufacturing canned food required considerable imports, necessitating a fifteen-fold increase in American sugar imports between 1800 and 1890. So much sugar came into the United States, in fact, that by 1889 the tariff on sugar raised $50 million a year for the government, roughly one-sixth of all federal revenue. The result was a whopping budget surplus.[7] American exports of manufactured foods, not just in Chicago but in most major canneries in the country, depended on imported cane sugar. When Congress tinkered with the cane sugar tariff, it would bring down Chicago's White City and cause the real city next to it to come tumbling down.

The concentration of American manufacturing in food also concentrated wealth and political power. One of the most powerful trusts in the country had its headquarters on Wall Street and its manufacturing base on the docks of Williamsburg, New York's waterfront. Henry O. Havemeyer's sugar-refining industry relied on patented techniques for refining cheap, low-grade sugar into sugar cubes. His sugar cubes had made the family one of the richest in the world, friends of the Morgans and darlings of New York society. The family's fascination with impressionist paintings—previously dismissed by art connoisseurs—had turned the New York art world on its head. At the beck and call of New York's sugar baron was Senator Nelson W. Aldrich of Rhode Island, chairman of the Finance Committee. Aldrich was one of the most powerful men in Congress, and because Congress had seriously weakened the presidency during Reconstruction, that made him one of the most powerful men in the country. Aldrich's precipitate actions on Havemeyer's behalf would bring about the nation's next financial panic.[8]

Havemeyer and his allies formed the Sugar Trust, which depended on a sugar tariff that blocked cheap imports. "The Mother of all Trusts," the sugar baron frankly stated later, "is the Customs Tariff Bill." However, they faced a new competitor in Claus Spreckels, whose California Sugar Refinery stretched out on a spit of land near San Francisco. Spreckels had a close friendship with the king of Hawaii and an 1875 reciprocity treaty with the kingdom that excluded the island nation from the sugar tariff. The Sugar Trust, having no ability to adjust the treaty, fumed. Exemption from the tax allowed Spreckels to ship sugar more than twenty-four hundred miles from his plantations in Hawaii to San Francisco at a price that let him undersell the high prices set by the Sugar Trust. Because of cheap Hawaiian sugar, the Sugar Trust's monopoly stopped just east of the Sierra Nevada. When Spreckels threatened to expand his operation to the Midwest in the late 1880s, the Sugar Trust fought back.[9]

In a bold move Havemeyer pushed Senator Aldrich to rewrite the tariff. The McKinley Tariff, proposed by the congressman and future president William McKinley, would eliminate the tariff on raw sugar. This gambit would eliminate the Hawaiian price advantage. Spreckels would continue to ship without a tariff from faraway Hawaii, but the Sugar Trust would pay almost nothing by comparison to import from nearby Cuba. Senator Aldrich could make this drastic move in part because of new operational rules in Congress, passed in 1890, when Republicans finally regained control of the House of Representatives, the Senate, and the presidency. It was the first time they had controlled both the legislative and the executive branches of government since the panic of 1873. Under the "Reed Rules," passed in the House in 1890, and a comparable set of rules in the Senate, congressional majorities could virtually eliminate all the procedural maneuvering that Democrats had used for thirty years to block Republican legislation. The majority party in Congress became suddenly, surprisingly, efficient.

The Sugar Trust could sell the new tariff policy neither as free trade—which Republicans rarely supported—nor as a means to destroy its California rival. Rather, Aldrich argued, the sugar duty taxed consumers too much. Lifting the tariff would deliver a "cheaper breakfast." To enlist the support of legislators from Louisiana, which produced sugarcane, and from the Midwest, where sugar beets grew, Republicans offered a two-cent-per-pound government subsidy for all raw sugar produced at home.[10]

Some questioned the logic of rapidly drawing down federal revenue with a sudden drop in the sugar tariff and a government subsidy for beets. "Why should the government appropriate annually from the Treasury $7,000,000 to give to the Sugar Trust and not grant the same favor to every American industry?" blasted the *Wheeling Register*.[11] But the new tariff would do just that. Congress also resolved to further spend its surplus down by buying silver from the politically powerful western states of Nevada, Colorado, and Arizona, whose power in the Senate was strong and whose population in the early years depended almost entirely on silver mining. Because western mining states generally favored attempts to "inflate" the currency with silver, congressmen paired this Sherman Silver Purchase Act with the McKinley Tariff favored by congressmen in northeastern states. The two measures together would ensure support from inflators and deflators, high-tariff and low-tariff men.

This sugar-and-silver recipe rapidly drained the federal budget. The

McKinley Tariff surrendered $50 million a year in sugar duties and then doled out millions more in a subsidy to the few dozen Louisiana plantations that produced sugar commercially; the Sherman Act committed the federal government to buying—at inflated prices—$50 million worth of silver every year. The bill created a separate silver-backed currency called Treasury notes but prevented the government from forcing these notes into circulation.[12] The Treasury notes, because they would have traded at a substantial discount, scarcely entered circulation at all. In this double stroke more than $100 million flew out of the federal budget each year.

But in a country where manufactured food and its sugar were such vital parts of the economy, this tinkering had drastic effects on the international scene and among American voters. Sugar plantation owners in Hawaii, to start with, determined that if the United States were to annex Hawaii, they would get the same subsidy that Louisiana received. The planters promptly fomented a revolution against the Hawaiian queen.[13] Once McKinley's tariff caused total yearly expenditures to exceed $1 billion, Democrats labeled the Republican-dominated Congress the Billion-Dollar Congress. Between the fall of 1890 and the spring of 1892 more revelations emerged of the Sugar Trust's purchase of Republican votes in Congress. Democrats made the Sugar Trust's purchase of votes in Congress the keystone of their 1892 platform. The platform called the McKinley Tariff a "fraud on the labor of the great majority of the American people" and "the culminating atrocity of class legislation." Even the Republican stalwart Carl Schurz shocked his party when he declared the McKinley Tariff "a bill to reward the signers to the campaign fund and to induce further contributions." In the Sugar Trust's corruption of Congress, Democrats found an issue that helped them win elections.[14]

Even as Democrats gained control of Congress in the elections of 1892, the actions of the Billion-Dollar Congress continued to create difficulties for the federal government that helped push the U.S. economy toward crisis. For one, the ratio of silver to gold values had been established since the days of Andrew Jackson as sixteen to one. But silver strikes in Nevada, Colorado, and Arizona, along with advances in mine engineering, threw vast quantities of silver on the market. Congress wrote the Silver Purchase Act to buy most of the silver the nation produced and thus prop up its value. Despite the exorbitant prices the government paid, it did nothing to stanch silver's declining value.[15]

As the mint gained silver, it lost gold, which was a serious problem. Ever since the 1820s the United States was prone to raids on its gold reserves. With a bimetallic currency and a fixed relationship between the metals, Americans who came to the mint with national currency could demand payment in silver or gold.[16] With hard silver artificially overpriced given its declining value, they invariably demanded gold, making the silver deposits in the mint almost useless. Between 1870 and 1890, Prussia, France, Austria-Hungary, Russia, and India converted from a partial silver currency to an entirely gold-backed currency, further lowering the value of silver. These countries briefly paid premiums for gold in order to acquire the reserves necessary to switch to the gold standard. Because America alone allowed the free export of gold, the U.S. Mint became the preferred source for international gold purchases. On its own this may not have been a problem, but the government was also losing revenue.[17]

Gold exports from the U.S. Mint occurred at the same time as the fiscal draining of the federal government. From 1890 to 1893—with sugar now on the free list—the federal government went from having an embarrassing budget surplus to an embarrassing deficit. The gold and fiscal drain came together in late April 1893 when the value of gold in U.S. vaults dropped below the magic number of $100 million, the number that most foreign bankers believed would allow the government to simultaneously pay its debts and guarantee its currency. In the universe of national and international trade $100 million in gold was a tiny store of value, but it was an important proxy for the stability of U.S. dollars.

In the 1890s the U.S. Treasury had none of the tools that European central banks had to protect their gold supplies. Because the Bank of England and other European banks used their vault assets to accept bills of exchange (thus acting as lenders), they could raise or lower the percentage they charged to ensure that gold did not flow out too quickly. If gold reserves dropped, the national banks could demand higher rates for lending and thus keep more gold in vaults. The U.S. Treasury could not do this. Following Jackson's bank war in the 1830s, an irritated Congress had created a so-called Independent Treasury that was firewalled from the rest of the banking system. It was designed to prevent a recurrence of Jackson's "pet banks," where the banks of political allies received federal deposits. Thus the Treasury had its own vaults and could not ordinarily deposit funds in banks or accept deposits from them. It largely paid government bills, collected customs and other taxes, and provided gold for dollar bills.[18] It could not loan money on its assets.

With no interest-rate lever to affect the gold reserves, the Treasury was important to the American economy but weaker than any bank in controlling its reserves. Even though the gold assets in federal vaults were a tiny sum compared with the overall economy, that gold that the United States received for its tariffs ultimately guaranteed the stability of American dollar bills. Any foreign banker knew that he could redeem dollars for gold if he needed it. But because gold was so easy to export from the United States, any sufficiently large European central bank could buy up American gold to support its own currencies. Here was trouble.[19]

EUROPEAN BANKS WERE already edgy by 1893. Through the 1870s and 1880s the Baring Brothers had been investing spectacular sums in Argentina, hoping to reproduce in Buenos Aires the Chicago miracle of a food surplus and fantastic growth in manufactured food exports. In the Barings' eyes, first Argentine wheat, then Argentine beef, would flow from the pampas and make fortunes for all who invested in the magical city of Buenos Aires. Their hopes proved premature: the Argentine pampas could produce less than one-tenth of the U.S. wheat harvest and thus had little influence over global wheat prices.[20] The Buenos Aires market followed global prices set in Chicago rather than having the power to raise them by strategically reducing exports. Then, in 1890, a bloody revolution, crop failures, and rampant inflation in Argentina caused a dramatic decline in Baring fortunes. Baring Brothers was the Goldman Sachs of its day, an unassailable name in Atlantic finance, but with the "Baring panic" of 1890 those days were over. Between 1890 and 1893 the Bank of England and a coalition of London merchant bankers allowed Baring Brothers to temporarily reorganize into a joint-stock firm and issue shares to its debtors to raise capital.[21] The firm that had negotiated the Louisiana Purchase, survived 1837 unscathed, and watched its competitors crumble in 1857 had finally been brought down a peg. Investors throughout Europe, fearing that the Barings' woes would spread, began selling off securities—especially American securities—for gold.[22]

Luckily for the United States, the Chicago miracle kept on ticking for a few years between 1890 and 1893. A famine in southern Russia caused wheat prices to shoot up, buoying international demand for American breadstuffs and ensuring that gold and credit were still available. But in 1893, Argentina exported a huge percentage of its total wheat production to obtain currency to pay off the Baring loans. A fantastic harvest in Russia saw wheat production shoot up 38 percent in the same year, causing a glut in the world wheat supply. This glut of 1893 established what merchants throughout the world agreed would now be a new and lower floor for the international price of wheat.[23] At the end of the nineteenth century a new and lower floor in international wheat prices could cripple the American economy. American railroads, midwestern banks, western banks, and urban crossroads cities like Chicago all depended on $1 wheat bushels. Just as American institutions before 1819 had depended on $1 flour barrels and American institutions before 1837 had depended on cotton at twenty cents a pound, so the sudden drop in wheat prices had a similar effect on mortgages.[24] Banks in Omaha, Kansas, and California that had issued farm mortgages to wheat growers began defaulting.[25] Only Philip Armour and Gustavus Swift—who fattened their animals on cheap feed—were smiling.

As news of the Treasury Department's problem became visible, Americans developed an obsession with precious metals. Fights over silver and gold became frequent. According to one Populist newspaper, Republicans traveled the country declaring that if the Treasury Department purchased any more silver, "the country will go to the devil as if greased for the occasion."[26] Congressional Republicans and Democrats clung to the belief that one party or the other had screwed up the reserve currency, and thus the money supply, and thus the standing of America in the world economy. Many "goldbugs," strongest in the Northeast, blamed the silver in the Treasury vaults, regarding it as inflationary. Many southerners and westerners blamed the Treasury Department's stubborn commitment to gold. According to them, a lack of currency in the Midwest and the South caused farmers to sell instantly at harvest rather than holding back reserves to wait for price increases. They regarded gold as deflationary and the cause of cheap wheat and cheap cotton.

Like many modern economists, goldbugs and silverites overstated the influence of the money supply on the overall economy. They turned to supposedly eternal verities, proverbs, and finger wagging. As the goldbug Elijah Morse of Massachusetts put it, "Hercules on his journey once came to a point where there were two roads. . . . [W]e have come to two roads. Sound finance beckons us on to prosperity and national honor; 'free silver' and a debased currency beckon us on to financial ruin, dishonor, and disgrace."[27] Southern Democrats and western Republicans meanwhile raised the rooftops to demand an "honest dollar," one not made crooked by deflation. Senator John P. Jones of

Nevada declared, "If you have borrowed a dollar, and through a badly regulated money system are made to pay a dollar worth twenty-five per cent more than the dollar you borrowed, you are not paying the best money, but the worst money; not an honest dollar, but a swindling, dishonest dollar." Jones, it should be pointed out, owned the largest silver mine in Nevada.[28]

As congressmen debated silver and gold, unemployment in major American industries followed the panic of 1893, though the numbers unemployed can be only guessed at. Estimates range from two to four million. In 1933, Albert Ross Eckler of the Census Bureau created a simple method of measuring depressions. He made an "index" of six measurements, including railway receipts, imports, coal production, and pig iron production. This single and simplistic measurement would eventually be called the gross domestic product, or GDP. By Eckler's measure the 1893–1895 depression saw a 26 percent decline in GDP, a fall nearly as drastic as the 32 percent decline of 1873–1877.[29] But Eckler's numbers tell us effects, not causes.

The year 1893 in Europe, by comparison, saw no significant downturn in commodity prices or employment. France and Germany, both having put up tariff walls after the 1873 downturn, were aggressively seeking markets outside Europe but passed through 1893 without noting any substantial difference from previous years.[30] In 1893 few could explain why the United States seemed to be the peculiar sufferer internationally, though Australia did experience a banking crisis at about the same time. In the United States, no important drop in production or employment appeared before the crash. Nor did there seem to be investment mania as there was before 1837, 1857, or 1873, though railroads were probably overbuilt. Most recognized that the new depression had something to do with the awkward position of the U.S. Treasury. But after agreeing on that, silver fiends and goldbugs could not settle their differences.

In modern terms the 1893 American crisis resembles the sequence of capital flight, balance-of-payments crisis, and credit crunch that hit Mexico in 1994 and much of Asia in 1997. Distinctively American, it grew out of the machinations of a Sugar Trust intent on adjusting a U.S. tariff to secure its monopoly on American sugar imports. However, sugar was a crucial if little understood import that profoundly affected America's export sector in manufactured food, its relations with Hawaii, and its relations with Cuba. When the U.S. tax on sugar disappeared in 1890, it threatened the federal government's ability to pay its debts three years later. If the gold dollar became a weaker silver dollar, American dollar payments for debts to Europe would shrink in value. Those doubts about Americans' willingness to pay in gold combined with a sudden and irreversible drop in the price of wheat in 1893. It was America's first balance-of-payments crash since 1819.

Perhaps only Tony Cermak noted the irony: May 9 was his twentieth birthday. On that day the Chemical National Bank, one of Chicago's largest, failed catastrophically, inaugurating a string of business failures in the city.[31] It was twenty years almost to the day after the emperor's Vienna Exposition and the panic of 1873.

DEMOCRATS RESPOND TO THE PANIC

PRESIDENT GROVER CLEVELAND, a Democrat, had just been inaugurated to lead a party recently victorious in Congress but now in disarray because of the panic. Cleveland owed his 1893 return to the presidency (he had been president four years earlier) to midwestern defections: Republican voters who left to join the newly formed Populist Party. With Cleveland winning the three-way race, Democrats gained the presidency, the House, and the Senate for the first time since before the Civil War. A New York political reformer whose interest in reform stopped at crippling Tammany Hall's control of New York, Cleveland was close friends with New York lawyers and bankers. But for all that, he understood that the financial crisis had to do with international doubts about Americans.

After he was inaugurated in March, Cleveland called a special session of Congress in June to push through a repeal of the Silver Purchase Act, effectively splitting his own party over the issue of silver.[32] Yet by the fall of 1893 the repeal had done nothing to revive the American economy. That winter Jacob Coxey planned the first march on Washington, an "Army of the Commonweal," as he called it, made up of farmers, workers, and veterans who wanted the federal government to intervene in the economy with pensions, or public works jobs, or anything. By January 1894 it had become clear that at least seven separate Armies of the Commonweal composed of tens of thousands of men and women would converge on Washington to confront Congress.

In that same winter, President Cleveland arranged for U.S. bond sales in Europe through the J. P. Morgan syndicate. A large bond sale in Europe, Cleveland reasoned, would bring gold back to the Treasury and reassure European investors. The tough terms Morgan demanded from the government for selling its bonds netted him tens of millions of dollars and turned the Democratic Party even more strongly against its president. Yet the continued infusions of gold from Europe and a recovering U.S. Mint did little to bring investors back. The symbolic doubt about the value of the American dollar had made the American crash its own self-fulfilling prophecy.

As Cleveland saw it, European bondholders feared a replay of the American greenback days of December 30, 1861—that a U.S. Congress with a new party in control of the House, Senate, and presidency might declare silver-backed dollars to be payable for all debts public and private. For any foreign loan denominated in dollars, Americans would pay less. Fear of the convertibility of dollars, and fear of an Argentina-style inflation, led Europeans to redeem American debts for gold in April 1893 when they could be sure to get it.

So a few things—the sugar subsidy drain on the Treasury, a collapse in wheat prices, and a fear of how a Democratic Congress would manage the dollar—together led to a collapse in railroad bond prices, then American banks, then American stock prices. European bondholders had been cashing in debts since 1890, but by 1893 European grain dealers and millers were paying very little for America's wheat. Days after the gold reserves dropped under $100 million (April 30), the New York stock market crashed (May 5). "Capital refused to invest further and loans were called in," recalled the New York congressman George Washington Ray. "Depositors became panic-stricken and withdrew their deposits. Chimney nooks and old ladies' stockings became the banks of deposit."[33]

With no end to the panic in sight, Congress, controlled by Democrats, convened in August 1893. First on its list was to undo the budget deficit. Determined not to increase the excise tax on beer, Democrats settled on a progressive income tax, the first income tax to be passed in a time of peace. At the same time they would cut down the tariff whose complex rate structure seemed to tax poor consumers while benefiting the trusts in sugar and steel. After stout Republican resistance in the House and the Senate, Democrats pushed an income tax bill through Congress in early 1894, a 2 percent rate for incomes of more than $4,000. Four thousand a year was then a princely sum that exempted about 98 percent of Americans. Republicans and Democrats in New York, Massachusetts, and Pennsylvania cried out that this was sectional legislation. "The income tax is favored by the South," complained Congressman Ray of New York, "because it knows that it will not pay over from 3 to 5 per cent of it, and that the Republicans of the

North will have to pay for the great part of it."[34] Indeed the emergency income tax passed in the Civil War had drawn 60 percent of its revenue from New York, Massachusetts, and Pennsylvania.[35] It hardly mattered. A Republican-dominated Supreme Court declared the income tax unconstitutional the following year. The Wilson-Gorman tariff bill slightly revised the McKinley Tariff and reimposed a tariff on sugar to raise revenue. It seemed to have little effect at first, though it would soon spur a revolution in Cuba.

THE SUMMER OF CHICAGO

IT MAY HAVE been the Pullman strike in May 1894, which began eight miles south of the Columbian Exposition, that most shaped the post-panic landscape. It began as a local conflict. In response to the panic, Pullman cut wages in his company town without a corresponding cut in the rents he charged workers to live there. The carpenters, painters, and foundry workers who manufactured Pullman's famous sleeper cars had little in common with the engineers, firemen, and brakemen who had formed the American Railway Union (ARU), but because the union's leader, Eugene V. Debs, believed in setting up a wide tent for railway workers, he saw the benefits of allowing Pullman's workers to join. When Pullman's workers struck, the ARU (against Debs's wishes) called a sympathy strike to block the passage of Pullman's cars over any railroad in the country. By late June 1894 strikers had successfully blocked most of the railways going in and out of Chicago. Americans around the country felt it, as ARU strikers blocked regular trains bound for destinations as far away as Boston, Texas, and Arizona.[36]

Cleveland's attorney general, Richard Olney, intervened by telling railway officials to attach mail cars to stopped trains. The stopping of U.S. mail service—a federal offense—gave Olney the justification he needed. Olney, formerly counsel for the Chicago, Burlington and Quincy Railroad and still on retainer for the firm, persuaded Cleveland to ignore the state's governor (who called for neutrality) and to order federal troops into Chicago. While the Pullman strike had been peaceful enough, the arrival of federal troops in Chicago on July 5, against the orders of the Illinois governor, caused mayhem. On the day they arrived, angry townspeople set boxcars on fire, and troops fired into crowds. The White City finally felt the effects of the downturn when persons unknown set a fire in the World's Columbian Exposition, burning seven buildings to the ground.

Circuit and federal judges ordered the sympathy strike stopped; a later ruling on July 10, 1894, called for Debs and three other leaders of the strike to be imprisoned for contempt of court. Federal officers then subpoenaed the records of the Western Union Telegraph to produce all the telegrams that Debs and his strike coordinators had sent to strikers so that Olney could prepare the state's case. Rumors flew back and forth, including claims by the Chicago chief of police that the federal troops were hastily mustered hooligans who were suspiciously close to boxcars that had just been set alight. The Chicago chief believed the federal soldiers had set the fires themselves to justify their occupation of the city. As John Altgeld, the Democratic governor of Illinois, pointed out in his telegraphed protests to President Cleveland, "The Government, in enforcing the law, can not afford to be itself lawless." Lawlessness, it turned out, was a flexible category.

As the Chicago reformer Jane Addams recalled, "There had been nothing in my experience [before 1894] to reveal that distinct cleavage of society, which a general strike at least momentarily affords. . . . [D]uring all those dark days . . . the growth of class bitterness was most obvious." She admired Pullman and knew his workers well but was shocked to discover the growing gulf between her upper-class friends and Chicago's workers as the strike progressed through June and July.[37] An appalled Texas governor who had traveled to Chicago to visit the Columbian Exposition had seen the conflict firsthand. He declared the strike peaceful and the president's calling of troops both disorderly and a violation of states' rights. "This strike is but the preliminary of terrible times in this country," he declared when he returned to Texas. "Unless a change is made those fourteen-story buildings in Chicago will be bespattered with blood, brains, hair, hides, livers, and lights, and the horrors of the French revolution will be repeated two-fold."[38]

For many who did not see the strike firsthand, the mobs, soldiers in the streets, and reports of fires in Chicago reminded them of the violence of 1877. Both political parties outside Chicago lined up against the strikers. The House and the Senate almost unanimously supported Cleveland's actions. The following year a Republican-dominated Supreme Court ruled that while the Sherman Antitrust Act had been passed in 1890 to regulate railroad rates, it actually gave the president authority to put down strikes. When one federal circuit court judge gasped that this ruling was simply "government by injunction," the name stuck.

Chicago's long and ugly summer of discontent eventually brought reforms. In December 1894 the nonpartisan U.S. Strike Commission visited Chicago, interviewed strikers and owners, and largely blamed Pullman and the interstate railroads for refusing to meet with representatives of the union.[39] By 1895, Massachusetts, Indiana, New York, and Illinois had created state boards of conciliation and arbitration to deal with disruptive strikes.[40] In 1896 the Illinois Supreme Court declared that Pullman's company-owned town was illegal. A town, they declared, "where the streets, alleys, schoolhouses, business houses, sewerage system, hotel, churches, theaters, waterworks, market places, dwellings and tenements are the exclusive property of a corporation is opposed to good public policy and incompatible with the theory and spirit of our institutions."[41]

Pullman was forced to sell his suburban utopia to his own workers and watch as they built their own churches, barrooms, and theaters in the land where he had once been lord and master. In 1898 the Erdman Act passed by Congress created a board that established binding arbitration between laborers and management in disputes involving railroads. It would last for many years, becoming the framework for future arbitration for strikes in other industries, though enforcement of its provisions would take almost thirty years.[42]

PARTISAN SHIFTS: THE AVALANCHE OF 1894 AND THE POPULIST MOVEMENT

THE FATE OF the political parties changed decisively after Chicago's unruly summer. While anger at the Sugar Trust and the Billion-Dollar Congress after 1890 had helped bring Democrats to power before the panic, the panic and the American Railway Union strike led to widespread dismay among Democrats. Pennsylvania's Republican congressman (and songwriter!) Marriott Brosius predicted a Republican "Avalanche" in November 1894. Republicans circulated a campaign pamphlet titled *What Congress Has Done*. All the pages were blank. Voters defected from the Democratic Party and toward Republicans and recovery. In the words of a song that Brosius composed, anger at a Democratic Congress would bring the avalanche:

> *Another day of crashing banks, of mills a-shutting down*
> *From rock-ribbed old New England to Kansas prairies brown;*
> *For idle men in cities, and idle men in farms,*
> *More reinforcements of idle men in empty-handed swarms;*
>
> . . .

Courage, honest son of labor, vainly hustling for a job.
(Perchance with vacant stomach, weary brain, and empty fob);
Though the actors are disgusting, and the drama long and tame,
Yet the powers that be are moving, and we'll get there just the same.

. . .

But the voters will be heard from ere this devil's work is done,
With an avalanche of ballots that will startle Washington;
November's blasts will chill their souls, from Congressmen to bums,
And they'll hustle for the cellars
When
The
Big
Storm
Comes.[43]

Eighteen ninety-four was and still is the largest shift in congressional power in American history. Before the midterm election the Democrats had majorities in both houses of Congress. After the 1894 election Republicans controlled the Senate and had two-thirds of the House. Though the Sugar Trust had persuaded Republicans in the Billion-Dollar Congress to eliminate a sugar tariff in 1890, which helped cause the government's fiscal crisis, Democrats, after all, controlled the presidency, the House, and the Senate in 1893 and had apparently done nothing substantial to resolve the panic. A Democratic attorney general who acted lawlessly on behalf of Pullman and the railroads embittered urban workers to the Democratic Party as a whole. Republicans courted workers by endorsing binding arbitration in future strikes. These concessions helped many urban workingmen desert the party of Cleveland.

But if the 1893 panic showed a revulsion against Democrats, it was not just a pendulum swing. Eighteen ninety-four also proved a time ripe for third-party politics and new issues, a fracturing and rebuilding of both Republican and Democratic Parties. Third-party politics blossomed just as it had in previous panics; Americans blamed both parties for formulaic responses to real suffering. The People's Party, or Populists, which had emerged in the South and the West in 1889 hoped that the 1893 panic would give it the opportunity that the new Republican Party had seen in 1857—to build a new party committed not just to stimulus but to a radical reshaping of the body politic.

From its beginnings the Populist Party had the overtones of a radical, leveling Christianity. It was a mode that went back to the Taborites of Bohemia and the Puritans of Britain's Commonwealth era, if not to the time of the prophets themselves. When the Kansas Populist Jerry Simpson complained that his rival in a congressional election wore silk stockings, the rival accused him of having no socks at all. Kansas Populists sent "Sockless" Jerry Simpson to Congress.

In matters of financial policy some of the Populists may have been more advanced economic thinkers than goldbugs or silver fiends. Many Populists wanted neither silver nor gold to back currency; instead, they wanted a federally controlled currency whose volume could be contracted in booms, when prices rose too rapidly, and expanded during depressions, when prices were dropping and interest rates were too high.[44] Goldbugs and silver fiends—each believing that money needed limits imposed by nature—scoffed at such schemes. Although the Populists' financial logic was often sophisticated, they also circulated conspiracy theories that sometimes strained credulity. Sarah E. V. Emery's *Seven Financial Conspiracies Which Have Enslaved the American People,* published in 1894, retold the legend of an 1873 conspiracy in which the Bank of England allegedly sent a lobbyist with $500,000 to Washington to bribe congressmen to demonetize silver. This "Crime of 1873," according to some Populists, had caused the rapid decline in wheat prices that marked 1873 and all the years afterward.[45]

A year before the panic, Populists assembled in Omaha laid out their demands for government reconstruction. In that year farm radicals—men and women—proposed a graduated income tax, direct election of senators, federal ownership of railroads, and a new banking system organized under the Post Office. Calling on workers to join them, they asked for additional planks and an endorsement of their program. The Populists represented women more fully in their party than in any that had preceded it, more so than the Republicans of the 1850s. Black Alliance locals drew on independent black voters and leaders as well, especially in North Carolina, Georgia, and Alabama, though the white rural Populist insurgency sometimes had ugly racist overtones.[46] This diversity in the political organization allowed many fault lines that the two established parties tried to exploit. Thus a reporter from the Salina *Weekly Republican* described the Populist Mary Lease at the time of the convention in the most unflattering terms, seeking to embarrass men who listened to a fiery and "mannish" female orator:

She could set on a stump in the shade and keep the cows out of a 100 acre corn field without a gun. She's got a face that's harder and sharper than a butcher's cleaver. I could take her by the heels and split an inch board with it. She's got a nose like an ant-eater, a voice like a cat fight and a face that is rank poison to the naked eye.[47]

While the criticism from both parties continued to heap scorn on the Populists, the panic changed the movement, infecting it with radical ideals from the German and Austro-Hungarian exiles from central Europe. It was the Springfield, Illinois, meeting of the Cook County People's Party in May 1894 that laid out the party's boldest attempt to build a coalition of farmers and workers. It would form the basis of what would later be called American liberalism. In that year, radical urban workers (mostly from Chicago) added new demands to the Populist platform, including municipal ownership of street railway, gas, and electric companies; a fund to pay for occupational injuries; an eight-hour workday; sanitary inspection of factories and homes; compulsory public education; and a tax on speculative landholdings.[48] Although Democratic and Republican political leaders declared them to be absolute lunacy, most of these reforms would be passed in the next two decades.[49]

The Populist movement's infection of the Democratic Party was obvious to everyone. William Jennings Bryan became the Democrats' standard-bearer for president in 1896. Populists endorsed him for president, choosing their own vice presidential candidate. Bryan brought the language and spirit of the Populist critique into the center of the Democratic Party even as he abandoned most of the planks of the Populist movement except the free coinage of silver. The crusading language he kept. In attacking the gold standard in his Chicago party address, he railed, "You shall not press down upon the brow of labor this crown of thorns, you shall not crucify mankind upon a cross of gold." Despite mentioning labor repeatedly, Bryan left little room in his jeremiad for urban workers who worried that inflationary measures would make their pay worth less:

> You come to us and tell us that the great cities are in favor of the gold standard; we reply that the great cities rest upon our broad and fertile prairies. Burn down your cities and leave our farms, and your cities will spring up again as if by magic; but destroy our farms and the grass will grow in the streets of every city in the country.

While Bryan helped bring Populism into the Democratic Party, his was the distinctively rural Populism that Republicans lampooned.

From 1893 to 1929 it spread like a brush fire among politicians in the rural South and Midwest while barely smoldering in the cities.

A political insurgency in the South could be a dangerous thing. After the 1873 depression the southern Democratic Party had used gun clubs to overturn Republican rule in Louisiana, Mississippi, and South Carolina. Twenty years later, the party was just as inclined to forcefully put down Populists. The threat of a Populist insurgency had led to a furious campaign of race-baiting by Democratic demagogues, none more frightening than that of Governor "Pitchfork Ben" Tillman of South Carolina. Tillman sought to kill the Populists as an independent party by race-baiting, declaring that while Populists may make lynching illegal in South Carolina, he would be the first in line if a black man raped his daughter. Indeed, lynching reached its peak in the South in the years of the Populist challenge and the reemergence of a new and more demagogic Democratic Party. Tillman led the southern Democratic Party in its turn toward disenfranchisement and formal segregation of all public facilities.[50]

And yet for all the race-baiting, the southern Democrats after the panic also embraced Populist demands for reform. In the South the party devoted itself to breaking the monopoly of the Southern Railway on state politics and passing more humane hours and labor legislation to avert the bloody horrors of 1894 Chicago.[51] Their 1896 platform called on the Supreme Court to embrace the federal income tax, "to the end that wealth may bear its due proportion of the expense of the government." Southern Democrats were also the partisans most committed to casting the harshest light on what they called the "robbery and oppression" of the railroad, sugar, steel, and oil trusts in Congress.[52]

In northern cities Populist Democrats found deep roots in immigrant workingmen's movements. In Democratic-stronghold cities like Tony Cermak's Chicago, the panic, the Pullman strike, and the Chicago conflagration led to Populist reform. These Populists became "Reform Democrats" who successfully drew German and Austro-Hungarian immigrants like Cermak into a party that had largely been Irish-American. The longest-lived standard-bearer for the Reform Democrats started in the West and moved east to follow and then shape the rise of Reform Democracy in Chicago. He was J. Hamilton Lewis, a trim, toupeed, redheaded scion of a prominent Virginia family who moved from his home in Georgia to Washington Territory in the 1880s, where after a brief and unhappy time as local counsel for the Northern Pacific Railroad he soon embraced the entire Populist

cause, but in the name of the Democratic Party. From his days as a corporate lawyer he retained his pin-perfect tailored clothing, erect bearing, spats, and trademark umbrella. A congressman from Washington
Territory elected to the House in 1896, he found his radical demands
for municipal ownership of utilities, factory inspection, home inspection, and the eight-hour workday largely stifled by opponents of reform
in both parties, the so-called Bourbon Democrats and Old Guard
Republicans.

By 1901, Lewis had come to see Chicago as the center of Reform
Democracy. He was attracted by the Populist-inspired municipal and
state reforms proposed after the 1894 conflagration. He relocated
there in 1903 to help Reform Democrats build a stable and strong party
structure committed to genuinely Populist principles. Ten years later
he would represent Illinois as a senator and become the first Democratic "whip," the man who established party unity in the Senate. His
southern drawl, his Confederate ancestry, his stirring speeches, his
wide-ranging knowledge of the classics, and his understanding of all the
parliamentary maneuvers ever tried in Congress made him invaluable
to the Reform Democrats when they returned to Congress in the second decade of the twentieth century. He was the most vital living link
between the Populist radicalism that followed the 1894 upheaval and
the Progressive and New Deal coalitions that followed. Twenty years
later Lewis would, in fact, draw the connection between the transformation that Reform Democrats in Chicago had promised and failed
to deliver on in 1894 and the one that Democrats would bring in the
1930s.[53]

The Populism of the 1890s did not flow just into Democratic
reform circles. In Republican-stronghold states like Wisconsin, Michigan, Kansas, and Iowa, Populism formed the seedbed of an important
insurgent movement inside the Republican Party. A group of Republican reformers, borrowing many organizing strategies from the Populist
movement and many planks from the Populist platform, took advantage of the convulsion of 1893 and the Republican avalanche of 1894 to
burrow through the Republican Party from within. After 1894, especially at the state level, these reform Republicans created what they
called the "Wisconsin Idea," a commitment to binding arbitration in
strikes and nonpartisan review of state functions. They broke up the
Republican caucus and party structure that had returned Old Guard
Republicans again and again to the House and the Senate. It was this
Populist-inflected Republican insurgency in the Midwest that first irri-

tated, then transformed a dyed-in-the-wool Republican named Theodore Roosevelt. No one hated the Populists more than Roosevelt, but his fear of the Wisconsin Republicans helped make him a reformer, then a trustbuster, and finally a Progressive.[54]

The 1893 panic did not kill the Populist movement; Populists and their fellow travelers the Georgeites, the Single-Taxers, the Christian Socialists, and the Greenbackers, would soon abandon the Populist Party to become reforming activists in both parties. Over the next two decades Progressive reformers on both sides of the aisle would attack the entrenched position of the Sugar Trust, the Rockefeller Trust, and the railroads. By the time of the short-lived panic of 1907, the power of the Democratic Bourbons and the Old Guard Republicans would crumble.[55] Despite all predictions of a growing conservatism after the panic of 1893, more and more Americans called for direct regulation of public corporations, packaged food, housing, and utilities. Two Progressive Era reforms in the Constitution—the direct election of senators and a progressive income tax—finally killed the trusts' dependence on the tariff and their lock on the Senate. Just as Republican stalwarts predicted, the Republican avalanche had come in 1894, but avalanches, like brush fires, do not choose their victims.

PERHAPS THE MOST enduring legacy of the 1893 depression was the "tramp," the man who rode the rails in search of work. The terms "tramp" and "bum" went back to the panic of 1873, but by the panic of 1893 the tramp had become the symbol of everyman, used by novelists like Robert Herrick in his *Memoirs of an American Citizen* (1905) to describe the dangers of the city from a tramp's-eye view. The tramp became the "shabby-looking young man" in Charles Monroe Sheldon's novel *In His Steps,* one of the best-selling novels of all time. A former printer thrown out of employment by the Linotype machine, Sheldon's tramp asks difficult questions of Henry Maxwell's congregation. "I've tramped through this city for three days trying to find a job," he tells the worshippers, "and in all that time I've not had a word of sympathy or comfort except from your minister here." Comparing his own wandering for work to the wandering of Jesus, he asks, "What do Christians mean by following the steps of Jesus?"

> I see the ragged edge of things a good deal. I understand there are more than five hundred men in this city in my case. Most of them

have families. My wife died four months ago. I'm glad she is out of trouble. My little girl is staying with a printer's family until I find a job. Somehow I get puzzled when I see so many Christians living in luxury and singing, "Jesus, I my cross have taken, all to leave and follow thee," and remember how my wife died in a tenement in New York City, gasping for air and asking God to take the little girl too.

The difficult question from the "shabby-looking young man," who dies shortly afterward, forces the preacher to ask himself, "What would Jesus do?" The wanderer's question sends the preacher to wander the country too, asking others the same question. In the novel, a newspaper editor decides not to advertise a brutal prizefight; a manager decides to make his workplace more livable; an office worker discovers that his railway is providing illegal rebates to a monopolist and decides to risk his job by handing the information over to the Interstate Commerce Commission. Jesus was a tramp, but he was also a whistle-blower.

If some writers romanticized the plight of the tramp, or used the lives of the tramps around them to ask hard questions, others recognized that it was hardly romantic to wander the country searching for work. Anton Cermak, who had ridden the freight cars from Braidwood to Chicago, would surely have agreed. One extremely popular song that Harry "Haywire Mac" McClintock composed shortly after 1893 is best understood as a song of caution about tramping. In the 1890s jockers, or older hoboes, tried to lure uprooted young men into their lair with stories of the open road. But the "lemonade springs where the bluebird sings" were seldom to be found, McClintock sang. Instead, as the older and bawdier versions of the song claimed, the boy was more likely, after having "hiked and hiked till my feet are sore," to end up "buggered sore like a hobo's whore/In the Big Rock Candy Mountain."[56] The open road, it seems, was dangerous.

FINALLY, the aftermath of the panic of 1893 saw a decisive shift in the organization of corporate America. Sugar had paved the way in 1891 when Havemeyer converted the Sugar Trust into a "holding company." In the trust, the member companies delivered a controlling share of stocks to trustees, who could sell those stocks only in certain cases; in the holding company, the member companies entirely transferred stock ownership to a unitary corporation. The individual manufacturers in the holding company could maintain the separate manufacturing facilities that had grown up in the competitive years, but there would be a single institution for marketing and sales. A New York City head-quarters would set prices, divide up markets, and punish competitors. In day-to-day operations the difference between trust and holding company was not that significant, but as public relations it was price-less. Havemeyer made the case when Congress called him to testify in 1899:

> You take a large corporation, and its stock is in the hands of the public; the public owns the company. [T]he public, the seventy-five millions of people . . . stands a pretty good chance of knocking out a man who has all his money in one thing. Eleven thousand [stock-holders are] almost enough to take Cuba, and they would take it if they could.[57]

According to Havemeyer, a corporation with stockholders was a rough and unruly democracy; he neglected to mention that his family con-trolled most of the preferred shares.

While the Sherman Antitrust Act of 1890 had originally threat-ened to break apart any "contract, combination, or conspiracy" like the Sugar Trust, the Supreme Court provided relief with its 1895 deci-sion *United States v. E. C. Knight*. It would pave the way for the mod-ern, multidivisional corporation. The Court declared that because Havemeyer's newly incorporated sugar cartel was a corporation with thousands of stockholders, and the corporation had openly purchased majority control of competitors' stocks, the firm's action could not be a contract, combination, or conspiracy even if the firm later shut down competitors. The Constitution's commerce clause, the Court contin-ued, let Congress regulate commerce but not manufacturing or refin-ing. The holding company, in manufacturing at least, was exempt from antitrust.[58]

The 1895 *E. C. Knight* decision gave the trusts reason for hope after the depression of 1893. The great merger wave of 1895 to 1907 ensued as trusts converted themselves into holding companies following patterns set just before the panic by General Electric and American Telephone and Telegraph. Consumer prices set by sugar, matchbook, and rope manufacturers would rise rapidly between 1895 and the 1920s. Con-sumers learned to their chagrin that holding companies like American Tobacco and American Sugar Refining would establish a uniformly high rate for goods sold in the United States and a competitively low rate for goods they sold abroad, increasingly in Central and South America.[59]

After the 1893 downturn, monopolists in oil, steel, coal, and even matchstick manufacture also learned that a properly formed monopoly or oligopoly could go directly to capital markets on the stock exchanges. To prepare stocks and bonds for those markets, new syndicates of banks—first organized by Kidder, Peabody—provided short-term loans for the period after the stocks and bonds were printed but before the syndicates sold them. The New York banks discovered in syndicate financing a new short-term loan that seemed rock solid, at least until 1929. Banks and big corporate firms became closely intertwined after 1894 as bank executives for the syndicates demanded seats on the governing boards of the biggest firms. A new market for "industrials," as opposed to railroad bonds, increased after 1894. Dow, Jones took a dozen of the biggest corporate industrial trusts and averaged their stock values. This "Dow Dozen" soon became the Dow Jones Industrial Average in May 1896, a number that millions of Americans began to equate with the health of the overall economy.[60]

As the market for industrial stocks and bonds grew, the internal structure of the largest corporations changed. Setting the pattern that would be adopted by others, J. P. Morgan reorganized the three score competing American railroads into seven major firms with regional monopolies over particular corridors: Alabama to Chicago, Chicago to central California, Atlanta to Richmond, or Seattle to Kansas City. This restructuring required the consolidation of functions, the creation of company-wide policies, and the firing of unnecessary workers. Newspapers called it "Morganization." While the consolidated railroad lines continued to compete for the service between Chicago and New York, each set prices inside its private corridors with little fear of competition.

Only in 1911 would a new Supreme Court take antitrust suits seriously again, when it approved the breakup of Standard Oil. The Court then established a "rule of reason" that applied when restraint of trade was obvious and egregious. Of course, proving the case of monopoly was difficult when the actions of holding companies were still largely hidden from scrutiny.

Did the rise of the modern, multidivisional corporation end the panic of 1893? Probably not. The simplest explanation for the recovery of the U.S. Treasury is the discovery of gold in Alaska, which led to a boom in the Pacific Northwest and eliminated foreign bankers' concerns about the gold supply in the U.S. Treasury.

. . .

WHAT BECAME, then, of the world of Tony Cermak, former hoodlum and now a wealthy, well-connected Chicago businessman? As in previous panics, alcohol consumption among America's workers rose, a fact that helped Cermak. Tony, it was alleged, could hold his liquor better than any politician in Chicago and knew all of the city's secrets, making him a perennial candidate for elective office. He was elected to the state legislature in 1902. In 1905, after Chicago's Anti-Saloon League forced the city council to close saloons on Sunday, Cermak was instrumental in creating a mass movement of tens of thousands of Chicagoans who opposed the saloon closings. They called themselves the United Societies for Local Self-Government. Cermak soon became the permanent secretary of this multiethnic political movement that forced the city council to overturn its Sunday ban. Funded in part by the breweries of Chicago, the United Societies became Cermak's route to a position as alderman, municipal court bailiff, and, by 1922, president of the Cook County Board of Commissioners. In Chicago, saloons were there to stay. The company town of Pullman soon saw working-class bars on its main street. Working-class organizations would continue to form in America's cities, most of all in its taverns.[61]

The Democratic Wilson-Gorman Act reimposed the tariff on raw sugar and shrunk the bounty on local sugar. Democratic congressmen were persuaded it would draw in $40 million a year in revenue. Hawaii, still independent and not yet an American territory, was once again exempt from the tariff and quickly recovered. However, the newly imposed tariff walloped Cuba, causing Cuban sugar exports to America to decline by 50 percent in 1895. As prices fell and plantations cut wages, revolutionary movements in the Cuban countryside quickly followed, including the bombing of Cuban train stations. Spain's brutal attempts to put down the Cuban rebellion led to nearly 100,000 fatalities. The conflict led large Cuban plantation owners to appeal to the United States for invasion and annexation. Continued appeals for an American intervention in Cuba came from an unlikely coalition of sugar refiners, American imperialists, journalists, and humanitarians.[62]

And so adjusting a tariff on sugar had caused a revolution in Hawaii, a depression in the United States, a bitter railroad strike in the Midwest, and a revolution and then a war in Cuba. After Spain surrendered to the United States, Cuba became an American protectorate, and Hawaii became a territory, meaning that both Cuban and Hawaiian sugar would pass duty free into the United States. Duty-free sugar significantly dropped the price of producing beer and liquor, as well as the cost of making canned food. The base of American industrialization was safe again.

Of course, the United States had once again lost its most important single source of revenue—the sugar tariff. The federal government, still operating at a deficit and now massively in the red because of the war against Spain, needed to find an object to tax. The Supreme Court in 1895 had already declared the income tax to be illegal. Taxing in the wake of a depression was a tricky business. The Whiskey Rebellion of 1793 and the fracturing of the Democratic coalition after 1819 testified to that. While the tussle in 1890 between eastern and western sugar barons had drained the U.S. Treasury and helped cause a financial panic and two revolutions, it became clear that Congress needed a new and higher excise tax on liquor and beer to sustain the federal government. Congressmen agreed that it was better to tax at the top of America's manufactured food production chain than at the bottom. In the long term the Sugar Trust lost its pride of place. It fell off the Dow Jones Industrial Average soon after 1900. Meanwhile, reformers in both parties began to question congressional supremacy, the power of corporations, and judicial intervention into the other two branches of government. Sugar would never hold the power it did before the panic of 1893, however vital it was to America's role as a nation that exported calories. From their perch in Chicago, Armour, Swift, and Cermak felt certain that America would forever be the land of canned fruit, potted ham, and the cocktail, but a world war would change all that.

CHAPTER ELEVEN

Who Put the Roar
in the Roaring Twenties?

FTER 1893, AS gold became the coin of the planet, Britain kept its place as a center of world trade. Despite the Baring crisis in 1890, sterling bills of exchange from British firms like Baring and Brown had the same luster they had had in the 1820s. Traded without discount in Macau, Madagascar, or Maui, they were the world's currency, irritatingly so for American bankers. A Boston merchant buying coffee beans in Venezuela could not close the deal without the guarantee of a *British* merchant on the top of his invoice. Britain's bills ruled the waves.

U.S. bankers wanted nothing less than a high-powered American currency that traded internationally. They sought to turn American bills into money that could be spent anywhere. Only by doing so could they avoid what the banker Lawrence Jacobs called the "considerable annual tribute" that American traders paid to English bankers.[1] This was a goal that burned in the brains of American bankers, traders, and wholesalers. A solution—a new instrument called the banker's acceptance—began to form in the wake of the panic of 1907.

The panic of 1907 had grown out of the failure of a number of "bank and trusts" in New York that had neither bank charters nor standing in the New York Clearing House. Once the panic began, hastily formed bank clearing houses had formed around the country. They sought to introduce liquidity by creating quasi-monies. A Republican-dominated Congress cracked down on these clearing houses, a move that helped split the Republicans into two parties and allowed Democrats to gain control of Congress and the presidency. The final product of the 1907 panic was the Federal Reserve, an institution that created the banker's acceptance, the instrument that would soon make United States dollars the preferred currency for the planet.

The New York Clearing House had stood on hand in the event of financial panics since 1857. In times of panic it would create a loan committee to help distressed banks. Banks turned in loans, had them evaluated by the committee, and received "loan certificates" in exchange that traded as bank certificates for the duration of the crisis. The system had worked well enough in 1857, and in 1873 the stability of the loan certificates had protected New York banks at the expense of Philadelphia banks. During the 1893 panic the Clearing House further solidified the power of Morgan's Chase Manhattan Bank, making Morgan into New York's bank maker and bank breaker. But in 1907 the New York Clearing House would fail abysmally.[2]

Two related problems called American banking and American dollars into question in 1907. First, a new and little-regulated shadow banking system had emerged after 1893, called "bank and trusts," which accepted deposits, cleared checks, and invested the proceeds of hundreds of depositors. They were much like the hedge funds of their day. Offering a higher rate for depositors than traditional banks, they had become popular in New York and Chicago. As trusts, they were subject to neither national nor state banking regulations. In the spring of 1907, the Knickerbocker Trust tried and failed to corner the international market on copper. Within days lines of Knickerbocker Trust depositors circled the main branch office seeking to withdraw their deposits. The firm suspended on October 22. On the twenty-third, the Clearing House discovered that the Knickerbocker's failure had led to doubts about the entire banking system as the Trust Company of America, Mechanics' & Traders' Bank, and the Oriental Bank failed. On the twenty-sixth the Clearing House authorized loan certificates for beleaguered member banks, including some of the trusts that were not in the Clearing House Association. When members of the loan committee for the Clearing House belatedly examined the books of the trusts, they found that many had assets that were not recoverable and few had any gold reserves. Dozens of these trusts failed in November 1907. Between October and March stock prices in New York dipped 45 percent, then slowly recovered over 1908. As a result of the panic, the New York legislature demanded that "bank and trusts" keep cash reserves.[3]

In 1907, however, the use of loan certificates by the Clearing Houses had further contributed to economic uncertainty. The cure might have appeared worse than the disease, as loan certificates quickly became a quasi-money. The New York Clearing House had intended the loan certificates to act as money only to be exchanged between member banks during the crisis. The smallest denomination was $5,000. But many of the other Clearing Houses, especially in Atlanta, San Francisco, and

Seattle, issued loan certificates in 1907 in denominations as small as $1 to be used as a citywide currency. It prompted fears of a massive inflation and the threat that the United States might leave the gold standard entirely. In response to the proliferation of this quasi-money, a Republican-controlled Congress passed the Aldrich-Vreeland Act of 1908. The act declared these city monies of the Clearing Houses to be illegal. Congress then suggested replacement with an emergency currency issued by newly created national currency associations of ten or more national banks. Replacing the authority of the city Clearing Houses with the authority of the federal government, these currency associations would value the securities and other assets of a particular bank and then authorize the bank to issue emergency currency. When the crisis passed, the banks would pay off those emergency notes by reimbursing the national currency association. The Aldrich-Vreeland Act passed on a party-line vote, with no Democrats sustaining it. President Roosevelt signed it that evening.[4]

The 1908 response to the 1907 crisis again raised the fundamental question that every panic had posed: What was American currency? Was it backed by gold? Could it be an international currency with the status of the British currency, British sovereigns, and the sterling bills of exchange? In response to these larger questions, a Republican-dominated Congress formed a national monetary commission comprising figures from Wall Street, Harvard, and Princeton. Over the next three years the commission collected twenty-five hundred books and then published thirty-three of its own. The committee finally recommended three general principles: ending the independent, firewalled Treasury; weakening national banking rules on deposits in times of crisis; and creating an American version of a European central bank. It called its proposed bank the National Reserve. The institution would be similar to the Bank of England. It would control the nation's gold supply and set interest rates, as well as act as a national version of the New York Clearing House that bailed out banks in times of financial stringency.[5]

The report of the commission might have created this kind of national bank, similar to the First and Second Banks of the United States, only with expanded powers. But the 1907 panic and the unpopular Republican response to it had helped bring dozens of Democrats to Congress. A sharp split in Republican ranks followed in the presidential election of 1912, forcing Republican voters to choose either the standard-bearer, William Howard Taft, or the "Bull Moose Party" candidate, Theodore Roosevelt, in the general election. That split in Republican ranks helped put the Democrat Woodrow Wilson in the White House.

Thus, in 1912, when the monetary commission finally made its recommendations, the Democrats, who dominated both houses of Congress, demanded something different. They recognized that American banks were flawed, but Democrats—heirs to the party of Jefferson and Jackson—had their doubts about a national bank hatched on Wall Street. They responded to the monetary commission's call for a central bank by creating the Pujo Committee of 1912–1913.

The committee's investigation exposed a vast "interlocking directorate" of hundreds of mining, transportation, and banking firms all controlled by what investigators called "the inner group" of bankers that included J. P. Morgan & Co., Chase National Bank, National Bank of Commerce, and National City Bank (now Citi).[6] This inner group, the Wall Street "money trust," controlled the banks of New York through its power over the New York Clearing House. If a bank, for example, offered lower rates to customers for checks, the Clearing House would eject it from the association. This was classic monopoly behavior: ejection from the cartel for lowering prices. Membership in the New York Clearing House Association was vital for banks because it provided safety from bank panics. Without access to asset-backed loan certificates, a nonmember bank would fail.[7] The Pujo Committee also found that the inner group used the Clearing House's loan committee to punish member banks that threatened their power, effectively devaluing their assets in times of crisis. The Pujo Committee suggested public incorporation and control of these Clearing House associations but said that the Republicans' hastily created national currency associations of 1908 were the wrong institutions. Instead, a single public institution would distribute these securities. It would be the germ of a bank managed by the U.S. government. By May 1913 a Democratically controlled Congress rejected the monetary commission's proposed National Reserve with a base on Wall Street. Instead, it favored an institution with member branches in twelve regions of the country. Democrats in Congress called it the Federal Reserve.

Agrarian, Progressive, and southern Democrats demanded that this Federal Reserve have regional branches that could act as a counterweight to Wall Street. Wilson for his part sought a board of governors to which he would have the power to appoint at least some members. In backdoor negotiations with President Wilson's secretary, William

Jennings Bryan required that even more of the members be federal appointees. Bryan also demanded that the certificates traded between banks be not gold notes but "Federal Reserve notes." The name demonstrated to him that banks were not supreme but ultimately drew their prestige directly from the federal government. All these proposals and demands shaped the Federal Reserve bill. With the help of the Populist faction of Democrats, Wilson guided the act through Congress. Twenty years after the failure of the Populist subtreasury plan that had proposed national notes guaranteed by American commodities, Congress built a bank that it felt certain could never become a Wall Street puppet, a reserve not just for J. P. Morgan but one that represented bankers in Chicago, Richmond, and San Francisco. It would be a bank that would build American exports and fund American imports.[8] Banking based on American farm exports had seemed a pipe dream in the 1880s and 1890s.

As the House concluded its work on the Federal Reserve Act, Congressman "Cotton Tom" Heflin of Alabama stood up to announce the great works of the Democratic Party, now in control of Congress. With a low tariff and the Federal Reserve in place, he declared, "this Republic can shake off temporary business disturbances like dew drops from a lion's mane. . . . [L]et the calamity howlers howl. Let the croakers croak, and the chronic kickers kick. Labor is employed, wages good, the earth yields abundantly, the Democratic Party is in control, God reigns, and all is well with the Republic."[9] Founded just before Christmas in 1913, the Fed seemed prepared for any financial conflagration. It wasn't.

Indeed, the conflagration came just six months later. The Washington journalist Mark Sullivan recalled that the predawn hours of June 28, 1914, must have seemed like any other Sunday morning to most Americans. At 5:00 a.m., the slow clip-clop of the milk wagon announced the coming of dawn in cities on the East Coast. In rural homes, mothers, wives, and bachelors added wood to their stoves to prepare biscuits, ham, and coffee. Talk of "the war" in the newspapers referred to the revolution in Mexico. The generals in the headlines were Venustiano Carranza and Pancho Villa. There were few references to any conflict in Europe.[10]

But half a world away it was afternoon in Sarajevo, the capital of Slavic Bosnia. A student named Gavrilo Princip, along with other members of a Slavic nationalist group called the Black Hand waited there for the arrival of Archduke Franz Ferdinand, eldest nephew of the emperor

Franz Joseph and heir apparent to the throne of Austria-Hungary. The bewhiskered emperor's control of his empire had been precarious ever since the humiliation of the 1873 Vienna Exposition and the bank panic of the same year. While the emperor's forcible annexation of Bosnia from the Ottoman Empire in 1908 was intended as a show of strength, Bosnia remained a hotbed of Slavic nationalist sentiment.

Austria-Hungary's oppressive police had sought to clamp down on Slavic nationalists for decades. By the first decade of the twentieth century Slavs in Bosnia had formed violent paramilitary training camps to prepare young militants for suicide missions against the emperor. Among these was the Black Hand, a group committed to a Slavic Bosnia. The Black Hand's members were not loners: they had funding from the military government in neighboring Serbia, which in turn had considerable support from imperial Russia. Slavic subjects versus German emperors: it was precisely the conflict that had driven Anton Cermak's neighbors and relations out of Kladno and Prague to Chicago, and it still boiled in the Czech, Slovak, and Bosnian lands ruled by the German-speaking emperor.

On the afternoon of June 28, 1914, these Bosnian students, supplied with Belgian revolvers and handheld Serbian bombs, watched the arrival of the archduke at the end of a parade of newfangled luxury motorcars in Sarajevo. One threw a bomb that missed its mark but caused the motorcade to scatter. Shortly afterward, Princip found the archduke's open sedan stalled on a side street. He fired his revolver into the carriage, killing Ferdinand and his wife, the duchess of Hohenberg. The Serbian bombs seized by police were just a few of the objects that showed the hand of the Serbian military government, a government with close ties to the Russian Empire. Austria-Hungary declared war on Serbia; Russia took Serbia's side. Prussia and Austria-Hungary collected allies to compose the Central powers. The United Kingdom, France, and Russia became the Triple Entente. Over the month of July the assembled powers mobilized for the bloodbath that would be called the world war.

In Britain the first day of August 1914 had the popular name St. Lubbock's Day after an 1871 act proposed by Sir John Lubbock that suspended regular banking for one day each season to give tellers a rest. The Bank of England used the August 1 holiday for an emergency meeting to deal with the international war that Princip's revolver had begun. Fearing that depositors would want to withdraw their funds in gold and hoard it for the duration of the war, the bank took the unprecedented step of declaring all standing transactions in English bills of exchange suspended for a month. It later suspended all payments in gold indefinitely. The English bills of Baring, Brown, and Rothschild were frozen and would not be guaranteed until the end of the war.[11] The St. Lubbock's Day suspension saved Baring, Brown, and Rothschild fortunes but destroyed the future standing of their bills. With all gold payments stopped, Britain's Treasury began issuing £1 notes that the public called "Bradburys" after the crudely engraved signature of Britain's Treasury secretary on the bottom right of the bill. Though the bill declared "these notes are a legal tender for a payment of any amount," outside Britain a Bradbury was worthless. In the financial center of the world, the gold standard had become an empty promise.[12]

THE BANKER'S ACCEPTANCE

INTO THE BREACH stepped the American Federal Reserve with a new financial instrument to replace Britain's sterling bill of exchange, the banker's acceptance, or BA. The banker's acceptance was the Fed's solution to the problem of how to create an American promise that could earn interest and be spent everywhere. Economists seldom mention objects, but this little American object laid the groundwork for the triumph of American money in the world economy. Adapted from an older practice in banking, the American BA was just like the sterling bill of exchange that had been involved in the 1837 panic. The American acceptance differed in two particulars from the sterling bill: it was denominated in dollars (not pounds sterling), and banks marked their unconditional obligation to pay the bill by stamping "Accepted" on the face of it. Even if the person who issued the bill defaulted, the accepting bank was still obligated to pay. The authors of the National Bank Act of 1864, presumably remembering the experience of defaults on cotton bills of exchange in 1837, had prevented banks from doing this kind of business. The practice was still common in Europe. The Federal Reserve allowed it again. Another way of thinking of the acceptance is as a postdated check that earned interest and was denominated in dollars, endorsed by a Federal Reserve member bank, and due in less than three months. It was designed for international trade.[13]

Any Federal Reserve branch would buy an American acceptance at a discount rate that was publicly posted. This federal discount rate—agreed upon by the regional banks—was distributed internationally.[14] Two weeks after St. Lubbock's Day, when Britain entered the war, Congress allowed the Fed to perform an act of transubstantiation: acceptances, redeemable at the Fed, would be as good as gold. These new American promises could compose as much as 50 percent of vault revenue in any member bank.[15] Treasury bills were to be a minor part of the Fed's reserves. Acceptances, because they represented the promise of a "real" transaction between a buyer and a seller, were declared better than money.[16] Given the way banks were regulated under the Federal Reserve, a bank with such promises in its vaults could issue four or five times the value of its acceptance in checks and deposits.

The acceptance, taken by any member bank that had gold at its command, was a creature of the world war. As an interest-bearing note, it created a ready international market for American dollars, allowing an American importer to pay a Venezuelan or Peruvian merchant instantly without the stamp of an English bank. The local merchant could immediately sell an acceptance in his home country for local currency. The Federal Reserve's published interest rate immediately calmed the market for American short-term notes, which since the Revolution had traded at interest rates that varied with the seasons: 8 percent in the spring, upward of 15 percent during the fall harvest, when money was tight, even higher in American cities during the Christmas buying season.[17] It did not eliminate these variations, but it smoothed them out.

Federal intervention to moderate seasonal interest rates surely benefited the nation as a whole. The stability of interest rates attracted investors who might previously have held cash to wait for seasonal and cyclical surges in interest rates. It also made planning easier for large institutions that needed to borrow.[18] In the words of a Marshall Field executive in 1925, the Federal Reserve now acted as a "shock absorber" for yearly variations in interest, one that prevented the "bearings in individual businesses" from becoming "burned out."[19] The stability of the acceptance was guaranteed with the weight of the Federal Reserve's gold supplies held by the Treasury.[20] The signature of a Baring, Brown, or Rothschild lost pride of place. The Fed ruled the waves.

Just as the Napoleonic Wars diminished English naval supremacy and made the First Bank of the United States possible, so World War I knocked down English monetary supremacy around the world and allowed the Federal Reserve to become a globe-trotting enterprise. The Fed established regular correspondent relationships with banks in Yugoslavia, Hong Kong, Peru, and Brazil. Banks like National City Bank and Morgan Guaranty established branches in Rio de Janeiro, Montevideo, Havana, and Hong Kong.[21] By the armistice of 1918, the Bank of England, with the pound now discredited, had no way to easily pick up the pieces. For more than a decade after the end of World War I, American commodity, stock, and bond markets boomed with this flood of new and flexible money: convertible to gold at the U.S. Mint, cheap to borrow, standard in form.

With the instrument of the acceptance, the Fed paved the way for a massive increase in American imports and exports.[22] Just as in the years before 1873, American exports surged. After 1914 they flowed not just to Europe but to the world. Between 1913 and 1925 combined American imports and exports nearly doubled from $37 billion to $60 billion.[23] The largest increases appeared in some of the most distant reaches of the globe, including Japan, British Malaya, China, Dutch India, Australia, South Africa, and Argentina.[24]

Fugitive gold from banks around the world raced toward the new monetary center in America.[25] Some came as payments for American goods; some came as investment through European correspondent relationships with other banks. A great deal of capital came directly through foreign branches of American banks that the Fed had encouraged, like the International Banking Corporation in China, a bank acquired by National City Bank in 1915.[26] Many, many deposits came to New York because the interest rates its banks offered to depositors were relatively high.

Before 1913, New York banks depended for liquidity on the New York Clearing House, and that liquidity was available only as loan certificates in times of crisis. Under the Federal Reserve System, participating New York banks could buy U.S. Treasuries and then write multiple "checks" whose assets ultimately relied on the U.S. Treasury's gold. These "checks" were themselves promises that other banks could and did hold, and they operated as further reserves to increase the banks' own lending. The U.S. Treasury was no longer firewalled from the banking system, as it had been for seventy years; it now offered hard collateral for nearly any business that banks wanted to do. The short-term liquidity the New York banks got from the Federal Reserve was unparalleled and put banks on what can only be regarded as a lending spree.

The United States, a borrower from Europe since before the Revolution, suddenly became a lender. Before Princip fired his pistol in 1914, Americans collectively owed foreigners $3.7 billion. When the Allies fired the last howitzer into Metz in 1919, foreigners owed Americans $12.6 billion.[27] This rapid change in indebtedness contributed to such a gold surge in the United States that America went from having one-quarter of the world's monetary gold in 1914 to nearly half by 1920, a billion-dollar increase.[28] If we count the acceptances and the gold together, the American monetary base more than quadrupled. When the war ended in 1919, a brief postwar downturn followed in 1920–1921, but the money did not stop coming, in part because the Fed refused to raise the interest rate.[29]

Under the spur of cheap credit from the Federal Reserve an American boom, the Roaring Twenties, had begun.[30] It was a unique period of galloping productivity, low inflation, and low interest rates made possible because the rest of the world—directly and indirectly—invested in America. This was partly direct investment, partly portfolio investment, and partly what bankers called a forced loan. That is, foreign bankers held dollars because of their comparative stability even though they did not earn interest.[31] At first, American bankers like Charles Rhoads of Girard Trust in Philadelphia resented the cheapness of Federal Reserve credit, believing that a low interest rate would "spoil the rate" banks charged their own customers, but New York banks had already discovered how to profit from a low Fed rate.[32] They could borrow and borrow and borrow again. While banks in the reserve system were expected to hold the acceptances of *other* banks, in fact they discovered that banks could write themselves banker's acceptances on the sly during times of monetary tightness.[33]

American investment patterns had also changed. Frederick Jackson Turner was right when he had declared at the Columbian Exposition of 1893 that the American frontier was closed. American investments for the previous four hundred years had most often been in untilled land in the West. Others had held gold, silver, and banknotes, a good idea during the deflationary 1870s, 1880s, and 1890s. But the prices for staples had started rising in the early twentieth century, then doubled during World War I. With little land available at the minimum government prices, a family needed to put its "nest egg" into something that appreciated every year just to match inflation. By the early 1920s, families converted American silver, antiques, and property into cash for investment in stocks or bonds that could beat inflation.[34] British, French, and German banks, meanwhile, proved unable to catch up to the lead that American financial institutions and American industries had taken during the war. Allied debts to America continually pulled gold back to the American banks that had funded the Allied powers.

The U.S. boom took place partly in industries that would make the United States famous. Before the war Henry Ford had produced an army of cheap, identical black automobiles, the Model A and then the Model T. While Ford had relied on the stock and bond markets to raise funds, after the war National City Bank and others aggressively sought to loan to new enterprises that would in turn loan to potential customers.

One of the New York banks' most important customers, General Motors, produced a very different kind of credit-financed car after 1920. Unlike the $310 Model T, GM cars were more expensive and came in a dizzying variety of colors and models. With access to cheap credit from National City Bank, GM created the General Motors Acceptance Corporation (GMAC), which provided financing for would-be buyers who could not afford to pay $400 all at once. Seeing the success in cars, GM's president, William Durant, then applied the same model in 1920 to electric washing machines and refrigerators with a company he called Frigidaire. Durant recognized that cars, washing machines, and refrigerators were similar devices: a metal case and an electric motor. With bank financing, Maytag too began to use the same model of aggressive advertising, assembly-line production, and credit financing.[35]

The banker's acceptance helped these assembly-line industries reach an international market. GM, Frigidaire, and Maytag all used the U.S. Commerce Department to find international retailers. These retailers took loans from U.S. manufacturers who borrowed from National City Bank and others, who then borrowed from the Fed. An American market of consumers grew up side by side with an international market of retailers.[36]

While the United States boomed, Europeans suffered. Central Europe's troubles were perhaps the most pronounced. On top of the massive debt Germany and Austria had contracted to fight the war, the victors France and England demanded more than $30 billion in reparations. Austria, then Germany, responded with the printing press. Austrian krones and then German marks became like Monopoly money. "Because Austrian money melted like snow in one's hand," wrote the Austrian writer Stefan Zweig, "everyone wanted Swiss francs or American dollars and foreigners in substantial numbers availed themselves of the chance to fatten on the quivering cadaver of the Austrian krone."[37] In 1921, Bavarian Germans crossed the border every weekend to drink Austrian beer made cheap by currency depreciation. By evening some were too drunk to stand and had to be hauled by hand truck to the trains that took them back to Germany.

The following year, when the krone stabilized and the German mark inflated, Austrians crossed into Germany to do the same thing. By 1923 both countries had resorted to barter. In August 1923 it took 620,000 German marks to make an American dollar; by November it took 630 billion. The rate was so favorable to visitors that the English unemployed could use their dole payments to vacation in the most expensive hotels in Germany. A Texan spent $100 to hire the entire Berlin Philharmonic Orchestra to perform one evening. To buy food, "the city dwellers hauled out to the farms whatever they could get along without—Chinese porcelain vases and rugs, sabers and rifles, cameras and books, lamps and ornaments. Entering a Salzburg peasant's home," Zweig exclaimed, "one might be surprised by a staring Indian Buddha or a rococo book case with French leatherbound books."[38]

In Germany, the national debt was denominated in marks. Thus, when hyperinflation from 1922 to 1924 caused marks to become worthless, the government canceled the debt by destroying the value of German bonds, wiping out the funds of pensioners, capitalists, and hundreds of schools, clubs, and banks in the Prussian Empire. Austrian and German reparations to England and France, denominated in gold, remained a costly burden.[39]

This environment of powerful American dollars and weak European currencies encouraged American artists and writers to hang around Europe after World War I and into the 1920s, soaking in the atmosphere of Viennese coffeehouses and Left Bank brasseries.[40] The so-called Lost Generation of America's great writers—Hemingway, Fitzgerald, Gertrude Stein, and John Dos Passos—were hardly lost at all; they lived it up in an environment where American dollars stretched further than ever before.

As late as 1924, Germany's financial problems continued to fester. In that year the Chicago banker Charles G. Dawes went to Paris as a private citizen to provide a solution to Germany's problem. The United States had a massive pile of money; Germany had a massive pile of debt. With the help of the State Department, Dawes put together a syndicate of banks to lend Germany $200 million for reconstruction at 7 percent. Dollar loans—denominated in American dollars and drawing payments directly out of German tariffs—promised immunity to German currency inflation while giving Germany needed funds for reconstruction.[41] The language of the Dawes Plan also appeared to guarantee that these bond payments would take precedence over German reparations.[42] Americans with dollars rushed to the gates, taking $110 million in German bonds. Hundreds of investors were turned away.

American banks sitting on huge pools of money quickly saw the opportunities: the Dawes Plan of 1924 was the starting gun of the fateful bond boom of the late 1920s. This boom, perhaps more than the stock market crash, would be responsible for America's next great depression. For while American investment in Germany helped stop hyperinflation, many of these foreign investments were of dubious value. The architects of the bond boom were companies whose names should sound familiar: National City Bank of New York; J. P. Morgan & Co.; Chase Manhattan Bank; Kuhn, Loeb; and the Bank of America of California. These banks are now called Citi, Morgan Stanley, Morgan Chase, and Bank of America. Kuhn, Loeb became the financial arm of Lehman Brothers. It packaged the financial instruments for sale to other banks.[43]

If they were Federal Reserve member banks, they could not legally issue bonds.[44] But years earlier these banks had learned to create "security affiliates" as a way to evade state and federal oversight.[45] National City Bank created National City Company in 1911; Chase National Bank created Chase Securities Corporation in 1917; Bank of America created Bancamerica in 1928.[46] These institutions churned out off-balance-sheet bonds that relied on the good name of their federally regulated parent banks. After 1924 affiliates proved the perfect vehicles for pushing loans onto European municipalities and states, which they then resold to other banks desiring high-yield bonds and to their own banking customers.[47] Of course, Europeans were no more reliable than Americans at repaying their loans. From 1791 to 1920, pushy American banks had been overestimating the value of flour barrels, land patents, cotton bales, and railway mortgages when they sold their debt to Europeans. Now American bankers were prepared to export that sales technique abroad as they overestimated the payoff from swimming pools, municipal buildings, and harbors from Peru to Potsdam. These security affiliates now persuaded Americans, not Europeans, that their banks could rest on inflated promises.

Those who examine the 2008 crisis may notice similarities between the security affiliates of the 1920s and the so-called structured investment vehicle (SIV) of the late twentieth century. Formed by Citigroup in 1988, the SIV allowed banks to create off-balance-sheet institutions that borrowed in the short-term markets while lending on longer-term investments, including real estate mortgages. The opaque practices of the off-books enterprise allowed these large banks to lend far beyond their means. In particular these practices allowed them to skirt section 5200 of the Fed's statutes, which was designed to prevent banks from over-leveraging.[48]

The bond boom did not just endanger the banks in the Federal Reserve System; risky bonds were accumulated outside that system. Smaller midwestern banks with large numbers of German-speaking customers were especially attracted to German loans. These smaller midwestern banks came to rely on foreign bonds as seemingly stable long-term investments. In the trunk of promises, these bonds provided a high yield.

Larger banks convinced the smaller banks that because bond prices were regularly listed in newspapers, these new foreign bonds would be liquid—that if patrons of the bank suddenly demanded their deposits, the small banks could instantly sell the foreign bonds at par. City Bank in particular pushed these bonds throughout the Midwest using salesmen. In the words of one former National City Bank bond salesman, his bank's job was "hatching up every conceivable kind of a security with every variety of trimmings and then scattering it all over the country by means of high-pressure selling."[49] In an early variant of what is now called modern portfolio theory, the big banks convinced the smaller midwestern banks that bond yields would go up when stock prices went down and that investments in local projects would be counterbalanced by risks in foreign loans.[50] The idea was safety in diversification, but because their portfolios contained so many risky German loans, these midwestern banks—even more than the Fed banks—would be ground zero for the bank failures of October 1930.[51]

From 1924 to 1928 the so-called bond men of the big American banks swarmed the governors and mayors of Germany, Austria, Yugoslavia, and France, searching for borrowers. They offered American funds for municipal, state, and federal promises. Europeans called these dollar-denominated bonds "dollar loans." In Germany alone, according to the country's ministerial director for economics, foreign loans went to "federal states, provinces, counties (Kreise), communities, associations of communities, church organizations, and to undertakings partly public, partly private."[52] As one critic noted later, "Bankrupt German municipalities and disrupted German industries had not to beg foreign bankers for advances; they were actually besieged by those bankers until they accepted loans."[53] American banks also swarmed Argentina, Chile, Cuba, and Peru to plan vast state expansion projects.[54] Latin American governments called the period the "dance of the millions." These instruments were created with little oversight and then quickly unloaded onto unsuspecting banks.[55]

What confused monetary economists then and now was why American banks continued to attract capital from around the world from 1924 to 1929. Why should capital flow to America, and why should American investments be so important for the long-term stability of

Germany? By the so-called rules of gold standard banking, gold *should* have flowed from American banks, where the official Fed rate was low, to English and German banks, where rates were higher.[56] But interest rates are only part of the story. Today, interest rates are low in America and high in Afghanistan, but little investment flows to Afghanistan. Capital does not simply flow to the highest rates; it also seeks the fewest regulations and the greatest safety. Capital controls imposed inside Germany, France, and England in the mid-1920s limited the scope of direct investment in Europe. Foreign accounts held in America, by comparison, had almost no controls at all.[57] For the decade after World War I, America seemed a safe haven for capital. Few understood that the capital was then reinvested through unstable instruments in unstable regions.

FALL OF 1928, FALL OF 1929

IN THE LATE fall of 1928, the dancing stopped. Long-term loans to Germany and the rest of the world plummeted from $1.5 billion a year to just over half a billion.[58] The reasons were varied. One reason was the opposition of the German finance minister, who publicly complained about the loans, fearing that some municipal loans might never be repaid.[59] Shortly afterward, the German Loan Council (Beratungsstelle) began to closely examine bond issues coming out of Germany.[60] Attempts to renegotiate the Dawes Plan raised the specter of default. Negotiations in Geneva in September 1928 suggested that the Americans might be asked to buy billions more in German bonds and that the funds generated would then pay off the German reparations to France and England.[61] As a reporter for the *Washington Post* put it, "The allies, having cashed their bonds would be quits with both Germany and the United States. If Germany should default, the American citizens would be 'holding the bag.' "[62] For Americans who had already seen the German government "revalue" their bonds into nothing in 1922, talk of renegotiating the agreement sent a chill through the markets that no amount of marketing by National City Bank could warm up.[63] The bloom was off the rose on foreign loans to Germany, an event that would cause a fiscal crisis in Germany and lead to the rapid rise of the National Socialist Party, which promised to default on these "Jewish" loans, then restore Germany to prosperity without them.[64]

In America, the problem of the dubious German loans made private investors and bankers skittish about lending abroad. With foreign bonds plummeting, banks had to put depositors' investments somewhere. By the summer of 1928 all that capital went into the New York stock market. In June 1928 rates for deposits were 5.5 percent and rising.[65] From the fall of 1928 to the fall of 1929 more and more of these deposits went directly into loans to brokers, who then lent the money short term to stock market speculators. At the beginning of October 1929 an internal investigation by the American Bankers Association estimated that New York banks had $6.8 billion invested in brokers' loans, double the total invested in December 1927.[66] As in the 2008 crisis, money market rates in New York began to rise higher than the official Fed rate, approaching 20 percent by early October 1929.[67] Some banks grew suspicious and pulled out of the brokers' loan market, causing premiums for brokers' loans to soar into the double digits. But given the high rate participating banks offered their depositors and the apparent safety from European conflict, hot money from around the world rushed to America.[68] From the fall of 1928 to the fall of 1929 the valuation of stocks on the New York Stock Exchange doubled. It was a classic stock market bubble.

In the spring of 1928, the Federal Reserve tried to stop the stock bubble by raising the discount rate, a move that should have restricted the money supply and drawn gold into Federal Reserve coffers. Indeed, many economists believed that this relatively minor increase in the discount rate caused the stock decline. But these economists failed to account for or even understand the role of banker's acceptances in inflating the money supply.[69] Banker's acceptances skyrocketed as National City Bank's acceptances rose from $49 million in 1926 to $99 million in 1927 to $140 million in 1928, even though international trade was declining.[70] By using the banker's acceptances, the New York banks with security affiliates produced money even as the Fed tightened lending, allowing the largest member banks like National City Bank and Bank of America to ignore the discipline that the Federal Reserve's discount rate might have provided.[71]

Then, on October 23 and 24, as regular stock investors became increasingly suspicious of the high price of stocks, the market crashed. When stock values dropped far below the loans brokers had issued to buy them, brokers automatically sold the borrowers' stocks. These margin calls further contributed to the vertiginous decline in stock prices. But stock market declines, even rapid ones, do not cause panics. It was the fundamental instability of the foreign bonds, the assets in the trunks of American banks, that would lead to massive bank failures a year later.

America's problems were not just with its oversized money supply, its international presence, and its sudden halting of foreign loans. Something was rotten in what "Sunshine Charley" Mitchell of National City Bank called "the credit structure of the country."[72] The banker's acceptance created by the Federal Reserve continued to float around in bank coffers as high-powered money. While banker's acceptances were supposed to be short-term loans for actual international trade, the New York banks had learned by 1928 that they could simply issue them to themselves on a ninety-day leash. They could effectively write checks to themselves when no one else had credit, then use them for three months or more as vault stock. So while the Fed became a source of credit, it did so only for the largest New York banks with international operations that could use the distant banks as straw lenders.[73] The banker's acceptances provided a way for the rest of the operators who built unsound assets in the early 1920s to avoid default themselves.

Thus in 1929, with international trade declining, banker's acceptances were unaccountably growing. As one internal memorandum in the Federal Reserve noted, "In recent months the volume of credit has been increasing more rapidly than appears to have been required for the needs of business."[74] In effect, the largest banks were handing bad bonds over to affiliate banks and taking short-term loans from their affiliates. This simultaneously hid bad loans and allowed banks to increase their monetary base.[75]

This problem with banks' underlying assets, more so than the stock market crash, caused the Great Depression. Of course, declines in stocks did lead directly to declines in the purchase of raw materials that in turn depressed commodity prices, especially wheat, steel, and aluminum. President Herbert Hoover noted this transmission from stock prices to commodity prices the day after the 1929 crash, but he believed that rapidly declining commodity prices would simply buoy up the economy. "The fundamental business of the country," he stated with certainty, "that is the production and distribution of commodities, is on a sound and prosperous basis."[76] As in the previous American depressions, however, declines in commodity prices tended to make buyers hold cash, delay purchases, and wait for prices to fall further. Hoover may have been right, that an equilibrium was possible with commodity and stock prices. But it would be a long wait before people seeking bargains eventually came in to buy.

There were deeper problems too with American bonds. In 1931, many sovereign states in central Europe and Latin America began to default on their loans, loans that took the form of the bonds held by small banks in the American Midwest. By the summer of 1932, nearly 20 percent of the roughly $7.5 billion in foreign loans were in default.[77] By 1933, American banks faced a default rate approaching 35 to 40 percent. In that year the Nazi regime declared that it would unilaterally renegotiate all the dollar loans and determine whether, or how much, lenders would be paid. Although the stock market crash led to relatively few bank failures at first, the failure of the bonds in 1931 helped cause a cascade of bank failures that spread fears about the stability of all banks in the United States.[78]

The originating banks whose shaky bonds had caused the crisis got off scot-free. National City Bank of New York's own stock dropped, but in 1929 its foreign operations ultimately helped it to survive the crash. China, which had moved off the silver standard, had large stores of silver available for purchase. When FDR came into office, he remonetized silver in order to restore confidence in bank reserves. Because National City Bank had offices in China, it could purchase silver bars in China, smuggle them out past an imperial ban on silver exports, and sell them at a high premium in London and New York.[79] The international crash provided opportunities for those who could predict how news would affect the relative value of currencies. The biggest New York banks netted millions in dollar-mark-pound-gold arbitrage, buying gold as it increased or shorting currencies they knew to be failing. Meanwhile, midwestern banks faced rack and ruin, crumbling in the mid-1930s and carrying down the U.S. economy with them.

Americans blamed Hoover not for the crash but for his failure to respond to it. In October 1930, Hoover blamed declines in the commodity markets on short-sellers. "If these gentlemen have that sense of patriotism which outruns immediate profit," he thundered, "and a desire to see the country recover, they will close up these transactions and desist from their manipulations."[80] As the newspaper columnist and cultural critic H. L. Mencken remarked in 1931, Hoover's sponsors called him a financial "master mind" because of his Commerce Department experience, "and he himself let it be known that he was loaded for any kind of economic bear that might come down from the woods." After the crash of 1929, however, Hoover's weaknesses became more obvious: "When the bears actually appeared he turned out to be quite helpless before them, and his friends are finding it hard today to show that his panicky shots have really drawn any blood."[81] Or more succinctly, "Harding, confronting public problems of grave importance, met them like an idiot, but Hoover has met them like two idiots."[82]

Mencken's comment was strangely prescient, for Hoover seemed blithely ignorant of the bond problems until late in 1932, when he blamed the crisis on the "concentration of catastrophes from abroad such as we have not experienced in the whole of our economic history."[83] Yet as secretary of commerce under Harding, he himself had had a hand in causing those catastrophes. His office had refused to pass judgment on the international loans between 1924 and 1928, though it had been asked to do so.[84] Parker Gilbert, the American agent-general in charge of overseeing German reparations, was especially irate at Hoover's letters, which appeared to approve the loans. The State Department did issue a covering letter that asserted that loans should be repaid. But Gilbert complained that the letter "ought to be set to music, and it is on such a high moral plane that nothing less than a pipe organ would do for the purpose." Yet after this morality lesson Gilbert wrote that Hoover's letter "proceeds to relieve itself of all responsibility by a closing sentence to the effect that, no question of Government policy being involved, it raises no objection! What a wonderful little tail for all that dog!" Hoover, Gilbert felt, was plainly irresponsible.[85]

When Hoover finally responded in 1930, he approved just a smidgen more than $100 million for public works projects and created the Reconstruction Finance Corporation to help unfreeze bank assets. That was all. Mencken was right: Hoover *was* an idiot twice, and by 1930 he reaped the troubles he had helped sow as commerce secretary. Of course, while Hoover the commerce secretary had allowed the bond men to create troubled assets from unlikely promises made all over Europe and Latin America, he may not have understood how much damage it would do to the nation's banking infrastructure by 1930.

By then, hundreds of thousands of laid-off workers were riding the rails in search of work. Squatters established shantytowns they dubbed Hoovervilles. A newspaper was dubbed a "Hoover blanket," the emptied pockets of a man's trousers were "Hoover flags," and armadillos or rabbits caught for food were "Hoover hogs." Songs like "My Great Depression Is You" and "I'm Goin' Coo-Coo for the Want of Somethin' to Do" filled the radio airwaves. Tramping reemerged as a way of life for millions of people old enough or young enough to move.

CRASH COMES TO CHICAGO

IN THE LARGEST American cities, crash politics brought the nation a new political coalition forged in the late 1920s. Anton Cermak helped organize one of the first and most important in Chicago. Back in the Roaring Twenties, the years of Republican dominance and Prohibition, Cermak and his allies' principal opponent was the Chicago mayor "Big Bill" Thompson. Between 1915 and 1931—except for a brief intermission—Thompson, a six-foot Republican, had built up a powerful, violent Republican Party machine that kept him in power. Built with money from the electrical power titan Samuel Insull and muscle from the gangland boss Al Capone, local Republicans had made Chicago into the legendary "Guntown."[86] Thompson's Chicago was the Chicago of the 1919 race riot, the Tommy gun, the speakeasy, the St. Valentine's Day Massacre, and the "Pineapple Primary" of 1928, where Thompson's supporters freely used hand grenades against his political opponents.[87] By 1928, Democrats like Cermak had managed to build up a base in Cook County that opposed Thompson's rule. Cermak courted traditionally Republican middle-class voters by preserving wooded areas in the suburbs, integrating reformers into public institutions, and organizing to defeat the influence of Al Capone.[88]

Cermak was no saint. Chicago Democrats too had decades-old connections to breweries, organized crime, and gambling, but Cermak had helped push the party to branch out from its stable base among Irish voters. The Democratic Party was becoming, as he called it, "a house for all peoples."[89] He did this through the late 1920s by carefully courting historically Republican ethnic voters: African Americans, Swedes, Germans, and white Protestants. Decades before, Cermak had already cemented his reputation as a popular opponent of Prohibition.

Cermak's campaign for mayor in the spring of 1931 has become the stuff of legend. In the primaries, Thompson rode a horse onstage at the Cort Theatre and led around town a menagerie of animals, including a jackass, a burro, an elephant, and a camel that he labeled as his opponents.[90] Friends dissuaded him from his plan of finding the biggest hog in the Chicago stockyards and calling it Cermak.[91]

By 1931 unemployment in Chicago had already reached close to 40 percent. Cermak's own life story made him particularly suited to the campaign. Here was a man thrown out of employment in Braidwood for asking for a raise in the 1880s who then arrived in Chicago by boxcar. Embarking on a career with a horse and buggy in the depression of 1893, Cermak had somehow succeeded. For a city in which two of every three people were immigrants, many voters hoped his was a universal story. The Cermak Troubadours sang his praises on the radio every night, though they competed song for song with Thompson's police quartet.[92]

On Monday, March 23, 1931, when Tony Cermak addressed a crowd of twenty-six thousand in Chicago's newly built hockey stadium on Madison Street, he made sure ethnic Germans, Swedes, and Jews preceded him onstage. "This great city," shouted Dr. Herman Bundesen, "that has more Catholics than Rome, more Jews than all of Palestine, more Irish than Dublin, more Scotch than Edinburgh, more Welshmen than Cardiff, more Poles than Poznan, more Swedes than Malmo, and more Germans than Kiel, is not going to permit any group to remain in power that would endeavor to replace Chicago's magnificent slogan: 'I Will!' "[93]

One of the most significant speeches that night came from Senator J. Hamilton Lewis, the old Populist-turned-Democrat who had fought for years as a Reform Democrat and Senate whip. He declared that Cermak represented something different. He coined a new term by saying that Cermak would bring a "new deal" for the people of Chicago, that only Cermak could "resurrect and revive" the city. This gambling phrase, coined by Lewis in 1931, stuck with other Democrats that night. It suggested two things: a shuffling of the established order with a Czech candidate in an Irish party who was backed by Italians, Jews, Germans, Swedes, and some black voters; and a new beginning. Cermak countered Thompson's attempts to pit ethnic groups against one another by pledging to put black men and women on school boards, to revise the municipal tax code to benefit small homeowners, and to build a subway underneath State Street.[94] Thompson had promised the subway in the last election but had failed to deliver. The project required the guidance of the electrical power titan Samuel Insull, who was otherwise occupied. Cermak promised to see it through and won by a landslide.[95] While fulfilling his promise would be nearly impossible, Cermak created a party machine that has lasted for generations.

While the term "New Deal" was first used to describe his brand of politics, Anton Cermak did not create the so-called New Deal coalition by himself. It had been forming since the 1920s among immigrants who felt burned by the promises of the old political machines, both Democratic and Republican. In New York City, Detroit, Minneapolis, Pittsburgh, and Cleveland, workers' movements grew up first, a new party affiliation grew up afterward.[96] These newer immigrants sought a New Deal long before the phrase was articulated by Senator Lewis or swiped by Franklin Roosevelt.

When Cermak was elected in Chicago, his promise to build a subway proved one of the most visible parts of his New Deal, but it was a sticky problem. Even before the Depression, Samuel Insull had become a bugbear for Chicago Democrats, an example of the dangers of private ownership of utilities. Throughout the Midwest, Insull built his monopolies by bribing freely and frequently for concessions from municipalities and states. He used a dizzying array of newspapers, holding companies, and trusts to maintain his hold and to fight off the encroachment of eastern railway, bank, and utility combinations. Insull's admission in 1926 that he had paid $125,000 to the Republican Frank L. Smith so that Smith could become Illinois's senator prompted the Senate to refuse his swearing in and to begin an investigation of what it labeled the "power trust." In the salad days of the late 1920s, political insiders in Chicago called Illinois's Republican governor, Len Small, and Mayor Thompson "Insull's Siamese Twins" who would have to ask Insull what to think before they planned any public works projects.[97]

At first, the crash of 1929 barely slowed Insull down. The unscrupulous bond agency of Halsey, Stuart had seen to that, for the firm had mastered the use of the radio in Chicago. Every Thursday night from 1928 to 1931 "the Old Counsellor," a professor at the University of Chicago, gave financial advice on twenty-nine radio stations across the Midwest. He invariably suggested the stability of Insull's bonds. The Old Counsellor was actually a professor of public speaking at the university whose smooth voice made him a perfect tout for Insull.[98]

The poet Edgar Lee Masters compared the seventy-year-old Chicago billionaire with the drooping white mustache to the thirty-year-old Chicago crime lord Al Capone. Both were businessmen who had kept Republicans in power in Chicago in the 1920s. Both did not care much for the law. But as Masters wrote, "Capone's career may furnish a theme for comedy or comic opera, such as Robin Hood." Insull had no colorful backstory. "There is as much romance to the life of Insull," Masters wrote, "as in that of an octopus lying behind a rock with concealed tentacles, waiting for an unwary fish to swim near."[99] The unwary fish proved to be Chicago families who believed even after the crash of 1929 that Insull's increasingly leveraged empire would pay dividends.

When England went off the gold standard in September 1931, it led many British investors to sell Insull bonds for hard specie. As sales increased, bond yields rose, making it difficult for the utility empire to sell new bonds in Britain. Without the continued cash infusions, Insull's utility empire collapsed. Insull's failure took investors for more than $1.5 billion. His status, deserved or not, as a greedy and remorseless monopolist who had ruined those who trusted him galvanized even more members of the Democratic Party, including Franklin Roosevelt, who called for public ownership of utilities. The idea had been important to urban Democrats from the 1890s to the 1930s, but FDR now added his voice to the chorus.[100] After the fall of 1932, when revelations about Insull's manipulation of information about his bonds hit the news, FDR used his lectern to explain how Insull had used subsidiaries to milk proceeds from other subsidiaries whose dividends were paid directly out of stock purchases.[101] Public construction of utilities became a key part of the New Deal coalition's promises to Americans, as important in Chicago as it was in New York, Detroit, Cleveland, and Cincinnati.

Investigations into the Insull monopoly began in Congress in the winter of 1931. In September 1932, Insull escaped to Greece, which did not have an extradition treaty with the United States. New York bankers jumped on the Insull failure—happy to promote a story that shifted blame for financial skulduggery off them and onto others.

FDR's newfound populism helped consolidate the two wings of the Democratic Party that had failed to find common ground after the panic of 1893. The lily-white southern wing of the Democratic Party had for more than a century been committed to Populist-style financial reform. It had galvanized the party of Jefferson after the 1792 panic, had sealed the Jacksonian party after 1819, and had drawn rural voters toward William Jennings Bryan after 1893. But in 1896 most urban and ethnic workers had found little to love in Bryanite panegyrics. In the early 1920s, H. L. Mencken had memorably stereotyped the two factions as the southern "Yahoos" versus the urban "gangsters." Only with the panic of 1929 could FDR's party succeed in linking the anti–national-bank populism of the southern and western farm states with the urban, multiethnic machine that endorsed public ownership of utilities. Certain wedge issues separated the two—Prohibition (Yahoos for, gangsters against) and black suffrage (Yahoos against, gangsters for)—but the Depression brought them together long enough to make a president.

If Cermak was the Moses of the new multiethnic reform party, like Moses he got only a glimpse of the promised land. Few in the party doubted that Cermak's political machine had helped deliver the votes that elected FDR. After the election, Cermak and the president-elect sought to iron out their differences in a brief meeting in Miami. Cermak in particular sought municipal funding for a State Street subway in Chicago. With the Insull empire collapsed, he hoped that the

Hoover-sponsored Reconstruction Finance Corporation (RFC) would provide funds to begin digging. There was no company to reconstruct, but Cermak made the case that Hoover's RFC—now under Democratic control—could initiate projects on its own, especially in a city with such staggeringly high unemployment. The RFC would create the Chicago Transit Authority, a model for other public utilities. But as Cermak and FDR sat side by side in a Miami motorcade, Giuseppe Zangara, a deranged and unemployed gunman, drew close to the roadster and fired into the car. Cermak received two bullets in the chest. Roosevelt cradled him in his arms while Secret Service agents rushed the pair to the hospital. Cermak died shortly afterward.

Many of the reforms that the New Deal coalition passed in Roosevelt's first one hundred days are still with us, including procedures for full disclosure of bond issues (Securities Act), the creation of publicly owned utilities (Tennessee Valley Authority), farm subsidies (Agricultural Adjustment Act), and public insurance for depositors (Federal Deposit Insurance Corporation). A dubious Supreme Court, chosen mostly by Republicans in the earlier, prosperous years, overturned other parts of the party's New Deal.[102] This so-called First New Deal seemed to have little effect on the U.S. economy, as the number of unemployed went from 4.8 million in 1930 to 14.5 million in March 1933.[103]

As Congress sought to reshape the financial and economic landscape, ordinary Americans found ways to make use of free time necessitated by underemployment and unemployment. New and cheap leisure activities dominated the 1930s. Pinball machines replaced gambling as a pastime for anyone with a penny and an hour to kill. Reform organizations saw these mechanical devices as little more than personalized pool tables, a gateway to more dangerous gambling. But pinball machines were probably less dangerous than the cramped juke joints of Depression-era America. For those juke operators who could not afford to hire a musician, the jukebox emerged as a cheap physical replacement. It made use of amplifiers (only recently invented) to broadcast music inside the cramped little buildings. By the 1930s the U.S. Mint was forced to produce millions more nickels to keep up with the craze. Furiously resisted by musicians' unions, the jukebox nonetheless emerged as the purveyor of cheap music. The jukeboxes were also readily adopted because they did not have a race, and so could perform anywhere. They helped broaden the appeal of African-American blues and jazz musicians among white audiences, a mechanical contraption that in its own perverse way helped unsettle segregation in the North and the South.

Miniature golf, which had been a popular enough attraction at swanky hotels throughout Europe in the 1920s, became an American phenomenon during the Depression. Like the jukebox and the pinball machine, it allowed one to while away hours for small change. While the pinball machine was considered a man's device and the jukebox an especially notorious device for introducing couples to each other, miniature golf appealed to families who had a little change and lots and lots of time. Likewise, Catholic churches short on funds were quickly drawn to an old carnival game that was updated by an entrepreneur who figured out how more than two hundred people could sit with numbered cards and chips all waiting for a big prize. He called it bingo, and it too became a Depression sensation. Likewise, the "supermarket" extended the revolution that had been brought twenty years earlier with the automobile. The post-1930 supermarket had parking lots, metal carts, and rectangular paper bags. It became a family attraction offering self-service, low prices, and one-stop shopping. Here one could spend hours shopping while spending less.

As these new pastimes suggest, many Americans were convinced that the First New Deal had little effect in restoring business confidence. Total production fell 25 percent from 1928 to 1933; prices fell by nearly 9 percent per year in the early 1930s. Continuing deflation like this increased the weight of existing debt (dollars owed became more valuable). This debt-deflation spiral served to hammer industries, banks, and individual borrowers alike.[104]

Recently, Amity Shlaes and other pundits have suggested that New Deal interventions in the economy introduced rigidities that may have hindered recovery. The National Industrial Recovery Act and the Agricultural Adjustment Act certainly suggest this. Both were mechanisms that rewarded owners with higher prices if they scaled back production and raised wages. This was certainly a peculiar way to stabilize prices. Often manufacturers in durable goods accepted higher wages for employees while making do with fewer workers; manufacturing productivity actually exploded in the 1930s for this reason. Of course, because firms did not hire back laid-off workers, it helped to deepen unemployment.[105] Similarly, when southern planters were paid by the New Deal Agricultural Adjustment Act to grow less after 1933, they took their allotment payments and dismissed hundreds of thousands of sharecroppers, hiring them back only during the short harvest season.[106]

For unemployed workers, rural tenants, and sharecroppers, tramping for work after 1933 was substantially different from 1893. In the

1890s boxcars were the primary mode of transit for those in financial peril, making mobility a difficult option usually reserved to single men. But by the 1930s, after Ford and GM had put millions of Americans in inexpensive gas-powered automobiles, regional mobility was more possible for unemployed families with a little means. The photographer Dorothea Lange paired up with her partner, Paul Taylor, to track the migrants on what they called the "American Exodus." As eroded topsoil mixed with dry conditions to produce a "dust bowl" in 1934 and 1935, many hundreds of thousands of farm families in the region surrounding the Oklahoma Panhandle gave up the land they had rented or owned to find work in sunny California.[107] Her memorable photographs of impoverished families on the move provide the most enduring picture of the migration that the Depression started. Of course, to move required some means. Farmers whose families remained in Oklahoma joked that "the rich 'uns had pulled up and gone to California to starve" while "the poor folks just stayed hungry where they were."[108] Californians called them Okies, though many came from Texas, Kansas, and Colorado. They traveled in beat-up Model Ts with families in tow. Panicked Californians created a border patrol on California's eastern border to stop the Okies from coming but found that stopping automobiles was more difficult than checking boxcars. Many settled into Southern California to pick fruit for abysmal wages. The Oklahoma radical and songwriter Woody Guthrie saw himself as their troubadour, singing about the plight of rural and urban workers in what became a folk music revival. A few of these workers might have sung along, though many might have strongly disagreed with him about the solutions to their problems. Within twenty years these impoverished Southern California migrants would become the base for a California brand of evangelical religion, country-western music, and conservative politics.[109]

Continuing poverty and unemployment helped engender political threats from inside and outside the Roosevelt coalition, especially the strike wave of 1934 and the political threat of the Louisiana governor and U.S. senator Huey Long. Important too was the emergence of John Maynard Keynes, a British economist whose work radically reshaped the economics profession. The attack from the left, and the influence of intellectuals like Keynes, pushed the president and Congress to intervene even more directly in the economy in what came to be called the Second New Deal.

How new was federal intervention in the economy? In one sense it was not new at all. Since the time of the Land Act of 1800, the federal government had provided credit to private borrowers for land purchases. Since the colonial period, townships and cities had built workhouses for the poor and created temporary public works projects for seasonally unemployed artisans and sailors. After the 1857 downturn, the Republican Party intervened in the economy through free grants of land, in subsidies to semipublic institutions like railroads, state universities, and banks, and finally with generous welfare provisions for veterans. What was new in the 1930s were federal attempts to invest in, tax, and reform the industrial workplace.

Two changes had occurred since 1893 to broaden federal officials' palette of opportunities for responding to the next panic. The first was the bolstering of executive power, usually symbolized by the emergence of Theodore Roosevelt as a trustbuster, sponsor of the Panama Canal, and advocate for national parks. But in 1901, Teddy Roosevelt took over a state that was already growing. An already active "administrative state" had begun to emerge in the 1880s with a large force of nonpartisan experts. It had grown with the broadening of Treasury powers, the Secret Service to stop dollar counterfeits, a veterans' pension bureau, the National Park Service, the Food and Drug Administration, and the Internal Revenue Service to collect taxes on cotton (immediately after the war), then liquor and tobacco, and finally (after 1913) federal income taxes. Forty years of growing faith in federal professional expertise made possible the post-1934 interventions in the economy.

The second change was the presence of a Federal Reserve that could affect interest rates. In previous panics conventional economic ideas focused on adjusting the interest rate. In extraordinary situations in the United States, the Treasury was expected to buy back federal debt. This happened in 1792, 1873, and 1893. (There was no debt to buy in 1837.) This purchasing of federal debt would sponge away the safer debt and in this way encourage conservative holders of capital (who held increasingly scarce Treasuries) to spread their investments into riskier private enterprises, thus bringing interest rates down. If the panic price to borrow ended and interest rates dropped, borrowers could get loans to build, buy, and plan again. Central banking countries in Europe had an additional spigot to turn, as did the newly created Federal Reserve. They could indirectly control interest rates through a central bank. If the bank intervened to lower the interest rate, or tried to hold it down, gold might flow out of the central bank, but the low rate would presumably encourage wary investors to reenter stock and money markets. What economists found in the early 1930s, however, was a low interest rate, gold flowing *into* the federal Treasury as people bought bonds instead of investing, and no visible upturn in private investment. Some blamed a new American tariff; others blamed a widespread anxiety about the future.

It was in this confusing period in 1934 that Keynes came to America to argue that the classical model of money supply–focused economics was broken. He made the case for deficit spending in a depression. He differed from traditional economists in a few important ways. First, he ignored individual prices of commodities, trying to combine them into overall aggregate prices. Second, he rethought how interest worked, arguing that from 1930 the United States was caught in a "liquidity trap," where, even though interest rates were low, investors preferred liquid funds to investment. Third, he disputed economists' arguments that unemployment was caused by workers' unwillingness to accept lower wages. Finally, he argued for new government spigots to break unemployment logjams. If the government bravely embraced deficit spending on public works, he promised, this would have a "multiplier" effect that would encourage people to buy things again. In June 1934, Keynes made a whirlwind tour of America, visiting economists, government administrators, and congressmen. He assured them that if the United States spent only $200 million a month, it would go back into the worst of the Depression; if it spent $300 million a month, it would break even; if it spent $400 million, it would bring full recovery. His elaborate formula, which few fully understood, seemed persuasive.[110]

Keynes's clear expository writing, combined with a seemingly scientific formula of prices, wages, supply, and demand, provided an important economic rationale for the direct public investment that a New Deal Congress and president were already planning. Rather than focusing on the supply side and encouraging capitalists to invest, Keynes called for an emphasis on the demand side in getting consumers to buy again. This required getting people back to work. Given that interest rates and money supply tinkering were apparently not working, Congress focused on what came to be labeled the problem of underconsumption. In justifying federal intervention, New Dealers borrowed a concrete metaphor familiar to rural farmers: pump priming. If you had a water pump that stopped delivering, farmers understood that you needed to pour water into the pump. This effectively broke an air-pocket vacuum that prevented the pump from pulling water out. Thus the government needed to pour some money into a broken economy to get it working again.

By 1935 this combination of attacks from the party's left wing and new ideas about economics had helped justify and bring about the Second New Deal reforms, including the National Labor Relations Act, the Social Security Act, the Works Progress Administration, and the Fair Labor Standards Act. All seriously and irreversibly committed the federal government to intervening in the industrial sector of the economy.[111] Minimum wage, collective bargaining, and Social Security became regular features of the industrial sector of the American economy. While the Agricultural Adjustment Act and the Soil Conservation Act (a program that continues today) provided subsidies to farmers, Congress excluded agriculture from much of the rest of this legislation. Because of the agricultural exclusions, most African-American and Latino workers were left out of the most interventionist parts of the Second New Deal. This was intentional: Southern and southwestern Democrats were happy to increase costs for primarily northern and midwestern manufacturing industries. They would not support pensions or collective bargaining for their mostly rural laborers. Most, after all, could not vote.[112]

Still, the poor rural South and West did change under the Second New Deal. The Tennessee Valley Authority (TVA) and other rural electrification projects brought electrical power to rural areas. Given the colossal, destabilizing failure of the Insull utility empire, few Democrats or Republicans believed that public utilities in private hands would succeed, especially in the rural South.[113] The TVA created a new batch of consumers for washing machines, radios, and lightbulbs, helping bridge the vast gulf between rural and urban consumers. For all its faults, the TVA helped integrate the rural South into the still-struggling national economy.

WHEN GREECE FINALLY agreed to turn him over in 1934, a defiant Samuel Insull, then seventy-four, had difficulty explaining how his pyramided utility empire worked. His lawyers succeeded in blaming "Old Man Depression" for his ills. By then public, not private, utilities had become one of the defining features of a post-panic America. Insull became immortalized as one of the inspirations for Orson Welles's *Citizen Kane,* though Insull's sometime ally William Randolph Hearst was probably more important. Insull was also immortalized with the board game that became one of America's favorite pastimes during the Depression: Monopoly. With his trademark droopy mustache, silk hat, striped pants, and spats, Insull became the symbol of corporate excess.

Players moved around Atlantic City to acquire properties and utilities and to avoid going to jail. It was a zero-sum game that had only one winner, no matter how often you played it.

The game had Monopoly money, but it was not based on a reserve of banker's acceptances and Treasury bills. The supply of money did not expand rapidly as the game progressed, and an inner circle of players could not invest in speculative enterprises in Germany or Peru, then foist them on unsuspecting players who walked up to watch the game. It did not end with frayed fortunes, escalating conflicts between players, a major rewriting of the rules, and a second world war. Still, it seemed like a model of an economy that anyone could play. After 1934 millions of Americans had considerable time on their hands. They played it over and over again.

CHAPTER TWELVE

Conclusions, Conclusions

NDREW JACKSON and Anton Cermak could never have met, but both became standard-bearers for the Democratic Party, and both came to represent crucial political turning points during America's economic crises. Both believed strongly in the spoils system and were sincerely committed to a unified executive, mayor or president, with complete power. Yet put in a room together, the two men would almost certainly have come to blows. Cermak had a very quick temper: as a member of the Cook County Board of Commissioners, he more than once threatened to take an argument outside the hall to be settled with fists. Andrew Jackson would have been delighted to oblige him.

Their differences, of course, are vast. Jackson was trained in a North Carolina school for gentlemen, however rough he was around the edges. Cermak had learned little but reading and arithmetic in his two or three years in Braidwood public schools. He found public speaking difficult and had little of Jackson's personal magnetism.

What really made them both Democrats was a commitment to Jefferson's idea of a "Democratic" party—a coalition of those who fought against entrenched economic interests. Democrats from the days of Jefferson became committed to a state that would abolish power concentrated in a single American bank. The party Jackson and Cermak shared was forged in Jefferson's time around a newspaper and a group of elite men who opposed a Federalist political machine they saw consolidating around the First Bank of the United States. In this little crusade Democrats were surely right, though Jeffersonians' attempts to deprive the bank insider William Duer of his financial power created an even greater bank panic than might have occurred otherwise. Rescued by a revolution in France, the Bank of the United States became a safe spot for European investors and a source of funds for Yankee merchants and smugglers. After the Land Act of 1800 the Jeffersonians would create a "bank" in the U.S. Land Office that would loan to everyone regardless of his ability to pay. In this, Jefferson's Democratic Party was probably wrong.

As a lender, the U.S. Land Office probably distributed economic benefits far more broadly than the Federalists could have or would have. Here was the birth of federally insured mortgage credit. The expression "doing a land-office business" came to mean doing a great deal of business. But although it made a great deal of revenue, it actually lost more than it made in the course of its existence. And of course, its largesse depended on the defeat or removal of the Indians who occupied the land. Each major defeat of Indian landholders put millions of acres for sale that Americans would voraciously buy on mortgage in booms and rapidly sell for pennies in busts.

With the death of the First Bank in 1811, a large and chaotic banking system emerged in each of the states. Its unruly notes led to widespread inflation. While it provided opportunities for fraud and chicanery, it may also have broadened and deepened economic relationships between Americans. Attempts by the newly formed Second Bank of the United States to destroy the "caterpillars" while stabilizing the "pillars" of the community proved nearly impossible. These new banks helped create a "jobber" system that distributed foreign commodities like monkey jackets far into the American interior. Here was the birth of easy consumer credit. New York banks and their jobber clients created a credit, distribution, and intelligence-gathering system that replaced the European system of factors, creditors, and staple commodities. They helped the country escape the system of imperial credit that has hobbled every other former colony for more than a century.

But this rapid expansion of land and the rapid increase in credit also fed an asset bubble that ballooned from 1815 to 1818. Directors of the Second Bank, with its hastily devised charter, created super-leverage for some directors of regional branches, including the Federalist Edward King in Ohio and the Democrat Wilson Cary Nicholas in Virginia. The underlying asset in many of these member banks was land, yet the price of land varied more than anyone recognized. As Indian removal allowed the government to open more and more land for settlement to eager borrowers in Ohio, Kentucky, and Alabama, trouble emerged. A trade war over the Caribbean between the United States and Great Britain caused flour prices to tumble. As flour prices declined, the price of uncleared land quickly followed. In 1819 land prices dropped 30 to 40 percent in Cleveland, Louisville, and Huntsville. A few complicated factors pricked the asset bubble: a trade war between the United States and Great Britain foremost, but also the shift to a gold standard in Britain and revelations about fraud inside the bank. The 1819 panic, more than anything, brought forth a politics of anger that made Jackson its central figure.

Jackson's inheritance from Jefferson was a sense that power was clustered around Britain and the British banking system. He was not entirely wrong. The 1819, 1837, 1873, and 1893 panics had much to do with rapid increases in interest rates set by the Bank of England. As the Massachusetts congressman Benjamin Gorham observed in Jackson's time, "The barometer of the American money market hangs up at the Stock Exchange in London."[1] The nastiness of partisan politics in America drew from a deep well of pain suffered from the consequences of panics and anger at those who profited from them. This was certainly Jackson's world. It was also Anton Cermak's.

It may seem peculiar that it was the Jackson party's "arrangement" in 1830 that healed trade tensions with Britain and built a new financial bond forged of cotton between Britain and America. It seems especially peculiar given Jackson's part in the War of 1812 and his even uglier war against the "English" bank after 1831. Part of Jackson's anger was personal, to be sure: the bank president, Nicholas Biddle, did more than run the bank in a way that benefited himself; he committed considerable resources to funding Jackson's opposition, building what became the Whig Party.

The financial bond between the United States and Great Britain that sustained the Second Bank of the United States had everything to do with cotton. The agency banks established in the South, competing alongside the Bank of the United States, helped promote an 1830s credit bubble in which the profits came from future cotton prices, the security came in slaves, and the capital came from overstuffed credit markets in formally antislavery Britain. Jackson's Specie Circular, the turn to gold, and the removal of deposits certainly pricked the bubble, drastically so, but so did the Bank of England's questions about the financial instruments held by banks in the North of England. English and American concerns about a credit chain forged out of slaves, agency banks, Biddle's Bank, and cotton led to the nation's third crash and the second major cascade of bank failures in 1837. Crash politics brought Jackson's opponents the Whigs into being.

While bank security in Andrew Jackson's day had much to do with a staple item (cotton) that required a consumer item (slaves) that Americans would rather not think about, the 1857 panic had much more to do with land. The collateralized debt obligation in land made its first real appearance in the bonded debt of American railroads. And the ugly scramble for the best lands to collateralize and sell to European investors led to a nasty blowup in Kansas. In the deepest sense it brought into focus two systems for creating securities out of the prospects of future production—one based on using enslaved workers as an asset, the other based on using the future value of immigrant family labor on federal land as an asset. It was a controversy that would lead to civil war. It also led to a rather farsighted attempt by a cranky and vituperative socialist actuary to make socialized debt a public good that would be liable to public inspection. First applied to insurance company assets, it would by the 1930s become the model for asset analysis of modern corporations.

Jackson's Ahab-like obsession with gold dollars and killing the bank carried the hope that destruction of these institutions would break the stranglehold that English bankers had on the American economy. Ironically, of course, the severing of the bank from the Treasury, and the Treasury from the executive, and the unwillingness to regulate American banks made English banks all the more powerful. The United States did have a central bank after 1837. It was the Bank of England. The 1873, 1893, and 1907 panics made that perfectly clear.

Eighteen seventy-three, the year of Tony Cermak's birth, demonstrated that abject dependence on Britain. Because Americans borrowed so much from Britain, U.S. interest rates depended on English rates. When American shippers drastically underbid the price of food in Europe after 1871, it led to instability in European banks. This instability caused the Bank of England to raise its rates. High rates clobbered banks and railroads that were borrowing in England to lend in America.

Beyond the nation's dependence on English capital markets, the American asset bubble of 1873 proved yet again the dangers of debt obligations built on unproven or invented assets: whether personal notes in 1792, bills of exchange in 1819, bank drafts in 1837, railway mortgages in 1857, or second- and third-mortgage railway bonds in 1873. Symbolic doubt emerged when lenders could not distinguish golden opportunities from gilt-edged monstrosities. When it came to handing out blame in 1873, American crash politics diverged most strongly from the European variety, as many Europeans blamed Jews for the panic. Many native-born Americans blamed the wandering workers who had come from across the ocean. Americans went back again, as they had before, to heavy drinking.

But 1873 had other scapegoats in America as well. If the crash politics of 1857 had helped bring about a war that led to the liberation of slaves, the crash politics of 1873 allowed the reemergence of southern Democrats devoted to preventing former slaves from ever voting again. Southern Democrats' power in Congress finally allowed the last southern states to overturn the experiment in black voting and begin the process of formalized disenfranchisement. It established the outer limits of how much former slaves would benefit from a war over slavery: they would have nothing but freedom.[2] Their savings, meanwhile, would be destroyed by the connivance of an insider who squandered the assets of tens of thousands of black families: Jay Cooke.

But if panics kill dreams, they also bring new possibilities. Tony Cermak, born in the center of the 1873 panic, helped bring, with his father, brothers, and sisters, a new understanding of public and private institutions that Jacksonian Democrats would not have recognized and would certainly have disliked. Andrew Jackson's strategy for interrupting the corrupting power of insiders was to destroy national semi-public institutions like the Second Bank of the United States. Jackson did believe that federal institutions like the United States Treasury could shape interest rates. But Cermak went further. He came to represent the many immigrants and workers who favored a different way: municipal and state ownership of utilities, old-age pensions, factory inspection, protection of unions, and income taxes. These immigrant workers' demands emerged publicly in Chicago after 1893, though they had first surfaced in the mines of Kladno in the late 1860s. That new radicalism was part of the reason the emperor Franz Joseph was happy to see those miners immigrate to America. Andrew Jackson, hearing Tony Cermak's demands for state ownership or control in the name of the Democratic Party, would have asked for a brace of dueling pistols.

The 1893 panic assured that Reform Democrats' first attempt to restructure the economy would fail catastrophically. New competitors in wheat sales, a crash in Argentina, and a budget move that eliminated the American tax on sugar led to a fiscal crisis in the U.S. Treasury after 1891 that caused foreigners to doubt Americans' willingness to pay their debts in gold by 1893. European mistrust of a Democratic Congress, combined with a bitter and prolonged strike in Chicago, saw Democrats like Jackson and Cermak fall from grace. Cermak personally made a fortune in the panic, but a Republican revival and a sharp turn against radical reform in the Supreme Court ensured that financial reform efforts would take place at the state level after 1893. Democratic reformers like J. Hamilton Lewis and Republican reformers like Robert La Follette transformed both parties from within.

For Democrats in the space between Jackson and Cermak, a new whale had emerged by the 1890s: J. P. Morgan. To kill him, an even larger whale had to be created. After the 1907 panic demonstrated Morgan's power to make and break banks in New York, Democrats in 1913 committed to creating a twelve-part, decentralized, non–Wall Street institution, the Federal Reserve. They hoped the Federal Reserve would take power away from Morgan, who had been using the New York Clearing House and the other Clearing House Associations to concentrate financial power in his own hands. The Federal Reserve instead created a complex and competitive inner circle: half a dozen bankers rather than one. Within a few years Wall Street banks had removed most of the federal oversight powers (over open market operations, for instance) and kept the infrastructure, thank you very much.

Democratic strategy from Jackson to Cermak changed because the Federal Reserve changed everything in regard to American panics. After the Federal Reserve, seasonal fluctuations in interest rates dropped quickly, a drastic monetary expansion followed, and a U.S. credit system began to move worldwide. But rather than the caterpillar banks of 1816–1819, or the agency banks of 1833–1838, the success of New York banks backed by the Federal Reserve attracted gold from around the world. Gold surged into the safe haven of the United States. It is true that German U-boats, American battleships, a trench in Belgium, and rifled artillery helped gold develop its sudden attachment to American shores. Apparently safe, nationally guaranteed, relatively unregulated: the Federal Reserve helped change the international flow of capital. After more than a hundred years as unsteady borrowers, Americans would become lenders. For more than ninety years after 1914, American banks would seem safe havens.

Every crisis is unique, with origins that differ one from the other. There are not and never have been "cycles" dictated by an inexorable ebb and flow of investment. When financial instruments break—usually because of poor construction, weak oversight, and miscalculations of risk—they break everything. With the exception of the 1893 crisis, high-yield financial instruments became the central assets of banks. Banks before each crisis worried more about their own expansion, margins, and balance of assets than about the possible instability of the high-yield instruments that their lending rested upon. Bankers failed to see that if they ran a bank that was a pawnshop for promises, the stability of the promises meant everything. More than the overall money supply, more than its liabilities, more than the overall terms of trade, every part of the institution was leveraged on a collection of interest-bearing promises. And during asset bubbles certain promises were likely to be broken.

What happened in 1929–1931 was especially peculiar because American banks rested on Treasury bonds combined with two new promises: dollar loans abroad and banker's acceptances. Treasury bonds did not break, but in 1928 the dollar loans did, and then the banker's acceptances proved to be an accounting trick that a few well-connected New York banks could use to tread water while smaller banks failed. By 1933, American officials had determined that the dollar loans abroad were dangerous. Dangerous indeed. American bankers had through the 1930s sought federal gunboats to ensure that Peru, Venezuela, and Argentina made payments on their bonded debts. In fascist Europe, the German government insisted that its invasion of Poland was simply to ensure that defaulted loans were repaid. It was a move that helped bring about World War II.

After World War II the United Nations would create the World Bank to ensure that banks would no longer make desperate foreign loans and then push sovereigns to use tanks, airplanes, and gunboats to enforce them as they had in the bond boom of the 1920s. After 1933 acceptances were eliminated from the portfolios of American banks as instruments too easily falsified by the banks. U.S. national debt in Treasury bills—the American government's promise—would be the basis for assets for national banks. This entire process provided stability for fifty years. Then, in 1987, the Federal Reserve began to reinterpret the phrase in Glass-Steagall that prevents commercial banks from being "engaged principally" in the securities business. By the 1990s, commercial banks using Federal Reserve assets could do as much as 25 percent of their business in securities underwriting. They could make new synthetic promises again, in the form of financial derivatives, and sell them to smaller banks, pension funds, insurance companies, and sovereign wealth funds.

With parts of Glass-Steagall removed, large banks began to create structured investment vehicles that resembled the security affiliates of the second and third decades of the twentieth century. Small banks and pension funds around the world—like the now-defunct midwestern banks of the 1920s—listened to the siren song of federally insured big banks that sold seemingly risk-free, high-interest-rate collateralized debt obligations, foreign exchange, and currency swaps. Some small banks and pension funds naturally wondered about the security of these new promises. The big banks introduced these banks to a new, entirely unregulated market that emerged after 1987: the over-the-counter derivatives market.

The derivatives market is a kind of virtual market where banks and others trade assets as if they owned them. The "as if" is important, because most countries prevent a banker from boarding an airplane with a million dollars of their currency without paying a tax. But a bank in Spain that worries about the declining value of the euro can enter a trade that protects it if the euro is in danger of devaluation. The Spanish bank can offer to pay the three-month interest on a million euros in exchange for an American bank's paying the three-month interest on the same amount in dollars. This is a forward euro-dollar swap. If euros drop in value in those three months, the Spanish bank makes a little from this trade by getting the interest in current dollars; if dollars drop in value, the American bank makes a little in this trade by getting the interest in current euros. These trades are payable not in dollars or euros but with AAA securities, usually U.S. Treasuries. This swap can act as a hedge for each bank in case its own currency drops in value; if it does, the trade makes the bank some money to counterbalance the risk. Hedge funds (which have capital and borrow from brokers) and shadow banks like Lehman Brothers (which borrowed on the money market) have large research departments that give them advice. They then speculate on currency movements. This vast currency and foreign exchange swap market is a perfect environment and has none of the messy regulations of the stock market (margins) or banks (reserve requirements) or even corporations (generally accepted accounting principles).

Being in the middle of a swap pool of swimming-around AAA securities is useful for a large bank if it suddenly needs to fill up the promises in its trunk. Indeed it can lend its Treasury bills *overnight* to any bank, hedge fund, or shadow bank that will pay an evening's interest to participate in this over-the-counter derivatives market. By the 1990s someone had figured that the derivatives market would be the perfect place for the newly created collateralized debt obligations. Using the model of the currency swap, shadow banks, hedge funds, and other entities (like AIG) created a "default swap" in which they would collect part of the interest if the bond paid off and they would pay part of the interest if the collateralized debt obligation, or CDO, failed. Many of these so-called CDO counterparties made promises in the tens of billions of dollars but had assets only in the millions.

Finding buyers and counterparties for new and high-interest collateralized debt obligations was easy; finding borrowers proved difficult. Agents of New York and international banks, resembling the "bond men" of the 1920s, rushed into America's heartland to push loans onto middle- and low-income home borrowers, including the so-called NINJA loans to those with "no income, no jobs or assets." The uncollectible German municipal 6 percents of the 1920s became the uncollectible home-mortgage 8 percents of the first decade of the twenty-first century. When the CDOs began to fail in 2007, the counterparties in this derivative "market" quickly folded. Banks, shadow banks, hedge funds, and pension funds quickly discovered what the midwestern banks had discovered in 1928: that this allegedly liquid market was not liquid at all. No one wanted to buy the CDOs because no one could price them. Markets seized up. Crash.

In August 2011, the AAA U.S. Treasuries that were at the heart of this derivatives market—with a nominal value of $600 trillion—shuddered again when congressional talks broke down over how to pay off the nation's spiraling deficit. The $14 trillion deficit is tiny. The $600 trillion market in derivatives is more than forty times the U.S. gross domestic product in one year. Yet again, in 2011, an entire market rested on a pinhead.

What is the problem with this derivatives market that (in early 2012) is still unregulated? Put simply, the biggest banks in the world have created—in the derivatives market—an entirely new supply of liquidity, of ready money. The move was analogous to the money supply created by the New York Clearing House in October 1853. On the first day of its operations, banks created an agreed-upon settlement document that announced what each bank owed to another. Each bank returned to its home bank to put that settlement document in the vault. On that day in 1853, the New York banks created a new form of money. The Federal Reserve took over that entire machinery of money creation when it was formed in 1913, because the American public believed it was operated on behalf of J. P. Morgan. Around 1987 the derivatives market, backed by U.S. Treasuries, created a much more complex money but nonetheless a newly minted document used to settle daily exchanges between banks. When a bank buys a position in the derivatives market using AAA collateral, new money is created. These positions in the derivatives market, which can be bought and sold instantly, are analogous to high-powered money. Comparable quasi-money booms occurred before 1819, 1857, and 1873, and they all ended badly. In the United States in 1857 such a boom ended in war.

While the Great Depression of 1929 offers us some guidance about the operations of banks, it gives us almost no guidance about the future. Because European and Latin American governments were the big borrowers and defaulters in the 1920s, the 1929 depression is a confusing analogue and makes that crash the wrong model for understanding our current crisis. In every other major panic described here, American consumers were borrowers. Sometimes they borrowed for planting wheat, sometimes for buying monkey jackets, sometimes for purchasing slaves, sometimes for the prospects of sod settlements on the plains of the Missouri River. But in the 1920s, Americans were lenders, and as new lenders they were pretty bad at it. Americans and small American banks, relatively new at lending, were persuaded by large American banks to lend abroad to places that would never repay.

ALL THE OTHER panics before 1929 have more to tell us about the current crisis, and the story should sound hauntingly familiar to those who went through the 2008 crisis. After all, American banks had had one hundred years to learn the art of making nonpaying American assets look attractive. They had the playbooks from Ohio's canal construction boondoggles of the 1840s, John Murray Forbes's 1857 Missouri fiasco, and Jay Cooke's Northern Pacific scam of 1873. For more than a century these banks had learned to package loans that were as valueless as the accordion file of bad debts in my father's Dodge Dart. Mostly these bankers sold them and shrugged when smaller banks choked on them.

But in the 1920s the borrowers and lenders were reversed. The lenders were midwestern American banks, whose depositors were midwestern Americans. Midwestern banks began to notice how unreliable those promises were only in 1928. When those banks and other lenders got scared, they plowed their lending into the stock market as the only available place for short-term loans. When prices began to collapse, National City Bank and others took rediscounts using banker's acceptances. They effectively borrowed from the Federal Reserve to prop up prices before they bailed themselves out. That *is* a familiar story in 2012. So how did Americans respond in Tony Cermak's day? They attacked privilege by imposing regulations, including Glass-Steagall and the federal Securities Act.

Things have changed drastically since Tony Cermak's day. Beginning in the mid-1990s the Democratic Party largely abandoned its commitment to attacking vested privilege. No more messianic struggles against "Anglocrats," corrupt bargains, white whales, Boston capitalists, robber barons, gold crosses, or public utility monopolists. The Democratic Party embraced Wall Street. Following in Bill Clinton's footsteps when the crisis of 2008 hit, President Obama and congressional Democrats did not reach for the boom stick. Instead, they sought the counsel of those Wall Street insiders who had demanded the deregulation of markets in the 1990s that helped cause the crash of 2008. They turned to Rahm Emanuel, Tim Geithner, and Larry Summers, who urged the federal government to absorb the bad debts by banks and to act as a central counterparty to guarantee all the derivative bets made by banks all over the world. As both Andrew Jackson and Tony Cermak would point out if they were alive today, shock at Wall Street presumption has lost its place in the Democratic Party.

The Tea Party movement, on one side, and the riots in Greece and London, on the other, are both refracted versions of the anger at entrenched privilege, at monopoly, and at Wall Street skulduggery that has followed America's panics since the crowd that gathered around Duer's jail in 1792. It is puzzling to see again in such different uniforms the ghosts of the old Democratic Party: of Andrew Jackson, "Sockless" Jerry Simpson, William Jennings Bryan, and Huey Long. But they are still with us, summoned up like spirits.

What has happened to the reformers who demanded transparency, public accounting, and direct federal oversight, men like Elizur Wright and Tony Cermak? When I finished the first draft of this book in 2009 I despaired that the shades of those courageous, angry, and righteously indignant gentlemen had left us behind. I should have had more faith. The Occupy Wall Street movement, for all its problems and contradictions, would have put a smile on their faces. Elizur Wright would have found someone to start an argument with. Tony Cermak would have hit a pub first, then started a proper brawl. Those ghostly malcontents are with us still. Listen.

Here Be Dragons

*What's Wrong with How Historians and Economists
Have Written About Financial Panics*

T THE RISK OF FURTHER irritating my colleagues, I would like to discuss a few problems with the way panics and economic history have been discussed in the past few decades. This is more free ranging and is more of a rant than a scholarly analysis. As the notes on the edges of medieval maps say, here be dragons. This discussion is speculative and probably uninformed, but I feel compelled to write about what has troubled me about much of the secondary material I have read after I have pored over the primary material. If you are not interested in history as a craft, you may safely ignore it. If you are a historian, you may want to tear these pages out of the book and stomp on them.

The first and primary problem with social historians (and I count myself among them) is that they have discussed the American economy as if farmers were self-sufficient yeomen breaking the wilderness. They regularly misunderstand how American stores provided consumer credit to farmers, plantation owners, and renters who settled the West. The store system of Andrew Jackson's day borrowed practices from the colonial store system that goes back to the seventeenth century, if not earlier. It was how the East India Company, the West India Company, and the Dutch East India Company profited. Credit provision by these transatlantic institutions was a crucial part of the slave trade. The store system allowed settlement in unsettled land.

I can think of a few reasons why historians miss the early and intimate relationship between Americans and credit: one is the continued attachment to Marx's idea of the conservative nature of merchant capital. Merchants, so the story goes, may engage in primitive accumulation but cannot create new forces of production. They are too conservative. While one might make such an argument about *encomienda* in the Spanish colonies, which *may* have relied on ancient forms of agricultural and mining practices, merchant capital as a concept does not really help us understand settler colonialism in the United States, Canada, Argentina, and Australia, which required a widespread destruction of local communities and lots of consumer credit.[1]

A related problem in the field is the use of the term "market revolution" to describe the period from 1819 to the 1840s. To me it has long lost its luster because it relies on the same binary divide between precapitalist and capitalist forms of agriculture. This depends on, I think, a misunderstanding of the intimate relationship between farming and commerce for most of the people who settled in the Americas.[2] If we are looking for alternative modes of agriculture, commerce, and trade, then the important anticapitalist movements in the wake of panics may be much more interesting. I include here not just the utopian and religious communities like Quakers, Shakers, and Oneidans but also the early Mormons, the Grangers, and the Populists. These people understood what it meant for banks and then railroads to extend credit through stores. They built their own associations that aimed to undermine or replace these institutions of credit (and they were institutions of credit) with locally managed cooperatives that distributed agricultural benefits in a way that served the broader community. Many of these communities regarded capital as a collective inheritance of an entire community, a storehouse of value that needed to be broadly shared. Marx hated such storehouses. Stalin sought to destroy them because he thought that the kulaks wanted to monopolize them. Elizur Wright liked them and believed that they were the basis of modern civilization. I don't feel so strongly about it, but I think that Marx's vision of accumulation as an evil obsession is peculiar. Our earliest stories—of Demeter, for example—are about how to accumulate virgin wheat (represented as Persephone) by burying it underground for three months. Accumulation saved lives in ancient rural communities. We can argue about how to share it, but to view accumulation as a disease seems silly to me.

Much of the crisis literature in the past fifty years has come from economic historians who, following Milton Friedman, begin as neoclassical economists but quickly adopt an Austrian-school attitude toward crises: that the state is to blame. While I'm more than willing to blame Franz Joseph and his state monopolies for the failure of the Austro-Hungarian Empire after the 1870s (and for the tackiness of the area inside the Ringstrasse), I'm not convinced that state institutions are to blame for any of the crises I've described here, with the possible exception of 1893. And in that crisis one could argue quite convincingly that private corruption of federal officeholders in the elimination of the sugar tariff caused the panic. Since Friedman, most economic historians have resisted any attempt to separate speculation from investment. How, according to Friedman, can we really separate the two? Doesn't speculation blend into investment? Don't markets need to clear with buyers who will come along to sweep up bargains?

This, to me, is a rather facile argument that attempts to explain away the problems of leverage that have contributed to most of the panics I discuss here. After 1929 the New York Stock Exchange increased the leverage requirements for stocks bought on margin from 10 percent to 50 percent. That is, you could borrow from your broker to buy stock, but 50 percent of the investment had to be your own money. Margin betting then gravitated to commodities, especially in Chicago, but failures on those exchanges led to new commodities regulations in the late 1980s, which chased it out again. In the 1990s, Congress allowed over-the-counter derivatives markets to emerge that had *no* regulation to speak of and *no* margin requirements. This is where margin speculation moved next. In 2010 that market had an astonishing notional value of $600 trillion. The biggest players in this over-the-counter market are the so-called G14 dealers that include Bank of America, J. P. Morgan, and Morgan Stanley.

Collateralized debt obligations were a sizable chunk of that over-the-counter market in 2008 before the Federal Reserve absorbed and canceled the toxic mortgage debt. In many cases the counterparties in those transactions (like AIG) could not pay on their side. Most of the over-the-counter derivates market moved to currency, interest rate swaps, and sovereign debt. The sovereign debt crisis of 2011 saw European banks sitting on Greek and Italian loans, with counterparties betting that they would not pay. But this over-the-counter market (as of 2012) still had no margin requirements. If the current Dodd-Frank Act, which was not fully implemented in 2012, imposed just a 1 percent margin requirement, that over-the-counter market could quickly absorb *all* of the AAA Treasuries issued by the U.S., German, Swiss, and Japanese governments just to keep functioning. When the S&P dropped the U.S. government AAA rating in August 2011, that nearly quintillion-dollar market shuddered. The sizable drops on the U.S. stock market were just aftershocks. Margins impose safety. We saw in 2011 that regulators cooled speculation in gold, silver, and oil markets by increasing margin requirements. It is clear that margin requirements can be a simple and effective method for trimming leverage and reducing risk.[3]

The other Friedman cul-de-sac is the obsession with the money supply. He and his followers have missed the fact that crises are and always have been crises in productive assets—the promises in the trunk. Those promises allow banks to function. Friedman's argument about the money supply's being the most important variable works only if we sharply divide "money" (expressed as any non-appreciating asset) from "appreciating assets." But as the Federal Reserve would have told you when it gave up trying to measure the money supply in the 1980s, there were so many competing non-moneys and semi-moneys that it found it was chasing after a chimera. Money is not really measurable, and it comes into Friedman's analysis to explain events that have bubbled out of control long before he gets to them.

SOME WILL THINK that this book is a warmed-over version of Joseph Schumpeter, who argued that business-cycle downturns came from periods of "creative destruction" in which new technologies undermined old ones. The old technologies, with millions invested in them, became instantly obsolete, leading to financial failures that cascaded to other industries. While I can't hate Schumpeter, I think there is a mechanistic fallacy in his argument, and of those who followed him. He and his followers scour the past for technologies that collapsed in each panic. While there may be something there, the whole account seems reductive and technologically determinist. Steamboats, canals, the Bessemer process, fractional distillation of oil, and washing machines are all technologies that flourished *during* the American panics, not before them. They swept away older technologies and older investments, but that sweeping away did not cause the panics. In fact, those new technologies often benefited by the uncertainty that panic created.

While I have read and sometimes profited from reading historical sociologists like Giovanni Arrighi and David Harvey, I am convinced that there is a kind of reductive story there also, a kind of latter-day Schumpeterianism. These historical sociologists posit a "spatial fix," a center of capitalism that then organizes and draws tribute from the rest of the world. For Arrighi it is a kind of pump that sucks assets; for Harvey it is an investment in a capital city (Amsterdam, London, New York) and a use of new communication technologies (telegraphs, telephones, the Internet) to draw higher profits everywhere else. But I think arguing that a "global market under U.S. hegemony" started after World War II is just plain wrong and suggests that they have not thought carefully enough about financial instruments and financial institutions of the Federal Reserve. Their story seems more or less political to me: American empire comes when Americans claim victory in World War II. The economic material seems to be used in the service of a story about the rise and decline of empires.[4] The American empire, if there was one, emerged *during* World War I, and it depended on particular institutions and particular instruments. The International Monetary Fund and the World Bank chartered after World War II were not conceived of as the path breakers of financial empire; they were chartered to restrain the dirty tricks of financial empires of the 1920s, including the gunboat diplomacy demanded by American banks in Peru or by Germans in Poland. When this financial empire falls, it will likely fall on the failure of those instruments just as France fell on the assignat, Britain on the sterling bill of exchange, and Russia on the ruble.

Regarding the history of American foreign policy, I am not ultimately persuaded by the Wisconsin school's account of American imperial adventures in the 1890s. Industrialists' obsessive search for international markets seems an idea in search of evidence. Carnegie hated empire; Rockefeller saw American empire as competition for his own efforts to control markets in Latin America. Minor Cooper Keith, vice-president of United Fruit, wanted to operate other countries (his "banana republics") as private entities. Many midwestern farmers who might have wanted foreign markets were isolationists. American empire was not accidental, but I think it had a lot to do with unexpected results of trade policy that then provided a pretext for presidential and congressional attempts to stir up voters on behalf of empire. This is something like what British historians call social imperialism, a kind of social bond to empire that draws some voters together.

Finally, I have learned something from the so-called cliometricians—the New Economic Historians who introduced economic modeling into American economic history. But I think that their work relied far too much on data that they didn't really understand. Their characteristic move was to attack all the economic historians who came before them as mandarins who knew the beginning and the end of a story and just guessed at the middle. By comparison, they looked at numbers and sought to reason from them. Their work almost entirely ignored the economic historians who came before them. There was something fresh about this approach in the 1970s, I suppose, and there were probably certain claims of the previous economic historians that did not bear close scrutiny: that slavery was not profitable, that railroads caused economic growth, or that Jackson's bank war alone caused the panic of 1837. But their work tended to reason from numbers whose provenance was much messier than they knew. This is especially true with international trade. In a certain sense I am trying to resurrect an older economic history that blends primary, secondary, and quantitative material, one that pays close attention to historians who are long dead. If I have succeeded, then lots of living historians will be angry with me for this attempt at a grand synthesis of disinterred scholarship. But if we are historians, we should listen carefully to the living and the dead. Perhaps this work will persuade scholars who follow that we can embark on the exploration of the places where maps have failed us. We push along in the dark anyway.

Acknowledgments

This book started as a Facebook posting. Jennifer Howard at *The Chronicle of Higher Education* saw my posting about how the panic of 1873 resembled the ongoing panic of 2008. She suggested I write an op-ed. Karen Leipziger masterfully edited the piece I wrote. That article, published online October 1, 2008, explained a few things about the ongoing downturn and predicted a few things that would happen in the world economy. They did happen. The article was translated by a dozen foreign newspapers in just over a week. Bloggers used the article to pick stocks; some used my article to make a great deal of money as the stock market was tanking. When banks began to call, write, and email me during that long October of 2008 their biggest question was: is there a book that explains the other financial panics the way that you did in your article? Jennifer and Karen: thank you.

I could not have written this without Cindy Hahamovitch. She put up with my disappearing to the Newberry library for one year and to Harvard for another year so that I could tackle this white whale. But above all, she read it and gave me voluminous comments. She did this twice, when the book was at its most ungainly and confused. Since 1981, when we first met, I learned from her most of what I know about being a scholar and an intellectual. She also married me, which made it easier for me to follow her around. She will doubtless roll her eyes at the knock-kneed farmers, monkey jackets, and other bits of overzealous and imaginative description in this book. She will know which of these sentences are her revisions of my spastic outbursts.

Paul Heideman, Greg Downs, Richard John, and Bruce Baker read this whole manuscript too, God help them. They pushed me to be clearer about financial history and reminded me when I was veering wildly into fields I did not fully understand. I took almost all of their sage advice. Alejandra Irigoin, Jess Lepler, Sandra "Dya" Englert, Leon Fink, Gary Gerstle, Josh Specht, Craig Kinnear, Shaun Nichols, Ryan

Quintana, and Richard H. Brown provided invaluable help with particular chapters. Nakul Kadaba and Peter Terenzio spent part of their summer helping me with some trouble spots, while Jo Guldi and Jean Russell helped me think through the process of breaking out of history as a discipline. Participants in the Newberry workshop put me through my paces about 1792, including Jim Grossman, Craig Koslofsky, Jen Hill, Susan O'Donovan, Greg Foster-Rice, Deborah Cohen, Bruce Calder, Danny Green, and Scott Stevens. Marla Miller and the history reading group at University of Massachusetts, Amherst did the same. David Zimmerman at the University of Wisconsin responded to my 1819 paper as did David Sicilia and the wonderful faculty who attended the Miller Center for Historical Studies seminar at the University of Maryland. Walter Johnson and the participants in Harvard's Justice, Welfare, and Economics Program helped me work on the panic of 1837. The Harvard Political Economy of Modern Capitalism workshop did the same for 1929. Thanks to Harvard fellows and organizers including Sandra Comstock, Sheyda Jahanbani, David Kinkela, Dayo Gore, Chris Capozzola, John Munro, Sarah Phillips, Andrew Zimmerman, Christine Desan, Sven Beckert, and Erez Manela.

Fellowships at the Newberry and Harvard's Warren Center made this book possible. A yearlong leave at the College of William and Mary allowed me to write the articles and grants that made those leaves possible.

The most useful thinking comes out when food is going in. Coffees with Leon Fink in Chicago made me think harder. Drinks with Lynn Hudson and Jane Rhodes, the other members of the "burn unit," made a dozen Chicago evenings without Cindy livable. Sandra Comstock, John Munro, and Andrew Zimmerman were always willing to get cappuccino at Harvard and let me try ideas on them. Fred Corney and Andy Fisher let me float an argument long enough to shoot it down for me. Kris Lane, Paul Mapp, Susan Kern, and Brett Rushforth listened to me talk about wheat; they pushed my arguments back while we digested our own wheaten delicacies. Eric Kades and Nate Oman: thanks.

Deirdre Mullane made me think like a writer. Her love of sublime sentences is infectious. She is the only person who edits me, and I think, "That sentence is so much better, but how did changing these two things make it better?" She is a fabulous agent and knows more about New York publishing gossip than one person can possibly know.

Andrew Miller is everything I had hoped for in an editor. I have never been pushed so hard to make my words do what they are supposed to do. His concentration, his attention to contradictions, and his unwillingness to put up with sloppy thinking have made this a much better book than it was as a manuscript. Three overhauls with comments on every page? You are the bomb. The copy editor for this project checked my footnotes, fixed incoherent phrases, and caught some embarrassing gaffes. Thank you.

Renny Hahamovitch and Annie Nelson put up with my singing to myself, talking to dogs that have long since died, wandering around in a daze, and generally being helpless as a father; that, and being gone for two years. They have borne it like farmers confronted with a lightning rod salesman: gamely, and with good humor. This book is dedicated to them.

Notes

PREFACE: A REPUBLIC OF DEADBEATS

1. The Gaussian copula function used by Barclays Bank to describe how default risk might spread in a mortgage market was just as ahistorical.
2. This was not always true: the Grange spread most rapidly after 1873, and the Congress of Industrial Organizations formed in 1932.
3. The Know-Nothings are not discussed here, however. Instead, I focus on the formation of the Republican Party.
4. Another important thread in this book is the importance of financial journalism, though it is patchier. Philip Freneau's *National Gazette* did not just set the low tone for political debate in American politics; it also set American newspapers on a path of exposing financial chicanery and political corruption. This investigative journalism proved important in identifying William Duer's wrongdoing, though it often made him a scapegoat for the panic while ignoring how Jefferson's party contributed to the financial instability. The panic of 1819 was certainly helped along by the insider account of bank dealings by the son of a teller, while the 1837 panic had much to do with Nicholas Biddle's corruption of the *New York Courier* editor James Watson Webb. While routine condemnations of the bank in *Niles' Weekly Register* or in Democratic Party organs can make for titillating reading, the journalism was not as thorough or reliable as we might hope. In comparison, the lucid analysis of Elizur Wright in the *American Railway Times* and Mark Twain's lucid analysis of Washington corruption in his 1854 articles (reused in his book *The Gilded Age*) have been fantastically detailed and careful. E. L. Godkin's analysis of the weakness of American railway bonds in 1873 was as clever and telling as it was prescient. H. L. Mencken is not just quotable; he is astute for the fallout from the 1929 panic. Was there a Cassandra for 1893? I cannot say.

CHAPTER ONE: DUER'S DISGRACE

1. Cathy Matson, "Public Vices, Private Benefit: William Duer and His Circle, 1776–1792," in *New York and the Rise of American Capitalism: Economic Development and the Social and Political History of an American State, 1780–1870,* ed. William Pencak and Conrad Wright (New York, 1989), 78–93; Robert

Francis Jones, *The King of the Alley: William Duer, Politician, Entrepreneur, and Speculator, 1768–1799* (Philadelphia, 1992). On the town house, see "William Alexander Duer, LL.D.," *Columbia University Quarterly* (March 1902): 148–49.

2. Kentucky abolished imprisonment for debt in 1821 after the 1819 panic. New York did so after 1831. Most of the rest of the states (except Massachusetts) did so after the 1837 panic. A national bankruptcy bill appeared briefly in 1800 and then again in 1841. See Charles Warren, *Bankruptcy in United States History* (Cambridge, Mass., 1935), chaps. 1–3.

3. Bruce Mann, *Republic of Debtors: Bankruptcy in the Age of American Independence* (Cambridge, Mass., 2002), 86–87; Robert F. Jones, "William Duer and the Business of Government in the Era of the American Revolution," *William and Mary Quarterly*, 3rd ser., 32, no. 3 (1975): 393–96.

4. On Duer's committing himself as a means of protection, see [William Findley], *A Review of the Revenue System Adopted by the First Congress Under the Federal Constitution* (Philadelphia, 1794), 34. The best description of the crowd scene described here is in Paul Gilje, *The Road to Mobocracy: Popular Disorder in New York City, 1763–1834* (Chapel Hill, N.C., 1987), 84. Quotations from *New Jersey Journal*, April 25, 1792; Steve Fraser also begins his story with Duer's mob in *Wall Street: America's Dream Palace* (New Haven, Conn., 2008), 1.

5. Jones, *King of the Alley*, 171–76; Joseph Stancliffe Davis, *Essays in the Earlier History of American Corporations* (Cambridge, Mass., 1917), 296.

6. Davis, *Essays in the Earlier History of American Corporations*, 297–98.

7. On Hamilton's version of a "Greenspan put," see Ron Chernow, *Alexander Hamilton* (New York, 2004), chap. 19. On interest rates, see *National Gazette*, May 24, 1792.

8. *Stockbridge (Mass.) Western Star*, May 8, 1792.

9. On Duer's position on financial instruments, see Matson, "Public Vices, Private Benefit." On the negotiable letters of credit, see Ned W. Downing, "Transatlantic Paper and the Emergence of the American Capital Market," in *The Origins of Value: The Financial Innovations That Created Modern Capital Markets,* ed. William N. Goetzmann and K. Geert Rouwenhorst (New York, 2005), 271–98.

10. Matson, "Public Vices, Private Benefit."

11. "About Swindlers!," *Boston Argus*, April 24, 1792.

12. Thomas M. Truxes, *Defying Empire: Trading with the Enemy in Colonial New York* (New Haven, Conn., 2010).

13. "Philadelphia," *Pennsylvania Evening Post*, Feb. 28, 1778.

14. E. Wayne Carp, *To Starve the Army at Pleasure: Continental Army Administration and American Political Culture* (Chapel Hill, N.C., 1990).

15. B. J. Lossing, "Continental Money," *Harper's New Monthly Magazine*, March 1863, 445.

16. John Bach McMaster, "Old Standards of Public Morals," *American Historical Review* 11 (April 1906): 517–18.

17. Thomas Paine, *Dissertations on Government* (Philadelphia, 1786). Benjamin Franklin disagreed, arguing that currency depreciation hit moneyed men hardest. See Max Edling, *A Revolution in Favor of Government: Origins of the U.S. Constitution and the Making of the American State* (New York, 2003), 294–95; Matson, "Public Vices, Private Benefit," 90–91.

18. Peter J. Coleman, *Debtors and Creditors in America: Insolvency, Imprisonment for Debt, and Bankruptcy, 1607–1900* (Madison, Wis., 1974); Edward Countryman, *The American Revolution* (New York, 1985), 165–66.

19. Barbara Allen Mathews, " 'Forgive Us Our Debts': Bankruptcy and Insolvency in America, 1763–1841" (Ph.D. diss., Brown University, 1994), 59–75.

20. Mason to Henry, May 6, 1783, in *The Papers of George Mason, 1725–1792*, ed. Robert A. Rutland (Chapel Hill, N.C., 1970), 2:771. For general background here, see Woody Holton, *Unruly Americans and the Origins of the Constitution* (New York, 2007).

21. My interpretation here is close to Max Edling's in *A Revolution in Favor of Government*. Federalists certainly aimed for a modern European-style state that could protect borders and finance future conflicts with a regular debt; Anti-Federalists differed about how extensive federal powers of taxation and military appropriation should be. I would further emphasize Federalists' distaste for the unruly multitude created by a revolution, a feeling they often stated privately.

22. Chernow, *Alexander Hamilton,* chaps. 1 and 2.

23. Quoted in Jackson Turner Main, *The Anti-Federalists: Critics of the Constitution* (Chapel Hill, N.C., 1961), 164.

24. Matson, "Public Vices, Private Benefit," 100.

25. The most detailed analysis of Duer's speculations are in Jones, *King of the Alley*. On the land riots and the Committee of Safety in New York, see Thomas Humphrey, "Poverty and Politics in the Hudson River Valley," in *Down and Out in Early America,* ed. Billy Gordon Smith (University Park, Pa., 2004), 235–61.

26. *Dunlap's American Daily Advertiser* (Philadelphia), May 8, 1792.

27. Woody Holton, *Abigail Adams* (New York, 2009).

28. On the Clinton machine, see Alfred Fabian Young, *The Democratic Republicans of New York: The Origins, 1763–1797* (Chapel Hill, N.C., 1967), chap. 2.

29. Stanley Elkins and Eric McKitrick, *The Age of Federalism: The Early American Republic, 1788–1800* (New York, 1995), 38–39; Rhys Isaac, *The Transformation of Virginia, 1740–1790* (Chapel Hill, N.C., 1982). On "ropes and chains," see speech of Patrick Henry in *Debates, Resolutions, and Other Proceedings . . . on the Adoption of the Federal Constitution,* comp. Jonathan Elliot (Washington, D.C., 1828), 2:68. One's position on the Constitution was not just based on region or class, of course. See Main, *Anti-Federalists*.

30. Alexander Hamilton, James Madison, and John Jay, *The Federalist Papers* (New York, 2008), 71, 114, 222.

31. Gordon Wood, *Revolutionary Characters: What Made the Founders Different* (New York, 2006), chap. 4.

32. My thanks to Rhys Isaac for suggesting the wording here.

33. "From the Virginia Gazette," *National Gazette,* Aug. 31, 1791.

34. Oliver Wolcott, *Memoirs of the Administrations of Washington and John Adams,* ed. George Gibbs (New York, 1846), 24.

35. Thomas Paine, *The Decline and Fall of the English System of Finance* (Paris, 1796), 31–32.

36. The cashier had latitude in assessing fees. For larger notes the board had to approve the discount. On 6 percent, see James O. Wettereau, "New Light on the First Bank of the United States," *Pennsylvania Magazine of History and Biography* 61 (July 1937): 263–85.

37. Banks today use LIBOR—the London Interbank Offered Rate—or the so-called prime rate, or some fraction over the official rate set by the U.S. Treasury.

38. While some nineteenth- and twentieth-century American bankers have used the term "bill of exchange" to refer to American notes discounted by American banks, this was not how most British and international bankers used the term. For them a draft or bill of credit required calculating a discount, while a bill of *exchange* involved calculating a discount *and* a foreign exchange rate. Of course the note could also be marked as acceptable from a merchant of known credit rather than a bank, as was surely common before the eighteenth century. On the American and European usages, see Joseph J. Klein, "The Development of Mercantile Instruments of Credit in the United States," *Journal of Accountancy* 12 (Dec. 1911): 601.

39. Alexander Hamilton, "Report on a National Bank" (1790), in U.S. Senate, *Reports of the Secretary of the Treasury of the United States . . . to Which Are Prefixed the Reports of Alexander Hamilton on Public Credit* (Washington, D.C., 1828), 1:55.

40. The best discussions of how merchants used banks are Thomas M. Doerflinger, *A Vigorous Spirit of Enterprise: Merchants and Economic Development in Revolutionary Philadelphia* (Chapel Hill, N.C., 1986); Stuart Bruchey, *Robert Oliver, Merchant of Baltimore, 1783–1819* (New York, 1979); and Janet Siskind, *Rum and Axes: The Rise of a Connecticut Merchant Family, 1795–1850* (Ithaca, N.Y., 2002).

41. Fareed Zakaria, "Worthwhile Canadian Initiative," *Newsweek,* Feb. 7, 2009.

42. The best description of the day-to-day mechanics of the discounting process is James S. Gibbons, *The Banks of New York, Their Dealers, the Clearing-House, and the Panic of 1857* (New York, 1859), chaps. 2 and 3. Interbank relationships are discussed in David Rice Whitney, *The Suffolk Bank* (Cambridge, Mass., 1878).

43. According to Secretary of the Treasury Albert Gallatin, local banks like the Bank of Pennsylvania discounted primarily for retail customers while "those for whom the Bank United States discounts are generally importers." See Gallatin to Thomas Jefferson, June 18, 1802, in *The Writings of Albert Gallatin,* ed. Henry Adams (Philadelphia, 1879) 1:80. The amount

of $6 million to $8 million comes from Edwin J. Perkins, *American Public Finance and Financial Services, 1700–1815* (Columbus, Ohio, 1994), 253. On the role of a bank as an investors' club, see Naomi Lamoreaux, *Insider Lending: Banks, Personal Connections, and Economic Development in Industrial New England* (New York, 1994). On the advantages of the Bank of the United States that induced Robert Oliver, trading in Baltimore, to switch from the Bank of Maryland to a branch of the Bank of the United States in 1799, see Bruchey, *Robert Oliver, Merchant of Baltimore*, 120.

44. Henry Thornton, *An Enquiry into the Nature and Effects of the Paper Credit of Great Britain* (London, 1802), chap. 4; Hamilton, "Report on a National Bank," 1:65.

45. On the customhouse, which collected 86 percent of federal revenue between 1789 and 1816, see Gautham Rao, "The Creation of the American State: Customhouses, Law, and Commerce in the Age of Revolution" (Ph.D. diss., University of Chicago, 2008).

46. The internal records of the First Bank of the United States have not survived, but a close analysis by James Wettereau of sample balance sheets in the Netherlands has shown that between 1792 and 1796 the bank's largest customer was the United States, with $6 million in government securities plus $2 million to $6 million in loans to the Treasury versus roughly $6 million in loans discounted. At the end of 1796, when the loans to Treasury were mostly paid, discounting increased considerably. Wettereau's analysis demonstrates that most of this discounting was for saltwater trade, though he does not say so explicitly. For example, specie reserves spiked during the embargo. Wettereau's work also shows how dependent the bank was on specie from Latin America. See Wettereau, "New Light on the First Bank of the United States."

47. Hamilton, "Report on a National Bank," 1:64–65; on the state of European banks and a careful account of the rise of country banks, see Thornton, *Enquiry into the Nature and Effects of the Paper Credit of Great Britain,* chap. 4; on Hamilton's influences, see Elkins and McKitrick, *Age of Federalism,* 227, and Charles Franklin Dunbar, "Some Precedents Followed by Alexander Hamilton," in *Economic Essays* (New York, 1904), 71–93.

48. T. H. Breen, *Tobacco Culture: The Mentality of the Great Tidewater Planters on the Eve of the Revolution* (Princeton, N.J., 1985).

49. It was also used for glass, soap, drugs, and explosives. John M. Dobson, *A History of American Enterprise* (Englewood Cliffs, N.J., 1988), 23.

50. This description is somewhat simplistic: a skipper did trade on his own account, but more often multiple traders consigned goods with tramp shippers. Collectively, the same problem prevailed, however. The trade imbalance could be settled with Americans trying to sell bills of exchange drawn on New York; this was technically possible, but few English merchants would take them. This situation prevailed through the 1920s. While bills of exchange drawn on London traded often in New York, bills

of exchange drawn on New York hardly ever traded in London. See Harold Glenn Moulton, *The Financial Organization of Society* (Chicago, 1921), 410–14. As a result, Americans needed some other financial instrument to represent their debt to English merchants. Between 1791 and 1811, Bank of the United States stock served that purpose.

51. British brokers confusingly referred to this American bank stock as bonds.

52. Jones to Madison, March 25, 1790, in *Papers of James Madison* (Charlottesville, Va., 1983), 13:119.

53. On the power of planters, see Isaac, *Transformation of Virginia;* Allan Kulikoff, *Tobacco and Slaves: The Development of Southern Cultures in the Chesapeake, 1680–1800* (Chapel Hill, N.C., 1986); and Breen, *Tobacco Culture.*

54. On the Scottish cargo trade, see Jacob M. Price, "The Last Phase of the Virginia-London Consignment Trade: James Buchanan and Co., 1758–1768," *William and Mary Quarterly,* 3rd ser., 43, no. 1 (1986): 64–98. On tobacco town formation, see Carville Earle, *Geographical Inquiry and American Historical Problems* (Stanford, Calif., 1992). William Byrd II's warehouse became the official inspection site for tobacco in the Richmond area. See James Sidbury, *Ploughshares into Swords: Race, Rebellion, and Identity in Gabriel's Virginia, 1730–1810* (New York, 1997), 151. On the economic position of Virginia tobacco planters generally, see Emory G. Evans, *A "Topping People": The Rise and Decline of Virginia's Old Political Elite, 1680–1790* (Charlottesville, Va., 2009), chap. 3.

55. Sally E. Hadden, *Slave Patrols: Law and Violence in Virginia and the Carolinas* (Cambridge, Mass., 2001). On the role of staples in the southern colonies, see John J. McCusker and Russell R. Menard, *The Economy of British America, 1607–1789* (Chapel Hill, N.C., 1985), and Jack P. Greene and J. R. Pole, eds., *Colonial British America: Essays in the New History of the Early Modern Era* (Baltimore, 1984).

56. The tax system in early Virginia set a tithe for adult white men and for adult slaves of both sexes. A slave patroller paid one tithe less for the adults in his household. See Hadden, *Slave Patrols,* 91. On taxation and slaveholders generally, see Robin Einhorn, *American Taxation, American Slavery* (Chicago, 2006).

57. In 1965, Georg Borgstrom coined the term "ghost acres" to define the acres of land a country would otherwise need to plant in order to gain the equivalent of its fishing and its imports. In this sense, slaves were voters whom politicians similarly did not have to cultivate in order to gain their representation. On Virginia, see Breen, *Tobacco Culture.* On the broader question of citizenship, representation, and the dangers of a democracy built on slavery, see Stephanie McCurry, *Masters of Small Worlds: Yeoman Households, Gender Relations, and the Political Culture of the Antebellum South Carolina Low Country* (New York, 1995), and Stephanie McCurry, *Confederate Reckoning: Power and Politics in the Civil War South* (Cambridge, Mass., 2010), especially chap. 1.

58. Cary Carson, Ronald Hoffman, and Peter J. Albert, eds., *Of Consuming Interests: The Style of Life in the Eighteenth Century* (Charlottesville, Va., 1994).

59. On the incentive to purchasers of federal land, see Daniel Feller, *The Public Lands in Jacksonian Politics* (Madison, Wis., 1984), 9.

60. Jones to Madison, March 25, 1790, in *Papers of James Madison,* 13:120.

61. H. W. Brands, *The Money Men: Capitalism, Democracy, and the Hundred Years' War over the American Dollar* (New York, 2006), 55.

62. Thomas Jefferson, "The Anas," reprinted in *The Writings of Thomas Jefferson,* ed. H. A. Washington (New York, 1861) 9:91–95. In describing the power of the Bank of the United States, Jefferson noted the institution's intense secrecy. To whom did it lend? What were its monthly returns? What was its reserve ratio? All of this, Hamilton had declared, was dangerous information to reveal to anyone, especially a new and notoriously leaky federal government. If a sister bank in New York knew that the Bank of the United States had a brief shortage of specie (gold and silver), that bank might set off a run on the bank. In fact, to this day the best information we have about the internal working of the Bank of the United States is in the Netherlands, because in the spring and summer of 1793 Dutch merchants suggested that they might buy Bank of the United States stock if they knew precisely how the bank operated. Someone at the Bank of the United States obliged by sending over confidential internal documents about monthly operations. The documents, which exist nowhere in the United States, are still in Amsterdam. See Wettereau, "New Light on the First Bank of the United States."

CHAPTER TWO: A BOTANIZING EXCURSION

1. They also called themselves Anti-Federalists, Democratic-Republicans, Republicans, and the Republican interest. I will use "Democrat" here but ask readers to recognize that that party has changed drastically during the past two hundred years and was not nearly as tightly organized as a national political party of the twentieth or twenty-first century. That said, I believe that many in the Democratic coalitions that organized and reorganized between 1790 and 1995 were anxious about the power of dominant banks. Some important exceptions—the Tilden and Cleveland years, for instance—may have helped solidify the extraparty opposition that became the Greenback, Granger, and Populist movements.

2. Elkins and McKitrick, *Age of Federalism,* chap. 6.

3. For the list, see *National Gazette,* Oct. 31, 1791.

4. Young, *Democratic Republicans of New York,* 194–96; Elkins and McKitrick, *Age of Federalism,* chap. 6.

5. Robert's brothers and cousins in the manor faction remained Federalists. Young, *Democratic Republicans of New York*; George Dangerfield, *Chancellor Robert R. Livingston of New York, 1746–1813* (New York, 1960).

6. Nancy Isenberg, *Fallen Founder: The Life of Aaron Burr* (New York, 2007), chap. 4.

7. John Marshall, *The Life of George Washington* (Philadelphia, 1807), 5:298.

8. "From the Virginia Gazette," *National Gazette,* Aug. 31, 1791.

9. Elkins and McKitrick, *Age of Federalism*; Raymond Walters Jr., *Albert Gallatin: Jeffersonian Financier and Diplomat* (New York, 1957).

10. Ford, *Writings of Thomas Jefferson,* 4:160.

11. Politicus [James Cheetham], *An Impartial Enquiry into Certain Parts of the Conduct of Governor Lewis, and of a Portion of the Legislature, Particularly in Relation to the Merchant's Bank* (New York, 1806), 9.

12. Ibid.

13. Albert Beveridge, *Life of John Marshall* (Boston, 1916–19), vol. 2, chap. 3.

14. Ibid., 84.

15. On Hamilton's analysis of Duer's strategy, see Hamilton to William Short, April 16, 1792, in *Works of Alexander Hamilton,* ed. John C. Hamilton (New York, 1850–51), 4:217–19. For stock provisions in the Bank of the United States, see Matthew St. Clair Clarke and David A. Hall, comps., *Legislative and Documentary History of the Bank of the United States* (Washington, D.C., 1832), 30–31; Davis, *Essays in the Earlier History of American Corporations,* 281–82. Cathy Matson has suggested that his final aim was to control the Bank of New York. See Matson, "Public Vices, Private Benefit," 105. Jones believes that Duer sought a corner on the U.S. 6 percents. See Jones, *King of the Alley,* 172–76.

16. *Philadelphia General Advertiser,* Feb. 11, 1792. Reprinted in *Connecticut Current,* Feb. 20, 1792; *Connecticut Journal,* Feb. 22, 1792; *Connecticut Gazette,* Feb. 23, 1792; *Providence Gazette,* Feb. 25, 1792; *Vermont Journal,* Feb. 28, 1792; *Connecticut Weekly Register,* Feb. 28, 1792.

17. Henry Knox, "Causes of the Existing Hostilities . . . ," Report to President Washington, Jan. 16, 1792, reprinted in *Federal Gazette,* Jan. 28, 1792.

18. *Connecticut Gazette,* Feb. 16, 1792; Congressional Research Service Report RL31836, *Congressional Investigations: Subpoenas and Contempt Power* (Washington, D.C., 2003).

19. William Seton to Hamilton, Jan. 22, 1792, in *Papers of Alexander Hamilton,* ed. Harold Coffin Syrett (New York, 1961–87), 10:528–30; Chernow, *Alexander Hamilton,* 381; Davis, *Essays in the Earlier History of American Corporations,* 295.

20. David J. Cowen, "The First Bank of the United States and the Securities Market Crash of 1792," *Journal of Economic History* 60 (2000): 1041–60. Alfred Young argues that this move was more financial than political in *Democratic Republicans of New York.* See also Jones, *King of the Alley,* 177.

21. Quoted in Davis, *Essays in the Earlier History of American Corporations,* 295.

22. Duer to Hamilton, March [12], 1792, in Syrett, *Papers of Alexander Hamilton,* 11:126–27n3.

23. *Dunlap's American Daily Advertiser,* May 8, 1792.

24. *Philadelphia Federal Gazette,* April 14, 1792.

25. Robert Eric Wright and David Jack Cowen, *Financial Founding Fathers* (Chicago, 2006), 72.

26. "A [*sic*] Act to Prevent the Pernicious Practice of Stock Jobbing . . . ," reprinted in *New York Daily Advertiser,* April 23, 1792; Perkins, *American Public Finance and Financial Services,* 315. Perkins argues that the panic did not spread past New York and was relatively short-lived, and he suggests that "crash" is not the right term for the 1792 downturn. On interest rates see letter of Elbridge Gerry, cited in Edward Channing, *A History of the United States* (New York, 1917), 4:102.

27. Walter Werner and Steven T. Smith, *Wall Street* (New York, 1991), 20–25. A great deal of legend has grown up around the origins of the New York Stock Exchange; Werner and Smith carefully sort through the primary sources.

28. *Philadelphia Public Advertiser,* April 4, 1792; *National Gazette,* April 23, 1792; "Observations on the Late Failures, &c.," *Claypoole's Daily Advertiser,* May 7, 1792. I disagree here with David Jack Cowen, who argues that Hamilton injected, then suddenly curtailed, liquidity, causing the panic of 1792, a story that is much like Milton Friedman's argument about 1931 in *A Monetary History of the United States* (Princeton, N.J., 1963). See Cowen's *Origins and Economic Impact of the First Bank of the United States, 1791–1797* (New York, 2000).

29. *National Gazette,* April 19, 1792.

30. On calling in loans, see *Charleston City Gazette,* April 9, 1792; on Philadelphia, see *National Gazette,* May 24, 1792.

31. Davis, *Essays in the Earlier History of American Corporations,* 303.

32. Fierce battles going back to the 1690s had split the Livingstons into bitterly opposed camps. The Livingstons tied up New York courts with their lawsuits against one another.

33. *New York Daily Advertiser,* March 26, 1792.

34. Philip Schuyler to Hamilton, March 25, 1792, in Syrett, *Papers of Alexander Hamilton,* 11:188–89; for the advertisement, see *New York Daily Advertiser,* March 26, 1792.

35. Gordon Wood, *Empire of Liberty: A History of the Early Republic, 1789–1815* (New York, 2009), 147–58.

36. "Observations on the Late Failures."

37. Madison to Edmund Pendleton, March 25, 1792, in *Letters and Other Writings of James Madison* (Philadelphia, 1865), 549.

38. Young, *Democratic Republicans of New York.*

39. Andrew Shankman, *Crucible of American Democracy: The Struggle to Fuse Egalitarianism and Capitalism in Jeffersonian Pennsylvania* (Lawrence, Kans., 2004), 56.

40. Ibid., 50–58; Roland M. Baumann, "Philadelphia's Manufacturers and the Excise Taxes of 1794: The Forging of the Jeffersonian Coalition," *Pennsylvania Magazine of History and Biography* 106 (Jan. 1982): 3–39; quotations come

from James Thomson Callender, *A Short History of the Nature and Conse-quences of Excise Laws* (Philadelphia, 1795), 66.

41. Aquiline Nimble-Chops, *Democracy: An Epic Poem* (New York, 1794). This poem has been attributed to the Democrat Brockholst Livingston, but Alfred Young rightly points out that the poem is a Federalist screed against the Jacobin societies Democrats formed in 1794. See Young, "The Mechan-ics and the Jeffersonians: New York, 1789–1801," reprinted in *The Labor History Reader,* ed. Daniel Leab (Urbana, Ill., 1985), 75.

42. Aquiline Nimble-Chops, *Democracy,* 6.

43. Germanicus [Edmund Randolph], *Letter to the Citizens of the United States* (Philadelphia, 1794); Beveridge, *Life of John Marshall,* 2:89.

44. Donald H. Stewart, "The Press and Political Corruption During the Feder-alist Administrations," *Political Science Quarterly* 67 (Sept. 1952): 431. Bruce Mann believes that Duer had no such plan. If a creditor-friend brought Duer to a New York sheriff with a mesne process, the friend could place Duer in debtors' prison for up to seven years, effectively suspending final execution for the debt. Other creditors, unable to reach him, would have their suits suspended and possibly extinguished. The limitations of the New York bankruptcy laws are described in Mann, *Republic of Debtors,* 192–98.

45. Donald Henderson Stewart, *The Opposition Press of the Federalist Period* (Albany, N.Y., 1969), 64; Mann, *Republic of Debtors,* 195.

46. Dangerfield, *Chancellor Robert R. Livingston,* 280.

47. Stewart, "Press and Political Corruption During the Federalist Administra-tions," 431.

48. Mathews, " 'Forgive Us Our Debts,' " chap. 4.

49. On the loan of $1.5 million, see Wettereau, "New Light on the First Bank of the United States," 269. James C. Riley argues for a drop in Dutch invest-ment in American securities in 1793 after the French declaration of war, but this may refer to direct investment negotiated through the State Depart-ment, not the indirect investment in Dutch mutual funds described by K. Geert Rouwenhorst in "The Origins of Mutual Funds," in Goetzmann and Rouwenhorst, *Origins of Value,* 249–69. These Dutch funds would have invested in U.S. stocks and bonds through foreign agents in a way that may not have been captured by the Dutch statistics Riley uses. See Riley, *Inter-national Capital Finance and the Amsterdam Capital Market* (New York, 1980), 187–97.

50. These funds were different in important ways from modern "funds of funds." They were one-off institutions that bought mortgages, then sold shares to smaller investors. Partly, they appear to have been designed to avoid the Dutch requirement that foreign stocks or bonds be registered and pay a large fee. These institutions bought mostly foreign obligations such as mortgages, loans, and Bank of the United States stock. They appear to have been pitched at those with smaller fortunes who wanted a diverse collection of assets. See Rouwenhorst, "Origins of Mutual Funds."

51. Quoted in Brooke Hunter, "Rage for Grain: Flour Milling in the Mid-Atlantic" (Ph.D. diss., University of Delaware, 2001), 254.

52. On English bases in the Napoleonic Wars, see Brian Lavery, *Nelson's Navy: The Ships, Men, and Organizations, 1793–1815* (Annapolis, Md., 1989), chap. 4.

53. Frank Lee Benns, *The American Struggle for the British West India Carrying Trade* (Clifton, N.J., 1972), 15–19. The Jay Treaty, signed in 1794 and in effect starting in 1796, formally negotiated U.S. entry into ports in the British West Indies. The trade had already begun in 1793, however. As Britain captured French sugar colonies, the number of open ports under this treaty proliferated.

54. On the bank's shift to merchants, see Perkins, *American Public Finance and Financial Services*. The Bank of the United States did see a drain in specie between 1804 and 1805, partly owing to Yankee merchants' growing demand for silver in their trade with China. See Wettereau, "New Light on the First Bank of the United States," 283; William Schell Jr., "Silver Symbiosis: ReOrienting Mexican Economic History," *Hispanic American Historical Review* 81, no. 1 (Feb. 2001): 110. On the cheapness of silver in the United States, see Thomas Paine, "Thoughts on the Establishment of a Mint in the United States," *National Gazette*, Nov. 17, 1791, 21; Robert Greenhalgh Albion and Jennie Barnes Pope, *Sea Lanes in Wartime* (New York, 1942), 65–94. Perkins argues that the United States purposely overvalued silver to encourage inflow into the United States.

55. On goods shipped, see Siskind, *Rum and Axes*, chap. 4.

56. James Stephen, *War in Disguise; or, The Frauds of Neutral Flags*, 3rd ed. (London, 1806), 20–21.

57. For 1.1 million tons, see William Cullen Bryant and Sidney Howard Gay, *Bryant's Popular History of the United States* (New York, 1881), 4:172; Benjamin W. Labaree, *Patriots and Partisans: The Merchants of Newburyport, 1764–1815* (New York, 1975), 131–36. The opening of Spain's ports provided sugar, an especially valuable commodity after the Haitian Revolution eliminated France's most important sugar colony. See Manuel Moreno Fraginals, *The Sugarmill: The Socioeconomic Complex of Sugar in Cuba, 1760–1860* (New York, 1976), 41–44; see also the account books in James O. Wettereau, *Statistical Records of the First Bank of the United States* (New York, 1985). I am indebted to Eric Kades at the William and Mary Law School for pointing out the role of the float, or interest in bonded duty, in supporting the Bank of the United States. On the role of trade generally in the American economy, see Claudia Goldin and Frank D. Lewis, "The Role of Exports in American Economic Growth During the Napoleonic Wars, 1793–1807," *Explorations in Economic History* 17 (Jan. 1980): 6–25.

58. Labaree, *Patriots and Partisans*, 126; Stephen, *War in Disguise*, 44, 50.

59. Jefferson to Albert Gallatin, Feb. 28, 1808, cited in Rao, "Creation of the American State," 327.

60. William Leete Stone, *Centennial History of New York* (New York, 1876), 213; Samuel Eliot Morison, *The Maritime History of Massachusetts, 1783–1860*

(New York, 1931), 130; George W. Sheldon, "Old Shipping Merchants of New York," *Harper's New Monthly Magazine*, Feb. 1892, 457–71.

61. J. C. A. Stagg, *Mr. Madison's War: Politics, Diplomacy, and Warfare in the Early American Republic, 1783–1830* (Princeton, N.J., 1983).

62. I am thinking also of Salem's Jacob Crowninshield and Philadelphia's John Swanwick. See John Reinoehl, "Some Remarks on the American Trade: Jacob Crowninshield to James Madison, 1806," *William and Mary Quarterly*, 3rd ser., 16, no. 1 (1959): 83–118; Roland M. Baumann, "John Swanwick: Spokesman for 'Merchant-Republicanism' in Philadelphia, 1790–1798," *Pennsylvania Magazine of History and Biography* 97 (April 1973): 131–82. See also Wood, *Empire of Liberty*, 169–73.

63. John D. Haeger, *John Jacob Astor* (Detroit, 1991). On Astor as a Democrat, see *Philadelphia Weekly Aurora*, Jan. 15, 1811, 161–62.

64. Gallatin wrote to President James Madison, "Mr. Astor sent me a verbal message that in case of non-renewal of the charter of the Bank United States all his funds and those of his friends, to the amount of two millions of dollars, would be at the command of government, either in importing specie, circulating any government paper, or in any other way best calculated to prevent any injury arising from the dissolution of the bank. Mr. Bentson told me that in this instance profit was not his object, and that he would go great lengths, partly from pride, and partly from wish to see the bank down." Gallatin to Madison, Jan. 5, 1811, in Adams, *Writings of Albert Gallatin*, 1:495.

65. Astor inadvertently gives a very detailed description of his affairs in a public letter complaining about the Bank of the United States' having closed his account. See Astor to Gallatin, Dec. 21, 1810, Albert Gallatin Papers (Wilmington, De., 1985), reel 21.

66. John Kuo Wei Tchen, *New York Before Chinatown: Orientalism and the Shaping of American Culture, 1776–1882* (Baltimore, 2001), 45–47.

67. John Kendrick Bangs, "A Historic Institution: The Manhattan Company, 1799–1899," *Harper's New Monthly Magazine*, Dec. 1898, 971–76.

68. Quoted in Hamilton to Burr, June 20, 1804, in James Edward Graybill, *Alexander Hamilton: Nevis-Weehawken* (Albany, N.Y., 1898), 40.

69. Isenberg, *Fallen Founder.*

70. Historians of banking have tended to focus on things that call themselves banks rather than things that act as banks. The land office has escaped their notice. On the terms the land office provided, see Malcolm J. Rohrbough, *The Land Office Business: The Settlement and Administration of American Public Lands* (New York, 1968), 22–59. Quotations from p. 43.

71. C. L. R. James, *A History of Pan-African Revolt* (Washington, D.C., 1969), 38.

72. Timothy Pitkin, *A Statistical View of the Commerce of the United States of America . . .* (New Haven, Conn., 1835), 373; Hunter, "Rage for Grain."

73. Quoted in Kevin Gannon, "Calculating the Value of Union: States' Rights, Nullification, and Secession in the North" (Ph.D. diss., University of South Carolina, 2002), 34.

74. Dumas Malone, *Jefferson and His Time* (Boston, 1948), 5:584, 572; "Farmers of New Hampshire," *New Hampshire Gazette,* Nov. 1, 1808.

75. Nicholas B. Wainwright, *History of the Philadelphia National Bank* (Philadelphia, 1953), 32–33; *National Aegis* (Worcester, Mass.), Feb. 8, 1809; "Philadelphia," *New York Gazette,* Feb. 3, 1809; Paul A. Gilje, *Liberty on the Waterfront: American Maritime Culture in the Age of Revolution* (Philadelphia, 2004), 143–44.

76. *New York Public Advertiser,* Sept. 13, 1809.

77. "Dover Farmer," *New Hampshire Gazette,* Nov. 1, 1808; "No Monopolist," *American Commercial Advertiser,* Sept. 29, 1808; *New Hampshire Gazette,* Sept. 27, 1808; remarks of Senator Samuel Smith, *Annals of Congress,* Senate, 11th Cong., 3rd sess. (Feb. 16, 1811), 240–50.

78. Jesse Atwater, *Considerations on the Approaching Dissolution of the United States Bank in a Series of Numbers* (New Haven, Conn., 1810), 4. Henry Clay referred to opponents of the embargo as supporters of a phantom of "English pride" that "incessantly pursues us. Already has it had too much influence on the councils of the nation." *The Works of Henry Clay,* ed. Calvin Colton. (New York, 1863), 1:162.

79. Clay is quoted in Kendric Charles Babcock, *The Rise of American Nationality* (New York, 1969), 55. On the turn against the bank in 1810, see Bray Hammond, *Banks and Politics in America: From the Revolution to the Civil War* (Princeton, N.J., 1957), 209–26.

80. "The Memorial of the Inhabitants of Pittsburg, Pennsylvania, Against the Renewal of the Charter of the United States' Bank . . . ," 11th Cong., 3rd sess., S. Doc. 313 (Feb. 4, 1811), 479–80.

81. Astor to Gallatin, Dec. 21, 1810, Gallatin Papers, reel 21. For an extended discussion of Astor's side of the conflict, see "Review of Bank Pamphlets, No. IV," *Weekly Aurora,* Jan. 15, 1811. This was also reprinted in the *Richmond Enquirer,* Jan. 17, 1811. See also Haeger, *John Jacob Astor,* 139.

82. Astor to Gallatin, Dec. 21, 1810.

83. Remarks of Senator William Branch Giles, *Annals of Congress,* Senate, 11th Cong., 3rd sess. (Feb. 14, 1811), 206.

84. Speech of Senator Giles in Clarke and Hall, *Legislative and Documentary History of the Bank of the United States,* 352.

85. Astor to Gallatin, Jan. 14 or 21, 1811, Gallatin Papers, reel 22.

86. Donald R. Adams Jr., *Finance and Enterprise in Early America: A Study of Stephen Girard's Bank, 1812–1831* (Philadelphia, 1978). On the conflict about the bank, see Walters, *Albert Gallatin,* chap. 19.

87. Comptroller of the Currency, *Annual Report,* 44th Cong., 2nd sess., H.R. Executive Doc. 3 (Washington, D.C., 1876), 40; Perkins, *American Public Finance and Financial Services,* 258.

88. *Newark Centinel of Freedom,* Jan. 1, 1811.

89. Hamilton, Madison, and Jay, *Federalist Papers,* 49.

90. Pitkin, *Statistical View,* 408. On American smuggling during the War of 1812 generally, see Rao, "Creation of the American State," chap. 8.

91. Bryant and Gay, *Bryant's Popular History of the United States,* 4:208.

92. Stephen Shapiro, *Culture and Commerce of the Early American Novel: Reading the Atlantic World-System* (University Park, Pa., 2008).

93. On the fiscal-military state, see John Brewer, *The Sinews of Power: War, Money, and the English State, 1688–1783* (New York, 1988), and Edling, *Revolution in Favor of Government.*

CHAPTER THREE: MONKEY JACKETS, THE UNCORKED MISSISSIPPI, AND THE BIRTH OF CATERPILLAR BANKS

1. Michael Zakim, *Ready-Made Democracy: A History of Men's Dress in the Early Republic, 1760–1860* (Chicago, 2006).

2. "French Goods at Auction in Boston, Allen Melville Will Sell at Auction . . . ," *New England Palladium,* April 6, 1810.

3. Napoleon to War Minister Déjéan, Nov. 4, 1808, in *Confidential Correspondence of the Emperor Napoleon and the Empress Josephine . . . ,* ed. John S. C. Abbott (New York, 1858), 222, quoted in Philip J. Haythornthwaite and Mike Chappell, *Uniforms of the Peninsular War in Colour, 1807–1814* (London, 1995).

4. On the manufacturing process in Yorkshire and the West of England, see Adrian Randall, *Before the Luddites: Custom, Community, and Machinery in the English Woollen Industry, 1776–1809* (Cambridge, U.K., 1991), 14–21.

5. On the bulk of goods flowing west and the sensitivity of these flows to financial booms and busts, see Thomas Senior Berry, *Western Prices Before 1861: A Study of the Cincinnati Market (Cambridge, Mass., 1943),* 327–32.

6. Gerald Carson, *The Old Country Store* (New York, 1954).

7. On Andrew Jackson's intertwined dealings in English provisions, western staples, and land deeds, see Robert Remini, *Andrew Jackson and the Course of American Empire, 1767–1821* (New York, 1977), vol. 1, chaps. 7–9.

8. *Brooks Brothers, Centenary, 1818–1918: Being a Short History of the Founding of Their Business Together with an Account of Its Different Locations in the City of New York During This Period* (New York, 1918), 15.

9. Remini, *Andrew Jackson,* vol. 1, chaps. 7–9.

10. Alan Taylor, *The Civil War of 1812: American Citizens, British Subjects, Irish Rebels, and Indian Allies* (New York, 2010).

11. Adams, *Finance and Enterprise in Early America,* 41–46.

12. Treasury Department circular, Dallas to Bank Presidents, Oct. 12, 1815, Gallatin Papers, roll 28, frame 129; Ralph C. H. Catterall, *The Second Bank of the United States* (Chicago, 1902), 17; Davis R. Dewey, "The Second United States Bank," in John Thom Holdsworth and Davis R. Dewey, *The First and Second Banks of the United States* (Washington, D.C., 1910), 157–59.

13. John Thom Holdsworth, "First Bank of the United States," in Holdsworth and Dewey, *First and Second Banks of the United States,* 105–6.

14. On Alexander Brown & Sons' successes in 1815–16, see Edwin J. Perkins,

Financing Anglo-American Trade: The House of Brown, 1800–1880 (Cambridge, Mass., 1975); Norman Sydney Buck, *The Development of the Organisation of Anglo-American Trade, 1800–1850* (New Haven, Conn., 1925); Ralph W. Hidy, *The House of Baring in American Trade and Finance: English Merchant Bankers at Work, 1763–1861* (Cambridge, Mass., 1949).

15. "Memorial of the Subscribers, Merchants, and Traders, Convened at the City Hotel . . . ," *Country Courier,* Jan. 13, 1817. On the trunks of British dry goods in New York, see William E. Dodge, *Old New York: A Lecture* (New York, 1880), 11.

16. On the new production methods in woolens, see Randall, *Before the Luddites.* On the problem of British shippers' bringing in finished, dressed, and napped goods as raw manufactures, see "Duties on Imports," *Niles' Weekly Register,* Feb. 7, 1818, and "Letter from the Secretary of the Treasury," *National Register,* Feb. 7, 1818.

17. "Memorial of the Subscribers, Merchants, and Traders." On the origins of "job" as a one-horse cartload, see *Oxford English Dictionary,* 3rd ed., s.v. "job."

18. John M'Cready, *A Review of the Trade and Commerce of New-York, from 1815 to the Present Time with an Inquiry into the Causes of the Present Distress . . .* (New York, 1820). The new trading system is described in Buck, *Development of the Organisation of Anglo-American Trade,* chaps. 5–6. The activities of jobbers and their assistants are vividly described in Charles F. Briggs, *The Adventures of Harry Franco: A Tale of the Great Panic* (New York, 1839). Briggs's father failed in 1819. Jobbers sometimes held the notes and sometimes turned them over to banks for ready cash. Complaints about the reorganization of trade in the 1830s suggest that jobbers before 1833 or so were "content to keep the country dealer's note, payable in New York, in his pocket-book." In the following season the jobber would receive either cash or bills of exchange for produce shipped to New York. "Exchange," *Columbian Register,* July 15, 1837.

19. Jehanne Wake, *Kleinwort, Benson: The History of Two Families in Banking* (New York, 1997), 41.

20. The classic statement of this argument is Robert Greenhalgh Albion, *The Rise of New York Port, 1815–1860* (New York, 1939). The best contemporary explanation is "A Scheme for Rebuilding Southern Commerce," *Southern Literary Messenger,* Jan. 1839, 2. Rohit Aggarwala has refined this considerably, arguing that New York's provision of merchant services generally was critical to New York's supremacy over Philadelphia. He rightly points out that Albion's is a technological determinism. I would add that New York's unwillingness to regulate its banks, its friendliness to aristocratic Britons, and its understandable bankruptcy laws made it more amenable as well. See Aggarwala, "Seat of Empire: New York, Philadelphia, and the Emergence of an American Metropolis, 1776–1837" (Ph.D. diss., Columbia University, 2002). While Albion and the article in the *Messenger* ascribe the

Black Ball Line to Jeremiah Thompson, the earlier role of Kleinwort is briefly described in Sheldon, "Old Shipping Merchants of New York," and in Wake, *Kleinwort, Benson.*

21. Comptroller of the Currency, *Annual Report* (1876), 30; America's 246 banks in 1816 claimed a capital of just under $90 million. In 1817, that sum leaped up to more than $125 million. Charles Clifford Huntington, *A History of Banking and Currency in Ohio Before the Civil War* (Columbus, Ohio), 50–51. On the litter of banks, see Frederick Jackson Turner, *Rise of the New West, 1819–1829* (1906; New York, 1962), 107.

22. Mr. Smith of Maryland in Clarke and Hall, *Legislative and Documentary History of the Bank of the United States,* 636.

23. Pitkin, *Statistical View,* 430–31.

24. "Editorial Address," *Niles' Weekly Register,* Feb. 28, 1818.

25. Ibid. *Niles* was quoting Washington Irving's pseudonymous Jeremy Cockloft, the Younger, who defined an American town as "the accidental assemblage of a church, a tavern, and a blacksmith's shop." See *The Complete Works of Washington Irving in One Volume* (Paris, 1834), 17. See also William O. Scroggs, *A Century of Banking Progress* (Garden City, N.Y., 1924), 17.

26. "Editorial Address."

27. I here depart from the argument made by Glenn Porter and Harold Livesay in *Merchants and Manufacturers* (Baltimore, 1971), as well as the whole tradition that spreads from Alfred Chandler's *Visible Hand* (Cambridge, Mass., 1977), which sees continuity in the form of the merchant network from the colonial period through the Civil War. They argue that mercantile credit extended directly from manufacturers and that *naturally,* and over time, the supply chain became more specialized. Jobbers and brokers were just individual representatives of some enormous and automatic expanding division of labor. In fact, the jobbers and brokers emerged because there was a break in the credit at the point of auction. This is similar to the reason that cities formed at the falls of rivers: the break in transportation allowed hotels, taverns, stables, and other specialized institutions to form. As I will show, the new American banks actually provided the mercantile credit for the inland trade by discounting promissory notes and inland bills of exchange. State-chartered banks, not manufacturers, acted as enforcers of mercantile credit between manufacturers and jobbers, and often between jobbers and retailers. The Porter and Livesay and Chandler accounts leave the state out of the history of capital formation and merchant banking. For them, the state is only an intruder. In fact, the several states were critical to the creation of a modern inland trading network and helped to build its debt collection system.

I have some personal background in the retail-wholesale chain and the uniqueness of the American experience in it. In the 1970s my father was a foot soldier in debt collection at what network engineers now call "the last mile." My dad foreclosed on customers for Woolco, but the banks foreclosed on Woolco.

In Toronto from 1991 to 1992, I worked as a network architect for Dylex, a company that owned most of the clothing stores in Canada. I learned there what was distinct and peculiar about American credit provision and the American merchant network because Dylex sought to emulate it completely. While as an engineer I helped stabilize their point-of-sale authorization and product-performance tracking network, the Gap and other American firms had better access to American bank credit for goods in the warehouse, goods in transit, and goods on the shelf. The Gap and other American firms ate Dylex's lunch, and the company filed for bankruptcy. This American system of internal merchant credit was not new; it went back to the second decade of the nineteenth century.

28. Henry Wisham Lanier, *A Century of Banking in New York* (New York, 1922), 38; Ira Cohen, "The Auction System in the Port of New York," *Business History Review* 45 (Winter 1971): 488–510. "In almost all instances, up to the termination of the year 1816, the avails of goods sold on a credit were anticipated by the importers, from ninety days to four months, through the medium of the banks." M'Cready, *Review of the Trade and Commerce,* 22.

29. A solid but rather romantic and racist account of the bloody Natchez Trace is Jonathan Daniels, *The Devil's Backbone: The Story of the Natchez Trace* (New York, 1962).

30. It was also called country money or country paper.

31. On the mechanics of river money and river trading, see Treasury Department, *Condition of the State Banks,* 26th Cong., 1st sess., H.R. Treasury Doc. 172, 528–32, 596–98. On river banks see, for example, "An Imposition," *New-York Columbian,* Nov. 12, 1819.

32. "Dying Confession of Joseph Hare," *New York Commercial Advertiser,* Sept. 29, 1818. The editor points out that Joseph Hare's robberies on the Natchez Trace could not have taken place recently because of the prevalence of currency.

33. Fulton and Livingston claimed a steamboat monopoly on the Mississippi River from 1811 to 1816. In 1816 a state court in Louisiana overturned the monopoly. The Fulton and Livingston monopoly was decisively broken on the East Coast by *Gibbons v. Ogden* in 1824. S. L. Kotar and J. E. Gessler, *The Steamboat Era: A History of Fulton's Folly on American Rivers, 1807–1860* (Jefferson, N.C., 2009), 22–28.

34. On disposing of boats, see Jonathan S. Findlay to James Findlay, May 26, 1818, reprinted in *Quarterly Publication of the Historical and Philosophical Society of Ohio* 6 (1911): 49. For a description of trade and commerce on the Mississippi River before and during the steamboat era, see William F. Switzler, *Report on the Internal Commerce of the United States* (Washington, D.C., 1888). See also Richard C. Wade, *The Urban Frontier: The Rise of Western Cities, 1790–1830* (Cambridge, Mass., 1959), and Andrew Robert Lee Cayton, *The Frontier Republic: Ideology and Politics in the Ohio Country, 1780–1825* (Kent, Ohio, 1986). Modern historians of this period have tended to follow the Austrian-school economist Murray Rothbard in criticizing the banks as

profligate pushers of paper while marveling at the economic dynamism connected with steamboats, a rise in the river trade, and manufacturing in places like Cincinnati. The New Economic Historians, on the other hand, have praised the free banking of the post-1815 period as stimulating the economy while generally ignoring the important changes in merchandising, credit provision, and international trade. This post-Keynesian macrolevel analysis that focuses on GDP, GNP, exports, commodity prices, and per capita consumption buries the complexity that the Austrian-school economists like Rothbard embraced. Finally, the Schumpeterian framework of "creative destruction" (or the Trotskyite framework of "uneven development") has focused on technological developments like the steamboat and the packet ship but has tended to divorce them from the innovations in credit, wholesaling, currency, and store operations. This is partly why the 1819 panic has proved nearly impossible to understand. In the end, the Austrian school, the New Economic Historians, and the Schumpeterians cannot all be right, yet most accounts of this period tend to throw them all together. This account risks doing that as well, but by following the money (or in this case the monkey), we can at least establish some issues of timing.

35. Atwater, *Considerations on the Approaching Dissolution of the United States Bank in a Series of Numbers*, 8–9.

36. "Cheap Goods," *Boston Weekly Magazine,* March 1, 1817.

37. Ibid.

38. Joseph Bishop, "Inauguration Scenes and Incidents," *Century Magazine,* April 1897, 735.

39. New York Session Laws, sess. 41, chap. 26 (March 8, 1818), sess. 41, chap. 239 (April 21, 1818), sess. 41, chap. 257 (April 21, 1818), and sess. 42, chap. 101 (April 7, 1819), which finally abolished "imprisonment for debt in certain cases." All cases available in the series *Session Laws of American States and Territories.*

CHAPTER FOUR: THE SECOND BANK, THE MONKEY
JACKET WAR, AND TENSKWATAWA'S REVENGE

1. In this account of banking, I am attempting to tell, in abbreviated form, the biography of an object: the paper dollar note. My accounts in this book of monkey jackets, cotton bales, dollar bills, and wheat kernels rely very loosely on Arjun Appadurai, ed., *The Social Life of Things: Commodities in Cultural Perspective* (Cambridge, U.K., 1988); and "Adventures of a One Dollar Note," *Port Folio,* March 1817, 242–48. On oyster cellars, see John McMaster, *History of the People of the United States* (New York, 1917) 4:537–39. On coins in circulation, see U.S. Mint, "Assays of Foreign Coins," 15th Cong., 2nd sess., S. Finance Doc. 540 (1818).

2. James William Gilbart, *The Principles and Practice of Banking* (London, 1873), 42.

3. Adams, *Finance and Enterprise in Early America*, 41–48.

4. Catterall, *Second Bank of the United States*, 17–18.

5. On the difference in how the two banks settled accounts, see Wettereau, "New Light on the First Bank of the United States." Catterall argues that an important factor here was the ignorance of banking of William Jones, president of the Second Bank of the United States, who did not compel the offices to settle their accounts. Catterall, *Second Bank of the United States*, 30–31.

6. "Specie . . . becomes scarce when there is a great foreign demand for it, or when upon one part of the same Country there is a great demand for it to be transported to another part. The former has been the condition of the Atlantic States in relation to foreign countries; the latter is the condition of the Western section in relation to the Eastern." In Clay to Langdon Cheves, Dec. 13, 1819, in *The Papers of Henry Clay*, ed. James F. Hopkins (Lexington, Ky., 1959–92), 2:729.

7. Hammond, *Banks and Politics in America*, 215.

8. J. David Lehman, "Explaining Hard Times: Political Economy and the Panic of 1819" (Ph.D. diss., University of California, Los Angeles, 1992), 217.

9. House Committee to Investigate the Books of the Bank of the United States, *Bank of United States, Investigation of Books and Financial Operations . . .* , 15th Cong., 2nd sess., Finance 547, p. 307. For a justification of using land as security, see Jacob Burnet, *Notes on the Early Settlement of the Northwestern Territory* (Cincinnati, 1847), 407–9.

10. Rufus King to Edward King, April 5, 1818, in Rufus King, *The Life and Correspondence of Rufus King* (New York, 1894–1900), 6:134; William H. Crawford, Secretary of Treasury Report, 1820, in *Reports of the Secretary of the Treasury . . .* (Washington, D.C., 1837), 2:175.

11. *American Beacon*, Feb. 5, 1817.

12. Catterall, *Second Bank of the United States*, 33–36.

13. Ludwell H. Johnson III, " 'Sharper Than a Serpent's Tooth': Thomas Jefferson and His Alma Mater," *Virginia Magazine of History and Biography* 99 (April 1991): 153; Malone, *Jefferson and His Time*, 6:303–4. Nicholas's request for a loan was on April 19, 1818.

14. *American National Biography*, s.v. "Nicholas, Wilson Cary."

15. Patrick Gary Bottiger, "Two Towns, Multiple Places: Race and Identity on the Early Republic's Frontier" (Ph.D. diss., University of Oklahoma, 2009), 119.

16. Daniel S. Dupre, *Transforming the Cotton Frontier: Madison County, Alabama, 1800–1840* (Baton Rouge, La., 1997).

17. On British Corn Laws as a reaction to post–Napoleonic War prices, see Vassilis Kardasis, *Diaspora Merchants in the Black Sea: The Greeks in Southern Russia, 1775–1861* (Lanham, Md., 2001), 113, and Cheryl Schonhardt-Bailey, *From the Corn Laws to Free Trade: Interests, Ideas, and Institutions in Historical Perspective* (Cambridge, Mass., 2006), 10. The best primary source is

William J. Patterson, *Statements Relating to the Home and Foreign Trade of the Dominion of Canada, Also, Annual Report of the Commerce of Montreal for 1869* (Montreal, 1870). The best account of the timing of English legislation is Arthur Barker, *The British Corn Trade from the Earliest Times to the Present Day* (London, 1920), chap. 5.

18. In peacetime, the European market for American wheat and flour was minimal. But because the U.S. Treasury's annual statement of exports initially included Spanish and French colonies in the tables for trade to Spain and France, it is easy to overestimate the significance of the European market in the early nineteenth century. Flour going to "Spain" in the tables was usually going to Cuba; flour going to "France" was likely going to Martinique. For much more complete American export figures, see Pitkin, *Statistical View*, 96–100, 119–21. In 1815, the year the Corn Laws were passed but before they were enforced, Great Britain received more than 100,000 barrels of flour from the United States. After that year the Canadian colonies' import of American flour went from a bit more than 10,000 to over 100,000 barrels, suggesting that at this early date American flour exports to Britain were effectively smuggled through Canada.

19. "London, Saturday, May 3, 1817," *London Times*, May 3, 1817; "Ad Valorem Duties," *Niles' Weekly Register*, May 17, 1817; Benns, *American Struggle for the British West India Carrying Trade*, 53.

20. Benns, *American Struggle for the British West India Carrying Trade*, 53.

21. McMaster, *History of the People of the United States*, 4:485.

22. *American Beacon*, July 24, 1818; *Boston Daily Advertiser*, Sept. 7, 1818.

23. *Grotjan's Philadelphia Public Sale Report*, March 29, 1819.

24. For average prices between 1794 and 1818, see *Memorial of the Chamber of Commerce of the City of Philadelphia*, 16th Cong., 1st sess., S. Doc. 124 (April 28, 1820), 20, 3–5. Discussion of Britain's 1818 trade barriers to American wheat exports to the British West Indies seems entirely absent from the current literature about Anglo-American trade. See the much older work in McMaster, *History of the People of the United States*, 4:485, which relies on William Graham Sumner, *Andrew Jackson as a Public Man: What He Was, What Chances He Had, and What He Did with Them* (New York, 1882), 164–68.

25. Andreas Andreades, *History of the Bank of England* (London, 1909), vol. 1, chap. 5.

26. Lehman, "Explaining Hard Times," chap. 4.

27. Malone, *Jefferson and His Time*, 6:304; Adams, *Finance and Enterprise in Early America*, 64; Davis R. Dewey, *Financial History of the United States* (New York, 1934), 152; John McMaster, *Life and Times of Stephen Girard, Mariner and Merchant* (Philadelphia, 1918), 2:353.

28. *Times* (London), Feb. 16, 1819.

29. Tammany Society, *Address of the Society of Tammany, or Columbian Order, to Its Absent Members and the Members of Its Several Branches Throughout the United States* (New York, 1819). Henry Clay later used this pamphlet to sug-

gest that Tammany supported protectionism until Andrew Jackson came along to change its position. While one section does endorse protection of domestic manufactures, the Tammany Society blamed first "the first restrictive measure down to the termination of the late war, owing to the restraint of remittances and outward cargoes, and the embarrassments in procuring foreign receipts." The figure of 20 percent comes from Paul Gates, "Research in the History of the Public Lands," *Agricultural History* 48 (Jan. 1974): 31–50. On the depths of this depression, see Clyde A. Haulman, *Virginia and the Panic of 1819: The First Great Depression and the Commonwealth* (London, 2008), chap. 2. Percentages come from *Historical Statistics of the United States* (1949), ser. L 1–14, 232.

30. William M. Gouge, *The Curse of Paper-Money and Banking . . .* (London, 1833), 71.

31. Malone, *Jefferson and His Time*, 6:303–4.

32. Berry, *Western Prices Before 1861*, 387. Berry cites Catterall, who says the bank acquired fifty thousand acres, but a quick tally of the acreage (apart from city lots) in the original report suggests just over sixty-six hundred acres. See Nicholas Biddle, *Documents . . . in Reply to the Resolutions Offered by Mr. Benton*, 22nd Cong., 1st sess. (1832), S. Doc. 98, 8–38.

33. Charles Theodore Greve, *Centennial History of Cincinnati and Representative Citizens* (Chicago, 1904), 571.

34. Richard E. Ellis, *Aggressive Nationalism: McCulloch v. Maryland and the Foundation of Federal Authority in the Young Republic* (New York, 2007).

35. Ibid., 98.

36. Ibid., 137–53.

37. *Newark Centinel of Freedom*, June 1, 1819.

38. Stephen S. L'Hommedieu, "Inaugural Address," *Cincinnati Pioneer* 3 (April 1874): 14.

39. Gouge, *Curse of Paper-Money*, 72.

40. On the time lag from the East to the Midwest, see Haulman, *Virginia and the Panic of 1819*.

41. "Another Text for 'Homo,'" *City of Washington Gazette*, Aug. 28, 1820.

42. George W. Warren wrote reminiscences—presumably from his father—that were reprinted in *History of Cincinnati, Ohio, with Illustrations and Biographical Sketches*, comp. Henry A. Ford and Kate B. Ford (Cincinnati, 1881), 71.

43. Greve, *Centennial History of Cincinnati*, 571.

44. Frederick D. Buchstein, "Josiah Warren: Peaceful Revolutionist," *Cincinnati Historical Society Bulletin* 32 (1974): 61–71.

45. Dupre, *Transforming the Cotton Frontier*.

46. Condy Raguet et al., "History of the Money Crisis of 1818," in *A Treatise on Currency and Banking*, ed. Condy Raguet (Philadelphia, 1840), 290–91; J. David Lehman corroborates these high unemployment figures in "Explaining Hard Times," 284–96.

47. Matthew Warner Osborn, "The Anatomy of Intemperance: Alcohol and

the Diseased Imagination in Philadelphia, 1784–1860" (Ph.D. diss., University of California, Davis, 2007), chap. 2.

48. Bryant and Gay, *Bryant's Popular History of the United States,* 4:245.

49. Pitkin, *Statistical View,* 373.

50. W. Harrison Bayles, chap. 12 of *A History of the Origin and Development of Banks and Banking,* published serially in *McMaster's Commercial Cases* (1915): 129–328; Whitney, *Suffolk Bank,* 7.

51. John L. Brooke, *The Refiner's Fire: The Making of Mormon Cosmology, 1644–1844* (Cambridge, U.K., 1994); Richard L. Bushman, *Joseph Smith and the Beginnings of Mormonism* (Urbana, Ill., 1984).

52. Donal Ward, "Religious Enthusiasm in Vermont, 1761–1847" (Ph.D. diss., University of Notre Dame, 1980).

53. Pitkin, *Statistical View,* 373.

54. See remarks of William Bowman Felton, April 7, 1826, in *Report from the Select Committee on Emigration from the United Kingdom,* House of Commons Parliamentary Papers (May 26, 1826), 58. He describes how American flour housed in a Quebec warehouse became Canadian flour and free from tariff until the Canada Trade Act of 1822. See Lord Stanley's remarks to Parliament about the "uniform and unvarying practice" of treating American wheat ground into Canadian flour as Canadian produce in *Times* (London), May 20, 1843. He remarked in 1843 that this "back door" had been open for as long as anyone could remember.

55. Quoted in Greve, *Centennial History of Cincinnati,* 570.

56. "A Scheme for Rebuilding Southern Commerce," *Southern Literary Messenger,* Jan. 1839, 2–14.

57. Lanier, *Century of Banking in New York,* 38.

58. Leland Hamilton Jenks, *Migration of British Capital to 1875* (New York, 1927), 78; Mira Wilkins, *The History of Foreign Investment in the United States, 1914–1945* (Cambridge, Mass., 1989), 55.

CHAPTER FIVE: THE POLITICS OF PANIC,
THE ECONOMICS OF RAGS

1. Washington Irving, *Astoria: or, Enterprise Beyond the Rocky Mountains* (Philadelphia, 1836); John Frost, *The Young Merchant* (Philadelphia, 1839); John Sanderson, *Biography of the Signers to the Declaration of Independence* (Philadelphia, 1820–27).

2. The federal government collected money by selling land, too, but it cost more to administer the sales than the government actually made from them, especially after the defaults in the panic of 1819.

3. I have been influenced here by the work of Jo Guldi on the relationships between banking and infrastructure in "The Road to Rule: The Expansion of the British Road Network, 1726–1848" (Ph.D. diss., University of California, Berkeley, 2008). The American research on state public investment

in infrastructure is vast. One should start with John Lauritz Larson, *The Market Revolution in America: Liberty, Ambition, and the Eclipse of the Common Good* (Cambridge, U.K., 2009).

4. On the role of cotton in the antebellum economy, see Douglass North, *The Economic Growth of the United States, 1790–1860* (New York, 1966).

5. Figures from Charles H. Evans, comp., *Exports, Domestic and Foreign*, 48th Cong., 1st sess., H.R. Misc. Doc. 492 (1884), 68. The latest *Historical Statistics of the United States* cannot be relied upon for the early nineteenth century. The 2011 edition lists wheat and flour exports as valued at less than $1 million (and therefore gives them the cryptic value "[Z]"), even though the yearly reports of the Treasury secretary show "wheat, flour, and biscuit" exports of more than $18 million for the year ending September 1817. The 1817 Treasury figures show "vegetable food" at $23 million and cotton at $22.6 million. It is important to note that Secretary of the Treasury William Crawford repeatedly overstated the value of cotton exports in the second decade of the nineteenth century. In 1817, for example, he lists U.S. exports of cotton by taking the total American cotton exports in pounds and multiplying them by their top prices: forty cents per pound for sea island cotton and twenty-five cents per pound for upland cotton. In addition, after 1817 wheat and flour exports are likely underestimates, given the widespread smuggling of flour to the Caribbean and through Canada. Caveat lector! Nonetheless, even Charles Pitkin, who uses his own sources for exports, sees wheat and flour exports halved in value in 1819.

6. Mitchell Wilson, *American Science and Invention* (New York, 1954), 79.

7. Margaret L. Coit, *John C. Calhoun: American Portrait* (Boston, 1950), 1.

8. George S. White, *Memoir of Samuel Slater, the Father of American Manufactures . . .* (Philadelphia, 1836), 367.

9. Cf. Angela Lakwete, *Inventing the Cotton Gin: Machine and Myth in Antebellum America* (Baltimore, 2003).

10. On Peterloo, see William Smart, *Economic Annals of the Nineteenth Century* (London, 1910), 720–21.

11. On the broadening of power looms past calicoes and fustians, see *Cotton: From the Pod to the Factory* (London, 1842), 44.

12. Calculated from James A. Mann, *The Cotton Trade of Great Britain . . .* (London, 1860), table 4, 99.

13. On the China market for British cotton goods, see Isaac Smith Homans, *A Cyclopedia of Commerce and Commercial Navigation* (New York, 1859), 469.

14. On the new strains of cotton produced, see Alan L. Olmstead and Paul W. Rhode, "Biological Innovation and Productivity Growth in the Antebellum Cotton Economy," *Journal of Economic History* 68 (Dec. 2008): 1123–71. On the role of long-staple cotton in power looms, see James Montgomery, *The Theory and Practice of Cotton Spinning; or, The Carding and Spinning Master's Assistant, Showing the Use of Each Machine Employed in the Whole Process . . .*, 2nd ed. (Glasgow, 1833), 324–26. On the teaseling of green-seed cot-

ton, see White, *Memoir of Samuel Slater,* 367. On the percentage of English cotton imports from the United States and supply considerations, see Mann, *Cotton Trade of Great Britain,* 40–44. Even today, cotton fields I have seen in Tidewater Virginia have the bolls very low to the ground and much more thinly spread than the cotton I have seen in black-belt regions.

15. Edward Baptist, "The Whipping Machine" (paper delivered at Slavery's Capitalism Conference, Harvard University, April 9, 2011).

16. On bumblebee cotton, see "A Cape Fear Fishing Point," *Forest and Stream,* May 29, 1890, 869. Until steam-powered gins pressed them and railroads transported them, bales were measurements of volume, though each had an estimated weight of four hundred pounds. See Secretary of the Treasury, *Communication . . . on Trade and Commerce . . . and a Paper on the Cotton Crop of the United States,* in 32nd Cong., 1st sess., S. Executive Doc. 112 (1853), 804–37; Cuthbert William Johnson and Gouverneur Emerson, *The Farmer's and Planter's Encyclopaedia of Rural Affairs* (Philadelphia, 1869), s.v. "gossypium."

17. These figures were not directly recorded. More than 85 percent of American cotton went to Britain, and yearly American cotton exports ranged from $29 million to $71 million in the 1830s and 1840s. Total American exports to England in those decades ranged from $26 million to $70 million. See Evans, *Exports, Domestic and Foreign,* 29–30, 78–79.

18. Ibid., 68–69.

19. Susan Lee and Peter Passell, *A New Economic View of American History* (New York, 1979), chap. 15.

20. Frank Moya Pons, *History of the Caribbean: Plantations, Trade, and War in the Atlantic World* (Princeton, N.J., 2007), chap. 8. As always, I am indebted to Kris Lane for helping me understand the role of the Caribbean in international commodity chains.

21. Of course a great deal of American wheat that went to Louisiana was still reexported to Caribbean sugar and coffee plantations. Douglass North neglected this reexport trade when he argued that American plantations were the chief consumers of midwestern flour. See North, *Economic Growth of the United States.*

22. *Niles' Weekly Register,* May 24, 1828, 201.

23. Calhoun to Adams, May 1820, quoted in Samuel Rezneck, "The Depression of 1819–1822," *American Historical Review* 39, no. 1 (Oct. 1933): 29.

24. Robert Remini makes the clearest case for this in *Andrew Jackson,* 3 vols.

25. Lynn Parsons, *The Birth of Modern Politics: Andrew Jackson, John Quincy Adams, and the Election of 1828* (New York, 2009). On American political coalitions forming before elections and American voting surges during presidential elections, see L. Sandy Maisel, *American Political Parties and Elections: A Very Short Introduction* (New York, 2007).

26. C. Edward Skeen, " 'Vox Populi, Vox Dei': The Compensation Act of 1816 and the Rise of Popular Politics," *Journal of the Early Republic* 6, no. 3 (Autumn 1986): 266.

27. George Cochrane Hazelton, *The National Capitol* (New York, 1914), 38.

28. Everett S. Brown, "The Presidential Election of 1824–1825," *Political Science Quarterly* 40 (Sept. 1925): 384–403.

29. Hershel Parker, *Herman Melville: A Biography* (Baltimore, 1996), 1:12.

30. *Memorial of a Convention of the Friends of National Industry . . . Delegates from Massachusetts, Rhode Island, Connecticut, New York, New Jersey, Pennsylvania, Maryland, Delaware, and Ohio,* 16th Cong., 1st sess., 31 H.R. Doc. 9 (Dec. 20, 1819), 3.

31. *Remonstrance of the Virginia Agricultural Society of Fredericksburg,* 16th Cong., 1st sess., H.R. Doc. 24(Feb. 2, 1821), 4.

32. Protection of Manufactures, Petition of Citizens of Pennsylvania, 16th Cong., 1st sess., Finance 569 (Jan. 17, 1820), 458; United Agricultural Society of Virginia, 16th Cong., 1st sess., Finance 570 (Jan. 17, 1820), 460.

33. James Schouler, *History of the United States of America Under the Constitution* (Washington, D.C., 1894), 3:100.

34. *Abridgement of the Debates of Congress* (New York, 1858), 4:677.

35. Lacy K. Ford, *Deliver Us from Evil: The Slavery Question in the Old South* (New York, 2009), 207–25; Michael P. Johnson, "Denmark Vesey and His Co-conspirators," *William and Mary Quarterly,* 3rd ser., 58, no. 4 (2001): 915–76; Sean Wilentz, *The Rise of American Democracy* (New York, 2005), 237–40.

36. Clement Eaton, *The Freedom-of-Thought Struggle in the Old South* (Durham, N.C., 1940).

37. Mathew Carey, *Three Letters on the Present Calamitous State of Affairs Addressed to J. M. Garnett, Esq., President of the Fredericsburg Agricultural Society* (Philadelphia, 1820), 33–34, 35.

38. "From the Pennsylvania Gazette," *Weekly Aurora,* Jan. 21, 1821.

39. "The Next President, No. III," *Augusta Chronicle,* Nov. 26, 1822; John C. Calhoun, *Report of the Secretary of War (in Obedience to a Resolution of the 29th Ult.),* 17th Cong., 1st sess. S. Doc. 38 (Feb. 1822), 2.

40. Ninian Edwards's Charges of Financial Mismanagement, 18th Cong., 1st sess., *American State Papers* 706 (April 19, 1824), 1–10.

41. On McDuffie, see John Edgar Dawson Shipp, *Giant Days; or, The Life and Times of William H. Crawford* (Americus, Ga., 1909), 176–77. Supporters of Calhoun called Crawford a radical; see "Mr. Calhoun," *Republican Star,* April 22, 1823.

42. Harry L. Watson, *Liberty and Power: The Politics of Jacksonian America* (New York, 1990); Shipp, *Giant Days.*

43. Henry Clay, *Mr. Clay's Speech in Support of an American System for the Protection of American Industry, Delivered March 30th and 31st, 1824* (n.p., 1824), 7.

44. Speech of William R. King, *Annals of Congress,* 18th Cong., 1st sess. (April 24, 1824): 572.

45. An Inhabitant of the South, *Letter to the Honorable James Brown.*

46. Greve, *Centennial History of Cincinnati,* 574.

47. Henry Shaw to Henry Clay, April 22, 1823, in Hopkins, *Papers of Henry Clay,* 3:185.

48. George Dangerfield, *Era of Good Feelings* (New York, 1960), 10–12.

49. I am indebted to Gregory Downs for reminding me how wide Adams's reach was in that election.

50. Watson, *Liberty and Power,* 82–84.

51. Speech of John Taylor, *Annals of Congress,* 18th Cong., 1st sess. (April 22, 1824): 556.

52. On the intention to surround Indian lands as early as 1790 by the use of the fraudulent Yazoo sales, see "To the Public," *Southern Centinel,* April 21, 1796, which asserts that Georgia used these sales to settlers for increasing the South's sectional representation and "bringing the Indians more within our power. They would be entirely inclosed within the settlements of the white people, and in case of war, be open to an attack on all sides."

53. William Garrott Brown and Albert James Pickett, *A History of Alabama* (New York, 1900), 150.

54. James Henry Rigali, "Restoring the Republic of Virtue: The Presidential Election of 1824" (Ph.D. diss., University of Washington, 2004), chap. 4.

55. Most helpful to me in thinking about how filibusters fit structurally into the U.S. state has been Thomas Ogorzalek of Columbia University in his "Filibuster Vigilantly: Private Action in Antebellum Expansion" (paper presented at the Social Science History Association Conference, Long Beach, Calif., Nov. 14, 2009).

56. The Southern letters in defense of Crawford were meant to help defend him against the two charges that hurt him in the South: radicalism and his apparent support for a tariff. See, for example, "To the People of South Carolina," *Richmond Enquirer,* Oct. 8, 1824. My understanding of radicalism has been greatly helped by Rigali, "Restoring the Republic of Virtue," chap. 4.

57. Robert E. May, *The Southern Dream of a Caribbean Empire, 1854–1861* (New Orleans, 1973); Robert E. May, *Manifest Destiny's Underworld: Filibustering in Antebellum America* (Chapel Hill, N.C., 2004).

58. "Supplement to Mr. Clay's Address," *Niles' Weekly Register,* July 5, 1828, 506.

59. Parsons, *Birth of Modern Politics,* chap. 3.

60. Ibid.

61. F. W. Taussig, *The Tariff History of the United States* (New York, 1914), chap. 2.

CHAPTER SIX: LEVIATHAN

1. Economic historians' historiography of the panic of 1837 is rather large. Reginald McGrane in his 1915 dissertation and 1924 book argued for the importance of Jackson's Specie Circular in causing the panic. Robert C. O. Matthews's 1954 book argued for a combination of a cotton slump and political factors like Jackson's redistribution of the bank deposits. Bray Hammond in his 1957 history of banking blamed the Specie Circular for the panic of 1837 and blamed the Bank of the United States, Pennsylvania, for the 1839 downturn. In 1960, Richard Timberlake blamed Jackson's surplus distribution for pulling specie out of the commercial banks in New

York. Thus a gold-and-silver drain caused the panic. In 1969, Peter Temin disagreed, arguing for an international origin to the panic but retaining the Timberlake story about a specie drain as central actor in the panic. Temin blamed two actions by the Bank of England: a discount rate hike in 1836 and a rejection of the bills of the seven houses. This, he suggested, was triggered by actions in China. Temin continues that the two actions by the Bank of England caused cotton prices to drop, leading cotton factors to fail, causing loans to go unpaid, causing bank failures. While historians like Alejandra Irigoin and others have since questioned the China story, I agree with Jessica Lepler's recent dissertation and forthcoming book that the seven houses and the English bank's lending practices were important factors triggering the 1837 crisis. Most important, I think, was the nonrenewal of the charter of the Bank of the United States, in 1836. The Bank of the United States had acted as a governor over bank issuance by deciding which notes were acceptable at the U.S. Land Office. Disputing Matthews, Temin argued that while a cotton boom in the early 1830s caused a land boom, the land boom must have increased cotton cultivation and pulled cotton prices down again, which should have retarded inflation. In following Timberlake, Temin's is an essentially monetary explanation of specie flow that does not attend to the role of these discounted notes in the overall economy. Temin and most economists post-1960 adopt an essentially monetary explanation for how banks work, one that misunderstands bank mechanics, the financial instruments that are their working assets, and the instruments' relationship to failures. What Temin and other economic historians also miss is how the cotton boom and the bust grew out of *politics*: Jackson's arrangement, new banking laws in Britain, the retirement of the American debt, the growing disquiet in Britain and America about the troubled relationship between English country banks and American cotton plantations, and finally the repeal of the charter of the Bank of the United States. The risks of a commodity-as-credit chain troubled all these actors. It was not just the Bank of England that raised these questions but also the English Parliament, English merchants, Andrew Jackson, and Americans themselves. The Bank of England's actions thus followed events rather than provoking them and spoke to concerns about politics, economics, and the intense and ugly way that English banking credit funded a cotton boom after 1830. For this reason I think the post-1960 dismissal of politics by economic historians, combined with their obsession with gold over working assets, has led them to miss most of the factors in the panic of 1837 and the depression that lasted until 1843. Historians, following these confusing goldbug stories among economic historians, have tended to give up on explaining the panic. And so in economists' obsession with gold we have lost one of the most important narratives for understanding America's relationship with banks. We have lost Jackson's obsession with the Second Bank, his own white whale.

2. The Russians were growing hemp too, and Kentuckians feared that cheap Russian ropes and bags would bind up any free-trade cotton.

3. Remini, *Andrew Jackson,* vol. 2.

4. Webb and Green exchanged barbs after Webb revealed some scandals in the navy in the New York *Courier.* For a copy of the Webb report, see *Boston Weekly Messenger,* July 2, 1829. For Green's response, see *Easton Gazette,* July 11, 1829. On Green's position as distributor of patronage, see Richard R. John, *Spreading the News: The American Postal System from Franklin to Morse* (Cambridge, Mass., 1995), chap. 6.

5. On New York, and Van Buren's position on internal improvements, see Daniel Walker Howe, *What Hath God Wrought: The Transformation of America, 1815–1848* (New York, 2007).

6. Homans, *Cyclopedia of Commerce and Commercial Navigation,* 881; John Stuart Mill, *Intercourse Between the United States and the British Colonies in the West Indies* (1828).

7. Andrew Jackson, Second Annual Message, Dec. 7, 1830, in *Register of Debates,* Senate, 21st Cong., 2nd sess. (Dec. 1830), 113.

8. British vessels coming from colonial possessions would be "subject to no other or higher duty of tonnage or impost, or charge of any description whatever, than would be levied on the vessels of the United States." *Register of Debates,* 22nd Cong., 1st sess. (May 27, 1830), 1138.

9. John A. Munroe, *Louis McLane: Federalist and Jacksonian* (New Brunswick, N.J., 1973), chap. 1; Beckles Wilson, *America's Ambassadors to England, 1785–1928* (n.p., 1928), chap. 10.

10. Munroe, *Louis McLane,* 271.

11. Henry Benjamin Wheatley, *A Dictionary of Reduplicated Words in the English Language* (London, 1866), 46; *Life and Letters of Washington Irving* (New York, 1857), 2:192–93.

12. By 1833 the price to ship cotton from New Orleans to Liverpool was five-eighths of a shilling per pound, only twice the price to ship from New Orleans to Boston or Providence. Testimony of Joshua Bates, *Report from the Select Committee on Manufactures, Commerce, and Shipping,* BPP-No. 690 (1833), 49–65.

13. *Register of Debates,* 21st Cong., 1st sess. (May 26, 1830), 1137; testimony of John Ewart, *Report from the Select Committee on Manufactures, Commerce, and Shipping,* 246–51.

14. "Mephistopheles" of the House Committee on Commerce, "Review of Mr. Cambreleng's Report from the Committee of Commerce," 21st Cong., 1st sess. (1829), 21.

15. Calculated from the appendix in C. Nick Harley, "Ocean Freight Rates and Productivity, 1740–1913: The Primacy of Mechanical Innovation Reaffirmed," *Journal of Economic History* 48 (Dec. 1988): 851–76.

16. Robert C. O. Matthews, *A Study in Trade-Cycle History: Economic Fluctuations in Great Britain, 1833–1842* (Cambridge, U.K., 1954), chap. 5.

17. Harriet Martineau, *Society in America* (New York, 1837), 1:75.

18. Thomas Roderick Dew, *Lectures on the Restrictive System* (Richmond, 1829), 42–43.

19. John Mayo, "The Development of British Interests in Chile's Norte Chico in the Early Nineteenth Century," *Americas* 57 (Jan. 2001): 363–94; Claudio Veliz, "Egaña, Lambert, and the Chilean Mining Associations of 1825," *Hispanic American Historical Review* 55 (Nov. 1975): 637–63; Alvaro Florez Estrada, *Mercantile Distress Experienced in Great Britain* . . . (London, 1826); Thomas J. Joplin, *Case for Parliamentary Inquiry into the Circumstances of the Panic* . . . (London, ca. 1832).

20. Henry Tucker Easton, *Banks and Banking* (London, 1896), 85–86. Henry Dunning Macleod, *The Theory and Practice of Banking* (London, 1856), 2:240–47. The 1824–1825 panic had devastated Cropper, Benson & Co., which had been so successful during the 1819 panic. See Vincent Nolte, *Fifty Years in Both Hemispheres* (New York, 1854), chap. 16. On the problems experienced in Chile, see Mayo, "Development of British Interests," and Veliz, "Egaña, Lambert, and the Chilean Mining Associations of 1825," who argues that in the Chilean enterprise the problems were mostly on the British side. For information on explosions in the Peruvian mines during the wars of independence, thanks to Carlos Galvez-Pena, personal communication, Oct. 26, 2011.

21. The most concrete discussion of the conversion of cotton into notes is in Nolte, *Fifty Years.* On the Atlantic side, see Ralph W. Hidy, "The Organization and Functions of Anglo-American Merchant Bankers, 1815–1860," in "The Tasks of Economic History," supplement, *Journal of Economic History* 1, no. S1 (Dec. 1941): 53–66. On transatlantic credit in the cotton South, see Richard Holcombe Kilbourne Jr., *Debt, Investment, Slaves: Credit Relations in East Feliciana Parish, Louisiana, 1825–1885* (Tuscaloosa, Ala., 1995), 16–48; Larry Schweikart, *Banking in the American South: From the Age of Jackson to Reconstruction* (Baton Rouge, La., 1987); and Harold Woodman, *King Cotton and His Retainers: Financing and Marketing the Cotton Crop of the South, 1800–1925* (Columbia, S.C., 1990). Few historians have connected the Atlantic credit network to the southern regional credit network. Jessica Lepler has pointed out to me that the seven houses were also involved in the Pacific trade. Jessica Lepler, personal conversation, May 23, 2011.

22. Jessica Lepler explained to me the significance of the sight bill versus the older bill of exchange. Lepler, personal communication, May 23, 2011.

23. According to Ralph Hidy, most bills of exchange before 1837 were "clean" bills, future promises that were not attached to bills of lading. He writes that after the panic, when Baring regained most of this trade, it required that all bills be attached to bills of lading. These were called "documentary" bills of exchange. Peter Austin argues that for certain merchants the Barings required documentary bills before 1837. Hidy, "Organization and Functions of Anglo-American Merchant Bankers"; Klein, "Develop-

ment of Mercantile Instruments of Credit in the United States," 594–607; Austin, *Baring Brothers and the Birth of Modern Finance* (London, 2007). On bills of lading as cash, see Thomas Roderick Dew, *The Great Question of the Day . . .* (Washington, D.C., 1840), 6.

24. Leone Levi, *The History of British Commerce and of the Economic Progress of the British Nation, 1763–1878* (London, 1880), 188–90; Andreades, *History of the Bank of England,* vol. 2, chaps. 1 and 2; John Giuseppi, *The Bank of England: A History from Its Foundation in 1694* (London, 1966), 91–93; W. Cunningham, *Modern Times,* vol. 3 of *The Growth of English Industry and Commerce* (Cambridge, U.K., 1903), 822–25.

25. Andreades, *History of the Bank of England,* vol. 2, chaps. 1 and 2; Giuseppi, *Bank of England,* 91–93; Cunningham, *Modern Times,* 822–25.

26. Samuel Gurney, a bill broker, described this process in 1833. A bank needing capital, like one of the seven houses or one of the manufacturing banks, would have Gurney discount its bills. Gurney provided cash for a note. Gurney would then sell these notes to a country bank in a rich agricultural area that wanted to lend. The country bank would return them to Gurney at the end of the ninety days for payment. Gurney himself would see to their redemption. Testimony of Samuel Gurney, House of Commons, *Report from the Select Committee on Manufactures, Commerce, and Shipping,* 1–16.

27. Lanier, *Century of Banking in New York,* 187–88. My choice of "agency house" may be confusing, given that Choctaw and Cherokee agencies in the Southwest were also called agency houses, but the term did have currency in the rest of the English-speaking world. More to the point, the literature on these South Asian and Chinese agency houses is quite extensive.

28. The mechanics of this limitation are described in Hidy, "Organization and Functions of Anglo-American Merchant Bankers," 53–66. See also Perkins, *Financing Anglo-American Trade.* Nolte was jailed for overcharging on his account. See Nolte, *Fifty Years.*

29. This was technically a sixty-day sight bill of exchange. The "sight" part ensured that the note was negotiable for many months in America before it became due in Britain. Lepler, personal communication, May 23, 2011.

30. Dew, *Great Question of the Day,* 8.

31. In some cases the agents were both bill broker and factor. Lepler, personal communication, May 23, 2011.

32. Stanley D. Chapman, *The Rise of Merchant Banking* (Boston, 1984), chap. 3; Nolte, *Fifty Years;* Perkins, *Financing Anglo-American Trade;* Rondo Cameron et al., *Banking in the Early Stages of Industrialization* (New York, 1967), 18–50; George D. Green, *Finance and Economic Development in the Old South: Louisiana Banking, 1804–1861* (Stanford, Calif., 1972), 72–79. See also Woodman, *King Cotton and His Retainers.* Many economic historians and historians of American banking post-1965 have discussed this but fail to understand how acceptance works, and so fail to understand what banks do.

33. Green, *Finance and Economic Development*, 77.

34. Dew, *Great Question of the Day*, 7.

35. Jessica Lepler, "The Pressure of 1836: Interpreting Atlantic Bank Wars" (paper presented at the Center for History and Economics Workshop, Harvard University, Dec. 3, 2009). Walter Johnson has pointed out to me that some of the most important planters retained title to their cotton as it was shipped and then settled when the price was set in Liverpool (personal communication, Harvard University, March 28, 2011). Doing this would have probably increased the risk to the seven houses if they advanced two-thirds on the cotton and the settled price was less than the agreed-upon guess of the price in New Orleans. Planters, lacking warehousing facilities in Liverpool, would have had to sell at the price on delivery and then would have had to pay back the houses for the difference, a scenario that may not have been imagined in the contract and may have been hard to enforce. If the seven houses held title, they could at least have held cotton for a month or so to wait for a rise.

36. On Baring's use of the bill of lading as security, see Austin, *Baring Brothers*, 79–83.

37. Felix Salmon, "Recipe for Disaster: The Formula That Killed Wall Street," *Wired*, Feb. 23, 2009.

38. Review of *American Prosperity*, by Edward Clibborn, in *Monthly Review* 3, improved ser. (1837): 127–39; on Irish origins, see *Sporting Magazine; or, Monthly Calendar of the Transactions of the Turf . . .*, Feb. 1805, 290.

39. Catterall, *Second Bank of the United States*, 106–8.

40. Biddle to John McKim, 1827, quoted in Catterall, *Second Bank of the United States*, 100.

41. Austin, *Baring Brothers*, chap. 2. The bank's power over other notes was in section 14 of the charter. See speech of Thomas Hart Benton, *Register of Debates*, Senate, 22nd Cong., 1st sess. (Jan. 20, 1832), 126.

42. On the controversy over Biddle's Federalism, see "The Ticket," *Franklin Gazette* (Philadelphia), Oct. 10, 1818.

43. Catterall, *Second Bank of the United States*, chap. 5.

44. Homans, *Cyclopedia of Commerce and Commercial Navigation*, 879–81; William Schaw Lindsay, *History of Ancient Shipping and Merchant Commerce* (London, 1874), 3:68–69. Homans's figures are for 1830 to 1840.

45. I am indebted to Alejandra Irigoin, who has worked with the Brown Brothers records, for her observations and criticism of this section. All faults in the interpretation are mine.

46. Walter Johnson, *Soul by Soul: Inside the Antebellum Slave Market* (Cambridge, Mass., 1999).

47. Quoted in Philip McMichael, "Slavery in Capitalism: The Rise and Demise of the U.S. Ante-bellum Cotton Culture," *Theory and Society* 20, no. 3 (June 1991): 330–31.

48. I am indebted to Bruce Baker for reminding me about the fictional

Yoknapatawpha County. See the brilliant analysis of tax and land records in Charles C. Bolton, *Poor Whites of the Antebellum South: Tenants and Laborers in Central North Carolina and Northeast Mississippi* (Durham, N.C.), chaps. 4 and 5.

49. Most historians have argued that Jackson hated the bank, and by extension hated banking, but through the time of his second State of the Union address he argued that a national bank was necessary. He complained that the Bank of the United States' private loans provided too many opportunities for private corruption (the objection he raised in the Maysville Road veto of 1830), and secondarily that an institution founded by Congress should not have been allowed to create branches in the states. Jackson's second State of the Union address can be found in *A Compilation of Messages and Papers of the Presidents, 1789–1902* (Washington, D.C., 1905), comp. James D. Richardson, vol. 3. Thomas Hart Benton's famous "moneyed tribunal" speech attacking the bank points out that Jackson's proposed bank would issue land scrip that would act as currency like the Mississippi scrip issued by the Treasury after the War of 1812. "If the Federal Government is to recognize any paper, let it be this. Let it be its own." The entire speech is in *Register of Debates,* Senate, 21st Cong., 2nd sess. (Feb. 2, 1831), 44–75; the reprinting of the speech is discussed in Remini, *Andrew Jackson,* 2:304; Burrows's letter to Biddle is quoted in Thomas P. Govan, *Nicholas Biddle, Nationalist and Public Banker, 1786–1844* (Chicago, 1959), 153.

50. For a very sympathetic biography of Webb, see James L. Crouthamel, *James Watson Webb: A Biography* (Middletown, Conn., 1969).

51. In an audit conducted in March and April 1832, a congressional committee discovered the deal. U.S. marshals sent to New York and Washington could not find Burrows to bring him to testify. Govan, *Nicholas Biddle,* 153–57; U.S. Congress, *Bank of the United States,* 22nd Cong., 1st sess. (April 30, 1832); Crouthamel, *James Watson Webb.* Crouthamel defends Webb, arguing that he did not personally know that Burrows's money was being pledged, but it seems highly improbable that Webb, the editor Mordecai Noah, and Burrows all met in Albany, New York, while lobbying the legislature and that Webb did not know that Burrows—who was there to support the bank—was not a lobbyist for the bank. Govan makes it clear that Biddle thought he was buying a change in the editorial position of the paper but also doubts that Webb understood the deal being made. The timing, the loan's being off the books, Burrows's written statement that he would speak only with Biddle about what he would do, and the *Courier and Enquirer's* change of position immediately afterward make a clear case for a conspiracy.

52. Jackson to White, April 29, 1831, in *Correspondence of Andrew Jackson* (Washington, D.C., 1929), 272, also quoted in Samuel Gordon Heiskell, *Andrew Jackson and Early Tennessee History* (Nashville, 1918), 177. The explanation most historians have given for Jackson's bizarre actions in 1831 is the Peggy

Eaton scandal; in the previous year the wives of his cabinet refused to visit Secretary of War John Eaton's vivacious wife. Publicly, Jackson refused to explain why he began asking for letters of resignation from some of his cabinet; the newspapers grabbed onto the so-called petticoat scandal because it sold papers. Cabinet members also preferred this story for explaining what was happening.

53. On the Kitchen Cabinet and Biddle's apparent coining of the term, see Remini, *Andrew Jackson*, 2:. 326–29.

54. Wilentz, *Rise of American Democracy*, 433.

55. Ibid., 369.

56. Ibid., 372.

57. *Augusta Age*, Oct. 3, 1832.

58. *New-Hampshire Patriot & State Gazette*, Oct. 15, 1832.

59. "Important Bank Arrangement: The Better Currency," *Washington, D.C., Extra Globe*, Sept. 11, 1835, 250–51.

60. Numbers are difficult to come by, but the best discussion of sources, with criticism of Jonathan Elliot's frequently cited sources, is *Annual Report of the Comptroller of the Currency*, 44th Cong., 2nd sess. (Washington, D.C., 1876).

61. Joseph Martin, *Martin's History of the Boston Stock and Money Markets* (Boston, 1898), 52.

62. Biddle to William Appleton, July 4, 1834, in *The Correspondence of Nicholas Biddle Dealing with National Affairs, 1807–1844*, 237.

63. R. Fisher to Biddle, July 7, 1834, in *Correspondence of Nicholas Biddle*, 242.

64. "The Bank's Arrangement," *Richmond Enquirer*, April 7, 1835.

65. Senator William Campbell Preston, S.C., *Register of Debates*, Senate, 23rd Cong., 1st sess. (March 13, 1834), 954. Portions quoted in Alan Heimert, "*Moby-Dick* and American Political Symbolism," *American Quarterly* 15, no. 4 (1963): 516. Though Heimert notes the symbolic connection to *Moby-Dick*, he misidentifies Preston as a Whig and the date as 1837 and argues that John C. Calhoun represented Ahab.

66. The official London discount rate remained at 4 percent from July 5, 1827, to July 21, 1836. See J. H. Clapham, *The Bank of England: A History* (New York, 1945), 2:429.

67. "Memorial of Merchants &c. of New York," *Register of Debates*, House, 23rd Cong., 1st sess. (Feb. 3, 1834), 2581.

68. Ibid., 2582.

69. *Register of Debates*, Senate, 23rd Cong., 1st sess. (May 26, 1834), 1808.

70. Ibid., 1807.

71. Catterall, *Second Bank of the United States*, 332–45.

72. The best statements of these three positions are Richard H. Timberlake, *The Origins of Central Banking in the United States* (Cambridge, Mass., 1978); Charles Sellers, *The Market Revolution: Jacksonian America, 1815–1846* (New York, 1991); and Howe, *What Hath God Wrought*.

73. Milton Friedman, *Money Mischief: Episodes in Monetary History* (New York, 1992), 56.

74. John Bach McMaster, *With the Fathers: Studies in the History of the United States* (New York, 1896), 231.

75. Remini, *Andrew Jackson*, 3:168–69.

76. *New Bedford Mercury,* July 25, 1834.

77. *Vermont Gazette,* June 10, 1834.

78. Statement of President of Philadelphia Board of Trade Frederick Fraley in House Committee on Coinage, Weights, and Measures, *Report and Hearings,* 51st Cong., 2nd sess. (1891), 129–30.

79. Huntington, *A History of Banking and Currency in Ohio,* 357.

80. The difficulties of the state banks are recounted in excruciating detail in the fifteen-hundred-page report of the Treasury secretary in House of Representatives, *Condition of the State Banks.* This condition resembles the problems Benjamin Bernanke describes in the early 1930s, when the "cost of credit intermediation" increased as untried lenders found few places to providently lend to, a condition he refers to as a "loss of information capital." See Bernanke, "The Macroeconomics of the Great Depression: A Comparative Approach," *Journal of Money, Credit, and Banking* 27 (Feb. 1995): 1–28.

81. Derived from Senate, *Report of the Secretary of the Treasury . . . of the Quantity, Surveys, Acquisitions, Sales, and Reservations of the Public Lands,* 27th Cong., 3rd sess., S. Doc. 249 (1843), 5–11. These numbers do *not* include land that was subsequently returned to the United States for nonpayment. On this process generally, see Rohrbough, *Land Office Business.*

82. Most state banks disallowed real estate as an asset but rather accepted bills, loans, and discounted notes as assets. Therefore, real estate on most banks' rolls was usually the result of liquidation and so, on most states' balance sheets, constituted less than 2 percent of assets. For a table of assets, see Treasury Department, *Condition of the State Banks,* 1362–63. Louisiana banks, however, had sizable real estate investments, up to 50 percent of nominal capital. In addition, they consolidated discounts "on real estate, and bills, and notes, including capital of branches," into one huge pot (463). Mississippi banks, meanwhile, had charters that allowed loans of up to two-thirds of the appraised value of lands. See ibid., 612. On this topic generally, see "Land Speculations," *Columbian Register,* May 13, 1837. Also see Edward Gaylord Bourne, *The History of the Surplus Revenue of 1837* (New York, 1885), 14. On banks as investment clubs in the nineteenth century, see Lamoreaux, *Insider Lending.*

83. While the newer Louisiana and Mississippi banks accepted slaves and land as collateral, most banks continued to discount bills of exchange. On the Louisiana and Mississippi loans, see Kilbourne, *Debt, Investment, Slaves,* and Edward E. Baptist, "Toxic Debt, Liar Loans, and Securitized Human Beings: The Panic of 1837 and the Fate of Slavery," *Common-Place* 10 (April

2010). On the loans in the rest of the country, see Treasury Department, *Condition of the State Banks,* which shows that 90 percent or more of most banks' resources came from "notes, bills of exchange, and all stocks and funded debts." Real estate comprised less than 5 percent of most banks' assets outside Louisiana and Mississippi. On railroads, see Catterall, *Second Bank of the United States,* 364.

84. Lawrence J. Kolitkiff, "The Structure of Slave Prices in New Orleans," *Economic Inquiry* 17 (Oct. 1979): 496–518; Ulrich B. Phillips, *American Negro Slavery* (New York, 1929); Green, *Finance and Economic Development in the Old South;* Walter Johnson, ed., *The Chattel Principle: Internal Slave Trades in the Americas* (New Haven, Conn., 2004).

85. Historians, particularly Peter Temin in *The Jacksonian Economy* (New York, 1969), used to argue that this was not the case, but more recent works by banking scholars have demonstrated that this is precisely what happened. See Lepler, "Pressure of 1836"; Jane Knodell, "Rethinking the Jacksonian Economy: The Impact of the 1832 Bank Veto on Commercial Banking," *Journal of Economic History* 66 (Sept. 2006): 541–74; Austin, *Baring Brothers.*

86. *Register of Debates,* Senate, 24th Cong., 2nd sess. (Jan. 11, 1837), 363.

87. John Joseph Wallis, "What Caused the Crisis of 1839?," *National Bureau of Economic Research Historical Working Paper Series* No. 133 (April 2001), http://www.nber.org/papers/h0133 (accessed July 2011).

88. On the back-and-forth between the president and the Senate before the Specie Circular was issued, see *Register of Debates,* Senate, 24th Cong., 2nd sess. (Jan. 11, 1837), 363.

89. W. Harrison Bayles, "The Panic of 1837," in *A History of the Origin and Development of Banks and Banking,* published serially in *McMaster's Commercial Cases* (1915): 129–328. Quotation is on page 223.

90. Lepler, "Pressure of 1836."

91. James William Gilbart, *A Practical Treatise on Banking* (New York, 1851), 55.

92. *Times* (London), June 17, 1836, quoted in Jessica Lepler, "1837: Anatomy of a Panic" (Ph.D. diss., Brandeis University, 2008), 70.

93. Clapham, *Bank of England,* 2:429.

94. Andreades, *History of the Bank of England,* 2:266.

95. Lepler, "Pressure of 1836," 20–21.

96. The 1836 report is reprinted in House of Commons, *Report from the Secret Committee on Joint Stock Banks* (1837), 465–69. Henry Moult testifies that when the Bank of England's confidential report was printed in September, he was unable to get cash ("discount") for any of his American bills of exchange. Ibid., 2.

97. Lepler, "Pressure of 1836," 72–80.

98. An Observer, "The Constitutional Currency," *Albany Evening Journal,* April 18, 1837.

99. Bayles, "Panic of 1837," 223.

100. Martin, *Martin's History of the Boston Stock and Money Markets,* 52.

101. *Baltimore Gazette,* May 17 and June 2, 1836.

102. An Examiner, *The Causes of the Present Crisis* (Philadelphia, 1837), 15; "States of Mississippi and Alabama," *Richmond Examiner,* May 5, 1837.

103. Biddle to Barings, Hottinguer & Co., Hope & Co., April 1, 1837, quoted in Hammond, *Banks and Politics in America,* 461–62.

104. On slaves as backing for cotton notes and other financial instruments, see Kilbourne, *Debt, Investment, Slaves.*

105. Thanks to Walter Johnson for pointing out the logic of Governor Alexander McNutt's message to the legislature. Walter Johnson, personal conversation, Dec. 3, 2009.

106. Lacy Ford, "Reconsidering the Internal Slave Trade: Paternalism, Markets, and the Character of the Old South," in Johnson, *Chattel Principle,* 143–64. Dunbar Rowland, *Encyclopedia of Mississippi History* (Madison, Wis., 1907), 2:199.

107. Jessica Lepler noted the term "absquatulate" in a financial crisis workshop at Harvard University, Dec. 3, 2009. On the land pledges to Texans, see Randolph B. Campbell, *Sam Houston and the American Southwest* (New York, 2007), 102.

108. William Clarence Webster, *A General History of Commerce* (Boston, 1918), 314.

109. Parker, *Herman Melville,* chaps. 4 and 5.

110. "To the Republicans of Virginia," *Richmond Enquirer,* Feb. 20, 1836.

111. The best account of the so-called panic of 1839 is Wallis, "What Caused the Crisis of 1839?"

112. Many historians have wondered why the great triumvirate, all of whom aimed for the presidency, never got there. The bank that tarred all three with infamy may be the missing fourth actor in the drama. On the great triumvirate, see Merrill Peterson, *The Great Triumvirate: Webster, Clay, and Calhoun* (New York, 2001).

113. Reginald McGrane, "Some Aspects of American State Debts in the Forties," *American Historical Review* 38 (July 1933): 680.

114. George Walton Green, *Repudiation,* Economic Tracts No. 11 (New York, 1883), 12.

115. Namsuk Kim and John Joseph Wallis, "The Market for American State Government Bonds in Britain and the United States, 1830–1843," *Economic History Review* 58 (2005): 736–64. Kim and Wallis demonstrate that, contrary to Leland Hamilton Jenks, Bray Hammond, and Biddle himself, the failures of 1841 and 1842 originated in the United States, not in British capital markets.

116. Green, *Repudiation,* 15. When the Mississippi legislature opposed the governor, a "Repudiation" party formed in the state and voted them out of office. Bessie C. Randolph, "Foreign Bondholders and the Repudiated Debts of the Southern States," *American Journal of International Law* 25, no. 1 (Jan. 1931): 70.

117. Martin, *Martin's History of the Boston Stock and Money Markets,* 32–33; Kim and Wallis, "Market for American State Government Bonds in Britain and the United States."

118. Sydney Smith, "Letters on American Debts," to the editor of the *Morning Chronicle,* Nov. 1843, reprinted in *Selections from the Writings of the Rev. Sidney Smith* (London, 1854), 1:131–47.

119. William Amasa Scott, *The Repudiation of State Debts* (New York, 1893), 248–49.

CHAPTER SEVEN: OF SWAMPS AND CALCULUS

1. This quote and much of the discussion of Elizur Wright that follows rely on Lawrence B. Goodheart, *Abolitionist, Actuary, Atheist: Elizur Wright and the Reform Impulse* (Kent, Ohio, 1990), 10–11.

2. Quoted in Philip Green Wright and Elizabeth Q. Wright, *Elizur Wright, the Father of Life Insurance* (Chicago, 1937), 48.

3. David French, "Elizur Wright, Jr., and the Emergence of Anti-colonization Sentiments on the Connecticut Western Reserve," *Ohio History* 85 (Winter 1976): 49–62.

4. Elizur Wright, Sept. and Oct. 1832, quoted in ibid., 64.

5. Ibid.

6. *New York Chronicle: An Insurance Journal,* Sept. 11, 1873, 161–62.

7. On the Tappans and failure generally in this period see Edward J. Balleisen, *Navigating Failure: Bankruptcy and Commercial Society in Antebellum America* (Chapel Hill, N.C., 2001).

8. Elizur Wright, describing actuaries in Great Britain, quoted in "Literary Record," *Independent,* Sept. 7, 1854.

9. Mike Davis, *Late Victorian Holocausts: El Niño Famines and the Making of the Third World* (New York, 2001).

10. On the prospect of selling midwestern wheat in Liverpool, see Frederick Merk, "The British Corn Crisis of 1845–46 and the Oregon Treaty," *Agricultural History* 8 (July 1934): 95–123. Merk points out that the abolition of the Corn Laws actually hurt the United States at first because it closed the back door that the United States had with Canadian millers. Previously, American wheat sent to Montreal became "colonial" flour and thus received preferential treatment over European wheat from the 1820s to the 1840s. Joseph Martin, on the contrary, sees the abolition of the Corn Laws as being as important to the Midwest as the invention of the cotton gin was to the South. As Martin suggests, the railroad and canal conflicts of the 1850s were mostly about the prospect of selling American wheat to Britain. While I agree with Martin that this was in their plans, I agree with Merk that sizable U.S. exports to Britain were in the future. As I will argue, they awaited the closing of the Mississippi River traffic in 1861.

11. "Technicalities of the Brokers," *American Railway Times,* March 26, 1857.

12. On the formation of the Ohio Life Insurance & Trust Company, see John D. Haeger, *The Investment Frontier: New York Businessmen and the Economic Development of the Old Northwest* (Albany, N.Y., 1981), chap. 3. The company accepted cotton notes from the firm of A. A. Gower, Nephews & Co.; see "Bank Items," *Bankers' Magazine,* Dec. 1847, 390. It also accepted checks drawn on pork vendors; see "Frauds on Bankers," *Bankers' Magazine,* Sept. 1854, 177. On the charter as a company with a land mortgage and a discount office, see H. F. Baker, "History of Banking in the United States: Ohio," *Bankers' Magazine,* Sept. 1856.

13. Perry McCandless, *A History of Missouri* (Columbia, Mo., 1972), 2:120; remarks of Hezekiah S. Bundy, *Congressional Globe,* House, 39th Cong., 2nd sess. (Jan. 5, 1867), 296.

14. "International Monied Relations," *Knickerbocker,* May 1839, 412.

15. "How Our Panic Affects England," *Philadelphia Press,* Sept. 24, 1857. The bank apparently traded at par in London until 1857.

16. "From Our American Correspondent," *Manchester Times,* Sept. 24, 1851; "The Money Market," *Leeds Mercury,* June 15, 1851; "Latest News," *Glasgow Herald,* Aug. 6, 1852.

17. This feature of the mortgage is explained in Richard Cobden's inspection report for the London bondholders and stockholders in 1859. "Not so much importance seemed to be attached to the punctual payment of promissory notes given for land as to the regular discharge of the interest; whilst the most essential condition of all was that the purchasers should be occupying and improving the land, which, under such circumstances, was estimated to double in value in five years." See "Illinois Central Railway," *Morning Chronicle* (London), July 14, 1859.

18. "Illinois Central Railroad," *Morning Chronicle* (London), June 11, 1852.

19. W. Harrison Bayles, "The Crisis of 1857," in *History of the Origin and Development of Banks and Banking,* published serially in *McMaster's Commercial Cases* (1915): 129–328.

20. "Financial and Commercial," *New York Herald,* Aug. 25, 1857.

21. Ibid.

22. Leonard L. Richards, *The Slave Power: The Free North and Southern Domination* (Baton Rouge, La., 2000).

23. William Earl Parrish, *David Rice Atchison of Missouri, Border Politician* (Columbia, Mo., 1961), 74–90; William Nisbet Chambers, *Old Bullion Benton, Senator from the New West: Thomas Hart Benton, 1782–1858* (Boston, 1956), 341–42.

24. Lewis H. Haney, *A Congressional History of Railways in the United States* (Madison, Wis., 1908), 2:13–15.

25. *Register of Debates,* 31st Cong., 1st sess. (June 21, 1850), 171; "Letter from Senator Atchison—Hannibal and St. Joseph Railroad," *Daily Missouri Republican,* Jan. 7, 1851.

26. On the grant, see Aug. 14, 1852, Hannibal & St. Joseph Railroad Co. Rec-

ords, Chicago, Burlington & Quincy Railroad Company Papers, Newberry Library, Chicago. On Douglas, see Tully R. Cornick, letter to editor, *Missouri Courier*, July 27, 1854.

27. Quoted in Perley Orman Ray, *The Repeal of the Missouri Compromise* (Cleveland, Ohio, 1909), 113.

28. Atchison quotes Guthrie's quotation of himself in "Atchison's Speech," *Missouri Courier*, July 7, 1853.

29. Ray, *Repeal of the Missouri Compromise*, 89.

30. "Atchison's Speech."

31. Minute book, March 17, 1854, Hannibal & St. Joseph Railroad Co. Records.

32. Minute book, March 17 and July 10, 1854, Hannibal & St. Joseph Railroad Co. Records. President R. M. Stewart laid out his justification of these events in *Reports of the President, Land and Fiscal Agents, and Chief Engineer of the Hannibal and St. Joseph Railroad* (St. Louis, 1854), in Hannibal & St. Joseph Railroad Annual Reports, Chicago, Burlington & Quincy Railroad Company Papers.

33. Edward L. Baker to Amos T. Hall (treasurer), Boston, Oct. 8, 1857; Baker, E. L., *Out-Letters*, June 12, 1857–Oct. 19, 1858, Chicago, Burlington & Quincy Railroad Company Papers.

34. Massachusetts Emigrant Aid Company (Boston, 1854), *American Broadsides and Ephemera*, ser. 1, no. 8937.

35. *Missouri Courier*, May 18, 1854.

36. *Reports of the President, Land and Fiscal Agents, and Chief Engineer of the Hannibal and St. Joseph Railroad*, 16.

37. A $4 million bond issue took place in 1856. See "Hannibal and St. Joseph Railway," *American Railway Times*, March 26, 1857.

38. "Squatterism in Kansas," *Floridian and Journal*, July 8, 1854.

39. Ibid.

40. "A Revelation," *Ohio State Journal*, Oct. 10, 1854.

41. "Our Railroad, Again," *Missouri Courier*, Sept. 28, 1854.

42. George W. Brown, *Reminiscences of Gov. R. J. Walker* (Rockford, Ill., 1902), 12.

43. *Missouri Courier*, Nov. 16, 1854; "The Hannibal and St. Joseph Railroad," *Missouri Courier*, Nov. 30, 1854.

44. Scott Reynolds Nelson and Carol Sheriff, *A People at War: Civilians and Soldiers in America's Civil War* (New York, 2007), chap. 1.

45. *Weekly St. Louis Pilot*, March 3, 1855; McCandless, *History of Missouri*, 2:264–66.

46. Richard C. Overton, *Burlington West: A Colonization History of the Burlington Railroad* (New York, 1967), 130–31.

47. *Report of the Commissioner of the General Land Office*, 35th Cong., 1st sess. (Nov. 30, 1857), 919 S.exdoc.11/4, 85–87.

48. I am indebted to Charles W. Calomiris and Larry Schweikart, "The Panic of 1857: Origins, Transmission, and Containment," *Journal of Economic His-*

tory 51, no. 4 (Dec. 1991): 807–34. They point out that railroad stocks and securities fell first, in the spring of 1857, and the Ohio Life Insurance & Trust Company followed afterward. They also discuss the call-loan market as a possible connection between railroads and banks. They do not discuss Ohio Life's somewhat unique role in the evolution of this new market or note that the call-loan market was primarily intended for railroads and only later became a vehicle for individual stock speculation. They suggest that the *Dred Scott* decision (March 6, 1857) might have been the cause of the drop in the railroad stock market. They did not discuss the Swamp Act, but the Swamp Act is—as far as I can tell—entirely absent from the vast historiography of Kansas and Nebraska. I learned about the Swamp Act from the Chicago, Burlington & Quincy Papers. It is discussed briefly in Overton, *Burlington West,* 130–31.

49. *Philadelphia Press,* Aug. 26, 1857; Frederic S. Mishkin, *Economics of Money, Banking, and Financial Markets,* 7th ed. (Boston, 2004), 192.

50. Timothy W. Hubbard and Lewis E. Davids, *Banking in Mid-America: A History of Missouri's Banks* (Washington, D.C., 1969), 77.

51. The mechanics of the Clearing House are described in "Important Actions of the New York Bank," *Albany Evening Journal,* Nov. 22, 1860; [Newton Squire], *The New York Clearing House, Its Methods and Systems . . .* (New York, 1888), 5–17; James Graham Cannon, *Clearing Houses,* 61st Cong., 2nd sess., S. Doc. 491 (Washington, D.C., 1910), 75–136. The Clearing House started at 14 Wall Street and moved to 82 Broadway the next year. It moved again in 1874 and 1894, presumably when downtown properties dropped in price. A solid account of the rise of the Clearing House is Fritz Redlich, *The Molding of American Banking: Men and Ideas* (New York, 1968), vol. 2, chap. 17. Redlich argues that in 1841, when Gallatin first proposed the New York Clearing House, Gallatin "drew a red herring across the trail" in suggesting that the Clearing House would need to create a common currency with a specie reserve. Yet the "loan certificate" was, I think, an almost necessary follow-on to the creation of the Clearing House. When you create an institution that clears balances between firms that would otherwise pass gold around, the receipt for clearance of balances quickly becomes a currency itself. The medium is the message. The bank is its printed money. The Clearing House is its certificates.

52. This is a bit like the asymmetric information theory of panics that the economists Charles W. Calomiris and Gary Gorton have proposed in their "Origins of Banking Panics: Models, Facts, and Bank Regulation," in *Financial Markets and Financial Crises,* ed. R. Glenn Hubbard (Chicago, 1991). They refer to bank assets in the free banking period and after. I use symbolic doubt to suggest that it is the fundamental illegibility of the document at issue, whether a dollar, a stock, a bond, or a debt obligation.

53. *Times* (London), Sept. 1, 7, 8, 1857; *Philadelphia Press,* Sept. 24, 1857.

54. Hubbard and Davids, *Banking in Mid-America,* 77.

55. I am indebted to my summer intern, Peter Terenzio, for his unpacking of the 1860 convention for me.

CHAPTER EIGHT: *CERES AMERICANA*

1. Dobson, *History of American Enterprise,* 91. My discussion of wheat relies on William Cronon, *Nature's Metropolis: Chicago and the Great West* (New York, 1991). This brilliant book greatly influenced how I think about the 1873 and 1893 panics as well.
2. *Congressional Globe,* Senate, 35th Cong., 1st sess. (March 4, 1858), 961.
3. May, *Manifest Destiny's Underworld;* Thomas Ogorzalek, "Filibuster Vigilantly: The Liminal State and Nineteenth-Century U.S. Expansion" (unpublished paper in author's possession). I am indebted to John Munro for pointing out how the Papineau revolt ended up on the license plate.
4. William Freehling, *The South vs. the South: How Anti-Confederate Southerners Shaped the Course of the Civil War* (New York, 2001), chap. 4.
5. Nelson and Sheriff, *People at War;* chap. 8; Charles P. Cullop, *Confederate Propaganda in Europe, 1861–1865* (Coral Gables, Fla., 1969), 77.
6. Denison to John C. Green, Oct. 17, 1871, John M. Denison, *Out-Letters,* vol. 10, Chicago, Burlington & Quincy Papers.
7. Anthony Trollope, *North America* (New York, 1862), 149.
8. John Bigelow's response to Congress's query about European railway building, quoted in remarks of Congressman Phelps in *Congressional Globe,* 37th Cong., 2nd sess. (April 9, 1862), 1591.
9. E. W. Hutter, "National Responsibility," *Philadelphia Inquirer,* Sept. 27, 1861.
10. "The War—the Ability of the North and South to Meet It Compared," *Philadelphia Inquirer,* Aug. 23, 1861. Also quoted in part in Heather Cox Richardson, *The Greatest Nation of the Earth: Republican Economic Policies During the Civil War* (Cambridge, Mass., 1997), 143.
11. Samuel Cox pointed out that the low tariff on flour and the high tariff on whiskey favored wheat over corn, which benefited the plains at the expense of the corn growers of southern Ohio, Indiana, and Illinois. Resolution of Samuel S. Cox, Lockbourne, Ohio, March 17, 1862, reprinted in *Congressional Globe,* 37th Cong., 2nd sess. (March 26, 1862), 1378.
12. On the importance of virgin land for wheat, see Alonzo Englebert Taylor, "Wheat and Wheat Flour," *Annals of the American Academy of Political and Social Science* 127 (Sept. 1926): 30–48.
13. William N. Parker, "Productivity Growth in American Grain Farming: An Analysis of Its 19th-Century Sources," in *The Reinterpretation of American Economic History,* ed. Robert W. Fogel and Stanley L. Engerman (New York, 1971), 175.
14. On wheat rust in Austria-Hungary, see U.K. Parliament, *Report by Her Majesty's Consuls on the Manufactures, Commerce &c. of Their Consular Districts,* BPP-C.828 (1873), 705–6. On the role of moisture in the buildup of wheat

rust, see Norman E. Borlaug, "Sixty-Two Years of Fighting Hunger: Personal Recollections," *Euphytica* 157, no. 3 (2007): 287–97.

15. Since the 1960s economic historians have suggested that the Civil War was a costly diversion of resources into industries that had no peacetime counterparts. This is a familiar neoclassical argument: that any federally funded investment will necessarily misdirect resources. The first foray in this direction began with Robert Fogel's argument that federally funded railroads misdirected resources and that canals would have been just as valuable. Any student of medicine or engineering would dispute this in that the most important advances in the sciences have come from wartime investment by states. One need only think of World War I (chemotherapy), World War II (penicillin, radar, and atomic energy), or even the Cold War (high-speed integrated circuits). On medicine and war, see Roger Cooter et al., eds., *War, Medicine, and Modernity* (Stroud, U.K., 1998).

16. Nelson and Sheriff, *People at War,* chap. 10.

17. Ibid., chap. 6; Richard Franklin Bensel, *Yankee Leviathan: The Origins of Central State Authority in America, 1859–1877* (New York, 1990). The best discussion of the political controversies about these notes is Richardson, *Greatest Nation of the Earth,* chap. 3.

18. On the timing of these events, see E. G. Spaulding, ed., *History of the Legal Tender Paper Money Issued During the Great Rebellion* (Buffalo, 1869), 11–15.

19. Richardson, *Greatest Nation of the Earth,* 94.

20. Frank M. Pixley, "A Tirade Against the 'Traitors' . . . ," *San Francisco Chronicle,* Sept. 16, 1862.

21. There were in fact two currencies: the currencies of the banks (which suspended specie payments in 1861) and the unbacked currency of the greenback. While greenbacks traded at a discount, so did the bank bills. Merchants with greenbacks who needed gold certificates or sterling bills of exchange to trade internationally (or those with gold bills who needed greenbacks) required the services of the Gold Room in New York, where the greenback discount was established by regular trading. See James McPherson, *Battle Cry of Freedom: The Civil War Era* (New York, 1988), 442–45; T. J. Stiles, *The First Tycoon: The Epic Life of Cornelius Vanderbilt* (New York, 2010), 351.

22. Joseph Camp Griffith Kennedy, *Agriculture of the United States in 1860* (Washington, D.C., 1864), xli–xlv.

23. Pennsylvania Railroad, *Sixteenth Annual Report* (Feb. 2, 1863), 9–13; Pennsylvania Railroad, *Eighteenth Annual Report* (Feb. 21, 1865), vi. The Erie began the war in receivership and finished the war profitably, though it continued to be plagued with massive debts. Edward Harold Mott, *Between the Ocean and the Lakes: The Story of Erie* (New York, 1908), 130–45; Chicago, Burlington & Quincy Railroad Company, *Report of the Directors* (June 19, 1863), 7–15.

24. A finely grained history of the elevator trade can be found in Guy A. Lee,

"History of the Chicago Grain Elevator Industry, 1840–1890" (Ph.D. diss., Harvard University, 1938).

25. George G. Tunell, "Transportation on the Great Lakes," 55th Cong., 2nd sess., H.R. Doc. 277 (1898), 4–6.

26. Albert Fink, *Report upon the Adjustment of Railroad Transportation Rates to Seaboard Cities* (New York, 1882), statement C.

27. H. R. Page & Co., *Atlas of Chicago* ([Chicago], 1879), Chicago Region Map Collection, Newberry Library.

28. "Agriculture in America," *Times* (London), Oct. 1, 1879.

29. Approximately two million bushels came across the Great Lakes and through Canadian ports in 1869. By the 1897–1898 season the United States was sending 510 million bushels of wheat to the world every year, though a growing portion was being consumed internally. William Crookes, *The Wheat Problem* (London, 1899), 10. I have relied on chapter 1 of William J. Hudson and Gary Vocke's provocative unpublished book, "World Grain Trade, 1850–2050." The rate war is described in Joseph Nimmo, *Report on the Internal Commerce of the United States,* 48th Cong., 2nd sess., H.R. Executive Doc. 7 (Dec. 31, 1884), 15. The effect of this storm of cheap wheat is described in Scott Reynolds Nelson, *Iron Confederacies: Southern Railways, Klan Violence, and Reconstruction* (Chapel Hill, N.C., 1999).

CHAPTER NINE: A STORM OF WHEAT

1. On the industrial history of Kladno and the industrial areas around Prague, see Jaroslov Purš, "The Situation of the Working Class in the Czech Lands in the Phase of the Expansion and Completion of the Industrial Revolution (1849–1873)," *Historica (Historical Sciences in Czechoslovakia)* 6 (1963): 145–237.

2. On the mines of Kladno, see T. Lindsay Galloway, "On the Present Condition of Mining in Some of the Principal Coal-Producing Districts of the Continent," *North of England Institute of Mining and Mechanical Engineers Transactions* 27 (1878): 193–94; on the use of Kladno's brown coals in steam engines, see W. A. Anderson, "Railway Apparatus," in *Reports of the United States Commissioners to the Paris Universal Exposition,* ed. Edward Henry Knight (Washington, D.C., 1880), 437–38.

3. *Denní Hlasatel,* April 7, 1915, translated in *Chicago Foreign Language Press Survey,* 1.

4. Purš, "Situation of the Working Class in the Czech Lands"; Thomas Čapek, *Bohemia Under Hapsburg Misrule* (New York, 1915).

5. On Louis Napoleon's role in reshaping Paris, see David Baguley, *Napoleon III and His Regime: An Extravaganza* (Baton Rouge, La., 2000), and Theodore Zeldin, *France, 1848–1945* (Oxford, U.K., 1977). On Louis Napoleon's role in creating the Crédit Mobilier, see "Express from Paris," *Morning Chronicle* (London), Dec. 1, 1852.

6. Victor Hugo, *Napoleon the Little*, in *The Works of Victor Hugo: Handy Library Edition* (Boston, 1909), chap. 6.

7. "Express from Paris"; "Housing for the Poor in Paris," *Leeds Mercury*, March 3, 1866; Roger Price, *An Economic History of Modern France, 1730–1914* (London, 1981), chaps. 1 and 2; David F. Good, *The Economic Rise of the Habsburg Empire, 1750–1914* (Berkeley, Calif., 1984), 78–96.

8. U.K. Parliament, *Report by Her Majesty's Consuls on Manufactures and Commerce &c. of Their Consular Districts* (1873), 703–20; Friedrich Kick and Henry Handley Pridham Powles, *Flour Manufacture: With Supplement, Recent Progress in Flour Manufacture* (London, 1888), 206–19; Dan Morgan, *Merchants of Grain* (New York, 1978), 50.

9. Fritz Stern, *Gold and Iron: Bismarck, Bleichröder, and the Building of the German Empire* (New York, 1977), 309.

10. On the French joint-stock banks like Crédit Foncier and Crédit Lyonnais formed in the 1860s, see Karl Erich Born, *International Banking in the 19th and 20th Centuries* (New York, 1983), 63–64, 104–5; Roger Price, *The French Second Empire: An Anatomy of Political Power* (New York, 2001), chap. 7. On the Prussian Hypothekenbanken after 1862 and Gründer banks after June 1870, see Born, *International Banking*, 86–87, 104–5.

11. Max Wirth, *Geschichte der Handelskrisen* (1890; repr., New York, 1968), 512; conversion to dollars in Lewis Heyl, *United States Duties on Imports, 1874* (Washington, D.C., 1874), 27.

12. Eric Hobsbawm, *The Age of Empire, 1875–1914* (London, 1987); Norman Stone, *Europe Transformed, 1878–1919* (Malden, Mass., 1999), chap. 1. On price convergence, see Kevin H. O'Rourke, "The European Grain Invasion, 1870–1913," *Journal of Economic History* 57 (Dec. 1997): 775–801.

13. They came from Jewish families, less exalted families than their financial competitors, the "high-finance" private bankers. The private bankers with exalted names—the Rothschilds, Barings, and Hopes—had tried to prevent the emergence of these newly rich financiers with their competing institutions. Still, they were obliged to do business with them.

14. In volume of exports to Britain, the United States exported about one-third of the Russian volume in 1867; by 1871 it was more than half; by 1873 it was more than double. The timing is confusing because American exports listed for 1873 are actually for July 1, 1872, to June 1873, while Russian figures are January to December. See Memorandum of the Odessa Committee on Trade and Manufactures, translated in U.K. Parliament, *Reports from Her Majesty's Consuls on Manufactures, Commerce &c. of Their Districts*, BPP-C.1427 (1876), 438–39.

15. On prices of wheat, rapeseed, flour, and bacon exported from Austria-Hungary, see U.K. Parliament, *Reports from Her Majesty's Consuls on Manufactures, Commerce &c. of Their Districts* (1873), 703–12. The consul from Austria-Hungary blames wheat rust and a cattle plague that crossed the border from Bosnia as well.

16. Report of Vice-Consul Webster in U.K. Parliament, *Reports from Her Majesty's Consuls on Manufactures, Commerce &c. of Their Districts* (1876), 454–56.

17. U.K. Parliament, *Reports from Her Majesty's Consuls on Manufactures, Commerce &c. of Their Districts* (1876), 431.

18. "The Grain Trade," *Massachusetts Ploughman and New England Journal of Agriculture*, Jan. 15, 1876.

19. Hugo, *Napoleon the Little*, chap. 6.

20. Wirth, *Geschichte der Handelskrisen*, 620.

21. Ibid.; *Times* (London), May 12, 1873.

22. "The Week," *Nation*, June 5, 1873.

23. Charles Kindleberger, *Historical Economics: Art or Science?* (Berkeley, Calif., 1990), chap. 14.

24. Wirth, *Geschichte der Handelskrisen*, 620.

25. On Kladno rents and crowding, see Purš, "Situation of the Working Class in the Czech Lands," 181–82, 224–26.

26. "MD (Mule Driver) Degree the New Mayor of Chicago Takes Pride In," *Boston Globe*, April 12, 1931.

27. *Historical Statistics of the United States* (Washington, D.C., 1949), ser. B, 304–30. While the *Historical Statistics of the United States* lists the majority of emigrants as German in the late 1870s and early 1880s, a substantial portion of the German totals were, like the Cermaks, subjects of the Austro-Hungarian Empire who left through the German cities of Bremen and Hamburg and were thus counted in the German totals. On attempts to correct these estimates, see Annemarie Steidl, Englebert Stockhammer, and Hermann Zeitlhofer, "Relations Among Internal, Continental, and Transatlantic Migration in Late Imperial Austria," *Social Science History* 31 (Spring 2007): 61–92.

28. "The Financial Crisis at Vienna," *Times* (London), May 12, 1873; Wirth, *Geschichte der Handelskrisen*, 473–78.

29. "Financial Crisis at Vienna."

30. "The Week in Trade and Finance," [dated Nov. 10], *The Nation*, Nov. 13, 1873, 328.

31. "An Unusually Transparent Scheme . . . ," *Financier*, April 13, 1872, 295.

32. Meade Minnigerode, *Certain Rich Men: Stephen Girard, John Jacob Astor, Jay Cooke, Daniel Drew* (New York, 1927), 79–82.

33. Jonathan Ira Levy, "The Ways of Providence: Capitalism, Risk, and Freedom in America, 1841–1935" (Ph.D. diss., University of Chicago, 2008), chap. 3.

34. Robert Sobel, *Panic on Wall Street: A History of America's Financial Disasters* (New York, 1968), 167–68; Ron Chernow, *The House of Morgan: An American Banking Dynasty and the Rise of Modern Finance* (New York, 1990), 35–36; Michael A. Bellesiles, *1877: America's Year of Living Violently* (New York, 2010), 2–4; "Railway Securities," *Railway Times*, Sept. 14, 1872, 37, reprinted from an August issue of *The Nation*.

35. Thomas A. Scott of the Pennsylvania Railroad faced this problem with his acquisition of the Texas & Pacific Railroad. He returned from England in the fall of 1873 without having sold his bonds and was forced to continue borrowing on the money market. "Week in Trade and Finance," 328. On the financial troubles of C. P. Huntington, see Scott Reynolds Nelson, *Steel Drivin' Man: John Henry, the Untold Story of an American Legend* (New York, 2006), chap. 6. On Scott and Huntington's problems generally, see Julius Grodinsky, *Transcontinental Railway Strategy, 1869–1893: A Study of Businessmen* (Philadelphia, 1962), 15–55. On Jay Cooke's financial troubles, see M. John Lubetkin, *Jay Cooke's Gamble: The Northern Pacific Railroad, the Sioux, and the Panic of 1873* (Norman, Okla., 2006).

36. Francis Murray Huston, *Financing an Empire: History of Banking in Illinois* (Chicago, 1926), 228.

37. Cannon, *Clearing Houses,* 83–90.

38. Nicolas Barreyre, "The Politics of Economic Crises: The Case of 1873," *Journal of the Gilded Age and Progressive Era* 10, no. 4 (Oct. 2011).

39. Edwin Jones Clapp, *The Port of Hamburg* (New Haven, Conn., 1911), 81–85. On the $10 steerage rate, see testimony of E. L. Boas in House of Representatives, *Testimony Taken by the Select Committee of the House to Inquire into the Alleged Violation of the Laws Prohibiting the Importation of Contract Laborers, etc.,* 50th Cong., 1st sess. (1888), 5.

40. Franz Kafka, *Amerika* (New York, 1996).

41. This is article 4 of the Austro-Hungarian constitution.

42. "Hungary: A Crisis in the Magyar Kingdom," *Chicago Tribune,* April 11, 1872.

43. E. L. Baker to J. Van Nortwick, Esq., Aug. 26, 1857, Baker, E. L., Out-Letters, June 12, 1857–Oct. 19, 1858, Chicago, Burlington & Quincy Railroad Company Papers.

44. J. M. Walker to William F. Weld, Dec. 23, 1873, Walker, J. M., Out-Letters, 1871–81, vol. 4, Chicago, Burlington & Quincy Papers.

45. Herbert G. Gutman, "The Braidwood Lockout of 1874," *Journal of the Illinois State Historical Society* 53, no. 1 (Spring 1960): 11.

46. The evidence is circumstantial, but CW&V apparently used the same agency that the railroad did in seeking farmers.

47. This "ticket business" would be separated from the "land business" after 1872. See C. R. Schaller (European commissioner) to George S. Harris (including underlines made by Harris), March 23, 1872, in Letters: Foreign, Sept. 11, 1869–Dec. 16, 1872, Land Department Records, Foreign Agencies, Burlington & Missouri (Iowa) Records, Chicago, Burlington & Quincy Papers.

48. On this delivery, see Gutman, "Braidwood Lockout of 1874," 5–28, and Herbert G. Gutman, "Labor in the Land of Lincoln: Coal Miners on the Prairie," in *Power and Culture: Essays on the American Working Class* (New York, 1987), 117–212.

49. The role of Castle Garden as an enclosed embarkation point that forced

workers into a particular position is discussed in Scott Reynolds Nelson, "After Slavery: Forced Drafts of Irish and Chinese Labor in the American Civil War; or, The Search for Liquid Labor," in *Many Middle Passages: Forced Migration and the Making of the Modern World,* ed. Emma Christopher, Cassandra Pybus, and Marcus Rediker (Berkeley, Calif., 2007). Buying a through ticket to Chicago in Prague was often cheaper than one bought in New York. Otherwise an immigrant who came to New York without an inland railroad ticket would be forced to buy a high-priced ticket from the Pittsburgh, Fort Wayne & Chicago, a Pennsylvania railroad affiliated with New York's Republican Party. This system predated the war. See "The Colonist," reprinted in *Message of the President . . . in Answer to a Resolution of the Senate, Calling for Information on the Subject of Contracts Made in Europe for Inland Passage Tickets,* S. Executive Doc. 26, 35th Cong., 1st sess. (1858), 27–44. On the Pittsburgh, Fort Wayne & Chicago's tight connection to Castle Garden, see "Victims of Vultures," *Chicago Tribune,* Oct. 19, 1872.

50. Gunther Peck, *Reinventing Free Labor: Padrones and Immigrant Workers in the North American West, 1880–1930* (New York, 2000).

51. C. R. Schaller (European commissioner) to George S. Harris, April 26, 1872, in Letters: Foreign, Sept. 11, 1869–Dec. 16, 1872, Land Department Records, Foreign Agencies, Burlington & Missouri (Iowa) Records.

52. "Declaration in Suit of Hiller vs. B&M R RR Neb, New York, State Supreme Court," Apportionment of Tickets folder, Miscellaneous Papers, 1873–1876, Land Department Records, Burlington & Missouri (Iowa) Records.

53. Maurice Baxter, "Encouragement of Immigration to the Middle West During the Era of the Civil War," *Indiana Magazine of History* 46 (March 1950): 30.

54. Quotation from Douglas Bukowski, *Big Bill Thompson, Chicago, and the Politics of Image* (Urbana, Ill., 1998), 232.

55. For the mechanics of delivery, see the reports of U.S. consuls stationed in Prussia and Austria-Hungary in House of Representatives, *Testimony Taken by the Select Committee of the House to Inquire into the Alleged Violation of the Laws Prohibiting the Importation of Contract Laborers,* 61–93.

56. On the HAPAG ships of the early 1870s, see Henry Fry, *The History of North Atlantic Steam Navigation* (London, 1896), 207–15.

57. On Cermak's first birthday in New York, see "Cermak's Career Is Story of Immigrant Boy's Rise," *Chicago Tribune,* March 6, 1933.

58. On the immigrant trains, see E. L. Boas testimony, House of Representatives, *Testimony Taken by the Select Committee of the House to Inquire into the Alleged Violation of the Laws Prohibiting the Importation of Contract Laborers,* 5. For descriptions see "Foreign Emigration," *Chicago Tribune,* Dec. 14, 1873.

59. Gottfried's biography suggests they stayed in Pilsen, where his father, Anton senior, worked on Thalia Hall, on "Alford Street" (this must be All-

port Street), but Thalia Hall was built in the 1890s. On the family's short delay in Chicago, see "Cermak's Career Is Story of Immigrant Boy's Rise."

60. Gutman, "Braidwood Lockout of 1874," 13–18. The company closed the mines on June 1; replacement workers began arriving on June 3, suggesting that the CW&V had cabled for them considerably earlier.

61. Ibid., 17.

62. Purš, "Situation of the Working Class in the Czech Lands," 216–17; Josef V. Polišenský, *Aristocrats and the Crowd in the Revolutionary Year 1848: A Contribution to the History of Revolution and Counter-Revolution in Austria* (Albany, N.Y., 1980), 212–14; Jaroslav G. Polach, "The Beginnings of Trade Unionism Among the Slavs of the Austrian Empire," *American Slavic and East European Review* 14, no. 2 (April 1955): 239–59.

63. Gutman, "Braidwood Lockout of 1874," 22–28.

64. Alex Gottfried, "A. J. Cermak, Chicago Politician: A Study in Political Leadership" (Ph.D. diss., University of Chicago, 1952), 66–67.

65. Kevin Kenny, *Making Sense of the Molly Maguires* (New York, 1998).

66. Gregory P. Downs, *Declarations of Dependence: The Long Reconstruction of Popular Politics in the South* (Chapel Hill, N.C., 2011).

67. Nelson, *Iron Confederacies;* Lou Falkner Williams, *The Great South Carolina Ku Klux Klan Trials, 1871–1872* (Athens, Ga., 1994); Eric Foner, *Reconstruction: America's Unfinished Revolution, 1863–1877* (New York, 1988), chap. 12; Brian Kelly, "Black Laborers, the Republican Party, and the Crisis of Reconstruction in Lowcountry South Carolina," *Internationaal Instituut voor Sociale Geschiedenis* 51 (2006): 375–414.

68. Cyrus McCormick was a trustee of the state-chartered Merchants' Savings, Loan & Trust Co. This trust company, chartered just before the panic of 1857, became the oldest trust company west of the Atlantic Seaboard. It continued to make payments in 1873 after nearly all other Chicago institutions suspended. See Edward Ten Broeck Perine, *The Story of the Trust Companies* (New York, 1916), 103–6, and Bessie Louise Pierce, *A History of Chicago* (Chicago, 1957), 3: 195.

69. David Nasaw, *Andrew Carnegie* (New York, 2006); Rolland Harper Maybee, *Railroad Competition and the Oil Trade* (Mount Pleasant, Mich., 1940).

70. Richard C. Lindberg, *The Gambler King of Clark Street: Michael C. McDonald and the Rise of Chicago's Democratic Machine* (Carbondale, Ill., 2009), 1–62.

71. Christine Sismondo, *America Walks into a Bar: A Spirited History of Taverns and Saloons, Speakeasies, and Grog Shops* (New York, 2011), 144–45.

72. Gerhard Hanloser, *Krise und Antisemitismus: Eine Geschichte in drei Stationen von der Gründerzeit über die Weltwirtschaftskrise bis heute* (Münster, 2003), 43–44.

73. Hans Rosenberg, *Große Depression und Bismarckzeit: Wirtschaftsablauf, Gesellschaft, und Politik in Mitteleuropa* (Berlin, 1967), 94–117.

74. Shelton Stromquist, "Traditions and Collective Action in Hornellsville," in *The Great Strikes of 1877,* ed. David O. Stowell (Urbana, Ill., 2008), 59; Rob-

ert Bruce, *1877: Year of Violence* (Chicago, 1970), 40; Henry Fink, *Regulation of Railway Rates on Interstate Freight Traffic* (New York, 1905), 25.

75. Bruce, *1877*, 40.
76. Dobson, *History of American Enterprise*, 148–61.
77. Allan Pinkerton, *Strikers, Communists, Tramps, and Detectives* (New York, 1878), 103–34; the testimony of Robert A. Ammon is in Pennsylvania General Assembly, *Joint Committee to Investigate the Railroad Riots in July 1877* (Harrisburg, Pa., 1878), 661–74.
78. David O. Stowell, *Streets, Railroads, and the Great Strike of 1877* (Chicago, 1999).
79. Matthew Wayne Shepherd, "Ten Tumultuous Months: Rutherford B. Hayes and the Limitations of 'Home Rule' in the Post-Reconstruction South, September 1878–June 1879" (master's thesis, College of William and Mary, 1998).
80. Foner, *Reconstruction*, 583.
81. Anthony DeStefanis, "Guarding Capital: Soldier Strikebreakers on the Long Road to the Ludlow Massacre" (Ph.D. diss., College of William and Mary, 2004).
82. Ira Katznelson, *City Trenches: Urban Politics and the Patterning of Class in the United States* (Chicago, 1982).

CHAPTER TEN: CROSSES OF GOLD

1. "MD (Mule Driver) Degree the New Mayor of Chicago Takes Pride In."
2. This and most of the discussion of Cermak that follows rely extensively on Alex Gottfried, *Boss Cermak of Chicago: A Study of Political Leadership* (Seattle, 1962), and "A. J. Cermak, Chicago Politician" (Ph.D. diss., University of Chicago, 1952).
3. Donald L. Miller, *City of the Century: The Epic of Chicago and the Making of America* (New York, 1996), 198–99. On beef, see Cronon, *Nature's Metropolis*.
4. Ibid., 200–2.
5. *Historical Statistics of the United States* (Washington, D.C., 1949), ser. M, 56–67.
6. Roy Rosenzweig, *Eight Hours for What We Will: Workers and Leisure in an Industrial City* (New York, 1985); Sismondo, *America Walks into a Bar*, 176–83.
7. The figure of $50 million is from Frederic Logan Paxson, *Recent History of the United States* (Boston, 1921), 148; one-sixth of revenue is from Jerome Sternstein, "Corruption in the Gilded Age Senate: Nelson W. Aldrich and the Sugar Trust," *Capitol Studies* 6 (Spring 1978): 18–19.
8. The Tenure of Office Act, passed in 1867 and revised in 1876, prevented the president from firing cabinet members or other federal employees without the consent of Congress. The Supreme Court overturned it in 1924. On the relative weakness of the president during the Gilded Age, see Wilfred E.

Binkley, "The President as Chief Legislator," *Annals of the American Academy of Political and Social Science* 307 (Sept. 1956): 92–105, and Robert W. Cherny, *American Politics in the Gilded Age, 1868–1900* (New York, 1997). On Havemeyer and Aldrich, see Sternstein, "Corruption in the Gilded Age Senate."

9. Testimony of Henry O. Havemeyer, June 14, 1899, in U.S. Industrial Commission, *Preliminary Report on Trusts and Industrial Combinations,* 56th Cong., 1st sess., H.R. Rep. 476 (Washington, D.C., 1890), 1:101; Sternstein, "Corruption in the Gilded Age Senate"; Jack Simpson Mullins, "The Sugar Trust: Henry O. Havemeyer and the American Sugar Refining Company" (Ph.D. diss., University of South Carolina, 1964), 75–81.

10. Sternstein, "Corruption in the Gilded Age Senate."

11. *Wheeling Register,* April 19, 1890.

12. On John Sherman's role, see Chauncey Depew, "Prospects of Free Trade in the United States," *Nineteenth Century* (Feb. 1894): 248, and George F. Parker, "The Cry for Fraudulent Money in America," *Nineteenth Century* (Oct. 1896): 521–22.

13. Once Hawaii won the subsidy, the drop in sugar prices contributed to a revolution in the Spanish colony of Cuba.

14. "Mr. Schurz on the Tariff," *New York Times,* Oct. 21, 1890; Sidney Ratner, *American Taxation: Its History as a Social Force in Democracy* (New York, 1942), 167. The Democratic platform was reprinted in "Protection Platforms of 1892," *American Economist,* May 29, 1896.

15. On the national production of silver, see Parker, "Cry for Fraudulent Money," 522.

16. The nation was effectively on a gold standard since Jackson's adjustment of the ratio of silver to gold in 1836. In 1873 the nation briefly went off gold and then returned to silver and gold in 1879, when the United States resumed specie payments for greenbacks.

17. On European countries selling silver to build up gold reserves, see Edward O. Leech, "The Doom of Silver," *Forum* 15 (Aug. 1893): 657–65; on the problem of gold raids and post-1893 proposals to give the Treasury expanded powers to prevent this, see "Editorial Comment," *Bankers' Magazine,* Jan. 1902, 1–13.

18. There were exceptions to this rule. Payments to veterans were made through depository banks, for example, and the Treasury made contracts with the Barings, Rothschilds, and Morgans for placing bonds in Europe.

19. Most historians credit the 1907 panic with proposals for a federal reserve, but bankers and the Treasury were seriously considering this at the turn of the century, partly in light of Populist proposals to create a subtreasury system.

20. The five-year average for wheat acreage was 49.2 million for the United States and 4.5 million for Argentina. India, however, had an average of 27.7 million acres under cultivation in those years. Helen C. Farnsworth, "Decline and Recovery of Wheat Prices in the 'Nineties," *Wheat Studies of the Food Research Institute* 10 (June and July 1934): 295.

21. Philip Ziegler, *The Sixth Great Power: Barings, 1762–1929* (London, 1988), chaps. 13 and 14; Austin, *Baring Brothers,* 191–93.

22. Chernow, *House of Morgan,* chap. 5.

23. Farnsworth, "Decline and Recovery of Wheat Prices," 348.

24. The Republican Chauncey Depew argued that the crisis was internal, not external. Fearing that President Cleveland and a majority-Democratic Congress would lower tariffs, jobbers in 1893 put off buying manufactured goods, which then lowered purchases from manufacturers and bank advances. This fear of free trade (which Cleveland and most Democrats agreed upon), not fear of free silver (which Cleveland and his party disagreed upon), then led to a crisis. This effectively exempts the Republican Party's actions in 1890 from any responsibility for the crisis. Cleveland's blaming the Silver Purchase Act of 1890 thus blames silverites and western and southern Democrats.

25. R. Hal Williams, *The Democratic Party and California Politics, 1880–1896* (Stanford, Calif., 1973), 178.

26. Floyd Benjamin Streeter, *The Kaw: The Heart of a Nation* (New York, 1941), 326.

27. Elijah Adams Morse, *The Democratic Party Platform* (Washington, D.C., 1893), 1.

28. *World's Congress of Bankers and Financiers* (Chicago, 1893), 129.

29. Albert Ross Eckler, "A Measure of the Severity of Depressions, 1873–1932," *Review of Economics and Statistics* 15, no. 2 (May 1933): 75–81.

30. Clive Trebilcock, *The Industrialization of the Continental Powers, 1780–1914* (London, 1981); Eugen Varga, *Mirovye ekonomicheskie krizisy* (Moscow, 1937).

31. Huston, *Financing an Empire,* 248–50.

32. J. Rogers Hollingsworth, *The Whirligig of Politics: The Democracy of Cleveland and Bryan* (Chicago, 1963), chap. 1.

33. *Congressional Globe,* House, 53rd Cong., 2nd sess. (Jan. 29, 1894), 1600.

34. Ibid., 1601.

35. Bennett D. Baack and Edward John Ray, "Special Interests and the Adoption of the Income Tax in the United States," *Journal of Economic History* 45 (Sept. 1985): 607–25.

36. *Dallas Morning News,* Aug. 1, 1894; *Arizona Weekly Journal-Miner,* Aug. 22, 1894; *Boston Daily Advertiser,* Aug. 23, 1894.

37. Jane Addams, *Twenty Years at Hull-House* (New York, 1911), 214.

38. *Dallas Morning News,* Aug. 1, 1894.

39. "The United States Strike Commission," *Advocate of Peace* 56 (Dec. 1894): 277–79.

40. Illinois State Board of Arbitration, *Seventh Annual Report* (Springfield, Ill., 1902), 190–95.

41. *People* ex rel. *Moloney v. Pullman's Palace Car Company,* 175 Ill. 125 (Oct. 1898), reprinted in *Report of Cases at Law and in Chancery Argued and Determined Before the Supreme Court of Illinois* (Springfield, Ill., 1899), 153.

42. In 1908 the Supreme Court struck down the section of the Erdman Act

that prevented yellow-dog contracts, in other words, contracts stipulating that workers not join a union. In 1932 the Norris-LaGuardia Act made yellow-dog contracts illegal.

43. *Congressional Record,* 53rd Cong., 1st sess. (Aug. 13, 1894), app., 1351.

44. On the origins of this view of financial panics after the panic of 1837, see Chester McArthur Destler, "The Influence of Edward Kellogg upon American Radicalism, 1865–1895," *Journal of Political Economy* 40 (June 1932): 338–65. On the sophistication of Simpson, see Gene Clanton, *Congressional Populism and the Crisis of the 1890s* (Lawrence, Kans., 1998), chaps. 2–4, and Charles Postel, *The Populist Vision* (New York, 2009).

45. On the "Crime of 1873," see Allen Weinstein, "Was There a 'Crime of 1873'? The Case of the Demonetized Dollar," *Journal of American History* 54, no. 2 (Sept. 1967): 307–26.

46. Compare Barton Shaw, *The Wool Hat Boys: Georgia's Populist Party* (Baton Rouge, La., 1984), with C. Vann Woodward, *Tom Watson: Agrarian Rebel* (New York, 1938). In describing Reconstruction, Populists tended to soft-pedal the attack on African-Americans and highlight the alleged ill effects of rule by "carpetbaggers." See Steve Kantrowitz, *Ben Tillman and the Reconstruction of White Supremacy* (Chapel Hill, N.C., 2000), 151–54.

47. *Salina Weekly Republican,* Oct. 28, 1892, quoted in John Erwin Hollitz, *Thinking Through the Past* (New York, 2000), 2:102.

48. Chester McArthur Destler, *American Radicalism, 1865–1901* (Chicago, 1966), 162–79.

49. Richard Schneirov, *Labor and Urban Politics: Class Conflict and the Origins of Modern Liberalism in Chicago* (Urbana, Ill., 1998); Georg Leidenberger, *Chicago's Progressive Alliance: Labor and the Bid for Public Streetcars* (Chapel Hill, N.C., 2006).

50. C. Vann Woodward, *Origins of the New South, 1877–1913* (Baton Rouge, La., 1971).

51. Josephus Daniels, *Tar Heel Editor* (Chapel Hill, N.C., 1939); Josephus Daniels, *Editor in Politics* (Chapel Hill, N.C., 1941); *The Presentation of the Portrait of the Late Benjamin Rice Lacy to the State of North Carolina* (Raleigh, N.C., 1929), Benjamin Rice Lacy Papers (1850–1930), North Carolina Division of Archives and History, Raleigh.

52. James M. H. Frederick, comp., *National Party Platforms of the United States* (Akron, Ohio, 1896), 89.

53. *National Cyclopedia of American Biography,* vols. 15 and 28, s.v. "Lewis, James Hamilton"; *Biographical Dictionary of the United States Congress, 1774–2005,* 1445; *Who Was Who in America,* vol. 1, s.v. "Lewis, James Hamilton"; *Congressional Record,* March 31, 1898, 3434.

54. George E. Mowry, *Theodore Roosevelt and the Progressive Movement* (Madison, Wis., 1946), chap. 1.

55. Kenneth William Hechler, *Insurgency: Personalities and Politics of the Taft Era* (New York, 1964).

56. Todd DePastino, *Citizen Hobo: How a Century of Homelessness Shaped America*

(Chicago, 2003), chap. 3; Todd DePastino, introduction to *The Road*, by Jack London (New Brunswick, N.J., 2006), xxvii; George Milburn, *The Hobo's Hornbook: A Repertory for the Gutter Jongleur* (New York, 1930), 61–62.

57. Havemeyer testimony, June 13, 1899, in U.S. Industrial Commission, *Preliminary Report on Trusts and Industrial Combinations*, 1:109.

58. For an alternative explanation for the emergence of the modern corporation in an international context, see Alfred D. Chandler, *Scale and Scope: The Dynamics of Industrial Capitalism* (Cambridge, Mass., 1990).

59. On prices, see Report of Senator Augustus Bacon, *Congressional Record*, 58th Cong., 2nd sess. (April 25, 1904), 5514–20.

60. William G. Roy, *Socializing Capital: The Rise of the Large Industrial Corporation in America* (Princeton, N.J., 2007); Thomas R. Navin and Marian V. Sears, "The Rise of a Market for Industrial Securities, 1887–1902," *Business History Review* 29 (June 1955): 105–38.

61. Paul M. Green, "Anton J. Cermak: The Man and His Machine," in *The Mayors: The Chicago Political Tradition*, ed. Paul M. Green and Melvin G. Holli (Carbondale, Ill., 2005), 100.

62. John Lawrence Tone, *War and Genocide in Cuba, 1895–1898* (Chapel Hill, N.C., 2006). More than a hundred years later, much of Spain's internal documentation on the reconquest of Cuba has still not been released to historians. Evelyn Jennings, professor of history, St. Lawrence University, personal communication, April 2002.

CHAPTER ELEVEN: WHO PUT THE ROAR IN THE ROARING TWENTIES?

1. Lawrence Merton Jacobs, *Bank Acceptances* (Washington, D.C., 1910), 13.

2. Cannon, *Clearing Houses*, 75–136.

3. Ibid., 169–79.

4. On the problems of the 1907 loan certificates, see ibid., 75–136. Arsène Pujo, *Report of the Committee . . . to Investigate the Concentration of Control of Money and Credit*, 62nd Cong., 3rd sess., H.R. Rep. 1593 (Washington, D.C., 1913), 13–32.

5. Robert L. Owen to Samuel L. Untermeyer, May 14, 1927, reprinted in Samuel Untermeyer, "Who Is Entitled to the Credit for the Federal Reserve Act? An Answer to Senator Carter Glass" (June 1927), Banks-U.S., 1924–1932, Misc. Pamphlets, Widener Library Pamphlet Collection, Harvard University.

6. In 1933 the Glass-Steagall Act separated these into J.P. Morgan & Co. into Morgan Chase and Morgan Stanley.

7. Albert Gallatin, Jefferson's Treasury secretary, then president of the National Bank of New York, suggested the creation of the Clearing House in 1841. It was chartered in 1853. See W. Harrison Bayles, "The Creation of the Clearing House," *McMaster's Commercial Cases* 19 (Oct. 1916): 252–65.

8. On the role of Bryan, see Untermeyer, "Who Is Entitled to the Credit for

the Federal Reserve Act?," and Joseph P. Tumulty, *Woodrow Wilson as I Know Him* (Garden City, N.Y., 1921), chaps. 21 and 22.

9. *Congressional Record,* 63rd Cong., 2nd sess., 1455, quoted in part in George Brown Tindall, *The Emergence of the New South, 1913–1945* (Baton Rouge, La., 1967), 12.

10. Mark Sullivan, *Our Times: America at the Birth of the Twentieth Century,* abr. ed. (New York, 1996), 323–34.

11. Liaquat Ahamed, *Lords of Finance: The Bankers Who Broke the World* (New York, 2009), chap. 2.

12. Giuseppi, *Bank of England,* 133–37.

13. Alexander Henderson, *Acceptances* (Boston, 1920), 11–13. Bills of exchange marked "Accepted" by a merchant house traded at a premium as early as the nineteenth century, and their use may go back to the thirteenth century or earlier. The Fed defined the American acceptance as a note accepted by a bank in its own system, and it pointedly sought to make a market in these instruments, sometimes holding as much as 50 percent of the acceptances that circulated. See Roger Wendell Valentine, "The Development of the Banker's Acceptance in the United States" (abstract of 1924 Ph.D. diss., University of Illinois, Urbana, 1928), 5–7 (in Harvard Widener Library Pamphlet Collection "Acceptances"). The Federal Reserve's Regulation J initially stated a three-month maturity; it was later extended to six months.

14. The conflicts about the rate and who controlled it roiled the Federal Reserve for many years. It may be one of the most important controversies for monetary economists. See, for starters, Milton Friedman and Anna Schwartz, *A Monetary History of the United States, 1867–1960* (Princeton, N.J., 1963), chaps. 5–7.

15. On the newness of the BA, see William Henry Kniffin, *American Banking Practice* (New York, 1921), 195–97. Kniffin says that a BA is simply a bill of exchange that has been accepted by a bank. The original Federal Reserve Act sought to define acceptances in two contradictory sections — sections 13 and 14. One limited the acceptance market to member banks, the other did not. After Congress revised the law in August 1914 to make the banker's acceptance more sweeping, the Fed acted by defining the BA precisely. On the change in the act, see "An Act Proposing Amendment to Section Nineteen of the Federal Reserve Act," Pub. L. No. 171 (1914), reprinted in Willis S. Paine, *Paine's Analysis of the Federal Reserve Act and Cognate Statutes* (New York, 1917), 33. The Fed promulgated circular number 5 on January 15, 1915; this was then superseded by Regulation J on April 2, 1915, which defined exactly what a banker's acceptance looked like. "The acceptance is still in its infancy in American banking," the Fed Board declared in circular number 11 on the same day, "but the development itself is certain." Regulation J and circular number 11 are reprinted in Paine, *Paine's Analysis,* 244–47.

16. According to Kniffin, "National Bank notes [are] secured by United States

Bonds; while the Federal Reserve notes are secured by gold and commercial paper" (*American Banking Practice*, 294).

17. Federal Reserve, *Of Service to Banks and Business: The Federal Reserve System* (1923). On Christmas, see "The Federal Reserve Banks and the Currency," *Monthly Review of Credit and Business Conditions*, May 1, 1921, quoted in Kniffin, *American Banking Practice*, 280.

18. Jeffrey A. Miron, "Financial Panics, the Seasonality of the Nominal Interest Rate, and the Founding of the Fed," *American Economic Review* 76 (March 1986): 125–40.

19. Forrest Crissey, *The Federal Reserve Bank System: An Interview with James Simpson, President of Marshall Field & Company* (Chicago, 1926), 8, Banks–U.S., 1924–1932, Misc. Pamphlets, Widener Library Pamphlet Collection, Harvard University.

20. The mechanics of this operation are described in Kniffin, *American Banking Practice*, 124–25.

21. Harold van B. Cleveland et al., *Citibank, 1812–1970* (Cambridge, Mass., 1985), chap. 4.

22. Fred I. Kent, "Acceptances in Foreign Trade," *American Industries* (Feb. 1922): 27–28.

23. This is indexed to 1925 dollars. See G. Bolwin, "Exchange of Merchandise Between Germany and the United States," in *German Commerce Yearbook 1928*, ed. Hellmut Kuhnert (Berlin, 1928), 225.

24. Ibid., 226–27.

25. Ranald C. Michie, *The Global Securities Market: A History* (New York, 2006), chap. 6. Thanks to Carl Strikwerda for assigning this in our global financial crisis reading group.

26. Zhaojin Ji, *A History of Modern Shanghai Banking: The Rise and Decline of China's Finance Capitalism* (Armonk, N.Y., 2003), 152–53; Cleveland et al., *Citibank*, 80–82.

27. George Henry Soule, *Prosperity Decade* (New York, 1947), 254–55.

28. The amounts are $1.5 to $2.6 billion using the 1934 valuation; see Federal Reserve System, *Banking and Monetary Statistics* (Washington, D.C., 1943), 536. Estimates of the world gold stock vary. The League of Nations estimated it at $7.7 billion in 1913 and $11.4 billion in 1929, according to Harold Bowen, "Gold Maldistribution," *American Economic Review* (Dec. 1936): 665.

29. Seymour Edwin Harris, *Twenty Years of Federal Reserve Policy* (Cambridge, Mass., 1933), 11–14.

30. Charles Lee Prather, "History of the Gold Policy of the Federal Reserve System" (Ph.D. diss., University of Illinois, 1929).

31. David Friday, "The Trend of Interest Rates," *Bankers' Magazine*, May 1928, 637–41.

32. Quotation from Jane W. D'Arista, *The Evolution of U.S. Finance* (Armonk, N.Y., 1994), 1:20.

33. Seymour Edwin Harris pointed out that Governor Benjamin Strong Jr. of the New York Fed continually asserted that banks like his were restrained from lending when the Fed raised the rate even slightly. "Governor Strong was aware, however, that member banks or the money market might obtain additional cash, when reserve banks sold securities, by selling acceptances to them [the Fed] instead of rediscounting. . . . The restraining effect of an increase of rediscounts is thus averted." Harris, *Twenty Years of Federal Reserve Policy,* 11. On the use of BAs by one's own bank, see ibid., 11, 317–18, and Valentine, "Development of the Banker's Acceptance," 6.

34. Vincent P. Carosso, *Investment Banking in America: A History* (Cambridge, Mass., 1970), chap. 12.

35. David E. Kyvig, *Daily Life in the United States, 1920–1940: How Americans Lived Through the "Roaring Twenties" and the Great Depression* (Chicago, 2002), chap. 2.

36. Cleveland et al., *Citibank,* chap. 5. Cleveland and one of his coauthors, Thomas F. Huertas, note Citibank's new customers, though they do not connect this to owner financing of merchandise.

37. Stefan Zweig, *The World of Yesterday* (New York, 1943), 292. The English unemployed stayed in the Hotel de l'Europe, the most fashionable hotel in Austria, because the English dole allowed them to live more cheaply in a hotel in Austria than in an English slum.

38. Ahamed, *Lords of Finance,* chap. 7; quotation from Zweig, *World of Yesterday,* 290.

39. Charles Kindleberger, *The World in Depression, 1929–1939* (Berkeley, Calif., 1986), 21, citing Paul Einzig, *World Finance Since 1914* (London, 1935), 177, describes how this period of inflation led the nations to abhor any currency depreciation.

40. Robert McAlmon, *Being Geniuses Together, 1920–1930* (Baltimore, 1977).

41. Senate Committee on Finance, *Sale of Foreign Bonds or Securities in the United States,* 72nd Cong., 1st sess. (1931), 25–26.

42. This, at least, was how the Germans viewed part 1, subtitle 3 of the Dawes Plan. See W. Reichardt, "Significance of the Loans Taken Up by Germany in Foreign Countries, Especially in the United States, After the Stabilization of Her Currency," in Kuhnert, *German Commerce Yearbook 1928,* 60.

43. Of the $7.8 billion in foreign bonds outstanding in 1930, member banks in the Federal Reserve held less than 10 percent, or $643 million. See testimony of Charles Mitchell, National City Bank, in Senate Committee on Finance, *Sale of Foreign Bonds or Securities in the United States,* 70.

44. J. P. Morgan did not participate directly in the Federal Reserve, nor did Kuhn, Loeb.

45. This was done initially to get around the bar against branch banking and overseas operations. In 1919 the Edge Act amended the Federal Reserve Act to allow overseas operations through federally chartered affiliates.

46. On National City Bank, see Senate Subcommittee on Banking and Cur-

rency, *Operation of the National and Federal Reserve Banking Systems,* 71st Cong., 3rd sess. (1931), 300–3. On Chase, see "Chase National Pays Dividend to Further Securities Corporation," *Financier, New York,* June 23, 1917, 1753. On Bank of America, see House Committee on Banking and Currency, *Branch, Chain, and Group Banking,* 71st Cong., 2nd sess. (1929), vol. 2, pt. 11, 1429–32.

47. Senate Subcommittee on Banking and Currency, *Operation of the National and Federal Reserve Banking Systems,* 1030–68.

48. As early as 1920, the Fed feared that acceptances allowed banks to skirt section 5200. See Valentine, "Development of the Banker's Acceptance," 6.

49. Julian Sherrod, *Scapegoats, by One of Them* (New York, 1931), 114.

50. "German Loans in Prospect," *New York Times,* Feb. 5, 1928; "Bonds and Bond Men," *Wall Street Journal,* Feb. 25, 1928.

51. On the sectoral center of the 1930 bank crisis, see Friedman and Schwartz, *Monetary History,* 308; Peter Temin, *Did Monetary Forces Cause the Great Depression?* (New York, 1976), 106–7; and Eugene Nelson White, "A Reinterpretation of the Banking Crisis of 1930," *Journal of Economic History* 44 (March 1984): 119–38.

52. Reichardt, "Significance of the Loans Taken Up by Germany in Foreign Countries," 50.

53. Quoted in Carosso, *Investment Banking in America,* 262.

54. Ibid., chap. 12.

55. The ugly details are in the 2,179 pages of testimony in Senate Committee on Finance, *Sale of Foreign Bonds or Securities in the United States.*

56. In addition, of course, the hoard of gold in American reserve banks and the U.S. Treasury should have made them safe enough to weather any financial storm, even the fateful stock market crash of 1929. Considerable gold did flow to France in 1927–1928.

57. Michie, *Global Securities Market,* 179–80. There were limits to how bank funds could be invested: no bank could directly invest more than 40 percent of its funds in a single enterprise, funds could not be lent on land, and call loans were subject to a limit of 50 percent of their market value. Banks imposed their own limits: drawing from a demand deposit account required advance notice, for example. But the federal government measured foreign investment only indirectly at this time.

58. Heywood William Fleisig, "Long Term Capital Flows and the Great Depression: The Role of the United States, 1927–1933" (Ph.D. diss., Yale University, 1969), 17.

59. "Would Curtail German Loans," *Wall Street Journal,* March 29, 1928.

60. "Exaggerate German Municipal Loans," *Wall Street Journal,* May 15, 1928.

61. "Europe Feels Need of America's Aid in War Debt Plans," *New York Times,* Sept. 16, 1928.

62. "Making Americans Pay," *Washington Post,* April 8, 1928.

63. "Germany's Reparation Bonds," *New York Times,* Sept. 30, 1928; Herbert

Feis, *The Diplomacy of the Dollar: First Era, 1919–1932* (Hamden, Conn., 1965), 45.

64. Fleisig, "Long Term Capital Flows and the Great Depression." Peter Temin and others would strongly disagree with this account, insisting that German problems were almost entirely domestic. For a survey of these debates, see Charles H. Feinstein, Peter Temin, and Gianni Toniolo, "International Economic Organization: Banking, Finance, and Trade in Europe Between the Wars," in *Banking, Currency, and Finance in Europe Between the Wars,* ed. Charles H. Feinstein (New York, 1995).

65. Claire Helene Young, *An Evaluation of Federal Reserve Policy, 1924–1930* (New York, 1992), 50.

66. Ibid., 56; Allan H. Meltzer, *A History of the Federal Reserve* (Chicago, 2003), 1:401.

67. Sidney Homer and Richard Sylla, *A History of Interest Rates,* 3rd ed. (New Brunswick, N.J., 1989), 349.

68. See Ranald C. Michie, *The London Stock Exchange: A History* (New York, 1999), 247–48, on New York's sucking in short-term funds from around the world. The rate on call loans was 12 percent in March 1929 and advanced that year to 15, 17, and 20 percent. See Soule, *Prosperity Decade,* 304, citing Francis W. Hirst, *Wall Street and Lombard Street* (New York, 1931), 304.

69. Perhaps this is because acceptances disappeared from Federal Reserve coffers after 1933 and were largely invisible to economists then and now. Appendix A of Friedman and Schwartz's *Monetary History* tries to cope with the acceptances and finally puts them down as liabilities. They were of course actually assets—part of the pawnshop of promises that made American banks work between 1914 and 1933.

70. Cleveland et al., *Citibank,* 126.

71. National City Bank and others admitted before Congress that since World War I they had frequently used their affiliates to boost stock prices, off-load bad bonds, and increase their reserve ratios. Some banks had their security affiliates buy their stocks when prices were low and sell them when prices were high. On banks' use of BAs to disguise their participation in the call-loan market and bond markets, see testimony of New York Reserve chairman George Harrison in Senate Subcommittee on Banking and Currency, *Operation of the National and Federal Reserve Banking Systems,* 47–52.

72. See Mitchell's testimony in ibid., 286.

73. Harris, *Twenty Years of Federal Reserve Policy,* 11, 317–18. Valentine described how New York banks used the banker's acceptances as a source of short-term credit in the 1920–1921 contraction in his "Development of the Banker's Acceptance," 6.

74. D'Arista, *Evolution of U.S. Finance,* 1:149. D'Arista, like Milton Friedman, notes this change without—I think—understanding it. She blames the "real bills doctrine" for being procyclical, which she argues caused acceptances to increase during upswings. If BAs were directly tied to international trade, this doesn't seem possible, because international trade was

declining rapidly in 1928. I am convinced that the acceptances—with lower interest rates—provided a back door to easy credit when the Fed raised rates. A closer analysis of internal Fed documents and internal National City Bank documents would resolve this question. I believe that the federal government's removal of banker's acceptances from Fed policy and Fed reserves after 1933 grew out of the recognition that these acceptances had been generated improperly.

75. Senate Subcommittee on Banking and Currency, *Operation of the National and Federal Reserve Banking Systems,* 301.

76. "Prosperity Unchecked," *Los Angeles Times,* Oct. 26, 1929.

77. Carosso, *Investment Banking in America,* 306.

78. Peter Temin finds that bonds held by banks may have been key to the Depression that followed the crash; he does not discuss the background of the international bond boom. See Temin, *Did Monetary Forces Cause the Great Depression?*

79. Ji, *History of Modern Shanghai Banking,* 153.

80. "Hoover Attacks Wheat Profiteers," *Boston Globe,* July 11, 1931.

81. H. L. Mencken, "The Hoover Bust," reprinting a column of Oct. 10, 1932, in *A Carnival of Buncombe* (Baltimore, 1956), 262.

82. Ibid., 267.

83. Herbert Hoover, *The State Papers and Other Public Writings of Herbert Hoover* (Garden City, N.Y., 1934), 269.

84. Feis, *Diplomacy of the Dollar,* 7–11. Feis argues that Hoover wanted the Commerce Department to look at the bond issues, though not to comment or pass judgment on them. Harding overruled him and gave the responsibility to the State Department.

85. William C. McNeil, *American Money and the Weimar Republic: Economics and Politics on the Eve of the Great Depression* (New York, 1986), 90–91.

86. On Guntown, see "New Mayor of Guntown," *Atlanta Constitution,* April 19, 1931.

87. Bukowski, *Big Bill Thompson, Chicago, and the Politics of Image.*

88. "Big Bill" Thompson did push for public ownership of trolleys and a five-cent fare in the 1920s, but he was considered beholden to Insull. As the former mayor Carter Harrison said, "Mr. Insull got an ordinance passed which he let the Mayor sign"; see "C. H. Harrison Tells Why He Is for Cermak," *Chicago Tribune,* April 4, 1931.

89. James L. Merriner, *Grafters and Goo Goos: Corruption and Reform in Chicago, 1833–2003* (Carbondale, Ill., 2004), 128.

90. Bukowski, *Big Bill Thompson, Chicago, and the Politics of Image,* 232.

91. "Cermak Ignores Personal Abuse in Mayor Race," *Chicago Tribune,* March 15, 1931.

92. "Thompson Wages His Hottest Fight," *Boston Globe,* March 29, 1931.

93. "Crowd of 26,000 Jams Stadium to Cheer for Cermak," *Chicago Tribune,* March 24, 1931.

94. Merriner, *Grafters and Goo Goos,* 128.

95. "Officials Doubt Transit Session Will Be Called," *Chicago Tribune,* April 14, 1928.

96. Lizabeth Cohen, *Making a New Deal: Industrial Workers in Chicago, 1919–1939* (New York, 1990); Joshua Freeman, *In Transit: The Transport Workers Union in New York City, 1933–1966* (New York, 1989); Gary Gerstle, *The Rise and Fall of the New Deal Order, 1930–1980* (Princeton, N.J., 1989); William Millikan, *A Union Against Unions: The Minneapolis Citizens Alliance and Its Fight Against Organized Labor, 1903–1947* (St. Paul, 2001).

97. "Officials Doubt Transit Session Will Be Called."

98. "Sound Business Demands Ample Reserves," *Chicago Tribune,* May 3, 1928 (advertisement); Edgar Lee Masters, *The Tale of Chicago* (New York, 1933), 324.

99. Masters, *Tale of Chicago,* 308–9.

100. Charles Merz, "Power Control: Will It Be a Fighting Issue in 1932?," *New York Times,* June 14, 1931.

101. In one of the strangest of ironies of Chicago politics, when Roosevelt reached Chicago in 1932, he refrained from attacking Insull. Insull, before he had crumbled, had given Mayor Cermak preferential prices for Insull bonds. FDR speech, "Campaign Address in Portland, Oregon, on Public Utilities and Development of Hydro-electric Power," Sept. 21, 1932, reprinted at the American Presidency Project, University of California, Santa Barbara, http://www.presidency.ucsb.edu/ws/index.php?pid=88390 (accessed Oct. 26, 2010); speculations about FDR's switch are suggested in Forrest McDonald, *Insull: The Rise and Fall of a Billionaire Utility Tycoon* (Chicago, 1962).

102. Congress's separation of banking from bond marketing (Glass-Steagall) was repealed in 1999, with effects that Senators Glass and Steagall might have predicted had they been alive to watch it.

103. Ratner, *American Taxation,* 453.

104. Ben S. Bernanke and Mark Gertler, "Financial Fragility and Economic Performance," *Quarterly Journal of Economics* 105 (Feb. 1990): 87–114; Irving Fisher, "The Debt-Deflation Theory of Great Depressions," *Econometrica* 1 (Oct. 1933): 337–57.

105. Amity Shlaes, *The Forgotten Man: A New History of the Great Depression* (New York, 2008); Alexander J. Field, "The Most Technologically Progressive Decade of the Century," *American Economic Review* 93 (Sept. 2003): 1399–413.

106. Pete Daniel, *Breaking the Land: The Transformation of Cotton, Tobacco, and Rice Cultures Since 1880* (Urbana, Ill., 1986).

107. Linda Gordon, *Dorothea Lange: A Life Beyond Limits* (New York, 2009).

108. Darren Dochuk, *From Bible Belt to Sunbelt: Plain-Folk Religion, Grassroots Politics, and the Rise of Evangelical Conservatism* (New York, 2011), 8.

109. Charles Shindo, *Dust Bowl Migrants and the American Imagination* (Lawrence, Kans., 1997); Dochuk, *From Bible Belt to Sunbelt;* Lisa McGirr, *Subur-*

ban Warriors: The Origins of the New American Right (Princeton, N.J., 2001).

110. John H. Williams, "Deficit Spending," *American Economic Review* 30 (Feb. 1941): 52–66.

111. Alan Brinkley, *Voices of Protest: Huey Long, Father Coughlin, and the Great Depression* (New York, 1982).

112. On the agricultural exclusions in the New Deal, see Cindy Hahamovitch, *Fruits of Their Labor: Atlantic Coast Farmworkers and the Making of Migrant Poverty, 1870–1945* (Chapel Hill, N.C., 1997).

113. Here I disagree with Amity Shlaes that the New Deal "snuffed out a growing—and potentially successful—effort to light up the South." Shlaes, *Forgotten Man,* 8. On the range of possibilities available for public utilities in this period, it is best to start with Richard John, *Network Nation: Inventing American Telecommunications* (Cambridge, Mass., 2010).

CHAPTER TWELVE: CONCLUSIONS, CONCLUSIONS

1. An Observer, "The Constitutional Currency," *Albany Evening Journal,* April 18, 1837.

2. Eric Foner, *Nothing but Freedom: Emancipation and Its Legacy* (Baton Rouge, La., 1983); Foner, *Reconstruction.*

POSTSCRIPT: HERE BE DRAGONS: WHAT'S WRONG WITH HOW HISTORIANS AND ECONOMISTS HAVE WRITTEN ABOUT FINANCIAL PANICS

1. James Belich, *Replenishing the Earth: The Settler Revolution and the Rise of the Anglo-World, 1783–1989* (Oxford, 2009).

2. This case is made rather well in Richard L. Bushman, "Markets and Composite Farms in Early America," *William and Mary Quarterly,* 3rd ser., 55, no. 3 (1988): 351–74. Thanks to Richard John for bringing it to my attention.

3. For a recent attempt to estimate collateral required, see Manmohan Singh, "Collateral, Netting, and Systemic Risk in the OTC Derivatives Market," IMF Working Paper, WP/10/99 (Washington, D.C., 2010). A somewhat more sanguine view is in Daniel Heller and Nicholas Vause, "Expansion of Central Clearing," *BIS Quarterly Review* (June 2010): 67–81.

4. Giovanni Arrighi, "The Global Market," *Journal of World-Systems Research* 5 (Summer 1999): 217–51; David Harvey, "Globalization and the 'Spatial Fix,'" *Geographische Revue: Zeitschrift für Literatur und Diskussion* 3, no. 2 (2001): 23–30.

Photographic Credits

[001] Author's private collection
[006] Courtesy of Earl Gregg Swem Library, College of William & Mary
[017] Author's private collection
[018] Courtesy of Library of Congress, New York World-Telegram and Sun
  Newspaper Photograph Collection.
All other images courtesy of Library of Congress

Index

accommodation bills, 105
Adams, Abigail, 11
Adams, John Quincy, 84, 90, 92, 93, 95, 125
Addams, Jane, 194
"Address to the People of the Southern
   States," 136
African-Americans, 174, 179, 226, 248, 235
agency banks, 164
Agricultural Adjustment Act, 230, 231, 235
AIG, 244, 251
Alabama, 65, 72, 83, 86, 87, 89, 90, 91, 100, 197,
   204, 238
Alarm Act, 89
Albany, N.Y., xi, 151
alcohol, xii–xiii, 73, 127, 176, 180–1, 205, 233,
   241
Aldrich, Nelson W., 184–5
Aldrich-Vreeland Act, 209
Alexander Brown & Sons, 52, 53, 55, 59, 77,
   101
Alexander II, Czar of Russia, 176–7
Altgeld, John, 194
American Bankers Association, 222
American liberalism, 198
American Railway Times, 132, 146–7
American Railway Union (ARU), 193, 195
American Revolution, 3, 5–6, 8, 18, 50, 56
American System, 89
Ames, Fisher, 42
Ammon, Robert, 177–8
Amsterdam, 5, 252
Anglo-American trade war, 60
Anti-Federalists, 10–11, 18, 265
Anti-Masons, 135
Argentina, 188, 192, 220, 241, 243, 249–50
Arkansas, 90, 124, 144
Armour, Philip, 155, 189, 206
arrangements, 103, 107, 239
Arrighi, Giovanni, 252
Astor, John Jacob, 38–9, 40, 44, 49, 50, 57,
   62–3, 64
Atchison, David Rice, 136–8, 140, 141, 142,
   143, 144, 151
Atwater, Jesse, 43, 59
Australia, 179, 190, 250
Austria, 217, 218, 220

Austria-Hungary, 154, 155, 158, 159–64,
   169–70, 171, 179, 187, 198, 212, 250
Austrian school of economics, 250, 275–6

Baltimore, Md., 30, 42, 51, 68, 132, 167, 178
Baltimore & Ohio Railroad, 132, 157, 177, 178
bank drafts, 107, 108, 115
banker's acceptances, xv, 207, 213–17, 222–3,
   236, 243, 246
Bank of Albany, 58, 156
Bank of America, 219, 251
Bank of England, x, xi, xv, 19, 68, 73, 100, 102,
   118, 119, 147, 164, 187, 197, 239, 285
Bank of Kentucky, 63, 66
Bank of New York, 25, 27, 30, 40
bankruptcy act of 1800, 34
banks of deposit, xi
banks of discount, 14
Barclays Bank, 259
Baring Brothers, 15, 18, 77, 101, 106, 188, 302,
   308
Bell, John, 151
Benton, Thomas Hart, 109, 116, 290
Bernanke, Benjamin, 292
Biddle, Nicholas, 75, 106, 107, 108, 112–13, 116,
   119, 120, 123, 239, 259
Bigelow, John, 153–4
bill brokers, xv, 29, 118
Billion-Dollar Congress, 186, 195, 196
bills of credit, 12
bills of exchange, xi, xv, 15, 16, 18, 44, 68, 101,
   103–4, 107, 207, 209, 213, 262, 263–4, 287,
   312
bimetallic currency, 186–7
Bismarck, Otto von, 161
Black Alliance, 197
Black Ball Line, 54–5, 60, 77
Black Friday, 163
Black Hand, 211, 212
black suffrage, 229
Blair, E. O., 108
Bleecker, Leonard, 30
Board of Treasury, 3, 9, 11
bonds, xi, 7, 12, 13, 59, 99, 102, 233, 243, 244, 245
   Duer's cornering of market in, 4, 26, 27–8
   railroads, xi, 133–5, 165, 166, 192, 240

A NOTE ABOUT THE AUTHOR

Scott Reynolds Nelson's *Steel Drivin' Man* won the National Award for Arts Writing, the Anisfield-Wolf Book Award, the Merle Curti Prize for best book in U.S. history, and the Virginia Literary Award for Nonfiction. His young adult novel *Ain't Nothing but a Man* (written with Marc Aronson) won seven national awards, including the Aesop Prize for best book in American folklore and the Jane Addams Prize for the best book on social justice.

A NOTE ON THE TYPE

This book was set in Hoefler Text, a family of fonts designed by Jonathan Hoefler, who was born in 1970. First designed in 1991, Hoefler Text was intended as an advancement on existing desktop computer typography, including as it does an exponentially larger number of glyphs than previous fonts. In form, Hoefler Text looks to the old-style fonts of the seventeenth century, but it is wholly of its time, employing a precision and sophistication available only to the late twentieth century.

Composed by North Market Street Graphics, Lancaster, Pennsylvania
Printed and bound by Berryville Graphics, Berryville, Virginia
Book design by Robert C. Olsson